STEAM 5.0 and Human-Centered Intelligent Learning Ecosystems

Jorge A. Ruiz-Vanoye
https://orcid.org/0000-0003-4928-5716
Universidad Politécnica de Pachuca, Mexico

Francisco R. Trejo-Macotela
https://orcid.org/0000-0003-2133-3456
Universidad Politécnica de Pachuca, Mexico

Martha Patricia Robles Gutiérrez
Universidad Politécnica de Pachuca, Mexico

IGI Global
Scientific Publishing
Publishing Tomorrow's Research Today

Vice President of Editorial Melissa Wagner
Director of Acquisitions Mikaela Felty
Director of Book Development Jocelynn Hessler
Production Manager Mike Brehm
Cover Design Jose Rosado

Published in the United States of America by
IGI Global Scientific Publishing
701 East Chocolate Avenue
Hershey, PA, 17033, USA
Tel: 717-533-8845 | Fax: 717-533-7115
Website: https://www.igi-global.com E-mail: cust@igi-global.com

Library of Congress Cataloging-in-Publication Data

LCCN: 2026038224 (CIP Data Pending)
ISBN13: 979-8-2600-3658-7
Isbn13Softcover: 979-8-2600-3659-4
EISBN13: 979-8-2600-3660-0
British Cataloguing in Publication Data
A Cataloguing in Publication record for this book is available from the British Library.

Table of Contents

Detailed Table of Contents

The advent of Artificial Intelligence (AI) has been widely associated with substantial changes in the educational landscape, contributing to the development of smart education, characterised by personalised learning, adaptive technologies, and data-driven teaching methodologies. Smart education is commonly understood as the integration of information technologies, AI, and advanced analytics to enhance learning experiences and outcomes (Liu & Ramakrishna, 2020; Weng et al., 2025). AI can support tailored educational experiences that adapt to different learning styles and paces. Research indicates that this technological integration may contribute to the development of interactive learning environments that could help prepare students for future challenges in a rapidly evolving job market (McDowall & Eames, 2006; Pears et al., 2019).

This chapter explores STEAM 5.0 as a human-centred reimagining of intelligent education, where science, technology, engineering, arts, and mathematics are no longer treated as separate domains but as interconnected spaces for creativity, ethical reasoning, and social responsibility. It examines how explainable AI can support personalized learning and assessment without reducing learners to data profiles or predictive categories. The chapter argues that intelligent learning ecosystems must remain transparent, inclusive, and pedagogically accountable, especially when algorithmic systems influence feedback, progression, and evaluation. Rather than celebrating automation as an educational cure-all, the discussion places human

Preface

INTRODUCTION

The accelerating convergence of artificial intelligence (AI), digital transformation, and interdisciplinary education is reshaping the ways in which societies prepare learners for increasingly complex technological, social, and economic realities. As education enters an era characterised by intelligent systems, ubiquitous connectivity, and data-driven decision-making, the challenge is no longer merely to adopt advanced technologies. It is also necessary to ensure that these technologies are designed and implemented in ways that enhance human potential. Against this background, STEAM 5.0 has emerged as an educational paradigm that extends beyond the integration of Science, Technology, Engineering, Arts, and Mathematics to encompass human-centred values, ethical responsibility, creativity, sustainability, and lifelong learning.

STEAM 5.0 and Human-Centered Intelligent Learning Ecosystems brings together contributions from an international group of scholars who examine how intelligent educational ecosystems can support inclusive, transparent, adaptive, and meaningful learning experiences. Taken together, the chapters investigate the intersections among artificial intelligence, explainable AI, Industry 5.0, immersive technologies, the Internet of Things (IoT), learning analytics, topology-based educational data science, and evidence-based pedagogical innovation. Throughout the volume, technology is treated not as an end in itself but as a means of supporting human development. The emphasis therefore falls on learner agency, collaboration, ethical reasoning, and social responsibility.

A central premise of this book is that the future of education depends on balancing technological innovation with educational values. Intelligent learning ecosystems should support not only personalisation and efficiency but also fairness, transparency, accessibility, and trust. As AI increasingly participates in assessment, curriculum design, learning support, and educational decision-making, educators, researchers, and policymakers need to develop frameworks that preserve human judgement while using computational intelligence to enhance learning.

The contributions assembled in this volume address this challenge from complementary perspectives. Some chapters establish the conceptual and theoretical foundations of STEAM 5.0, whereas others present practical educational strategies, technological architectures, empirical studies, and innovative analytical methodologies. Taken together, they suggest that a productive direction for education lies in collaboration between humans and intelligent technologies rather than in the replacement of one by the other.

This volume is intended for researchers, educators, graduate students, educational technologists, policymakers, and practitioners interested in the next generation of intelligent educational systems. It also contributes to ongoing discussions surrounding Education 5.0, Smart Education, digital transformation, sustainable development, ethical AI, and interdisciplinary innovation in teaching and learning.

CHAPTER OVERVIEW

Chapter 1, "STEAM 5.0: Foundations for Human-Centred Intelligent Educational Ecosystems", establishes the conceptual framework for the volume. It traces the evolution of smart education through the integration of artificial intelligence, adaptive learning technologies, and advanced educational analytics. The chapter introduces STEAM 5.0 as a human-centred educational paradigm that combines technological innovation with personalised learning, ethical considerations, and interdisciplinary collaboration.

Chapter 2, "STEAM 5.0 and Human-Centred Intelligent Learning Ecosystems", explores the philosophical and pedagogical dimensions of intelligent education. Its discussion centres on the responsible integration of explainable AI into educational environments, with particular attention to transparency, learner autonomy, ethical assessment, and the preservation of human judgement within increasingly automated learning systems.

Chapter 3, "STEAM Training to Master Industry 4.0 and 5.0: Human-Centred Skills for Industry 4.0–5.0", examines how STEAM education prepares learners for rapidly evolving industrial environments. The chapter considers the development of interdisciplinary competencies that combine technical expertise with creativity, sustainability, systems thinking, and ethical responsibility to support resilient and human-centred industrial transformation.

Chapter 4, "STEAM Skills to Meet Social and Productive Needs", examines how STEAM methodologies can address real-world societal and industrial challenges.

Through practical educational models and active learning strategies, the chapter considers how computational thinking, collaboration, and interdisciplinary problem-solving can be cultivated in response to contemporary technological demands.

Chapter 5, "STEAM as an Educational Strategy to Integrate Emerging Technologies", presents STEAM as a comprehensive educational framework for incorporating artificial intelligence, virtual and augmented reality, robotics, the Internet of Things, additive manufacturing, and other emerging technologies into higher education and lifelong learning. Particular emphasis is placed on the contextualised, ethical, and creative integration of these technologies.

Chapter 6, "Educational Strategies to Unleash Creativity and Soft Skills", focuses on the development of creativity, socio-emotional competencies, and transferable skills within competency-based education. Drawing on constructivist and evidence-based pedagogical approaches, it explores how curriculum design can intentionally cultivate communication, collaboration, self-regulation, metacognition, and lifelong learning capabilities.

Chapter 7, "Generative AI and Large Language Models in Smart Education for Metaverse-Based Learning", investigates the convergence of generative artificial intelligence, large language models, learning analytics, and immersive virtual environments. Combining conceptual analysis with empirical research, the discussion proposes architectures and ethical frameworks for AI-enhanced metaverse learning environments. It also addresses bias, privacy, hallucinations, and academic integrity.

Chapter 8, "IoT-Enabled and Explainable Smart Experimental Platforms for Multidisciplinary STEAM Engineering Training", examines intelligent laboratory ecosystems that integrate IoT technologies, explainable artificial intelligence, adaptive learning models, and cloud computing. The chapter indicates how smart experimental platforms can transform engineering education by supporting personalised, safe, collaborative, and multidisciplinary learning experiences aligned with sustainable development objectives.

Chapter 9, "Persistent Homology for Learning Trajectories with Cycles, Transitions, and Ruptures", introduces an innovative application of topological data analysis to educational analytics. By modelling learning trajectories as evolving geometric structures, the chapter presents reproducible methodologies for identifying complex patterns, transitions, and learning disruptions that traditional analytics often overlook. These methodologies may thereby provide interpretable and human-centred decision support for educational interventions.

CONCLUSION

Collectively, these chapters indicate that STEAM 5.0 represents more than an educational methodology; it embodies a vision of intelligent learning ecosystems in which technological advancement serves human development. By integrating artificial intelligence with creativity, ethics, sustainability, and interdisciplinary collaboration, the contributors present a comprehensive roadmap for designing educational systems that are adaptive, equitable, transparent, and resilient. It is our hope that this volume will help to inspire further research, foster international collaboration, and contribute meaningfully to the continuing transformation of education in the age of intelligent technologies.

Chapter 1
STEAM 5.0:
Foundations for Human-Centred Intelligent Educational Ecosystems

Jorge A. Ruiz-Vanoye
http://orcid.org/0000-0003-4928-5716
Universidad Politécnica de Pachuca, Mexico

Francisco R. Trejo-Macotela
http://orcid.org/0000-0003-2133-3456
Universidad Politecnica de Pachuca, Mexico

Martha Patricia Robles Gutiérrez
http://orcid.org/0009-0000-3143-9831
Universidad Politecnica de Pachuca, Mexico

Ocotlán Diaz-Parra
http://orcid.org/0000-0002-8740-3747
Universidad Politecnica de Pachuca, Mexico

Julio C. Ramos-Fernandez
http://orcid.org/0000-0002-9997-6550
Universidad Politecnica de Pachuca, Mexico

ABSTRACT

The advent of Artificial Intelligence (AI) has been widely associated with substantial changes in the educational landscape, contributing to the development of smart education, characterised by personalised learning, adaptive technologies, and data-driven teaching methodologies. Smart education is commonly understood as the integration of information technologies, AI, and advanced analytics to enhance learning experiences and outcomes (Liu & Ramakrishna, 2020; Weng et al., 2025).

DOI: 10.4018/979-8-2600-3658-7.ch001

AI can support tailored educational experiences that adapt to different learning styles and paces. Research indicates that this technological integration may contribute to the development of interactive learning environments that could help prepare students for future challenges in a rapidly evolving job market (McDowall & Eames, 2006; Pears et al., 2019).

1. INTRODUCTION

1.1 Context of Smart Education in the Era of AI

The advent of Artificial Intelligence has been widely associated with substantial changes in the educational landscape, contributing to the development of smart education, characterised by personalised learning, adaptive technologies, and data-driven teaching methodologies. Smart education is commonly understood as the integration of information technologies, AI, and advanced analytics to enhance learning experiences and outcomes (Liu, 2020). AI can support tailored educational experiences that adapt to different learning styles and paces. Research indicates that this technological integration may contribute to the development of interactive learning environments that could help prepare students for future challenges in a rapidly evolving job market (Isomöttönen et al., 2019).

In this context, the role of educators is also changing as they integrate digital technologies into pedagogical practice. Continuous professional development and collaborative professional networks can support educators in developing the competences required for interdisciplinary STEAM teaching. Communities of Practice provide spaces in which educators can exchange experiences, strengthen engagement, and support professional learning (Spyropoulou & Kameas, 2024).

Equity remains a central concern in STEAM education. Evidence from early childhood settings identifies limited resources, inequitable teacher–student interactions, and insufficient family involvement as barriers to equitable participation (Sun et al., 2025). In AI-enabled education, responsible implementation also requires attention to inclusion, data privacy, human agency, and equitable access (Miao et al., 2021).

1.2 The Emergence of STEAM 5.0

STEAM education extends STEM by integrating the arts and encouraging project- and problem-based learning across disciplinary boundaries. These approaches can combine technical knowledge with creativity and help learners engage with contemporary societal and workforce challenges (Liu, 2020; Pressick-Kilborn et al., 2021). In this chapter, the term STEAM 5.0 is used as a conceptual label for a human-centred extension of STEAM that incorporates interdisciplinary learning, critical thinking, and emerging technologies. This framing is consistent with research highlighting the value of dialogic STEAM activities, multiple ways of knowing, and inter- and transdisciplinary learning (Fernández-Cárdenas & Santillán-Rosas, 2025; Mejias et al., 2021).

Within the conceptual framework adopted in this chapter, STEAM 5.0 is associated with creativity, collaboration, critical thinking, and problem-solving, drawing on established STEAM scholarship. Evidence from dialogic STEAM activities suggests that relational dialogue and collaborative teacher–student engagement can support critical-thinking development, although the reported effects varied across participating schools (Fernández-Cárdenas & Santillán-Rosas, 2025). More broadly, STEAM education integrates the arts into STEM and creates opportunities for transdisciplinary learning focused on contemporary societal challenges (Pressick-Kilborn et al., 2021).

2. CONCEPTUAL FOUNDATIONS OF STEAM 5.0

2.1 From STEM to STEAM

The movement from STEM (Science, Technology, Engineering, and Mathematics) to STEAM reflects efforts to integrate the arts into STEM education and to recognise multiple ways of knowing within educational practice (Mejias et al., 2021). STEAM approaches can create opportunities for transdisciplinary learning and for framing project- and problem-based activities around contemporary societal challenges (Pressick-Kilborn et al., 2021). Through these approaches, learners can connect knowledge across disciplines and apply it to authentic educational problems.

STEAM 5.0

In this chapter, STEAM 5.0 is used as a conceptual label for integrating artificial intelligence into established STEAM principles while maintaining a human-centred pedagogical orientation. AI can support competency-based personalised learning through adaptive technologies, individualised learning pathways, and instruction tailored to learners' needs and abilities (Dastane et al., 2024). However, meaningful educational integration also requires educators to develop the pedagogical competence needed to evaluate and apply AI tools appropriately within teaching and learning practices (Zou et al., 2025).

2.2 Human-Centred AI in Education

Human-centred AI in education prioritises learners' needs while preserving human agency, ethical oversight, and the central role of educators (Miao et al., 2021). AI combined with agile teaching strategies may support responsive, personalised, and collaborative learning environments (Adenubi et al., 2024). Research in higher education also indicates that AI tools can support personalised learning and assessment, communication, engagement, collaboration, and instructional scaffolding (Msambwa et al., 2025). In addition, learning analytics can help educators monitor students' learning and persistence, evaluate pedagogical effectiveness, identify students who may require support, and inform timely interventions (Wong, 2017). Smart digital technologies may therefore enhance teaching and learning when they are thoughtfully integrated into broader pedagogical environments (Mhlongo et al., 2023).

2.3 Educational Ecosystems as Complex Adaptive Systems

Educational systems can be understood as complex and adaptive rather than linear, because learning and change emerge through interactions among people, institutions, practices, and contexts (Davis & Sumara, 2006). From this perspective, educational practices evolve through feedback, experimentation, and adaptation to local conditions. Educational outcomes are shaped by interacting social, cultural, economic, institutional, and technological factors. Inclusive and adaptive education ecosystems therefore require collaboration among stakeholders, the participation of end users, and the coordinated exchange of knowledge and resources (OECD, 2023; Robinson et al., 2016).

2.4 Principles of Personalised and Inclusive Learning

Principles of personalised and inclusive learning recognise learner variability and seek to reduce barriers to meaningful participation. Rather than assuming a single preferred way of learning, inclusive design provides multiple means of engagement, representation, and action and expression, while supporting learner choice, belonging, and equitable access (CAST, 2024). Technology can contribute to these aims when it is integrated into an equity-oriented pedagogical framework; smart digital technologies can provide multimodal and flexible forms of engagement and extend learning beyond conventional classroom environments (Mhlongo et al., 2023).

Learning analytics can help educators monitor students' learning and persistence, identify learners who may require additional support, and inform prompt interventions (Wong, 2017). AI combined with agile teaching strategies may also contribute to responsive, personalised, and collaborative learning environments (Adenubi et al.,

2024). Attention to learner identities, cultural relevance, and barriers to participation should therefore form part of the design of inclusive educational experiences.

3. INTELLIGENT LEARNING ECOSYSTEMS: THEORETICAL FRAMEWORK

3.1 Definition and Core Components

In this chapter, an intelligent learning ecosystem is conceptualised as an interconnected socio-technical environment comprising learners, educators, institutional arrangements, digital infrastructures, and data-informed processes. Within such environments, learning analytics can support personalisation and adaptation, although their implementation also raises concerns regarding privacy and data ownership (Siemens, 2013). When artificial intelligence is incorporated into educational processes, its design and governance should explicitly address fairness, accountability, transparency, bias, autonomy, agency, and inclusion (Holmes et al., 2022).

Within the context of STEAM 5.0, intelligent learning ecosystems are conceived as human-centred environments that align computational intelligence with creativity, ethics, and societal responsibility. These ecosystems integrate artificial intelligence (AI), learning analytics, immersive technologies, and collaborative platforms into pedagogical architectures that foreground agency, transparency, and inclusivity.

Core components typically include:

- Human actors: learners, educators, administrators, families, and community stakeholders.
- Data infrastructures: learning management systems, multimodal sensors, assessment tools, and interoperable databases.
- Computational intelligence layer: machine learning models, recommendation engines, adaptive algorithms, and explainability mechanisms.
- Pedagogical frameworks: curricular designs grounded in constructivism, inquiry-based learning, and interdisciplinary STEAM integration.
- Governance and ethical safeguards: privacy policies, fairness auditing, transparency protocols, and participatory oversight structures.

Table 1 summarises these components and their functions.

Table 1. Core Components of Intelligent Learning Ecosystems.

Component	Function	STEAM 5.0 Orientation
Human Actors	Co-creation of knowledge, feedback loops	Emphasis on creativity and collaboration
Data Infrastructure	Collection and integration of learning data	Interoperability and ethical data stewardship
Computational Intelligence	Adaptation, prediction, and recommendation	Explainability and human oversight
Pedagogical Frameworks	Structuring learning experiences	Interdisciplinary and problem-based learning
Governance Mechanisms	Ensuring fairness, transparency, and accountability	Ethical and socially responsible innovation

To further clarify the structure of intelligent learning ecosystems within the STEAM 5.0 paradigm, Figure 1 illustrates a layered conceptual architecture that integrates human, technological, and governance dimensions. The model highlights the interdependence between educational actors, data infrastructures, computational intelligence, pedagogical frameworks, and ethical governance mechanisms. Rather than operating as isolated components, these layers interact through continuous bidirectional feedback loops that enable adaptive learning processes, institutional oversight, and human-centred innovation. The architecture emphasises that computational intelligence should remain embedded within pedagogical and ethical structures, ensuring that technological optimisation supports meaningful learning rather than purely algorithmic efficiency.

Figure 1. Layered architecture of an intelligent STEAM 5.0 learning ecosystem integrating human actors, data infrastructures, computational intelligence, pedagogical frameworks, and ethical governance mechanisms

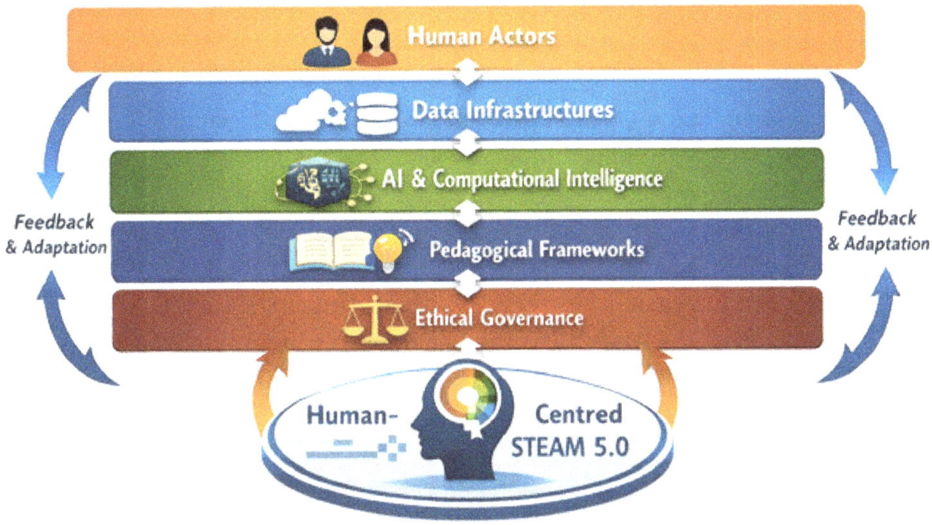

3.2 Socio-Technical Perspectives in Smart Education

Intelligent learning ecosystems should be understood through a socio-technical lens, in which technical components interact with organisational arrangements, professional practices, and stakeholder needs. Educational technologies are not neutral artefacts: decisions about their design, adoption, and use reflect values, judgements, and political choices (Selwyn, 2019). A socio-technical approach therefore requires technological development to be considered alongside organisational change and constructive engagement with users (Baxter & Sommerville, 2011).

In educational settings, AI may influence assessment, learner modelling, feedback, and curricular decision-making. Its design and deployment should therefore involve educators and other relevant stakeholders while retaining human responsibility for pedagogical decisions (Holmes et al., 2022; Miao et al., 2021). Rather than treating AI as an autonomous authority, educational institutions should maintain human oversight so that algorithmic outputs can be interpreted, questioned, and revised in context.

A socio-technical perspective also foregrounds issues of digital inequality, algorithmic bias, and cultural representation. When STEAM learning is mediated by AI-driven tools, educators must interrogate how data categories are constructed, whose knowledge is privileged, and how students' identities are represented computationally.

3.3 Integration of Cognitive, Pedagogical, and Technological Dimensions

An effective intelligent ecosystem requires alignment between three interdependent dimensions:

- Cognitive dimension: insights from cognitive science regarding memory, metacognition, and self-regulated learning (Winne & Hadwin, 1998).
- Pedagogical dimension: instructional design principles such as scaffolding, formative feedback, and collaborative inquiry (Luckin et al., 2016).
- Technological dimension: algorithmic modelling, adaptive interfaces, and multimodal interaction tools.

The integration of these dimensions prevents technological determinism. For instance, adaptive systems should not merely optimise content sequencing but should support metacognitive awareness by explaining why certain recommendations are made. In STEAM education, where creative and analytical thinking intersect, AI must accommodate divergent problem-solving pathways rather than enforcing linear progression models.

Constructive alignment between learning objectives, assessment strategies, and AI-driven adaptation mechanisms is essential. When computational models incorporate pedagogical theories explicitly, they become more interpretable and educationally meaningful.

3.4 Learning Sciences and Computational Intelligence

The learning sciences provide theoretical grounding for the application of computational intelligence in education. Principles such as knowledge construction, distributed cognition, and social learning inform the design of AI-driven environments (Sawyer, 2014).

Computational intelligence techniques—such as supervised learning, reinforcement learning, and natural language processing—enable real-time modelling of learner behaviour. However, the translation of behavioural traces into meaningful educational insights requires theory-informed interpretation. Purely predictive accuracy is insufficient; models must also align with valid constructs of learning.

The convergence of learning sciences and AI fosters what may be termed *theory-guided machine learning*, where algorithmic features correspond to pedagogically relevant constructs (e.g., persistence, conceptual change, collaborative engagement). This synthesis is foundational for STEAM 5.0, where technological sophistication must remain subordinate to human development and creativity.

4. EXPLAINABLE AI AS A PILLAR OF TRUSTWORTHY EDUCATION

4.1 Foundations of Explainable Artificial Intelligence (XAI)

Explainable Artificial Intelligence (XAI) encompasses methods and approaches designed to make the decisions and behaviour of AI systems more transparent and comprehensible to human users (Adadi & Berrada, 2018). In education, XAI seeks to clarify how and why algorithms generate predictions, recommendations, or classifications.

Foundations of XAI include:

- Model transparency (inherently interpretable models such as decision trees).
- Post-hoc explanation techniques (e.g., feature importance, local approximations).
- Interactive explanation interfaces enabling dialogue between user and system.

Within STEAM ecosystems, XAI extends beyond technical transparency to pedagogical intelligibility. Explanations should be tailored to diverse stakeholders: learners may require formative feedback explanations, whereas educators may need diagnostic or comparative insights.

4.2 Transparency, Interpretability, and Accountability in Learning Systems

Transparency and interpretability concern making the decisions and behaviour of AI systems understandable to human users (Adadi & Berrada, 2018). Floridi et al., (2018) frame explicability as an ethical principle that combines intelligibility with accountability, including mechanisms for scrutiny, the allocation of responsibility, and redress when AI systems produce harmful or erroneous outcomes. In educational contexts, these principles manifest in:

- Clear communication of data usage and consent.
- Explanation dashboards for educators.
- Auditing procedures to detect bias or disparate impact.

- Governance committees including diverse stakeholders.

Transparency without interpretability is insufficient; stakeholders must meaningfully understand how decisions are reached. Accountability frameworks should incorporate both institutional responsibility and technical safeguards, ensuring that AI augments rather than replaces professional judgement.

4.3 Pedagogical Implications of Explainability

Explainability has direct pedagogical implications. When students receive intelligible feedback from AI systems, they are better positioned to develop metacognitive skills and self-regulated learning strategies.

Moreover, transparent systems can foster epistemic trust. Learners are more likely to engage with adaptive tools if they understand the rationale behind recommendations. Conversely, opaque systems risk diminishing motivation or reinforcing deterministic labelling.

Educators benefit from explanatory insights that contextualise predictive analytics within broader classroom dynamics. Rather than merely identifying "at-risk" students, explainable systems can highlight contributing factors, supporting targeted interventions grounded in professional expertise.

4.4 Human-AI Collaboration in Educational Decision-Making

Human-AI collaboration reframes AI as a decision-support partner rather than an autonomous authority. In STEAM 5.0 ecosystems, collaborative intelligence emerges when educators interpret algorithmic outputs through pedagogical lenses.

Effective collaboration requires:

- Role clarity (AI as augmentation, not replacement).
- Reciprocal feedback loops (educators correcting or refining system outputs).
- Professional development to cultivate algorithmic literacy.

Such collaboration aligns with principles of responsible AI, ensuring that ethical judgement remains fundamentally human while leveraging computational efficiency.

5. PERSONALISATION IN STEAM LEARNING ENVIRONMENTS

5.1 Adaptive Learning Pathways

Adaptive learning pathways dynamically adjust content, pacing, and feedback according to learner profiles. Machine learning models analyse performance data to recommend tasks aligned with individual competencies.

In STEAM contexts, adaptation should accommodate both analytical reasoning and creative exploration. Over-personalisation may fragment shared learning experiences; therefore, hybrid models combining individualised tasks with collaborative projects are recommended.

Adaptive systems must remain transparent, allowing learners to understand progression criteria and to exercise agency in selecting alternative pathways.

5.2 Multimodal Learning Analytics

Multimodal learning analytics (MMLA) combines data from multiple sources—including digital logs, text, speech, gestures, eye-tracking, and biosensor data—to support more holistic analyses of learning processes in complex and open-ended environments (Blikstein & Worsley, 2016).

In STEAM laboratories or makerspaces, multimodal data can capture collaborative problem-solving and embodied cognition. However, ethical concerns regarding surveillance and privacy must be addressed. Consent procedures, data minimisation strategies, and anonymisation protocols are essential.

Figure 2 illustrates the conceptual data pipeline underlying multimodal learning analytics in STEAM environments. Multiple data streams—including textual interactions, speech signals, gesture data, and eye-tracking indicators—are captured during learning activities in digital and physical learning spaces. These heterogeneous signals are processed through multimodal data integration techniques that extract behavioural and cognitive indicators. The resulting features contribute to the construction of a dynamic learner model representing knowledge states, engagement patterns, and collaborative behaviours. AI-driven personalisation mechanisms subsequently use this model to generate adaptive recommendations and feedback. Importantly, explainable interfaces translate algorithmic outputs into interpretable insights for educators and learners, thereby supporting transparency and pedagogical decision-making.

Figure 2. Multimodal learning analytics pipeline illustrating the integration of heterogeneous behavioural data into a unified learner model for AI-driven personalisation in STEAM learning environments

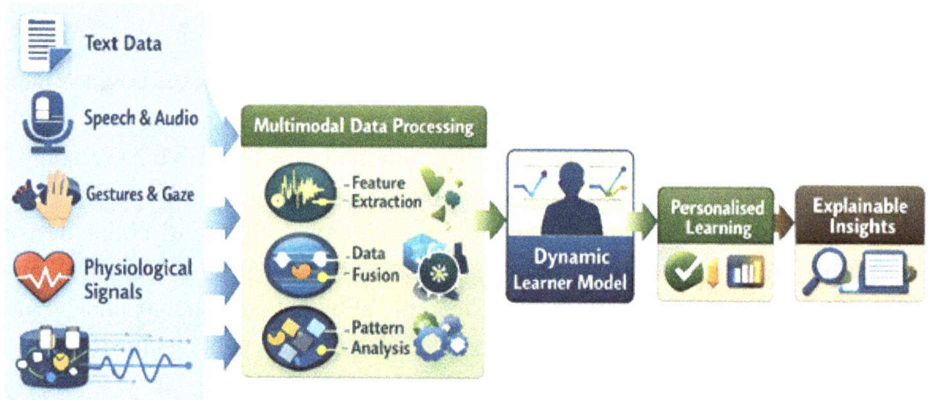

5.3 Student Modelling and Learning Profiles

Student modelling involves constructing computational representations of learners' knowledge, skills, preferences, and affective states. Contemporary approaches integrate cognitive diagnostic models with behavioural analytics.

Learning profiles in STEAM 5.0 should move beyond deficit-based classifications. Instead of labelling students as "low performing," models should identify strengths, interests, and growth trajectories. Incorporating learner voice into profile construction can mitigate misrepresentation.

Ethical modelling requires fairness-aware algorithms and continuous validation to prevent reinforcing systemic biases.

5.4 Equity, Accessibility, and Cultural Sensitivity

Personalisation should not exacerbate educational inequities. AI-enabled educational systems may reproduce or amplify biases related to gender, age, race, social status, and income when biased datasets or design assumptions influence their outputs (Holmes et al., 2022).

Equity-oriented design principles include:

- Inclusive datasets representing diverse populations.
- Accessibility standards aligned with universal design for learning.
- Culturally responsive pedagogical frameworks integrated into AI models.

STEAM 5.0 envisions intelligent ecosystems that promote social justice, ensuring that technological sophistication enhances, rather than undermines, equitable educational opportunity.

6. SMART EDUCATIONAL INFRASTRUCTURES

The rapid advancement in technologies such as the Internet of Things (IoT), Virtual Reality (VR), Augmented Reality (AR), and AI has had a substantial influence on educational methodologies. The integration of these technologies into learning environments has been associated with the emergence of innovative pedagogical practices that aim to address diverse learning needs and may enhance educational outcomes.

6.1 IoT-Enabled Learning Spaces

Internet of Things (IoT) technologies can connect devices, sensors, cloud services, and analytic platforms within smart learning ecosystems. When these components are integrated into an appropriate pedagogical framework, they can support flexible access, experiential activities, data-informed learning, and the provision of guidance and feedback (Benita et al., 2021). Research on IoT applications in education nevertheless remains predominantly focused on technical implementation, while its social and pedagogical dimensions require further investigation (Desai & Kim, 2023). In higher education, successful adoption also depends on factors such as privacy, infrastructure readiness, financial resources, faculty support, staff and student training, and network and data security (Madni et al., 2022).

6.2 Virtual and Augmented Reality Laboratories

Virtual reality (VR) and augmented reality (AR) can support experiential learning by enabling students to interact with immersive simulations and visualisations of complex content. In STEM education, students participating in a VR-supported hands-on activity achieved significantly better learning performance and practical abilities than those receiving lecture-based instruction (Chen et al., 2020). However, immersive technology does not automatically produce effective learning: its educational value depends on the alignment of learning content, technological design elements, and relevant learning theories (Radianti et al., 2020). Implementation may also be constrained by high costs, limited accessibility and scalability, and the need to adapt and customise applications for particular educational settings (Al-Ansi et al., 2023).

6.3 Robotics and Intelligent Tutoring Systems

Social robots can serve as tutors or peer learners, although their educational effectiveness depends on the adaptive, social, and pedagogical functions implemented in each system (Belpaeme et al., 2018). In one field study, a robot tutor that selected assistance according to learners' mastery and engagement produced greater learning gains than a robot using a fixed assistance policy (Ramachandran et al., 2019). Longer-term personalisation based on learners' skill profiles also resulted in stronger post-test performance than non-personalised curriculum sequencing (Leyzberg et al., 2018).

Intelligent Tutoring Systems (ITS) are related adaptive technologies, but they are not necessarily robotic. Julian and Smith (2019) developed a computer-based ITS for teaching cognitive and procedural skills in robotic-assisted surgery, whereas Hasan et al., (2020) reviewed the transition from conventional ITS to affect-sensitive tutoring systems incorporating emotion-recognition processes.

Social robots may also support collaborative and self-regulated learning. Adaptive robotic scaffolding produced stronger indicators of self-regulated learning among primary-school pupils (Jones & Castellano, 2018). In group learning, an empathic robot fostered meaningful discussions about sustainability, although a longer-term classroom intervention did not produce significant learning gains (Alves-Oliveira et al., 2019). Broader adoption nevertheless requires careful attention to technical reliability, classroom integration, and the availability of evidence from longer-term studies (Belpaeme et al., 2018).

6.4 Data Ecosystems and Interoperability

Data-driven educational ecosystems can combine information from learning and administrative systems to inform teaching, learning, and institutional decision-making. Human-centred learning analytics and artificial intelligence approaches emphasise stakeholder involvement and pedagogical contextualisation, as failure to address users' needs and trust may limit adoption in authentic educational settings (Topali et al., 2025).

Interoperability enables data from disparate digital tools to be combined and reused coherently and efficiently. Achieving it requires technical and semantic standards, together with organisational and legal alignment (OECD, 2023). Under these conditions, learning analytics can support the monitoring of student performance and persistence, the identification of learners requiring assistance, the evaluation of pedagogical practices, and timely institutional action (Wong, 2017). Nevertheless, legacy systems, privacy and security requirements, limited institutional capacity, and insufficient stakeholder coordination may constrain implementation (OECD, 2023; Topali et al., 2025).

In summary, the convergence of IoT, VR/AR, robotics, and AI is frequently discussed as offering transformative possibilities in educational settings. Although these technologies present advantages related to accessibility and engagement, their implementation requires careful consideration to address associated challenges and to support effective learning outcomes.

7. ETHICAL AND GOVERNANCE CONSIDERATIONS

7.1 Responsible AI in Education

The concept of ethics has evolved in society over time, but the fundamental principles of human integrity remain relevant today. However, ethics extends to deeper aspects of human development, because it not only focuses on morality but also integrates various disciplines such as justice and integrity, and above all, responsibility in the age of artificial intelligence (Bracho-Fuenmayor, 2024).

In higher education, ethics encompasses respect for the behavior of everyone from students to administrators, preparing future professionals who will practice their profession responsibly and diligently. Therefore, students' knowledge, conduct, and attitudes form the foundation for performing respectfully and effectively in the workplace, particularly in the use of technology (Carrillo-Velarde, 2020).

When technology is developed, the goal is always to improve people's lives in all areas of development. However, a lack of knowledge and the novelty of new discoveries often lead to a lack of regulation in their application, and, above all, a failure to prevent harm that was not initially foreseen.

Artificial intelligence can support teaching and learning when it is integrated into clearly defined pedagogical aims rather than treated as an end in itself (Miao et al., 2021). Active-learning approaches, meanwhile, emphasise learners' cognitive engagement, inquiry, experience, and self-regulation, and may offer advantages over traditional forms of instruction (Alomá Bello et al., 2022).

This is how artificial intelligence has broad capabilities and the potential to transform society; the challenge lies in determining where this strength can negatively impact its users. Therefore, it is crucial to analyze the ethical principles and approaches that underpin artificial intelligence (Pegoraro & Curzel, 2023).

Delgado-Quintero et al., (2025) conducted a bibliometric analysis of publications indexed in Scopus between 2013 and 2023 to map the multidimensional ethical issues associated with artificial intelligence across several disciplinary fields, including education.

The revealing data from mapping the ethical landscape in artificial intelligence came from humanities and technology fields such as Education, Engineering, Law, Philosophy, Computer Science, Business, and even Sociology. The findings showed that in 2020, a significant amount of research was conducted on the topic of ethics in artificial intelligence; another important aspect was the relationship between terms related to ethics; the authors termed these associations a "cluster".

From a human rights perspective, the principles related to artificial intelligence systems are as follows: respect for privacy and human dignity, the guarantee of transparency and accountability; other aspects that are integrated into the principles of artificial intelligence are related to the area of equity and non-discrimination.

Advances in artificial intelligence show their potential to change people's lives and be indispensable tools in various human activities, especially because they greatly improve the efficiency of processes, but also, from another point of view, the great potential of artificial intelligence can amplify existing injustices (Pegoraro & Curzel, 2023).

Ethical reflection provides a framework of values and principles for critically examining the effects of artificial intelligence on everyday life. AI should therefore be understood not merely as an advanced technological development, but also as a source of significant ethical and moral questions concerning its design and implementation (Guzmán-Brand & Gélvez-García, 2024).

Among the areas where artificial intelligence has the greatest impact is education; it has clearly been key to triggering new educational approaches related to better learning and a new educational stance, such as active, meaningful learning, as well as new roles for teachers.

In a recent investigation (Sánchez Islas & Rodríguez Betanzos, 2026) questionnaires were administered to 401 university students, where the results showed that they have a positive attitude towards the use of Artificial Intelligence because they recognize its potential and consider it positive for their learning because it allows for personalization and assistance to improve writing and ease of research and analysis; in turn, the work of Sánchez and Rodríguez also detected that, on the part of the students, they believe that excessive use leads to dependence and they lose their capacity for critical thinking.

Another noteworthy aspect of the work "Exploring the use of artificial intelligence in university students" is that they found that generative artificial intelligence tools are useful for analyzing complex ideas, searching for documents, and supporting research by students; however, they opined that the use of artificial intelligence will be effective if it is used with an ethical and responsible approach. Another relevant piece of information is their data, because 57% say that they have an improvement in their academic performance because their abilities to understand, analyze, organize and simplify tasks have been expanded with the use of artificial intelligence tools, especially generative intelligence (Sánchez Islas & Rodríguez Betanzos, 2026).

Gil Iranzo et al., (2024) examined the impact of artificial intelligence on higher education students and found that pedagogical approaches should explicitly incorporate ethical considerations to address digital inequalities and algorithmic bias. Among their findings, they also encountered the widespread opinion that the use of artificial intelligence promotes students' critical thinking, creativity, and digital literacy with a critical focus. The design of their research allowed them to identify that students initially generate skepticism and even anxiety, but eventually move towards clear empowerment and critical development.

Their conclusions were that it is necessary to integrate theoretical frameworks such as critical digital pedagogy and modulate human-computer interaction. This work points out technical and pedagogical aspects in its conclusions and considers it appropriate to integrate actions for the design of critical curricula, continuous training of teachers and broad collaboration with industry to focus on the characteristics of the transition between university and industry. Added to the previous finding is the approach that technological advancement must promote the pursuit of current and profound social equity in order to truly speak of educational innovation.

Nozato López conducted a study that consisted of a literature review on the use of artificial intelligence by higher education students, where he focuses the research point mainly on two aspects: pedagogical contributions and ethical challenges from an academic point of view, but also in the same document he integrates humanistic findings corresponding to digital inequalities and algorithmic systems (Nozato López, 2024).

The aspects explored by Nozato López were specifically the use of artificial intelligence, focusing on ethical considerations and the promotion of critical thinking; he took as references the recommendations issued by UNESCO, which recommends that artificial intelligence technologies and applications must respect human rights and contribute to well-being. Among the revealing points, it was identified that both students and teachers have a leading role in the use of this new technology; therefore, among the recommendations issued by educational institutions to focus on responsibility and ethics, is that teachers must guide students to reflective and ethical use; their teaching practice requires them to implement teaching-learning strategies situated in meaningful, critical, and reflective learning, as well as integrating new student-centered and integrative pedagogical approaches, such as STEAM education.

Within the field of digital skills, this document reflects on the fact that digital tools are inseparable from human activity and emphasizes that human development must integrate digital skills and socio-emotional skills of empathy and ethics to ensure equitable and sustainable progress (Robles Gutiérrez et al., 2025). They develop six digital competencies that integrate the use of various types of artificial intelligence tools with approaches to responsible technology use and digital ethics. The defined competencies are: Content creation, protection and security, information and data, digital environment, communication and collaboration, and finally, entrepreneurship. The competencies were developed with research from teachers, students, and employers.

The use of digital technology in most human activities forces universities to be concerned not only with knowledge, but also with the significant ethical considerations related to digital competencies supported by artificial intelligence tools, which are primarily data privacy, transparency in the structure and outcome of algorithms, equity and inclusion (Sánchez Islas & Rodríguez Betanzos, 2026).

Ethics and responsibility in education are defined in several studies as a powerful strategy to amplify learning and motivate new skills; the most prominent features are the personalization of learning and assistance to improve writing and ease in research and also in analysis. The main challenges focus on algorithmic biases, data privacy and security, transparency and accountability, data commercialization, and the role of teachers. This necessitates a new approach not only for universities in the educational field but also for society in establishing frameworks and criteria for the use of artificial intelligence.

7.2 Algorithmic Fairness and Bias Mitigation

Technological advances, especially those related to artificial intelligence, are always developed with the advancement of humanity and personal well-being in mind. In the field of algorithmic fairness, systems configured as algorithms based on artificial intelligence are expected to produce fair results, automatically avoiding or favoring groups of people or individuals.

People's characteristics are sensitive, such as gender, race, ethnicity, age, or any socioeconomic status. Several studies have shown that artificial intelligence algorithms produce information that is not neutral; It is important to analyze that these are pre-configured mechanisms that learn from historical data and can generate information about social contexts that have inequalities that were not initially foreseen.

The development of artificial intelligence systems and their use in public governance requires reviews to ensure compliance with aspects of fairness, transparency, and accountability (Bustelo Gracia, 2025) It points out that nowadays it is impossible not to apply digital systems in various processes; however, automation criteria and artificial intelligence algorithms tend to be discriminatory. Therefore, it is important to implement thorough audits and reviews to identify biases, in order to mitigate risks and ensure that artificial intelligence applications generate fair and ethical information.

AI-assisted decision-making in healthcare, including medical diagnosis and risk prediction, raises important concerns about fairness. Biases arising from unrepresentative data, algorithmic design, or human interpretation may produce discriminatory outcomes for under-represented groups, potentially restricting access to appropriate care or contributing to inadequate treatment. Similar risks arise in employment, criminal justice, lending, and credit scoring, where biased AI systems may reproduce or amplify existing inequalities (Ferrara, 2024).

On the other hand, the increasing trend of using predictive methods is generating concern in various sectors focused on equity; it turns out to be a crucial question: in what part of the organization and implementation is it necessary to train with real data and verify that they do not reproduce the social biases that arise in reality?. When performing predictive operations, it is possible that the datasets used in both training and real-world processes may contain unfair biases; these situations are similarly replicated when processing data with predictive models. Addressing this problem is urgent because the design of automated systems can perpetuate inequalities and discriminate against vulnerable groups for various reasons (Bergasa Sariego, 2024).

Causes of Biases in AI

In any process, however sophisticated, weaknesses are not immediately apparent, even after rigorous testing. Currently, artificial intelligence exhibits systematic errors in the final information of decision-making processes and, depending on the area in which it is implemented, it can generate unfair results. Several situations can lead to this, including poor data collection, inadequate algorithm design, and human interpretation (Ferrara, 2024).

Consequences of AI Bias

Several authors agree that one of the negative impacts of artificial intelligence bias is discrimination, because it can be long-lasting and also amplifies existing inequality. Another major concern is limiting people's access to essential services, which can range from healthcare to financial services. Gender stereotypes and discrimination: Today there are facial recognition developments that can confuse the features of men and women. The most vulnerable groups throughout the years have been those based on gender and skin color; stereotypes have been generated; for example, if you have dark skin, it is very likely that the systems will identify you as a criminal.

But if we talk about the use of artificial intelligence in government systems that serve citizens, it is possible that some citizens could be denied services, job placement, or even be taken to jail for having incorrect information. Several nations have worked hard on equity, equality, and inclusion to empower the entire population equally, but systemic biases make it impossible to achieve full development in society.

Mitigating Bias in Artificial Intelligence

Efforts have been made at prestigious universities to mitigate the biases of artificial intelligence; they focus on the aspects that cause the most bias, which are data preprocessing, model selection, and decisions generated after processing. The recent emergence of these new technologies means that there is a lack of experience and data to carry out training, and also a limited capacity to find and measure biases. Currently, there is a lack of knowledge about the types of biases and their consequences; therefore, actions cannot be prioritized.

However, identifying the causes and consequences allows us to develop strategies to mitigate the biases generated by the use of artificial intelligence and to build new approaches to make this new technology robust and truly ensure that it will be beneficial for society as a whole.

The issue of algorithmic fairness and bias mitigation, and its importance, is recognized by researchers, policymakers, and the academic community. There is still a long way to go before we can fully trust artificial intelligence; it is currently being studied and analyzed as we go, but the steps being taken are firm and will lead to foundations that will make artificial intelligence reliable and an advance with benefits for humanity now and in the future.

7.3 Data Privacy and Student Agency

Educational institutions face many challenges and responsibilities that extend beyond the educational process; they must also consider other aspects to maintain the trust of their users and society. One of the most sensitive issues is the privacy of student data, which leads to risks that compromise their identity through identity theft, cyberbullying, violation or intrusion of their privacy on social networks; this endangers the safety and well-being of students.

Student data privacy has always been a sensitive issue to handle, especially given the responsibility of educational institutions to report information and indicators to demonstrate their performance. The reports that need to be made range from grades, attendance, and even sensitive data such as family and socioeconomic information; all this information must be handled with responsibility, clarity, and ethical rules.

Schouten (2017) argues that educational data can inform teaching and academic advising by supporting predictions about suitable pedagogical approaches and student pathways. However, the use of aggregate data in higher education also presents moral risks and therefore requires careful professional judgement.

At the institutional level, clear governance policies should assign responsibility for data collection, preservation, anonymisation, and administration. Institutions should also communicate the sources and purposes of data use, establish appropriate access restrictions, obtain informed consent, and provide mechanisms through which individuals can challenge adverse consequences (Aznarte, 2020).

Learning analytics involves processing data about learners and their educational activities. Because these processes may involve sensitive personal information, including data relating to minors, they raise significant privacy, security, and legal concerns (Amo et al., 2020). Institutions should therefore evaluate the validity and representativeness of the data used and consider whether data-driven interventions could reinforce discrimination or existing inequalities (Aznarte, 2020).

The analysis of educational data in general is a sensitive and fragile data that must be handled with effort by various entities, both private and public, and also by various sectors, such as health, economic and especially educational. Thus, the use of educational technologies has implications and risks that, as technology advances and demands escalate, will become complex to address.

In education, the use of technology allows not only the creation of facilities to develop tools focused on learning, which is why new educational applications have been called Educational Technology, this educational innovation has made it possible to obtain data that allows verification of learning progress and attention to more educational approaches; with the use of systems that generate learning analytics assisted by artificial intelligence, the efficiency of the information has overcome all limits of difficulties.

Another very interesting aspect is the ability to retrieve, measure, store, analyze, and recover information that can be used to make decisions in large quantities, but because these technologies are of recent application, research studies identifying information about the vulnerability of personal and sensitive data have not yet been conducted.

Marín & Tur (2023) analyzed studies focused on the ethics of educational technology, identifying recommendations for data privacy in various aspects. However, they found no corresponding processes or methodologies for preventing vulnerabilities related to data privacy protection. The key takeaway regarding the potential of educational technology in the educational process is clear: it impacts both the process itself and its management. Since its inception, it has significantly strengthened its development, but most importantly, it allows us to measure aspects that can improve everything related to education.

The issue of data protection in the educational process is neglected due to the results it generates for educational decision-making, but from the students' personal point of view, it generates many problems that can be irreversible and traumatic. This opens up new areas of research and technical development to make the most of the benefits of technology and artificial intelligence, but also to protect the most vulnerable and strategic in the educational field.

The increasing use of digital technologies enables aspects of social and educational activity to be converted into data, a process commonly described as datafication. However, data should not be treated as neutral or self-contained, as their meaning depends on the social, cultural, and interpretive conditions in which they are produced, circulated, and used (Gindin et al., 2021).

It is clear that software programs designed for education use, collect, and analyze information ranging from educational assessments to personal data of the students who use them. Most commonly, they are used officially by educational institutions, but most implementations also use digital space (cloud), which at first glance seemed like a very flexible and convenient practice, without considering the vulnerability of sensitive data of the students who use these advances.

In e-learning environments, educational software and learning management systems collect substantial amounts of students' personal information and metadata. Much of this information is increasingly stored and processed by third-party cloud platforms, software-as-a-service providers, and learning-technology vendors, thereby reducing educational institutions' direct control over student data (Alier et al., 2021). These data may be used for educational research, institutional management, pedagogical development, learning analytics, and behaviour-informed learning tools. Nevertheless, such uses require explicit ethical, privacy, legal, and organisational safeguards, as technical capacity alone does not justify the collection and analysis of student data (Alier et al., 2021).

Educational technologies routinely collect and process students' personal data and metadata, often through cloud platforms and third-party service providers. Alier et al., (2021) argue that developments in educational technology over the previous 25 years have made student privacy increasingly difficult to ensure. They identify incentives to gather, mine, and exploit data from learners' online activity that may not align with students' interests or ethical principles, and they conclude that existing legal protections have not kept pace with technological change.

Similar concerns arise in digital social-protection systems. Such systems are frequently presented as neutral, objective, and efficient mechanisms for allocating services and benefits. However, in her analysis of Ecuador's Social Registry,

Science, technology and society studies analyze phenomena beyond the effect of protecting student data, focusing instead on issues of poverty that impact the definition of beneficiaries and non-beneficiaries. In other words, the aim is to improve the political dimension to achieve reliable data systems and thus ensure certainty in the relationship between the state and its citizens. It can be concluded that much remains to be done to protect and serve society through the full use of technology to visualize inequalities and exclusions and to contribute to the design of public policies in the new society.

Data privacy and student autonomy may seem like different issues, but they are closely related. In the educational and social spheres, they affect individuals as well as groups; this is how discrimination and violations of personal data arise. Several institutions have undertaken efforts on two fronts: to understand the negative effects of the use of digital technologies and how to regulate them and develop clear standards.

7.4 Policy and Institutional Frameworks

The origin of artificial intelligence and its application in all human activity has given humanity many benefits, but it has also revealed challenges related in general to society and in particular to the educational sector, especially in the ethical sphere. Today it has become clear that artificial intelligence has promoted personalized learning and generated all the facilities to develop critical thinking; the aforementioned capabilities are key in the new trend of education.

Given the above scenario, it is clear that it is necessary to regulate the use of new technologies in order to have a comprehensive benefit, that is, to take advantage of their benefits and control the risks with real and tangible proposals such as Ethical Frameworks, Regulations and Data Protection Laws (Nozato López, 2024).

Currently, the advances made have led to the term "ethical AI," which has integrated the most prominent ethical principles and has had a high degree of agreement among various initiatives from reputable institutions.

Floridi & Cowls (2019) conducted a comparative analysis of initiatives from various institutions to identify where they converge or diverge and to identify key points to establish a clear and current framework or standard for the use of artificial intelligence.

Likewise, Panadés Zafra et al., (2024) developed an in-depth evaluation framework regarding principles and statements focused on the use of technology in healthcare. Essentially, the relationship extends to the concept of digital health, grounded in bioethics, demonstrating a bridge between scientific orientations in medicine and the close connection to human values within the medical field.

In agreement with Panadés Zafra et al., (2024) analyzes from a biomedical point of view the principles and approaches of the Commandments of Asilomar with its 23 commandments, where they address commandments and challenges in relation to the medical field; Research goal, Link between science and policy, Research culture, Avoiding races, Security, Transparency in rulings, Judicial transparency, Accountability, Alignment of values, Human values, Personal privacy, Freedom and privacy, Shared benefit, Shared prosperity, Human control, No subversion, Arms race, Capacity for precaution, Importance, Risks, Recursive self-improvement, and Common good.

Panadés Zafra et al., (2024) analyzes and contrasts the Montreal Declaration, which establishes ten principles for ethical AI, summarizing them as follows: Principle of well-being, Principle of respect for autonomy, Principles of protection of privacy and intimacy, Principle of solidarity, Principle of democratic participation, Principle of equity, principle of inclusion of diversity, precautionary principle, principle of responsibility, and principle of sustainable development; this information can be expanded upon at the following site (Universidad de Montreal, 2018).

The WHO published a guide based on the ethics and governance of AI in Health; the analysis and progress that has been developed is an example to be taken as a basis since it integrates aspects such as; Promoting human well-being, safety, and the public interest; protecting human autonomy and data privacy; solidarity; ensuring inclusion and equity; human dignity; and fostering responsibility and accountability. Further information can be found at the following website (OMS, 2021).

In the medical field, the vision and development has been clear because it focuses on purely medical aspects based on respect for life and the integrity of people, but it also has a focus on avoiding inequalities and the privacy of the quality of data. The above data is fundamental to showing how to lay the foundations for a framework to regulate the use of artificial intelligence and ensure the exploitation of its benefits.

In various sectors and institutions, the importance of regulating the use of artificial intelligence has been recognized; these efforts have motivated international progress in formalizing key documents to regulate the use of artificial intelligence with rules and regulations. Such is the case of the United Nations General Assembly Resolution (ONU) en 2024. Vercelli (2025) refers to key areas of observation and development, which are: Recognition of the need for a global framework for the sustainable and comprehensive development of artificial intelligence. It emphasizes the protection of human rights, sustainable development, and international cooperation, advocating for the creation of ethical and technical standards that evolve through cooperation among member states. Vercelli (2025) examines in depth the key points of the document and the implications for those who must adhere to the regulations generated by this effort. The foundations for articulating regulation in international political and technological documents, however, are primarily focused on the point of "widely leveraging the opportunities of safe, secure, and reliable artificial intelligence systems for sustainable development."

Another aspect highlighted in this general observance document is the improvement of international cooperation for the development of artificial intelligence capabilities. It is important to note that the general pronouncements form the basis for protecting human rights; special emphasis is placed on avoiding technological gaps, algorithmic fairness, and mitigating biases, (Drnas de Clément, 2022) For more information, please visit the following website:(ONU, 2024).

The European Union has also generated criteria to standardize and regulate the use of artificial intelligence and has also developed studies and strategies to promote the development of standards that benefit technological development based on artificial intelligence under a regulatory instrument called a Regulation (UE) 2024 in the European Parliament and the Council, which integrates rules focused on harmonizing the development, marketing and above all the use of artificial intelligence systems in the member states that comprise it (Presno Linera & Meuwese, 2024). Another very important aspect of this effort is the classification given to artificial intelligence systems according to the level of development and contribution, but it focuses mainly on the risks it faces (minimal, limited, high and prohibited). The new 2024 regulation also imposes obligations regarding transparency, human oversight, and impact assessment. The European Union's Artificial Intelligence regulation is expected to be applied worldwide; for more information, please visit the website: (European Union, 2024).

In summary, it can be said that the United Nations (UN) has a global reach due to the very nature of the organization, but also because it focuses on data related to human rights, sustainability, and international cooperation. Similarly, the European Union (EU) operates within Europe, but this does not preclude it from promoting a global approach and focusing on clear legal norms regarding risk management and transparency.

8. FUTURE DIRECTIONS: TOWARDS HUMAN-AI SYMBIOTIC LEARNING

8.1 Intelligent Adaptive Ecosystems

In this chapter, intelligent adaptive ecosystems are conceptualised as educational environments that combine learner modelling, AI-enabled assessment, adaptive sequencing, personalised feedback, and human pedagogical judgement. Adaptive systems can adjust content, task sequence, pace, and feedback in response to learners' current knowledge, previous responses, and progress (Caspari-Sadeghi, 2023). Generative AI may further support dynamic content generation, customised feedback, and adaptive learning pathways within intelligent tutoring systems, although the available report presenting these applications remains an under-review preprint (Maity & Deroy, 2024).

Empirical findings should be interpreted in relation to their particular educational contexts. In a quasi-experimental study involving 40 secondary-school students,

Alenezi (2024) reported improved performance, particularly among lower-performing learners, together with increased student satisfaction. In a separate randomised study, mastery-based task selection in a mixed-reality science environment produced better learning of scientific principles than random task selection without reducing enjoyment (Yannier et al., 2024).

Adaptive technologies can also provide personalised feedback and update learning pathways as students progress. Their outputs may help educators make more targeted pedagogical decisions, but effective implementation still depends on teacher readiness, digital literacy, pedagogical alignment, and careful interpretation of learner data (Alenezi, 2024; Caspari-Sadeghi, 2023).

8.2 Lifelong and Continuous Learning Models

Lifelong learning extends beyond initial schooling and encompasses continuing educational opportunities across different stages of life and across formal, non-formal, and informal contexts. Educational institutions therefore need flexible pathways that enable learners to update their knowledge and skills in response to changing personal, social, and professional circumstances (UNESCO Institute for Lifelong Learning, 2022).

Artificial intelligence may support lifelong learning through personalised pathways that incorporate learner profiles, prior knowledge, progress data, adaptive sequencing, and flexible self-paced environments. However, the design of such systems should remain responsive to learners' evolving needs and educational goals. In technology-based learning environments, learning analytics may also support the assessment of learner progress and the adaptation of educational activities. For example, Baalsrud Hauge et al., (2015) proposed a learning-analytics architecture for monitoring and scaffolding learning experiences in serious-game environments. These context-specific findings should not, however, be generalised automatically to entire lifelong learning trajectories.

8.3 Emerging Technologies and Convergence Trends

Artificial intelligence, machine learning, and mixed-reality technologies can be combined to create adaptive educational experiences. AI-based assessment systems can diagnose learners' current knowledge, monitor progress, update learner profiles, and support personalised feedback (Caspari-Sadeghi, 2023). In a mixed-reality science environment, AI-enabled mastery-based task selection produced better learning of scientific principles than random task selection, without reducing learners' enjoyment (Yannier et al., 2024).

Technology-supported interdisciplinary approaches may also contribute to higher-order thinking. A meta-analysis of Indonesian studies reported a positive overall effect of STEM-based e-learning on students' higher-order thinking skills (Solehuddin et al., 2023). More broadly, STEAM education can provide opportunities for transdisciplinary, project- and problem-based learning, while dialogic STEAM activities may support the development of critical thinking through meaningful interaction (Pressick-Kilborn et al., 2021; Fernández-Cárdenas & Santillán-Rosas, 2025).

8.4 Vision for STEAM Education Beyond 2030

In this chapter, future STEAM environments are envisaged as flexible, interdisciplinary, and technology-enabled spaces in which physical design, pedagogy, and digital tools operate in an integrated manner. Open and multifunctional learning environments can support experiential, cooperative, and participatory activities when technology functions as a pedagogical resource rather than determining the educational process (Mondaini & Rosciani, 2021).

Adaptive learning technologies may also respond to differences in learners' knowledge, abilities, and progress by adjusting content and learning pathways (Jing et al., 2023). A case study involving primary-school pupils with learning difficulties demonstrated how content presentation can be adapted to identified learner requirements, although these findings should not be generalised beyond the context examined (Lancheros-Cuesta et al., 2014). Future STEAM initiatives should therefore combine technological flexibility with inclusive design and continuing human pedagogical oversight.

Education systems are likely to undergo significant transformation through the influence of intelligent adaptive ecosystems, continuous learning models, and emerging technologies. In considering educational trajectories beyond 2030, fostering a constructive relationship between human actors and AI may be important for supporting environments that remain adaptive, engaging, and aligned with the evolving needs of contemporary learners.

9. CONCLUSIONS

In this chapter, we mention that STEAM 5.0 is a smart, interdisciplinary and human-centred educational ecosystem. We also state that AI should complement, rather than replace, teachers, through human-AI collaboration and explainability. We also note that personalised learning is only valid if it incorporates equity, accessibility, privacy and the mitigation of bias. Furthermore, the future of STEAM 5.0 depends on ethical governance, continuous learning and responsible adaptive technologies.

REFERENCES

Adadi, A., & Berrada, M. (2018). Pecking inside the black-box: A survey on explainable artificial intelligence (XAI). *IEEE Access : Practical Innovations, Open Solutions*, *6*, 52138–52160. DOI: 10.1109/ACCESS.2018.2870052

Adenubi, A. O., Samuel, N., Oyenuga, A. O., & Adewale, K. A. (2024). Artificial intelligence with agile teaching strategies for personalized learning. *Nigerian Online Journal of Educational Sciences and Technology*, *6*(1), 364–379.

Al-Ansi, A. M., Jaboob, M., Garad, A., & Al-Ansi, A. (2023). Analyzing augmented reality (AR) and virtual reality (VR) recent development in education. *Social Sciences & Humanities Open*, *8*(1), 100532. DOI: 10.1016/j.ssaho.2023.100532

Alenezi, A. (2024). Evaluating the effectiveness of AI-powered adaptive learning systems in secondary schools. *International Journal on Studies in Education*, *6*(4), 686–700. DOI: 10.46328/ijonse.264

Alier, M., Casañ Guerrero, M. J., Amo, D., Severance, C., & Fonseca, D. (2021). Privacy and e-learning: A pending task. *Sustainability (Basel)*, *13*(16), 9206. Advance online publication. DOI: 10.3390/su13169206

Alomá Bello, M., Crespo Díaz, L. M., González Hernández, K., & Estévez Pérez, N. (2022). Fundamentos cognitivos y pedagógicos del aprendizaje activo. *Mendive. Review of Education*, *20*(4), 1353–1368. https://mendive.upr.edu.cu/index.php/MendiveUPR/article/view/3128

Alves-Oliveira, P., Sequeira, P., Melo, F. S., Castellano, G., & Paiva, A. (2019). Empathic robot for group learning: A field study. *ACM Transactions on Human-Robot Interaction*, *8*(1), 3. Advance online publication. DOI: 10.1145/3300188 PMID: 33829148

Amo-Filvà, D., Alier, M., García-Peñalvo, F. J., Fonseca, D., & Casañ, M. J. (2020). Privacidad, seguridad y legalidad en soluciones educativas basadas en blockchain: Una revisión sistemática de la literatura. *RIED. Revista Iberoamericana de Educación a Distancia*, *23*(2), 213–236. DOI: 10.5944/ried.23.2.26388

Aznarte, J. L. (2020). Consideraciones éticas en torno al uso de tecnologías basadas en datos masivos en la UNED. *RIED. Revista Iberoamericana de Educación a Distancia*, *23*(2), 237–252. DOI: 10.5944/ried.23.2.26590

Baalsrud Hauge, J. M., Stanescu, I. A., Arnab, S., Moreno-Ger, P., Lim, T., Serrano-Laguna, Á., Lameras, P., Hendrix, M., Kiili, K., Ninaus, M., de Freitas, S., Mazzetti, A., Dahlbom, A., & Degano, C. (2015). Learning analytics architecture to scaffold learning experience through technology-based methods. *International Journal of Serious Games*, *2*(1). Advance online publication. DOI: 10.17083/ijsg.v2i1.38

Baxter, G., & Sommerville, I. (2011). Socio-technical systems: From design methods to systems engineering. *Interacting with Computers*, *23*(1), 4–17. DOI: 10.1016/j.intcom.2010.07.003

Belpaeme, T., Kennedy, J., Ramachandran, A., Scassellati, B., & Tanaka, F. (2018). Social robots for education: A review. *Science Robotics*, *3*(21), eaat5954. Advance online publication. DOI: 10.1126/scirobotics.aat5954 PMID: 33141719

Bergasa Sariego, C. A. (2024). *Mejorando la equidad en algoritmos de aprendizaje automático usando un enfoque de transporte óptimo* [Master's thesis, Universidad de Chile]. DOI: 10.58011/5cew-3z19

Blikstein, P., & Worsley, M. (2016). Multimodal learning analytics and education data mining: Using computational technologies to measure complex learning tasks. *Journal of Learning Analytics*, *3*(2), 220–238. DOI: 10.18608/jla.2016.32.11

Bracho-Fuenmayor, P. L. (2024). Ética y moral en la educación superior: Una revisión bibliométrica. *Revista de Ciencias Sociales*, *30*(3), 553–568. DOI: 10.31876/rcs.v30i3.42695

Bustelo Gracia, J. L. (2025). Hacia una gobernanza algorítmica transparente: Auditoría de sesgo. Estudio de caso. *Cuadernos de Gobierno y Administración Pública*, *12*(1), e97604. Advance online publication. DOI: 10.5209/cgap.97604

Carrillo-Velarde, M. V. (2020). La ética y los valores en la educación superior. *Dominio de las Ciencias*, *6*(3), 1108–1117. DOI: 10.23857/dc.v6i3.1340

Caspari-Sadeghi, S. (2023). Artificial intelligence in technology-enhanced assessment: A survey of machine learning. *Journal of Educational Technology Systems*, *51*(3), 372–386. DOI: 10.1177/00472395221138791

CAST. (2024). *CAST Universal Design for Learning Guidelines version 3.0*. https://udlguidelines.cast.org/

Chen, J.-C., Huang, Y., Lin, K.-Y., Chang, Y.-S., Lin, H.-C., Lin, C.-Y., & Hsiao, H.-S. (2020). Developing a hands-on activity using virtual reality to help students learn by doing. *Journal of Computer Assisted Learning*, *36*(1), 46–60. DOI: 10.1111/jcal.12389

Dastane, O., Turner, J., & Nankervis, A. (2024). The trajectory of artificial intelligence for competency-based personalised learning: Past, present and future. *The International Journal of Information and Learning Technology*, *41*(5), 473–489. DOI: 10.1108/IJILT-07-2024-0162

Davis, B., & Sumara, D. (2006). *Complexity and education: Inquiries into learning, teaching, and research*. Lawrence Erlbaum Associates.

Delgado-Quintero, D. J., Sepúlveda-López, J. J., Pineda Romero, M. M., & Santos-Mendez, D. J. (2025). Mapping the ethical landscape in AI: A bibliometric analysis with educational insights. *INTELETICA*, *2*(3), 1–16. DOI: 10.4114/INTELETICA.vol2iss3pp1-16

Drnas de Clément, Z. (2022). Inteligencia artificial en el derecho internacional, Naciones Unidas y Unión Europea. *Revista Estudios Jurídicos. Segunda Época*, *22*(22). Advance online publication. DOI: 10.17561/rej.n22.7524

Fernández-Cárdenas, J. M., & Santillán-Rosas, I. M. (2025). Learning critical thinking through dialogic STEAM educational activities: A case of high school students in northeastern Mexico during pandemic times. *SAGE Open*, *15*(4), 21582440251388756. Advance online publication. DOI: 10.1177/21582440251388756

Ferrara, E. (2024). Fairness and bias in artificial intelligence: A brief survey of sources, impacts, and mitigation strategies. *Sci*, *6*(1), 3. Advance online publication. DOI: 10.3390/sci6010003

Floridi, L., & Cowls, J. (2019). A unified framework of five principles for AI in society. *Harvard Data Science Review*, *1*(1). Advance online publication. DOI: 10.1162/99608f92.8cd550d1

Floridi, L., Cowls, J., Beltrametti, M., Chatila, R., Chazerand, P., Dignum, V., Luetge, C., Madelin, R., Pagallo, U., Rossi, F., Schafer, B., Valcke, P., & Vayena, E. (2018). AI4People—An ethical framework for a good AI society: Opportunities, risks, principles, and recommendations. *Minds and Machines*, *28*(4), 689–707. DOI: 10.1007/s11023-018-9482-5 PMID: 30930541

Gil Iranzo, R., Gutiérrez-Ujaque, D., & Teixidó Cairol, M. (2024). De la ansiedad al empoderamiento: Impacto del uso de la inteligencia artificial en la percepción de los estudiantes en educación superior. *REDU. Revista de Docencia Universitaria*, *22*(2), 85–104. DOI: 10.4995/redu.2024.22009

Gindin, I. L., Cingolani, G., & Rodríguez-Amat, J. R. (2021). Autoridades interpretativas: Una perspectiva teórica sobre datificación y producción de sentido. *Palabra Clave (La Plata)*, *24*(3), e2436. Advance online publication. DOI: 10.5294/pacla.2021.24.3.6

Guzmán-Brand, V. A., & Gélvez-García, L. E. (2024). La ética y la responsabilidad en la implementación de la inteligencia artificial: Revisión sistemática. *Revista Ingeniería. Matemáticas y Ciencias de la Información*, *11*(22), 107–118. DOI: 10.21017/rimci.1081

Hasan, M. A., Noor, N. F. M., Rahman, S. S. B. A., & Rahman, M. M. (2020). The transition from intelligent to affective tutoring system: A review and open issues. *IEEE Access : Practical Innovations, Open Solutions*, *8*, 204612–204638. DOI: 10.1109/ACCESS.2020.3036990

Holmes, W., Porayska-Pomsta, K., Holstein, K., Sutherland, E., Baker, T., Buckingham Shum, S., Santos, O. C., Rodrigo, M. T., Cukurova, M., Bittencourt, I. I., & Koedinger, K. R. (2022). Ethics of AI in education: Towards a community-wide framework. *International Journal of Artificial Intelligence in Education*, *32*(3), 504–526. DOI: 10.1007/s40593-021-00239-1

Isomöttönen, V., Daniels, M., Cajander, Å., Pears, A., & McDermott, R. (2019). Searching for global employability: Can students capitalize on enabling learning environments? *ACM Transactions on Computing Education*, *19*(2), 11. Advance online publication. DOI: 10.1145/3277568

Jing, Y., Zhao, L., Zhu, K., Wang, H., Wang, C., & Xia, Q. (2023). Research landscape of adaptive learning in education: A bibliometric study on research publications from 2000 to 2022. *Sustainability (Basel)*, *15*(4), 3115. Advance online publication. DOI: 10.3390/su15043115

Jones, A., & Castellano, G. (2018). Adaptive robotic tutors that support self-regulated learning: A longer-term investigation with primary school children. *International Journal of Social Robotics*, *10*(3), 357–370. DOI: 10.1007/s12369-017-0458-z

Julian, D., & Smith, R. (2019). Developing an intelligent tutoring system for robotic-assisted surgery instruction. *The International Journal of Medical Robotics + Computer Assisted Surgery : MRCAS*, *15*(6), e2037. DOI: 10.1002/rcs.2037 PMID: 31509636

Lancheros-Cuesta, D. J., Carrillo-Ramos, Á., & Pavlich-Mariscal, J. A. (2014). Content adaptation for students with learning difficulties: Design and case study. *International Journal of Web Information Systems*, *10*(2), 106–130. DOI: 10.1108/IJWIS-12-2013-0040

Leyzberg, D., Ramachandran, A., & Scassellati, B. (2018). The effect of personalization in longer-term robot tutoring. *ACM Transactions on Human-Robot Interaction*, *7*(3), 19. Advance online publication. DOI: 10.1145/3283453

Liu, L. (2020). STEAM platform: Transforming youth leadership for a smart circular economy. In B. Panth and R. Maclean (Eds.), *Anticipating and preparing for emerging skills and jobs* (pp. 297–304). Springer. DOI: 10.1007/978-981-15-7018-6_36

Maity, S., & Deroy, A. (2024). Generative AI and its impact on personalized intelligent tutoring systems [Preprint]. arXiv. https://arxiv.org/abs/2410.10650

Marín Juarros, V. I., & Tur Ferrer, G. (2023). La privacidad de los datos en tecnología educativa: Resultados de una revisión de alcance. *Edutec. Revista Electrónica de Tecnología Educativa*, *83*(83), 7–23. DOI: 10.21556/edutec.2023.83.2701

Mejias, S., Thompson, N., Sedas, R. M., Rosin, M., Soep, E., Peppler, K., Roche, J., Wong, J., Hurley, M., Bell, P., & Bevan, B. (2021). The trouble with STEAM and why we use it anyway. *Science Education*, *105*(2), 209–231. DOI: 10.1002/sce.21605 PMID: 33250574

Mhlongo, S., Mbatha, K., Ramatsetse, B., & Dlamini, R. (2023). Challenges, opportunities, and prospects of adopting and using smart digital technologies in learning environments: An iterative review. *Heliyon*, *9*(6), e16348. DOI: 10.1016/j.heliyon.2023.e16348 PMID: 37274691

Miao, F., Holmes, W., Huang, R., & Zhang, H. (2021). *AI and education: Guidance for policy-makers.* UNESCO., DOI: 10.54675/PCSP7350

Mondaini, G., & Rosciani, M. (2021). Adaptive environments: New spaces for learning. In Scaradozzi, D., Guasti, L., Di Stasio, M., Miotti, B., Monteriù, A., & Blikstein, P. (Eds.), *Makers at school, educational robotics and innovative learning environments* (pp. 367–373). Springer., DOI: 10.1007/978-3-030-77040-2_49

Msambwa, M. M., Zhang, W., & Kangwa, D. (2025). The impact of AI on the personal and collaborative learning environments in higher education. *European Journal of Education*, *60*(1), e12909. DOI: 10.1111/ejed.12909

Nozato López, M. J. (2024). La inteligencia artificial en educación: Consideraciones éticas y fomento al pensamiento crítico. *RECIE. Revista Electrónica Científica de Investigación Educativa*, *8*, e2357. DOI: 10.33010/recie.v8i0.2357

Organisation for Economic Co-operation and Development. (2023). *OECD digital education outlook 2023: Towards an effective digital education ecosystem.* OECD Publishing., DOI: 10.1787/c74f03de-

Panadés Zafra, R., Amorós Parramond, N., Albiol-Perarnaub, M., & Yuguero Torres, O. (2024). Análisis de retos y dilemas que deberá afrontar la bioética del siglo XXI, en la era de la salud digital. *Atencion Primaria*, *56*(7), 102901. Advance online publication. DOI: 10.1016/j.aprim.2024.102901 PMID: 38452658

Pegoraro, R., & Curzel, E. (2023). Convocatoria de Roma por la ética de la IA: El nacimiento de un movimiento. *Medicina y Etica : Revista Internacional de Bioética, Deontología y Etica Médica*, *34*(2), 315–349. DOI: 10.36105/mye.2023v34n2.01

Presno Linera, M. Á., & Meuwese, A. (2024). La regulación de la inteligencia artificial en Europa. *Teoría y Realidad Constitucional*, *54*(54), 131–161. DOI: 10.5944/trc.54.2024.43310

Pressick-Kilborn, K., Silk, M., & Martin, J. (2021). STEM and STEAM education in Australian K–12 schooling. In *Oxford research encyclopedia of education*. Oxford University Press., DOI: 10.1093/acrefore/9780190264093.013.1684

Radianti, J., Majchrzak, T. A., Fromm, J., & Wohlgenannt, I. (2020). A systematic review of immersive virtual reality applications for higher education: Design elements, lessons learned, and research agenda. *Computers & Education*, *147*, 103778. DOI: 10.1016/j.compedu.2019.103778

Ramachandran, A., Sebo, S. S., & Scassellati, B. (2019). Personalized robot tutoring using the Assistive Tutor POMDP (AT-POMDP). *Proceedings of the AAAI Conference on Artificial Intelligence*, *33*(01), 8050–8057. DOI: 10.1609/aaai.v33i01.33018050

Robinson, J. P., Winthrop, R., & McGivney, E. (2016). *Millions learning: Scaling up quality education in developing countries*. Brookings Institution.

Sánchez Islas, M., & Rodríguez Betanzos, A. (2026). Exploración del uso de la inteligencia artificial en estudiantes universitarios. *Cuaderno de Pedagogía Universitaria*, *23*, e713. Advance online publication. DOI: 10.29197/cpu.v23i.739

Schouten, G. (2017). On meeting students where they are: Teacher judgment and the use of data in higher education. *Theory and Research in Education*, *15*(3), 321–338. DOI: 10.1177/1477878517734452

Selwyn, N. (2019). Should robots replace teachers? AI and the future of education. *Polity*.

Siemens, G. (2013). Learning analytics: The emergence of a discipline. *The American Behavioral Scientist*, *57*(10), 1380–1400. DOI: 10.1177/0002764213498851

Solehuddin, M., Sopandi, E., Saputra, D. G., Dhaniswara, E., Yulianto, S., Zhang, W., & Xu, S. (2023). Development of adaptive e-learning content to increase learning effectiveness. *Journal International Inspire Education Technology*, *2*(2), 101–112. DOI: 10.55849/jiiet.v2i2.457

Spyropoulou, N., & Kameas, A. (2024). Leveraging communities of practice for STEAM education: A study on engagement and professional development. *European Journal of Education*, *59*(4), e12806. DOI: 10.1111/ejed.12806

Sun, J., Zhang, Z., Hong, L., OuYang, L., & Lu, C. (2025). Collaborative optimization for interdisciplinary intelligent education systems: Algorithm design and application. In *Proceedings of SPIE* (Vol. 13808, Article 138081A). SPIE. DOI: 10.1117/12.3082466

Topali, P., Ortega-Arranz, A., Rodríguez-Triana, M. J., Er, E., Khalil, M., & Akçapınar, G. (2025). Designing human-centered learning analytics and artificial intelligence in education solutions: A systematic literature review. *Behaviour & Information Technology*, *44*(5), 1071–1098. DOI: 10.1080/0144929X.2024.2345295

UNESCO Institute for Lifelong Learning. (2022). *Making lifelong learning a reality: A handbook*. UNESCO Institute for Lifelong Learning.

United Nations News. (2024, September 19). *La regulación mundial de la IA es necesaria*. https://news.un.org/es/story/2024/09/1532941

Université de Montréal. (2018). *Déclaration de Montréal pour un développement responsable de l'intelligence artificielle*. https://declarationmontreal-iaresponsable.com/

Vercelli, A. (2025). Las inteligencias artificiales y sus regulaciones internacionales: Análisis de las resoluciones de la Asamblea General de la ONU en 2024. *SADIO Electronic Journal of Informatics and Operations Research*, *24*(2), 110–119. DOI: 10.24215/15146774e081

Wong, B. T. M. (2017). Learning analytics in higher education: An analysis of case studies. *Asian Association of Open Universities Journal*, *12*(1), 21–40. DOI: 10.1108/AAOUJ-01-2017-0009

World Health Organization. (2021). *Ethics and governance of artificial intelligence for health*. World Health Organization. https://www.who.int/publications/i/item/9789240029200

Yannier, N., Hudson, S. E., Chang, H. Y., & Koedinger, K. R. (2024). AI adaptivity in a mixed-reality system improves learning. *International Journal of Artificial Intelligence in Education*, *34*(4), 1541–1558. DOI: 10.1007/s40593-023-00388-5

Zhou, D., Liu, Y., Huang, J., Xiang, Y., Gu, R., & Liu, B. (2022). An intelligent tutoring system enhancing transdisciplinary problem-finding in design-led integrated STEM education. In *Proceedings of the International Conference on Intelligent Computing and Artificial Intelligence in Education (IC-ICAIE 2022)* (pp. 943–949). Atlantis Press. DOI: 10.2991/978-94-6463-040-4_142

Zou, D., Xie, H., & Kohnke, L. (2025). Navigating the future: Establishing a framework for educators' pedagogic artificial intelligence competence. *European Journal of Education*, *60*(2), e70117. DOI: 10.1111/ejed.70117

Chapter 2
STEAM 5.0 and Human-Centred Intelligent Learning Ecosystems

Mustafa Kayyali
http://orcid.org/0000-0003-3300-262X
Maaref University of Applied Sciences, Syria

ABSTRACT

This chapter explores STEAM 5.0 as a human-centred reimagining of intelligent education, where science, technology, engineering, arts, and mathematics are no longer treated as separate domains but as interconnected spaces for creativity, ethical reasoning, and social responsibility. It examines how explainable AI can support personalized learning and assessment without reducing learners to data profiles or predictive categories. The chapter argues that intelligent learning ecosystems must remain transparent, inclusive, and pedagogically accountable, especially when algorithmic systems influence feedback, progression, and evaluation. Rather than celebrating automation as an educational cure-all, the discussion places human judgment, empathy, imagination, and learner agency at the centre of technological design. By connecting STEAM 5.0 with explainable AI and ethical assessment, the chapter offers a reflective framework for building learning environments that are not only adaptive and efficient, but also humane, trustworthy, and intellectually liberating.

INTRODUCTION

The idea of STEAM 5.0 begins with a quiet dissatisfaction. For years, educational systems have spoken confidently about innovation, digital transformation, and

DOI: 10.4018/979-8-2600-3658-7.ch002

technological readiness, yet many classrooms still struggle with a stubborn question: *innovation for whom, and at what human cost?* The integration of science, technology, engineering, arts, and mathematics has already pushed education beyond narrow disciplinary borders. It has encouraged learners to think across systems, experiment with design, connect logic with imagination, and treat knowledge as something alive rather than fixed. Yet the arrival of artificial intelligence, particularly in its adaptive, predictive, and generative forms, has changed the stakes. STEAM education is no longer only about preparing learners to use technology. It is increasingly about preparing them to live, think, create, and make ethical decisions inside environments shaped by intelligent systems.

This chapter approaches STEAM 5.0 as a deeply human-centred stage in the evolution of STEAM learning. Unlike earlier models that often celebrated digital tools for their speed, efficiency, or novelty, STEAM 5.0 asks whether intelligent technologies can be designed around human dignity, creativity, empathy, transparency, and social responsibility. It moves away from the idea that education should simply become more automated or more data-driven. Instead, it suggests that the future of learning depends on a more delicate balance: the capacity of AI systems to support personalization and assessment, and the responsibility of educators to preserve the learner as a thinking, feeling, questioning human being.

At the heart of this discussion lies the concept of the human-centred intelligent learning ecosystem. Such an ecosystem is not merely a digital platform, nor is it a collection of smart tools placed around a traditional curriculum. It is a living educational environment where learners, teachers, algorithms, data, content, feedback, assessment, and institutional values continuously interact. In this kind of ecosystem, intelligence does not belong only to the machine. It is distributed across human judgment, technological assistance, social interaction, creative inquiry, and reflective practice. A well-designed intelligent learning ecosystem should not make students passive recipients of algorithmic guidance (Rajabi, 2025). It should help them become more aware of how they learn, why they make certain choices, how their work can improve, and how knowledge can be used responsibly in the world beyond the classroom.

The promise of explainable AI is especially important here. In many educational settings, AI systems are used to recommend learning materials, identify weaknesses, generate feedback, predict performance, or support assessment. These functions may appear helpful, even impressive. Yet when the reasoning behind AI-generated decisions remains hidden, education risks becoming strangely opaque. A student may be told that they are "at risk," "advanced," "weak in problem-solving," or "ready for the next level," without understanding how such judgments were made. A teacher may receive dashboards, scores, or alerts without knowing what assumptions shaped them. This is where explainability becomes more than a technical feature. It becomes a pedagogical and ethical requirement.

In STEAM education, explainability has an even richer meaning (Wang & Chen, 2024). Because STEAM learning is built around inquiry, experimentation, creativity, and interdisciplinary problem-solving, learners must be encouraged to understand processes rather than merely accept outcomes. If AI supports a design task, evaluates a mathematical model, recommends a scientific simulation, or comments on a creative project, its contribution should be open enough to invite questioning. Learners should be able to ask: Why did the system recommend this path? What evidence did it use? What possibilities did it ignore? Could there be another interpretation? Such questions are not distractions from learning. They are learning. They turn AI from an invisible authority into an object of reflection, critique, and dialogue.

However, the ethical challenges are serious. Personalization can easily become profiling. Assessment can slide into surveillance. Feedback can become over-standardized. Efficiency can be mistaken for educational depth. When learner data is collected, analyzed, and transformed into predictions, the educational system must decide whether it is using such information to support human growth or to classify students prematurely. This distinction matters. A humane learning ecosystem recognizes that students are never fully measurable. Their abilities are uneven, emerging, contextual, and sometimes hidden beneath anxiety, language barriers, social pressures, or prior educational wounds. To design intelligent systems responsibly, educators and developers must resist the temptation to treat data as destiny.

STEAM 5.0 therefore calls for a different educational imagination (Lampou, 2024). It invites institutions to design AI-supported environments where personalization does not isolate learners, where assessment does not flatten creativity, and where technology does not quietly replace the relational work of teaching. The teacher remains central, not as the sole source of knowledge, but as an interpreter, mentor, ethical guide, and designer of meaningful learning experiences. The learner also remains central, not as a user profile, but as a person capable of agency, curiosity, resistance, and transformation.

This chapter argues that the future of STEAM education will not be defined by how much AI can do, but by how wisely humans decide what AI should and should not do. The real challenge is not to build systems that are merely intelligent, but to create learning ecosystems that are understandable, trustworthy, inclusive, and emotionally alive. In that sense, STEAM 5.0 is not simply the next technological phase of education. It is a call to return intelligence to its fuller human meaning.

REFRAMING STEAM 5.0: FROM TECHNOLOGICAL INTEGRATION TO HUMAN-CENTRED EDUCATIONAL INTELLIGENCE

The discussion of STEAM 5.0 begins, perhaps, with a necessary unease (Gore et al, 2023). For decades, education has been told to integrate technology, to modernize, to digitize, to prepare learners for an economy that is always presented as arriving faster than schools can possibly respond. Computers entered classrooms, then smartboards, then learning management systems, then analytics dashboards, then adaptive platforms, and now generative and explainable artificial intelligence. Each wave carried its own promise: better access, greater efficiency, richer interaction, more individualized learning. Some of these promises were real. Others were exaggerated, hurried, or poorly understood. Yet beneath the enthusiasm, one question has remained rather stubborn: has education become more intelligent simply because it has become more technological?

STEAM 5.0 asks this question with unusual seriousness (Lampou, 2024). It does not reject technology, nor does it romanticize an earlier classroom untouched by machines. That would be naïve. Instead, it challenges the assumption that technological integration is, by itself, a sign of educational progress. A classroom may be full of devices and still remain intellectually thin. A platform may generate beautiful analytics and still fail to understand the fragile, uneven, sometimes contradictory nature of human learning. A student may receive instant feedback from an AI system and still feel unseen. This is the tension at the heart of STEAM 5.0: the shift from placing technology *inside* education to rethinking education through the lens of human-centred intelligence.

Earlier approaches to STEM and STEAM often emphasized competence, innovation, and employability (Montés et al, 2024). Learners were encouraged to solve problems, build prototypes, interpret data, and connect scientific and artistic modes of thinking. This was already a significant move away from rigid subject silos. The addition of the arts, in particular, widened the educational imagination. It allowed creativity, design, narrative, emotion, ethics, and cultural interpretation to enter spaces that had sometimes been dominated by technical rationality. STEAM, at its best, reminded educators that a bridge is never only an engineering structure, that an algorithm is never only a sequence of operations, and that a scientific discovery does not exist outside society. Knowledge breathes through context.

Yet the emergence of AI has complicated this picture. Intelligent systems do not simply provide tools that students use from the outside (Liu & Yu, 2023). They increasingly participate in the learning process itself. They recommend resources, generate explanations, adapt tasks, assess responses, predict difficulties, simulate environments, and even shape the kinds of questions learners are likely to ask. In such a setting, technology is not merely an instrument. It becomes an actor within the educational ecosystem. This is precisely why the language of "integration" starts to feel insufficient. Integration suggests addition: put the technology into the classroom, train teachers to use it, align it with curriculum, measure its impact. STEAM 5.0 requires something deeper and less comfortable. It asks how intelligence is distributed among human beings, machines, communities, and environments, and how that distribution should be governed.

The term human-centred educational intelligence is useful here because it resists the narrowing of intelligence into computation. Artificial intelligence can process patterns, generate outputs, and optimize pathways with extraordinary speed. But education is not only a pattern-recognition problem (Lei, 2025). It is also a moral, emotional, cultural, and relational process. A learner's hesitation may be cognitive, but it may also be personal. A weak answer may reflect misunderstanding, but it may also reflect fear, fatigue, linguistic insecurity, or lack of trust. A creative project may not meet a rubric neatly, yet it may contain the first trace of original thought. Human-centred intelligence begins from this messiness. It refuses to reduce learning to the visible residue of data.

This does not mean that data has no value. Quite the opposite. In a well-designed STEAM 5.0 ecosystem, data can reveal patterns that teachers may not easily notice (Szilágyi et al, 2024). It can help identify gaps, support timely intervention, make feedback more responsive, and offer learners multiple routes through complex material. In science education, AI-driven simulations can help students test hypotheses that would be impossible in a physical classroom (Kotsis, 2024). In engineering design, intelligent tools can support iteration and modelling. In mathematics, adaptive systems can diagnose misconceptions with impressive granularity. In the arts, generative technologies can become partners in exploration, provocation, and critique. These are not small contributions. They can make learning more vivid, more flexible, and more accessible.

The danger appears when these systems are treated as neutral, objective, or educationally self-sufficient. They are not. Every AI system carries assumptions: about what counts as progress, what counts as evidence, what counts as an error, what kind of learner is being imagined, and which forms of knowledge are easiest to measure. In STEAM contexts, where creativity and problem-solving often unfold in non-linear ways, such assumptions can quietly discipline the learner. The system may reward efficiency over exploration, correctness over curiosity, fluency over depth, or predictability over risk. Something vital can be lost without anyone openly deciding to lose it.

This is where explainable AI becomes central to the reframing of STEAM 5.0. Explainability is not merely a technical demand placed on developers. It is a pedagogical condition (Torres-Rivera et al, 2025). If an AI system guides a learner, assesses a performance, suggests a pathway, or flags a weakness, the reasoning behind that intervention should be open to scrutiny. Students should not be expected to obey algorithmic recommendations as if they were educational weather: mysterious, external, unavoidable. Teachers, too, need more than dashboards filled with coloured indicators. They need to understand the logic behind those indicators, the limits of the model, and the kinds of evidence being privileged. Without explainability, intelligent learning ecosystems risk becoming polished black boxes with pedagogical authority but little accountability.

A human-centred STEAM 5.0 classroom would look different from a classroom that simply uses advanced technologies (Agarwal et al, 2025). It would invite learners to question the tools themselves. Why did the model generate this design? Why did the system interpret this answer as incomplete? What data was used to personalize this task? What might the algorithm be missing? These questions turn AI from an invisible controller into a visible object of inquiry. They also strengthen STEAM learning because they connect technical understanding with ethical reflection. Students learn not only with AI, but about AI, around AI, and sometimes against AI. That small resistance matters. It keeps agency alive.

Teacher agency is equally important. There is a subtle danger in imagining AI as a compensatory mechanism for the limitations of human educators. Such thinking can lead institutions to underinvest in teachers while overinvesting in systems. But STEAM 5.0 should not be built on the replacement of professional judgment. Teachers remain interpreters of complexity (Spyropoulou & Kameas, 2025). They see contradictions that data may smooth over. They notice the classroom atmosphere, the unspoken frustration, the student who has gone silent, the group whose collaboration is technically successful but ethically uneven. Intelligent systems may assist this work, but they cannot carry its full human weight.

The arts within STEAM become especially valuable in this reframing. They disturb the cold elegance of purely technical solutions. They ask what a design feels like, whose story it tells, whose body it excludes, what memories it awakens, what social wounds it might deepen or heal. In a STEAM 5.0 ecosystem, the arts are not decorative additions to science and technology. They are ethical and imaginative engines. They remind learners that intelligence without empathy can become brittle, and innovation without human meaning can become strangely empty.

To reframe STEAM 5.0, then, is to move from fascination with smart tools toward a more mature concern with wise educational arrangements (SWARGIARY, 2026). It is to ask whether learning ecosystems make students more capable of judgment, not merely more efficient at completing tasks. It is to design AI-supported education that expands rather than narrows the learner's horizon. It is to accept that personalization must not become isolation, that assessment must not become surveillance, and that prediction must never be mistaken for destiny.

The promise of STEAM 5.0 lies in this difficult balance. It seeks an education where intelligent systems support creativity without scripting it, guide learners without enclosing them, and reveal patterns without flattening persons into profiles. Such an education would not worship technology, but neither would it fear it. It would treat AI as powerful, useful, partial, and deeply in need of human interpretation. At its most compelling, STEAM 5.0 is not a slogan for the next technological phase of schooling. It is a call to recover the fuller meaning of intelligence itself: curious, ethical, embodied, imaginative, relational, and always unfinished.

INTELLIGENT LEARNING ECOSYSTEMS: PERSONALIZATION, ADAPTIVITY, AND THE ETHICS OF LEARNER DATA

An intelligent learning ecosystem is often described through its visible features: adaptive platforms, AI tutors, learning analytics, automated feedback, dashboards, recommender systems, digital portfolios, and increasingly, generative tools able to explain, assess, and redesign learning tasks in real time. Yet this surface description, while useful, misses the deeper educational question. What makes a learning ecosystem truly intelligent? Is it the volume of data it can collect, the speed with which it can respond, or the sophistication of its algorithmic predictions? Or is intelligence, in the educational sense, something more demanding: the capacity to support human growth without enclosing it, to guide without overdetermining, to personalize without shrinking the learner into a behavioral profile?

This question sits at the heart of STEAM 5.0. In a human-centred intelligent learning ecosystem, personalization should not mean merely delivering different content to different students (Rüütmann & Läänemets, 2025). That is the thin version of the idea. It is useful, yes, but insufficient. A mathematics learner may need slower scaffolding in algebraic reasoning; an engineering student may benefit from simulation-based experimentation; a young designer may need feedback that helps them see the emotional texture of a prototype, not only its functional flaws. Personalization, in its richer form, recognizes that learners approach knowledge with different histories, anxieties, strengths, languages, cultural references, and ways of making meaning. It is not only about pace and difficulty. It is also about relevance, confidence, voice, identity, and the right to enter knowledge from more than one doorway.

Adaptive systems promise to make this possible. They observe patterns, detect gaps, recommend pathways, and adjust tasks according to learner performance. In STEAM education, such adaptivity can be genuinely valuable. A student working through a physics simulation can receive immediate prompts when misconceptions appear (Shernoff, 2024). A learner building a digital model can be guided toward alternative design decisions. A group project in environmental science may be supported by AI-generated resources that match students' developing questions. The ecosystem becomes responsive, almost conversational. Instead of waiting for end-of-term assessment to reveal what has gone wrong, teachers and learners can see traces of difficulty as they emerge.

Still, responsiveness is not the same as wisdom. An adaptive system can respond quickly and still respond narrowly. It may identify that a student has answered incorrectly, but not why the mistake matters. It may recommend simpler tasks, but unintentionally lower intellectual expectations. It may detect hesitation as disengagement, when the learner is actually thinking deeply. It may interpret silence in an online forum as absence, although the student is reading carefully, composing thoughts slowly, perhaps translating internally before speaking. Human learning is filled with these quiet ambiguities. Data captures some of them, distorts others, and misses many altogether.

The ethics of learner data begins precisely at this fragile boundary between what is visible and what is real (Guan et al, 2023). Intelligent learning ecosystems depend on data: clicks, response times, drafts, revision histories, quiz patterns, peer interactions, biometric signals in some experimental settings, and even affective indicators inferred from facial expression or tone. The educational appeal is obvious. With enough data, institutions hope to identify risk, reduce dropout, personalize intervention, and improve achievement (Cannistrà, 2023). Yet learner data is not innocent material waiting to be processed. It is produced within relationships of power. It is collected by institutions, interpreted by systems, accessed by teachers or administrators, and sometimes stored by private companies whose priorities may not be fully aligned with educational care.

This does not mean that learner data should be rejected outright. Such a position would be too easy, perhaps even irresponsible. Data can help teachers notice students who are quietly falling behind (Rodriguez, 2022). It can reveal unequal participation patterns in collaborative work. It can help institutions identify structural barriers faced by particular groups. It can support accessibility, differentiated instruction, and fairer feedback cycles. But ethical use requires a different posture: not data hunger, but data humility. A learning ecosystem should collect what is educationally necessary, explain why it is collected, protect it with seriousness, and avoid converting every trace of student activity into a permanent evaluative mark.

A troubling feature of many data-driven systems is their tendency to make learners excessively legible. The student becomes a score, a risk category, a competency map, a progress curve, a probability of success. These representations may help, but they can also harden. Once a learner is classified as weak, disengaged, advanced, creative, slow, or at risk, the system may begin to treat them through that frame. Teachers may unconsciously adjust expectations. Students may internalize the label.

The prediction begins to behave like a script. In education, this is dangerous because learning depends so heavily on becoming otherwise. A child who appears weak in one context may flourish in another. A student who resists conventional tasks may show remarkable inventiveness in open-ended design. A learner who fails early may later develop intellectual resilience precisely because someone refused to believe the early data was the whole story.

Personalization must therefore be protected from the shadow of profiling. The difference is subtle but crucial. Personalization opens possibilities; profiling narrows them. Personalization says: here are several pathways that may help you grow. Profiling says: this is the kind of learner you are (Facler, 2023). Personalization remains provisional, revisable, and dialogic. Profiling tends to become categorical, administrative, and quietly deterministic. In STEAM 5.0, where creativity, experimentation, and interdisciplinary problem-solving are central, the cost of premature classification is especially high. The learner needs room to surprise the system, the teacher, and even themselves.

Explainability plays an essential role in this ethical architecture (Ramachandran, 2025). If an intelligent ecosystem recommends a learning pathway, assigns a difficulty level, predicts risk, or generates assessment feedback, its reasoning should be understandable enough for meaningful human review. Not every learner needs access to the mathematical complexity of a model, but they do deserve intelligible explanations of decisions that affect their learning. Why was this task recommended? Which evidence shaped this feedback? Was the judgment based on one performance, repeated patterns, peer comparison, or previous data? Can the learner challenge it? Can the teacher override it? Can the system admit uncertainty? These questions may sound procedural, yet they are deeply pedagogical. They determine whether AI becomes a partner in learning or an invisible authority.

The teacher's role becomes more delicate, not less important. In intelligent learning ecosystems, teachers are not simply users of platforms; they are ethical interpreters of algorithmic suggestions (Airaj, 2024). A dashboard may flag a student as disengaged, but the teacher may know that the student is caring for siblings after school. An AI-generated assessment may praise the structure of a project while missing its cultural insensitivity. A recommender system may suggest remedial exercises, while the teacher recognizes that the student needs a different representation, a peer explanation, or simply a moment of encouragement. Such judgments are not sentimental extras. They are part of professional knowledge. A system that treats teachers as passive recipients of analytics weakens the very human intelligence it claims to support.

Learner agency must also be designed into the ecosystem, not added later as decorative rhetoric. Students should be able to see, question, and sometimes shape their own learning data. They should understand how their digital traces are used and what rights they have over them. They should be invited to reflect on the patterns produced by the system: Do these analytics match their lived experience of learning? What do they reveal? What do they hide? In a STEAM 5.0 environment, data literacy becomes more than a technical skill. It becomes a form of self-understanding and civic awareness (Hirzel, 2023). Learners who can interrogate educational algorithms are better prepared to navigate a wider world increasingly organized by automated judgment.

The issue of equity cannot be treated as an afterthought. Adaptive and personalized systems are often promoted as solutions to inequality, but they may also reproduce it. If training data reflects historical biases, if language models privilege dominant linguistic patterns, if access to high-quality devices and connectivity remains uneven, or if students from marginalized backgrounds are monitored more intensely under the banner of support, intelligent ecosystems may deepen the very divisions they promise to heal. Ethical design requires attention not only to the algorithm, but to the social conditions around it. Who has access? Who is watched? Who is trusted? Who is given creative freedom, and who is constantly corrected?

A humane intelligent learning ecosystem should be built around several quiet commitments (Lizzio, 2025). It should treat data as partial evidence, never as the full truth of a learner. It should make adaptive decisions explainable and contestable. It should preserve teacher judgment and student voice. It should use personalization to widen opportunity rather than automate sorting. It should protect privacy not merely as a legal requirement, but as a condition of dignity. Above all, it should remember that education is not the management of learning behavior. It is the cultivation of persons.

STEAM 5.0 offers a powerful opportunity to redesign learning environments around this broader understanding (Papadopoulou, 2024). Intelligent systems can help learners explore complex problems, receive timely feedback, and build connections across science, technology, engineering, arts, and mathematics. They can make education more responsive, inclusive, and imaginative. But they must be governed by ethical restraint and human purpose. Without that, personalization becomes quiet control, adaptivity becomes algorithmic steering, and learner data becomes a mirror that reflects only what the system has been trained to see.

The task, then, is not to make education simply smarter in a technical sense. It is to make intelligence more humane. That is the real promise of intelligent learning ecosystems in STEAM 5.0: not a classroom ruled by data, but one enriched by carefully interpreted evidence; not a learner reduced to patterns, but a person supported through them; not a future where machines decide what students may become, but one where intelligent technologies help keep the horizon of becoming open.

CREATIVITY, EMPATHY, AND CRITICAL AGENCY IN HUMAN–AI LEARNING ENVIRONMENTS

The promise of human–AI learning environments cannot be measured only by how quickly they deliver feedback, how accurately they predict performance, or how neatly they personalize content (Scholapurapu, 2025). These capacities matter, of course. They may reduce delay, widen access, and give learners forms of support that traditional classrooms, often constrained by time and resources, struggle to provide. Yet the more serious question is not whether AI can make learning more efficient. Efficiency is a thin ambition if it is left alone. The deeper question is whether human–AI environments can protect and strengthen the qualities that make education more than training: creativity, empathy, judgment, imagination, resistance, and the learner's ability to act as a conscious participant in their own intellectual formation.

In STEAM 5.0, creativity is not a decorative quality added after technical competence has been achieved. It is not a pleasant supplement to "serious" scientific or mathematical work. It is part of how knowledge becomes alive. A learner who builds a model, designs a prototype, composes a digital artwork, investigates an environmental problem, or experiments with a mathematical pattern is not simply applying information. They are entering a space of possibility. They are asking, sometimes without fully knowing they are asking it: What else could this become? What if this assumption were loosened? What if the problem is not where we first thought it was? AI can support this process by offering alternatives, generating examples, simulating outcomes, and pushing learners beyond the first obvious idea. But it can also flatten creativity if it makes the quickest solution appear to be the best one.

This tension is worth lingering over. Generative AI can produce endless variations, but abundance is not the same as imagination (Ervik, 2023). A system may generate ten design options, twenty titles, a hundred visual patterns, or a polished explanation in seconds. The learner may feel empowered, even dazzled. Yet genuine creativity requires more than variation. It requires selection, hesitation, discomfort, failure, revision, and attachment to meaning. It involves the strange human act of caring about one possibility more than another. If AI produces the first draft, the learner must still learn to ask: Why this? Why not that? What is missing? What does this output assume? Does it carry my intention, or merely imitate the surface of intention? In this sense, creativity in human–AI environments depends not on replacing human effort, but on deepening the learner's responsibility toward what is created.

The arts within STEAM are especially important here because they resist the reduction of creativity to productivity (Woodford, 2022). A painting, a story, a performance, a design object, or a multimedia project cannot be judged only by its technical correctness. It asks for interpretation. It holds ambiguity. It may be uneven, excessive, unresolved, or emotionally awkward, and still be meaningful. AI systems, trained to detect patterns and optimize outputs, may struggle with this unruly dimension of human expression. They may reward coherence while missing rupture. They may praise balance while overlooking the power of deliberate imbalance. They may suggest refinement when what the work actually needs is risk. Educators, then, must help learners treat AI-generated suggestions as invitations rather than verdicts. The machine can propose; the learner must decide.

Empathy enters human–AI learning environments in a more complicated way (Fraga do Nascimento, 2024). AI can simulate warmth. It can produce encouraging language, adapt tone, offer reassurance, and respond patiently to repeated questions. For learners who feel embarrassed to ask for help in front of peers, such responsiveness may be genuinely valuable. A student struggling with coding, geometry, chemistry, or design vocabulary may find in an AI tutor a low-pressure space for practice. There is something humane in that, even if the system itself does not feel. But simulated empathy must not be confused with relational understanding. AI does not know the learner in the way a teacher, mentor, or classmate might know them. It does not remember the tremor in a student's voice after repeated failure, the cultural weight behind a hesitant answer, the family pressures carried silently into a classroom, or the pride hidden inside a project that looks unfinished from the outside.

This is why empathy in STEAM 5.0 cannot be outsourced (Lampou, 2024). It must be designed into the ecosystem through human choices, institutional values, and pedagogical practice. Teachers need to ask whether AI-supported learning environments make students feel more visible or more monitored, more capable or more categorized, more willing to explore or more anxious about constant evaluation. A dashboard may show that a learner has not engaged with a platform for several days. The empathetic question is not merely "How do we increase engagement?" but "What is happening around this learner's life, confidence, access, and sense of belonging?" A system may detect errors; a teacher may detect discouragement. A system may suggest remediation; a peer may offer solidarity. Education needs both structure and tenderness, and tenderness is not easily automated.

Critical agency may be the most decisive quality of all. Without it, human–AI learning environments risk producing learners who are skilled at using intelligent tools but weak at questioning them. Critical agency means that students do not simply receive AI outputs, recommendations, or assessments as neutral facts. They learn to interrogate them. They ask how the system reached its answer, what data shaped its response, whose knowledge is represented, whose language is privileged, and what forms of intelligence are being ignored. This is not a minor technical skill. It is a civic and ethical capacity. In a world increasingly governed by algorithmic decisions, learners must understand that intelligent systems are not magic mirrors of truth. They are constructed, partial, and sometimes quietly biased.

In STEAM education, critical agency should be cultivated through practice, not preached as an abstract virtue (Dahal, 2022). Students can compare AI-generated solutions with their own reasoning. They can test machine explanations against experimental evidence. They can examine how a generative model responds differently to culturally varied prompts. They can identify when an automated assessment values formal polish over conceptual originality. They can redesign AI-generated prototypes to better serve excluded users. They can debate whether a technically efficient solution is socially acceptable. These activities move AI from the background of learning into the foreground of inquiry. The learner is no longer merely assisted by technology; the learner studies technology as part of the world they are learning to shape.

This shift is crucial because dependence can arrive quietly. At first, AI helps the learner begin. Then it helps organize. Then it helps phrase, calculate, design, correct, summarize, and decide. None of these acts is harmful in itself. The danger lies in gradual surrender: the slow fading of the learner's own struggle with uncertainty. Struggle is not always pleasant, and it should not be romanticized. Some forms of struggle are unfair, humiliating, or unnecessary. Yet a certain kind of cognitive friction is essential to learning. The pause before an idea forms, the clumsy first attempt, the frustration of not yet understanding, the revision that hurts a little because it reveals weakness—these experiences build intellectual muscle. Human–AI environments should reduce needless barriers, but they should not remove every difficulty that allows learners to become stronger thinkers.

A well-designed STEAM 5.0 ecosystem would therefore treat AI as a partner in inquiry rather than a substitute for judgment (Jamro & Jamro, 2023). It would encourage learners to use AI to expand possibilities, not to close them prematurely. It would invite students to create with machines while retaining authorship, to receive feedback without surrendering self-evaluation, to personalize learning without retreating into isolated pathways, and to question technological systems without falling into shallow rejection of them. This balance is delicate. It demands teachers who are not merely trained to operate platforms, but prepared to cultivate reflective, ethical, and imaginative forms of AI use.

There is also a collective dimension to creativity, empathy, and agency that should not be forgotten. Human–AI learning environments are often imagined as interactions between an individual learner and an intelligent system. That image is too narrow. Learning remains social. STEAM problems are rarely solved alone, especially when they concern climate change, public health, accessibility, urban design, sustainability, or digital justice. Students need spaces where they can argue, listen, negotiate, misread one another, repair misunderstandings, and build shared meaning. AI may support collaboration by organizing ideas or modelling alternatives, but it cannot replace the moral education that happens when learners encounter the perspectives of others. Empathy grows through contact with difference, not only through personalized support.

The human-centred promise of STEAM 5.0 lies in keeping these dimensions alive (Hasani et al, 2025). Creativity ensures that learners do not become mere operators of existing systems. Empathy ensures that intelligence remains connected to care, context, and human consequence. Critical agency ensures that students can question the systems that shape their learning and their society. Together, these qualities prevent human–AI education from becoming a sleek machinery of optimization.

The task ahead is not to make learners less dependent on technology by pretending AI does not matter. It matters profoundly. The task is to help them live with intelligent systems without becoming intellectually smaller in their presence. A learner in a STEAM 5.0 environment should come away not only with sharper skills, but with a more restless imagination, a more generous awareness of others, and a stronger capacity to ask difficult questions (Lampou, 2024). What is this tool helping me see? What is it hiding? Who benefits from this design? What kind of human being am I becoming as I use it?

Those questions may be uncomfortable, but education worth the name has always lived close to discomfort. Human–AI learning environments will be judged, eventually, not by how advanced their systems appear, but by whether they help learners become more fully human: inventive without arrogance, analytical without coldness, technologically fluent without obedience, and critically awake in a world that often prefers users to thinkers.

TOWARD SUSTAINABLE AND ETHICAL STEAM 5.0 ECOSYSTEMS: DESIGN PRINCIPLES, CHALLENGES, AND FUTURE DIRECTIONS

A sustainable and ethical STEAM 5.0 ecosystem cannot be built by simply adding advanced technologies to existing educational structures and hoping that intelligence will somehow emerge from the machinery (Torres-Rivera et al, 2025). That temptation is strong, especially now, when artificial intelligence is often presented as if it were a ready-made solution to almost every difficulty in teaching and learning. Yet education has seen this kind of technological optimism before. New systems arrive with elegant dashboards, bold promises, and a language of transformation, only to discover that classrooms are stubbornly human places. They are uneven, emotional, culturally layered, underfunded in some contexts, overregulated in others, and always shaped by the invisible weight of institutional habits. STEAM 5.0 must begin from this reality, not from a fantasy of frictionless innovation.

Sustainability, in this context, should be understood broadly. It is not only environmental sustainability, although that is increasingly urgent. It also includes pedagogical sustainability, ethical sustainability, social sustainability, and institutional sustainability. A learning ecosystem may be technologically impressive but pedagogically exhausting. It may be efficient but socially exclusionary. It may personalize learning while consuming vast quantities of data, energy, and human attention. It may promise inclusion while depending on devices, connectivity, and digital confidence that many learners do not possess equally. A truly sustainable STEAM 5.0 model must ask whether intelligent learning environments can endure without draining teachers, narrowing students, deepening inequalities, or quietly normalizing surveillance as a condition of educational support (Torres-Rivera et al, 2025).

The first design principle, then, is human purpose before technical function. Every AI-supported component in a STEAM 5.0 ecosystem should be justified by a meaningful educational need. This sounds obvious, almost too simple, but it is frequently ignored. Technologies are often adopted because they are fashionable, funded, marketable, or institutionally impressive. A human-centred approach asks different questions. What kind of learning does this tool make possible? Does it deepen inquiry, creativity, collaboration, reflection, or ethical reasoning? Does it give teachers better insight without reducing their professional autonomy? Does it help students understand themselves as learners, or does it merely produce more measurements about them? If a tool cannot answer these questions convincingly, its intelligence may be more decorative than transformative.

A second principle concerns transparency and explainability. In STEAM 5.0, learners and teachers should not be surrounded by systems that make consequential decisions in silence (Spyropoulou & Kameas, 2025). If an AI platform recommends a pathway, generates feedback, predicts risk, or evaluates performance, its reasoning must be open enough to be questioned. Not every explanation needs to be technically exhaustive; indeed, an explanation that overwhelms the user with model architecture and statistical terminology may fail pedagogically. What matters is usable clarity. Students should understand why they received a particular recommendation. Teachers should be able to inspect and contest algorithmic judgments. Institutions should know what data is being used, how long it is retained, and what assumptions shape automated decisions. Without this, intelligent ecosystems become theatres of trust, asking human beings to believe what they cannot meaningfully examine.

The third principle is data restraint. Modern educational technology has developed a habit of collecting more than it needs, partly because data has become an institutional currency. The more traces captured, the more “intelligent” a system appears.

But learners are not mines from which behavioral signals should be endlessly extracted. Ethical STEAM 5.0 ecosystems should collect the minimum data necessary for clear educational purposes, protect that data carefully, and avoid transforming every click, pause, draft, hesitation, and mistake into a permanent record of performance (Aguayo et al, 2023). There is something deeply unhealthy about a learning environment in which students feel continuously watched. Experimentation requires a degree of privacy. Creativity needs shadowed corners. Intellectual risk becomes harder when every attempt is recorded, scored, and fed back into a predictive profile.

Inclusivity must also be treated as a design condition rather than a rhetorical flourish. STEAM 5.0 ecosystems should be accessible to learners with different abilities, languages, cultural backgrounds, economic circumstances, and patterns of learning (Deák & Kumar, 2024). This requires more than compliance with accessibility standards, although those standards are necessary. It requires sensitivity to the ways learners actually encounter technology. Some students may have unstable internet access. Some may use shared devices. Some may be unfamiliar with academic digital tools. Others may speak in dialects, accents, or multilingual forms that AI systems handle poorly. A platform trained on narrow linguistic or cultural data may interpret difference as deficiency. Ethical design must actively guard against this. The question is not whether the system works for an imagined average learner, but whether it remains fair, flexible, and respectful when learners do not fit that imaginary centre.

Teacher empowerment is another essential pillar. A sustainable STEAM 5.0 ecosystem cannot depend on the quiet overburdening of teachers. Too many digital reforms ask educators to become curriculum designers, data analysts, platform managers, pastoral caregivers, technical troubleshooters, and ethical supervisors all at once, often without sufficient time, training, or recognition. If AI is introduced as yet another layer of responsibility, it will not humanize education; it will exhaust the very people expected to humanize it. Teachers need professional development that goes beyond button-clicking tutorials. They need space to understand algorithmic bias, interpret learning analytics, design AI-supported tasks, protect student agency, and decide when not to use AI. Sometimes the most ethical use of technology is restraint. Teachers must be trusted to make that judgment.

The environmental dimension deserves more attention than it usually receives. AI systems require computational infrastructure, energy, hardware production, cooling systems, and constant upgrading (Cruzes, 2025). A STEAM 5.0 ecosystem that speaks about sustainability while relying uncritically on energy-intensive technologies risks contradiction. Educational institutions should consider the ecological footprint of AI adoption, especially when tools are scaled across campuses, regions, or national systems. This does not mean rejecting AI, but it does mean asking uncomfortable questions about necessity, efficiency, procurement, repairability, and long-term environmental cost. A smaller, well-governed, purpose-built system may sometimes be more responsible than a spectacular platform whose hidden ecological demands remain conveniently out of sight.

The challenges are not minor. Bias remains one of the most persistent. AI systems may reproduce inequalities embedded in historical data or institutional practices. Predictive tools may label certain students as "at risk" in ways that follow patterns of class, language, disability, race, gender, or geography. Automated feedback may reward dominant writing styles or conventional problem-solving approaches. In creative STEAM tasks, systems may prefer polished outputs over strange, emerging, or culturally specific forms of originality. These harms may not appear as dramatic failures. They may accumulate quietly, shaping expectations and opportunities over time. Ethical governance must include regular auditing, diverse stakeholder review, and mechanisms through which learners and teachers can report harm or contest automated judgments.

Another challenge is the risk of dependency. When AI becomes too convenient, learners may gradually outsource not only routine tasks but also the productive struggle through which understanding develops (Aboodi, 2025). This is not a call for artificial difficulty or nostalgic hardship. It is a reminder that learning requires friction: the unfinished sketch, the failed experiment, the confusing equation, the first clumsy explanation, the argument with a peer that forces a clearer thought. STEAM 5.0 ecosystems should help learners move through difficulty, not erase every difficulty in advance. The goal is not comfort without growth. It is support without intellectual weakening.

Future directions should move toward participatory governance. Students, teachers, parents, technologists, ethicists, community representatives, and policy-makers all have a stake in how intelligent learning ecosystems are designed and used. Decisions about educational AI should not be left only to vendors, technical teams, or senior administrators. The people most affected by these systems must have a voice in shaping them. This is especially important in STEAM education, where the purpose is not merely to consume technology but to understand, critique, and redesign the technological world. Participatory design turns governance itself into a learning process.

Curriculum will also need to change. AI literacy, data ethics, sustainability awareness, design justice, and critical digital citizenship should become woven into STEAM learning rather than treated as occasional side topics. Students should learn how AI systems work, where they fail, how they shape knowledge, and how they might be designed differently. They should examine the social consequences of automation, the environmental cost of computation, the ethics of data extraction, and the politics of algorithmic classification. Such learning prepares them not only for future employment, but for responsible participation in societies increasingly shaped by intelligent systems.

The future of STEAM 5.0 should not be imagined as a gleaming automated classroom where every learner follows a perfectly optimized path (Bhattacharjya, 2025). That vision is too clean, too managerial, too poor in human texture. A better future is more complex: teachers supported but not displaced; students guided but not profiled; data used carefully but not worshipped; creativity amplified but not standardized; technology questioned as well as used. Sustainable and ethical STEAM 5.0 ecosystems will be those that remain open to revision, humble about their limits, and brave enough to place human dignity above institutional convenience.

The real direction ahead is not toward more intelligent machines alone. It is toward more intelligent educational relationships: between learners and teachers, between humans and technologies, between innovation and responsibility, between knowledge and care. STEAM 5.0 will matter only if it helps education become more humane, not merely more advanced (Lampou, 2024). That is its hardest promise, and also its most necessary one.

CONCLUSION

STEAM 5.0 invites education to slow down at the very moment when technology urges it to accelerate. This may seem paradoxical, but it is precisely the point. Intelligent systems can process data faster than any teacher, generate feedback in seconds, identify patterns across thousands of learner interactions, and personalize content with remarkable precision. Yet speed, by itself, is not wisdom. Nor is personalization automatically humane simply because it is adaptive. The deeper value of STEAM 5.0 lies in its insistence that education must remain anchored in human purpose, even as it becomes increasingly supported by artificial intelligence.

Throughout this chapter, the central argument has been that human-centred intelligent learning ecosystems must be built on more than technical capability. They require ethical imagination, pedagogical care, institutional accountability, and a clear understanding of what learning is meant to become. In STEAM contexts, this is especially important because learners are not only absorbing information. They are designing, experimenting, interpreting, building, questioning, and creating. They are learning how to connect scientific reasoning with artistic imagination, mathematical structure with social meaning, engineering design with human need, and technological innovation with ethical consequence. If AI enters this space without transparency or human guidance, it may support performance while weakening reflection. It may optimize tasks while narrowing thought.

Explainable AI offers one way to avoid this danger. Its importance does not rest only in making algorithms technically interpretable. Its educational value lies in making AI-mediated learning open to conversation. When students understand why a system recommends a task, flags an error, suggests a pathway, or evaluates a response, they gain more than feedback. They gain the possibility of critical engagement. They can compare machine judgment with their own reasoning. They can challenge assumptions. They can recognize bias, uncertainty, and limitation. In this sense, explainability becomes part of learning itself. It helps students develop not only knowledge of STEAM subjects, but also a more mature awareness of how intelligent systems shape knowledge, opportunity, and decision-making.

The same applies to assessment. Ethical assessment in AI-supported STEAM education cannot be reduced to faster grading or more detailed analytics. It must ask whether assessment protects learner dignity, recognizes diverse forms of intelligence, and leaves room for growth that cannot be easily predicted. A student's creative potential, collaborative sensitivity, ethical reasoning, or capacity for original thought may not appear neatly in a dashboard. These qualities often emerge slowly, unevenly, and sometimes unexpectedly. A humane assessment system must therefore treat data as evidence, not as final judgment. It must support teachers rather than replace them, illuminate learning rather than confine it, and encourage students rather than silently categorize them.

One of the strongest lessons of STEAM 5.0 is that intelligence should not be imagined as a property of machines alone. True educational intelligence is relational. It appears in the teacher who notices a student's hesitation before any system detects disengagement. It appears in the learner who combines a scientific principle with an artistic metaphor and suddenly sees a problem differently. It appears in a group of students negotiating design choices, failing, laughing, adjusting, and trying again. It appears when technology expands human possibility without swallowing human presence. This broader understanding of intelligence is necessary if educational institutions are to avoid building systems that are smart in function but poor in spirit.

Still, the path forward is not simple. Institutions will need to make difficult choices about data governance, algorithmic transparency, teacher training, digital equity, curriculum redesign, and the role of commercial AI platforms in public and private education. They will need to ask uncomfortable questions. Who controls learner data? Who benefits from predictive analytics? How can bias be detected before it harms students? How can teachers remain professionally empowered in AI-rich environments? How can learners be taught to use intelligent tools without becoming dependent on them? These questions cannot be answered through technology policy alone. They require educational philosophy, ethical leadership, and sustained dialogue among teachers, learners, researchers, designers, families, and communities.

The future of STEAM 5.0 should therefore not be framed as a race toward total automation. A richer and more responsible vision is possible. In that vision, AI becomes a companion to inquiry, not a hidden master of learning pathways. It helps teachers see patterns they might miss, but it does not replace their interpretive wisdom. It gives students feedback, but it also teaches them to question feedback. It supports personalization, but without trapping learners inside narrow profiles of ability. It makes assessment more responsive, but not less human. Most importantly, it keeps creativity, empathy, uncertainty, and moral judgment at the centre of education.

In the end, the measure of STEAM 5.0 will not be the sophistication of its platforms or the elegance of its algorithms. It will be found in the kinds of learners it helps form. Are they more curious? More thoughtful? More ethically awake? More capable of working across difference? More willing to ask not only *Can this be built?* but also *Should it be built, for whom, and with what consequences?* These are the questions that matter.

A human-centred intelligent learning ecosystem is not a finished model waiting to be implemented. It is an ongoing commitment. It must be revised, questioned, repaired, and reimagined as technologies and societies change. Its success depends on remembering that education is not merely the transmission of skills into future workers, but the shaping of persons who can live responsibly in a complex world. STEAM 5.0, at its best, offers that possibility: a future where artificial intelligence does not diminish the human learner, but helps create more transparent, creative, just, and deeply humane spaces for learning.

REFERENCES

Aguayo, C., Videla, R., López-Cortés, F., Rossel, S., & Ibacache, C. (2023). Ethical enactivism for smart and inclusive STEAM learning design. *Heliyon*, *9*(9), e19205. DOI: 10.1016/j.heliyon.2023.e19205 PMID: 37662760

Airaj, M. (2024). Ethical artificial intelligence for teaching-learning in higher education. *Education and Information Technologies*, *29*(13), 17145–17167. DOI: 10.1007/s10639-024-12545-x

Bhattacharjya, M. (2025). Future-proofing education: Developing transdiscipllinary STEAM models to prepare learners for a workforce in the forthcoming era of automation. *Transdisciplinary Journal of Engineering & Science*, *16*(6), 67–97. DOI: 10.22545/2025/00271

Cannistrà, M. (2023). Reducing dropout rates: the challenge of learning analytics in higher education institutions.

Cruzes, S. (2025). Data centers in the age of AI: A tutorial survey on infrastructure, sustainability, and emerging challenges. *Authorea Preprints*.

Dahal, N. (2022). Transformative STEAM education as a praxis-driven orientation. *Journal of STEAM Education*, *5*(2), 167–180. DOI: 10.55290/steam.1098153

Deák, C., & Kumar, B. (2024). A systematic review of STEAM education's role in nurturing digital competencies for sustainable innovations. *Education Sciences*, *14*(3), 226. DOI: 10.3390/educsci14030226

Ervik, A. (2023). Generative AI and the collective imaginary: The technology-guided social imagination in AI-imagenesis.

Facler, M. (2023). The personal learner profile, as the key component for shaping a personalized learning journey, in a learning management system in the digital era. In *INTED2023 Proceedings* (pp. 1336-1344). IATED. DOI: 10.21125/inted.2023.0387

Fraga do Nascimento, A. (2024). How can we rethink the digital space in online programs with the support of an Empathic AI to promote inclusion, designing enriched learning experiences that foster deeper connections between students and teachers?.

Gore, S. N., Chidhakwa, J., Mlilo, M., Magede, M., & Mpofu, V. (2023). Towards an Upper Middle-Class Economy: An Analysis of Zimbabwe's STEAM Education and Education 5.0 Frameworks. *Journal of Emerging Trends in Educational Research and Policy Studies*, *14*(3), 122–130.

Guan, X., Feng, X., & Islam, A. Y. M. (2023). The dilemma and countermeasures of educational data ethics in the age of intelligence. *Humanities & Social Sciences Communications*, *10*(1), 138. DOI: 10.1057/s41599-023-01633-x

Hasani, N., Hosseini, A., Ashjazadeh, Y., Diederichs, V., Ghotb, S., Riggio, M., Hansen, E., & Nasir, V. (2025). Outlook on human-centred design in industry 5.0: Towards mass customisation, personalisation, co-creation, and co-production. *International Journal of Sustainable Engineering*, *18*(1), 2486343. DOI: 10.1080/19397038.2025.2486343

Hirzel, T. (2023). AI-empowered Learning Models in Economy 5.0: Fostering Meaning Creation Beyond Literacy.

Jamro, M. Y., & Jamro, F. A. (2023). AI matters: Chatbot integration in holistic STEM Education.

Kotsis, K. T. (2024). ChatGPT in teaching physics hands-on experiments in primary school. *European Journal of Education Studies*, *11*(10). Advance online publication. DOI: 10.46827/ejes.v11i10.5549

Lampou, R. (2024). The role of STEAM education in curriculum 5.0. PENSAR MÁS ALLÁ EN EDUCACIÓN THINKING OUTSIDE THE BOX IN EDUCATION, 57.

Lei, M. (2025). Research on the Application of Artificial Intelligence Pattern Recognition Technology in University Training Laboratory. *International Journal of Advance in Applied Science Research*, *4*(8), 67–72.

Liu, M., & Yu, D. (2023). Towards intelligent E-learning systems. *Education and Information Technologies*, *28*(7), 7845–7876. DOI: 10.1007/s10639-022-11479-6 PMID: 36532790

Lizzio, A. (2025). From Artificial to Humane Intelligence (HI)–A Sociotechnical Framework for Co-Evolving AI. Available at *SSRN* 5373124. DOI: 10.2139/ssrn.5373124

Montés, N., Barquero, S., Martínez-Carbonell, A., Aloy, P., Ferrer, T., Romero, P. D., Millan, M., & Salazar, A. D. S. (2024). Redefining STEAM to STEAM∀ H (STEAM for all humanity) in higher education. *Education Sciences*, *14*(8), 888. DOI: 10.3390/educsci14080888

Papadopoulou, E. A. (2024). Advancements in STEAM education for 21st century learners. *International Journal of Education*, *16*(4), 39–70. DOI: 10.5296/ije.v16i4.22270

Rajabi, K. I. (2025). Beyond the LMS: How a Multi-Platform, AI-Enhanced Ecosystem Boosts Motivation, Interaction, Deep Learning, and Design Competence among Arabic-Speaking Graduate Students.

Ramachandran, M. (2025). AI Ethics by Design with AI Reference Architecture: Embedding Ethics by Design in AI Architecture. In *Engineering Ethics of AI by Design: Principles, Practices, and Frameworks for Responsible Artificial Intelligence* (pp. 409–464). Springer Nature Singapore.

Rodriguez, V., Rojas, N. M., Rabadi-Raol, A., Souto-Manning, M. V., & Brotman, L. M. (2022). Silent expectations: An exploration of women pre-Kindergarten teachers' mental health and wellness during Covid-19 and beyond. *Early Childhood Research Quarterly*, *60*, 80–95. DOI: 10.1016/j.ecresq.2021.12.006 PMID: 34955598

Rüütmann, T., & Läänemets, U. (2025). Generating Curricula: A Human-Centred Perspective in the Era of Artificial Intelligence. In International Baltic Symposium on Science and Technology Education. Scientia Socialis Ltd. 29 K. Donelaicio Street, LT-78115 Siauliai, Republic of Lithuania. DOI: 10.33225/BalticSTE/2025.180

Scholapurapu, P. K. (2025). Artificial intelligence-powered learning analytics and student feedback mechanisms for dynamic curriculum enhancement and continuous quality improvement in outcome-based education. *SSRN*, *10*, 9789349552531–06. DOI: 10.2139/ssrn.5382140

Shernoff, D. J. (2024). *Integrative STEM and STEAM education for Real-Life learning*. Springer. DOI: 10.1007/978-3-031-69824-8

Spyropoulou, N., & Kameas, A. (2025). AI and the future of teaching in STEAM: Competences, challenges, and opportunities. INTED2025 Proceedings, 4421-4427.

SWARGIARY, K. (2026). EDUCATION 6.0: Envisioning the Symbiotic Future of Learning and Innovation. ATLANTIS PUBLICATION HOUSE (RUSSIA).

Szilágyi, S., Körei, A., & Vaičiulytė, I. (2024). An innovative STEAM-based method for teaching cycloidal curves in engineering higher education. *Education Sciences*, *14*(10), 1087. DOI: 10.3390/educsci14101087

Torres-Rivera, A. D., Díaz-Torres, S. T., & Díaz-Torres, L. A. (2025). ENGINEERING EDUCATION FOR SOCIETY 5.0: A STEAM-BASED, ETHICAL AND SUSTAINABLE LEARNING MODEL INSPIRED BY THE "AULA SUSTENTABLE". In EDULEARN25 Proceedings (pp. 9127-9136). IATED.

Torres-Rivera, A. D., Rendón Peña, A. A., Díaz-Torres, S. T., & Díaz-Torres, L. A. (2025). Ethical integration of AI and STEAM pedagogies in higher education: A sustainable learning model for society 5.0. *Sustainability (Basel)*, *17*(19), 8525. DOI: 10.3390/su17198525

Wang, D., & Chen, G. (2024). Making AI accessible for STEM teachers: Using explainable AI for unpacking classroom discourse analysis. *IEEE Transactions on Education*, *67*(6), 907–918. DOI: 10.1109/TE.2024.3421606

Woodford, P. (2022). What are STEAM proponents thinking? on creativity, excellence, and measurement. *Diálogos Sonoros*, *1*(1), 1–15.

Chapter 3
STEAM Training to Master Industry 4.0 and 5.0:
Human-Centered Skills for Industry 4.0-5.0

Eric Simancas-Acevedo
http://orcid.org/0000-0001-7823-709X
Universidad Politécnica de Pachuca, Mexico

Omar A. Dominguez-Ramirez
https://orcid.org/0000-0002-9663-8089
Universidad Autónoma del Estado de Hidalgo, Mexico

Mario Alejandro Vega-Navarrete
http://orcid.org/0000-0003-2739-8840
Metropolitan Polytechnic University of Hidalgo, Mexico

Luis Enrique Ramos-Velasco
Consejo de Ciencia, Tecnología e Innovación de Hidalgo (CITNOVA), Mexico

Mayra L. González-Mosqueda
http://orcid.org/0009-0009-5125-7248
Tecnológico Nacional de México, Pachuca, Mexico

ABSTRACT

This chapter examines the role of STEAM education as a strategic response to the transformations driven by Industry 4.0 and the human-centered paradigm of Industry 5.0. It analyzes the evolution of industrial models, highlighting the integration of digital technologies such as artificial intelligence, the Internet of Things, and cyber-physical systems, alongside the growing importance of sustainability

DOI: 10.4018/979-8-2600-3658-7.ch003

and social well-being. The discussion emphasizes the need for interdisciplinary competencies that combine technical expertise with creativity, critical thinking, and ethical responsibility. It also explores how STEAM methodologies, including project-based learning, design thinking, and rapid prototyping, foster innovation and prepare professionals for complex industrial environments. The chapter addresses the integration of sustainability and circular economy principles as key training axes. Overall, it argues that education plays a central role in enabling a balanced interaction between humans and intelligent systems, supporting resilient and sustainable industrial development.

1. INTRODUCTION: INDUSTRIAL TRANSFORMATION AND THE ROLE OF EDUCATION

Industry is undergoing a significant transformation that is reshaping how value is created and maintained. Advanced digital technologies, intelligent automation, and data-driven decision-making now influence nearly every stage of industrial activity. At the same time, sustainability and social well-being have become central concerns in strategic planning.

The implications extend beyond production systems. These developments are changing the competencies organizations seek, reshaping professional roles, and creating new occupational profiles. Expertise that was considered sufficient a decade ago may no longer satisfy the requirements of today's interconnected environments.

Understanding the evolution of industrial paradigms is important for interpreting the challenges facing both industry and education. It also helps identify the learning frameworks and training strategies needed in a context of rapid technological change and rising societal expectations.

The following section reviews recent industrial models and considers how these transformations are influencing educational needs and workforce development priorities.

1.1 Evolution of Industrial Paradigms

Throughout history, industry has experienced profound transformations as part of its natural evolution. From the first attempts to mechanize production to the deployment of intelligent systems capable of streamlining and optimizing industrial operations, each milestone has been recognized as an industrial revolution and associated with a specific stage of industrial development. Industry 1.0 marked the first decisive turning point, replacing labor-intensive manual processes with mechanized production powered primarily by steam energy. Industry 2.0 emerged with the implementation of electricity, enabling the creation of assembly lines and the standardization of production processes. This led to Industry 3.0 with the incorporation of electronic and computer systems through programmable logic controllers (PLCs), which allowed for the automation of processes. More recently, Industry 4.0 emerged, characterized by its high level of digitalization. This led to the development of cyber-physical systems, the Internet of Things (IoT), Big Data, and artificial intelligence applications, all integrated into an intelligent digital ecosystem capable of making operational decisions with minimal human intervention (Schwab, 2017; Xu et al., 2018). Currently, we are discussing Industry 5.0, which integrates the human being as the focal point of the industry 4.0 ecosystem and is developed not only based on economic and industrial interests but also on social well-being and environmental sustainability (Xu et al., 2021). As Fogaça et al. suggest, in his work “What are Industry 4.0 and Industry 5.0 all about? Administrative Sciences” from 2025, the evolution of industry does not represent abrupt changes in production processes but rather the constant evolution of these processes in response to the necessary integration of the global problems of each industry, a complement to the previous one; this evolution is represented in Figure 1.

Figure 1. Evolution of industrial paradigms from Industry 1.0 to Industry 5.0.

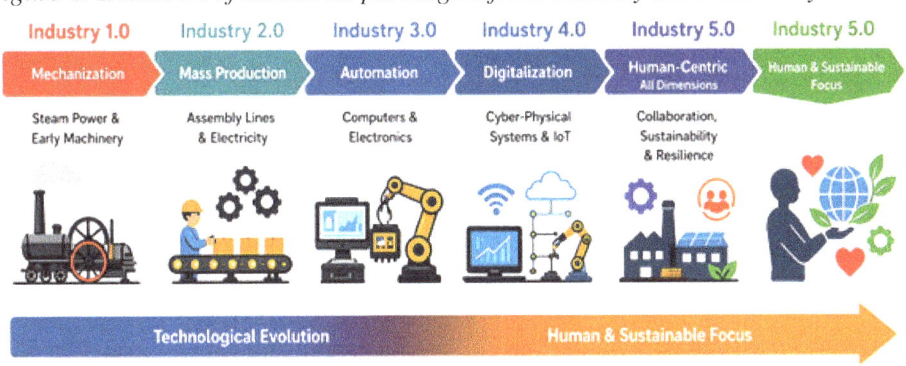

based on Schwab (2017), Xu et al. (2018), Xu et al. (2021) and Fogaça et al. (2025).

We can define one of the key factors in industrial evolution as the digitization of processes, as it enables global interaction among the various actors involved in industrial processes. Through diverse digital platforms, it allows for the real-time visualization, interpretation, and manipulation of data via global networks, facilitating the coordination of different groups involved without requiring them to be physically present in the same geographic location. This new form of intercommunication in industrial environments leads to several changes in the very structure of industrial processes. An example can be found in supply chains, where intelligent logistics platforms now enable more precise route planning and operational optimization. These capabilities facilitate the adoption of distributed manufacturing models, in which production activities are decentralized to lower operating expenses before converging in final assembly and integration stages. Greater digitalization also simplifies remote oversight, allowing specialists to monitor and coordinate processes across multiple locations at the same time.

Collectively, these transformations strengthen industrial performance and reduce vulnerability to disruptions arising from geopolitical uncertainties (Ivanov & Dolgui, 2020). Today, extensive digitalization has become a strategic cornerstone of industrial advancement, enabling access to vast volumes of data that can be rapidly processed by automated and intelligent systems. Analytical capabilities are substantially enhanced, supporting more informed decision-making from both economic and sustainability-oriented perspectives. This enhances operational efficiency without compromising social and environmental considerations (Wamba et al., 2017). These developments enable the automation of various tasks that were previously performed manually by a person. This level of automation, in turn, demands greater technological proficiency from users for effective interaction with automated processes. However, globalization and digitalization also highlight the need for soft skills, thus creating a demand for new profiles that are proficient in engineering, data management, and digital analytics, applying a sustainable approach. These observations are consistent with Aheleroff et al. (2022) who affirms that industry 4.0 and 5.0 are presented as frameworks that can contribute to sustainability and resilience since they allowed the reorganization of production systems focusing on social needs, considering automation through the implementation of strategic objectives that favor the transformation of systems around both areas.

Since 2021, the European Commission, and independent authors like Xu et al. have argued that industrial evolution cannot be represented solely as technological advancements applied to production processes, but rather as a strategic paradigm shift focused on incorporating technology from a human-centered perspective. This perspective suggests that Industry 5.0 does not seek to supersede Industry 4.0. It instead reframes and integrates its technological advances through a sustainability-driven lens. The objective is to cultivate a responsible industrial model guided by ethical principles and values that support long-term development. Within this framework, human beings recover a central role. Although digital technologies contribute to data processing, analysis, and interpretation, the ultimate evaluation of results—and their alignment with industrial needs and sustainability goals—remains a human responsibility. The outcome is a collaborative ecosystem in which people and technology complement one another, creating favorable conditions for creativity, adaptability, and the strengthening of soft skills. Table 1 presents a comparative overview of Industry 4.0 and Industry 5.0, emphasizing their differences in strategic orientation, human participation, production priorities, and sustainability focus, while also illustrating the technological and structural continuities that connect both paradigms within the broader evolution of industrial transformation.

Table 1. Differences and similarities between Industry 4.0 and Industry 5.0.

Dimension	Industry 4.0	Industry 5.0	Similarity / Continuity
Central focus	Digitization and automation of production processes.	Human centrality, sustainability and resilience.	Both seek to improve industrial competitiveness.
Key technologies	Cyber-physical systems, IoT, Big Data, AI, advanced robotics.	Collaborative AI, human-centered robotics, sustainable digital twins.	They share a digital technological base.
Worker role	Specialized operator with digital skills.	Creative collaborator who interacts with intelligent systems.	They require advanced technological training.
Productive objective	Efficiency, optimization and cost reduction.	Social value, human well-being and environmental sustainability.	Both pursue innovation and continuous improvement.
Innovation model	Techno-centric.	Human-centric and ethical.	Based on digital transformation.
Sustainability	Considered as a competitive advantage.	Structural strategic axis.	They integrate technologies to optimize resources.
Resilience	Focus on productive flexibility.	Systemic adaptability to global crises.	Use of digitization for anticipation and response.
Educational implications	Training in automation, data and intelligent systems.	Comprehensive STEAM training with an ethical and creative approach.	Need for lifelong learning.

Note: Based on Xu et al. (2021), European Commission (2021) and Aheleroff et al. (2022).

1.2 Industry 4.0: Digitization and Automation

Industry 4.0 arose from the need to integrate the various cyber-physical systems comprised of existing machinery equipped with sensors and automated actuators, developed during the industry 3.0 era, within a globalized interconnected environment. The solution to this need was digital environments, as these enable the creation of globalized operating cores where information from different cyber-physical systems can be accessed from any point on the network. Because these operating cores, developed on digital platforms, allow bidirectional communication with the interconnected cyber-physical systems, they globalize the ability to monitor processes, establish simulation environments for improvement proposals, and actively manage the automation and control processes of each cyber-physical system. The fundamental distinguishing feature of Industry 4.0 is the emergence of so-called smart factories (Zhang et al., 2021), which are basically industries that achieve adaptable and flexible automation depending on globalized contexts through the interoperability of equipment, production lines, and supply chains in a collaborative manner. This requires three fundamental elements, which are described below:

According to Lee (2008), the Internet of Things (IoT), which allows the connection of different actuators and sensors installed in cyber-physical systems with databases and control centers hosted in digital clouds via the internet, enabling the monitoring and manipulation of systems in real time. The cyber-physical systems themselves, which, being equipped with sensors interconnected by IoT, are approximated by mathematical and/or computational models that allow for the virtual evaluation of possible changes and improvements to the system, thus determining the feasibility of its real-world application. Various digital platforms, such as Big Data and Artificial Intelligence tools, which simplify the processing of large volumes of data in short periods of time, generating algorithms for predicting and optimizing the production and maintenance of cyber-physical systems, thereby reducing the possibility of unforeseen failures and interruptions to production lines. Zhang et al. In 2021, it already identified these parts as the fundamental basis of the so-called Industry 4.0, thereby defining the emerging need for advanced digital skills for it.

The integration of these three fundamental elements demonstrates that in Industry 4.0, evolution is moving towards the implementation of flexible models capable of being constantly and intelligently reconfigured (Kaihara, 2018). This intelligent reconfiguration enables systems to react with remarkable speed to shifts in market conditions or broader global circumstances affecting a given industry. As a result, a highly adaptive production ecosystem emerges, one capable of balancing the quantitative demands of manufacturing with the qualitative requirements imposed by its surrounding environment. Soori et al. (2024), in their work, define the industry 4.0 paradigm as one in which intelligent digital systems increase the precision of production systems while reducing the likelihood of workplace accidents by minimizing human interaction in repetitive tasks or hazardous environments. The inclusion of automated systems improves the standardization and optimization of production in relation to demand. The need for human collaboration with robotic systems is also highlighted, which requires the sufficient integration of sensors and security strategies based on digital systems such as artificial vision that allow the different tasks that integrate the human and cyber-physical factors to be executed in a way that guarantees the safety of human personnel as well as the correct operation of the cyber-physical systems.

In general, the evolution from Industry 3.0 to 4.0 is not simply a change in which process automation displaces human operators, but rather a transformation in which the nature of human work evolves from a manual labor profile to one based on qualitative skills such as data processing and analysis, and the programming and supervision of controllers incorporated into cyber-physical systems. This contrasts with the general societal perception that the incorporation of intelligent systems into production processes would lead to a decrease in jobs; however, it is now known that this change, in turn, results in the creation of new jobs with more specialized profiles, capable of actively participating in decision-making based on information analysis supported by intelligent systems for the establishment of continuous improvement (Miah et al., 2024).

The evolution of these jobs therefore creates a need to retrain personnel who are already highly specialized in the operation of cyber-physical systems so that they can refine new core competencies based on the implementation of intelligent digital tools. These needs are not only technical; the new profiles in demand require more robust soft skills training, as the results of analyses performed by digital tools demand personnel with critical thinking skills and the ability to propose solutions to complex problems. This is where new challenges arise, such as the need for digital literacy and continuous updating to achieve effective human-machine collaboration in the face of the rapid development of technological solutions (Van Laar et al., 2017). However, authors such as Grybauskas et al. (2022) demonstrate that this paradigm shift to Industry 4.0 generates negative implications from a social and sustainability perspective. This motivates the need to generate an ecosystem that effectively integrates engineering, management, ethics, and sustainability through an educational system focused on both technical skills and soft skills and sustainable policies.

Figure 2. Industry 4.0: technological components and training competencies.

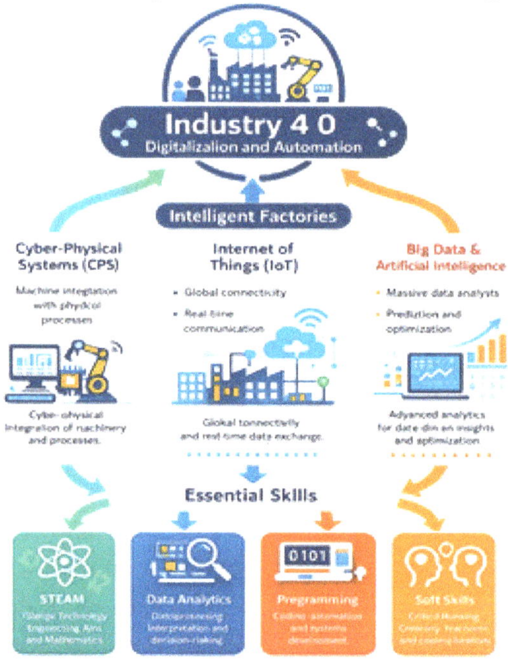

Based on Soori et al., 2024, Miah et al., 2024 and Van Laar et al., 2017.

Figure 2 synthesizes the core components of Industry 4.0, emphasizing the convergence of cyber-physical systems, the Internet of Things, and big data analytics as the technological backbone of smart factories. It also highlights the growing need for a workforce equipped with robust STEAM competencies, particularly in areas such as data analytics, programming, and the interpersonal skills required to operate effectively within increasingly complex industrial environments.

1.3 Industry 5.0: Human and Sustainable Approach

Fogaça et al. (2025) characterize Industry 5.0 as an axiological progression of Industry 4.0. Their perspective describes a transition away from an approach centered primarily on production output and technological deployment toward a human-oriented ecosystem that embraces sustainability-driven values and priorities, fostering not only industrial productivity but also socially responsible well-being. Although Industry 4.0 already revealed the growing importance of soft skills, this human-centered paradigm reinforces their relevance even further. As cyber-physical systems assume repetitive operations and tasks performed under hazardous conditions, people gain greater opportunities to channel their creativity into strategic initiatives, innovation processes, and continuous improvement efforts. The drive for innovation and continuous improvement in Industry 5.0 stems directly from human talent, based on its ability to apply critical thinking and collaborative work in a collaborative environment to achieve competitive advantages in production without compromising social and sustainable well-being on a global scale. Creativity and soft skills are fundamental pillars for the successful development of Industry 5.0 in the globalized context.

The European Commission (2021) defines the focal points of production systems in Industry 5.0 as security, as a necessity for reducing operational risks arising from cyber-physical systems; the continuous improvement of the quality of life of industry workers; and the well-being of society in general, with the understanding that industrialized development must be sustainable. This reaffirms that the integration of sustainable development and overall well-being goes beyond productive efficiency in a functional, human-centered ecosystem. In this Industry 5.0 ecosystem, a particularly important factor is the need for human-machine collaboration, in which the natural bridge of communication is established as human cognitive capacity enhanced by the implementation of intelligent digital systems capable of interacting in real time with operating cyber-physical systems, thus achieving an adaptable, resilient, and sustainable production model (Fogaça et al., 2025).

Within this paradigm, sustainability and human well-being are no longer viewed as matters of corporate responsibility or simple sources of competitive differentiation; rather, they are embedded as foundational principles guiding the evolution of production systems (Aheleroff et al., 2022). As a consequence, technologies such as IoT, data analytics, and intelligent automation are implemented according to new criteria systematically incorporated into industrial policies and decision frameworks (Fogaça et al., 2025). This transformation of production dynamics fosters an intrinsically resilient industrial model. As noted by Aheleroff et al., Industry 5.0 is expected to strengthen its ability to foresee environmental changes while responding and adapting to technological, economic, and ecological disruptions on a global scale. In this reconfigured landscape, the human being occupies a central position, within a collaborative ecosystem where sustainability, resilience, and innovation converge. This approach is summarized in the conceptual model presented in Figure 3.

Figure 3. Conceptual model of human-centered Industry 5.0 that integrates sustainability, resilience, innovation and human-machine collaboration

Based on the European Commission (2021) and Fogaça et al. (2025).

In Industry 5.0, resilience and sustainability can be considered the central axes that articulate production models around the human being, achieving a balance between industrial competitiveness and social well-being and environmental responsibility, thus achieving an industry strongly integrated with the human being, their social and economic well-being, as well as responsible for the care of the environment (European Commission, 2021; Fogaça et al., 2025).

1.4 STEAM Education as a Strategic Response

The constant evolution of Industry 5.0 has revealed the need to modify the training profiles of the workforce, as traditional training profiles are insufficient to meet the demands of this new approach. International organizations such as the World Economic Forum (2023) indicate that the most sought-after skills are analytical thinking, complex problem-solving, digital literacy, and creativity. However, these competencies cannot be treated as isolated constructs or developed in fragmentation; the European Commission (2021) emphasizes the necessity of establishing a coherent linkage between a human-centered industrial paradigm and the reinforcement of cognitive, social, and ethical capacities. From this standpoint, it becomes possible to infer the importance of embedding these skills within academic curricula both horizontally and vertically, ensuring a systemic integration that allows graduates to respond effectively to the evolving demands of Industry 5.0. These emerging demands, the STEAM approach (Science, Technology, Engineering, Arts, and Mathematics), understood as a pedagogical framework, fuses scientific and technological knowledge with creativity and soft skills within innovative learning environments (Perignat & Katz-Buonincontro, 2018). It actively brings industry-driven problems into the classroom through project-based learning, thereby strengthening creativity, critical thinking, and transversal competencies, which lie at the core of its educational design. Ramírez-Cedillo et al. (2025) argue that, in the shift from education toward Industry 5.0, training processes must weave together technical expertise, advanced digital literacies, and cognitive as well as collaborative capacities within immersive educational settings. The European Commission (2021) stresses that technological innovation should remain firmly human-centered, with creativity, well-being, and sustainability established as structural pillars of industrial progress. The transition from Industry 4.0 to Industry 5.0 is not merely a technical upgrade but a reconfiguration of the production paradigm, where digitalization, intelligent automation, and human-centered principles converge under the guiding axes of sustainability and resilience. This shift calls for professionals able to merge advanced technical competencies with critical thinking, creativity, ethics, and social responsibility. STEAM education emerges as a strategic educational lever, capable of connecting scientific and technological knowledge with soft skills and a humanistic outlook, thus enabling the formation of talent prepared to interact collaboratively with intelligent systems and to lead sustainable innovation processes. In this way, education does not merely accompany industrial transformation; it becomes a central axis in its responsible consolidation oriented toward social well-being.

2. FUNDAMENTALS OF STEAM TRAINING APPLIED TO INDUSTRY

STEAM education integrates science, technology, engineering, the arts, and mathematics into a coherent interdisciplinary framework, which is essential for mastering the paradigms of Industry 4.0 and 5.0 (Castillo-Castillo et al., 2025). This approach fosters collaborative skills that transcend isolated disciplines, preparing professionals capable of addressing technological disruptions and sustainability demands in smart manufacturing environments (Uniminuto Virtual, 2024). The change is significant: when each discipline is taught in isolation, students learn isolated pieces; when they are interwoven, competencies emerge that can be transferred from one problem to another and are indispensable in the face of technological disruptions, sustainability demands, and the growing complexity of cyber-physical systems (Lasi et al., 2014; Schwab, 2017). As a reminder: the Fourth Industrial Revolution took shape with the advent of the Internet of Things (IoT), artificial intelligence, big data analytics, and cloud computing (Xu et al., 2018; Atzori et al., 2010). The fifth, however, marks a shift and places people back at the center of production (Nahavandi, 2019). Below, we examine each pillar separately, drawing on comparative tables and figures that help ground these concepts in specific industrial and educational contexts.

2.1 Science and Evidence-Based Thinking

Every industrial plant is, at its core, a system full of questions: Why did this machine fail? What will happen if we raise the temperature? Is this change worth it? Science offers a disciplined way to answer these questions. Its method proceeds in steps: observe, formulate a testable hypothesis, experiment under controlled conditions, and analyze the results using rigorous statistics—and then start over as many times as necessary. In Industry 4.0, this evidence-based thinking processes massive volumes of data from IoT sensors, detecting predictive anomalies with accuracies exceeding 95%, validated through statistical significance tests ($p < 0.05$) (Bermúdez, 2023; Wuest et al., 2016; Wamba et al., 2017). Consider algorithms that recalculate probabilities in real time, such as Bayesian methods: by replacing gut feelings with a quantitative and reproducible model (Bermúdez, 2023; Kusiak, 2018). The benefit is twofold: on the one hand, it mitigates the biases inherent in any intuitive decision; on the other, it enforces standardized data collection protocols, without which traceability in global supply chains would be impossible. In STEAM education, students are trained to break down real-world problems—such as energy optimization—through controlled experiments that simulate digital factories, fostering a culture of empiricism and continuous validation that is essential for sustainable industrial innovation (Castillo-Castillo et al., 2025; Freeman et al., 2014).

The table summarizes the steps of the scientific method adapted to industrial environments where IoT data streams converge into predictive visualizations, illustrating the scientific cycle from sensors.

Table 2. The scientific method adapted to industrial environments

Step	Industrial Description	Example in Industry 4.0	Success Indicator
Observation	Multimodal data capture using IoT sensors	Machinery vibrations and thermal flows	Monitoring coverage > 99%
Hypothesis	Formulation of predictive models based on historical data	Correlation between temperature and failure	Falsifiable and testable hypothesis
Experimentation	Controlled (A/B) tests with isolated variables	Simulation of scheduled downtime	Control of confounding variables
Analysis	Regression and ANOVA with statistical significance ($p < 0.05$)	Validation using historical datasets	Model fit R2 > 0.85
Conclusion	Iterative implementation with continuous monitoring	Predictive maintenance optimization	Sustained performance improvement

Note: Prepared by the author based on Wuest et al. (2016), Bermúdez (2023), and Kusiak (2018).

2.2 Technology as an Enabler of Transformation

It would be a mistake to reduce technology to a set of tools. In today's industry, it functions more as an amplifier of what people and organizations are capable of doing. Digital twins, high-speed communication networks, and collaborative artificial intelligence free workers from the most routine cognitive load and redirect it toward higher-value tasks, in a back-and-forth relationship between the operator and the machine (Tao et al., 2019; Lu et al., 2022). Digital twins deserve a separate discussion. These are virtual replicas of a physical system that are updated with live data, making it possible to simulate, diagnose, and fine-tune a process without having to halt the production line (Kritzinger et al., 2018; Negri et al., 2017). Added to this are edge computing and software-defined industrial IoT architectures, which distribute decision-making throughout the entire cyber-physical ecosystem rather than concentrating it at a single point (Wan et al., 2016; Gubbi et al., 2013).

However, purchasing technology does not equate to transformation. A tool only delivers results if people accept it and make it their own. Davis (1989) put it clearly decades ago: the perceived usefulness to the user and the ease with which they believe they can use it carry more weight than any technical specifications. Hence, in smart factories, seamless interaction between operators and autonomous machines accelerates cultural adaptation and helps retain talent. STEAM education embodies this lesson through virtual factory prototypes where students manipulate real-time data flows and discover that technology, when properly embraced, empowers far more than it automates.

Table 3. From Instrumental Adoption to Transformational Empowerment

Dimension	Instrumental Adoption	Transformational Enablement	Key Reference
Focus	Efficiency in Isolated Tasks	Systemic cultural and organizational change	Lu et al. (2022)
Human impact	Replacement of repetitive tasks	Human-machine cognitive collaboration	Davis (1989)
Technology	Robots and static equipment	Digital twins and real-time AI	Tao et al. (2019)
Architecture	Centralized systems	Distributed decision-making (edge / IoT)	Wan et al. (2016)

Note: Prepared by the author based on Tao et al. (2019), Davis (1989), and Wan et al. (2016).

2.3 Engineering and the Systems Approach

Systems engineering deals with something that seems simple but rarely is: making many parts work together as a whole. To do this, it relies on frameworks such as model-based systems engineering (MBSE) or the classic V-model, which reduce unforeseen issues by taking seriously the nonlinear interdependencies and emergent properties of Industry 4.0's cyber-physical networks (Lee et al., 2015; Dintén et al., 2021). The strategy consists of breaking down complexity into hierarchical modules, each with well-defined interfaces, and honestly weighing the trade-offs between cost, performance, and sustainability (Lee, 2008). No system operates under ideal conditions, so adaptive feedback—advanced controllers that correct course on the fly—is key to maintaining stability in the face of disturbances and to predicting how, for example, a fleet of autonomous vehicles or an integrated logistics network will behave. And there is one aspect that cannot be put off: the security of these cyber-physical systems must be considered from the very first stage of design, not afterward (Humayed et al., 2017).

Bringing this into the classroom requires practice rather than mere discourse. Simulation workshops train students to look at the whole rather than the parts, to integrate disparate subsystems into scalable solutions, and to resist the reductionist temptation to isolate each component. Industrial and intellig l robotics, with its wealth of interactions, offers an unbeatable environment for practicing this systems thinking (Soori et al., 2024).

Table 4. Principles of the Systems Approach in Industrial Engineering

Principle	Industrial Application	Benefit	Tool / Reference
Holism	Interactions between Functions and Subsystems	Complexity management	MBSE (Lee et al., 2015)
Emergence	Non-obvious collective properties	Behavior Anticipation	Agent-Based Modeling
Feedback	Adaptive control in the face of disturbances	Operational stability	Advanced controllers
Hierarchy	Modules with defined interfaces	System scalability	Reference architecture (Dintén et al., 2021)
Security	Cyber-Physical System Security	Resilience and Trust	Security by Design (Humayed et al., 2017)

Note: Prepared by the author based on Lee et al. (2015), Dintén et al. (2021), and Humayed et al. (2017).

2.4 Arts, Creativity, and User-Centered Design

What role do the arts play in a factory? More than is usually assumed. Their contribution to the STEAM approach lies in user-centered design (UCD), a practice that refines human-machine interfaces (HMIs), makes them more user-friendly and easier to use, and reduces operational errors in situations where a poorly designed screen can be costly (Abras et al., 2004; Norman, 2013). UCD is not mere intuition: it is grounded in international standards that place the person at the center of the process (ISO 9241-210:2019) and in time-tested usability heuristics. When divergent ideation and rapid prototyping are applied to technologies such as augmented reality for maintenance, the abstract becomes manageable, and aesthetics are reconciled with cognitive ergonomics (Dym et al., 2005). One point is worth emphasizing: creativity is not the exclusive domain of artists. It is a cross-disciplinary skill that emerges—and grows—wherever it is intentionally fostered (Amabile, 1996; Florida, 2002).

That is why, in STEAM education, projects alternate between sketching and rounds of iteration guided by empathy, which opens the door to unconventional solutions designed for different types of users. The arts ultimately contribute something that no other discipline offers with the same ease: the visual and narrative language capable of transforming a mass of data into information that anyone can understand and use.

Table 5. Contributions of the Arts and User-Centered Design to Industrial Innovation

Element	Role in Innovation	Contribution to Industry	Key Reference
Visual communication	Data-driven infographics and dashboards	Better understanding of information	Norman (2013)
Creativity	Divergent and unconventional ideation	Generation of innovative solutions	Amabile (1996)
User-centered design	Empathy–prototype–testing cycle	Fewer errors and greater usability	Abras et al. (2004); ISO 9241-210 (2019)

Note: Prepared by the author based on Abras et al. (2004), Norman (2013), and Amabile (1996).

2.5 Applied Mathematics and Modeling

Behind every sound production decision there is usually a mathematical model. Differential equations, for example, capture continuous dynamics—such as how heat is transferred or how a fluid behaves—with a level of physical accuracy that rule-of-thumb methods can hardly match (Analuisa-Sánchez, 2025; Zavala Ortiz, 2020). When uncertainty is a concern, Monte Carlo simulations allow us to see how it propagates throughout a supply chain, and hybrid simulations reconstruct entire assembly processes. Bayesian calibration adds a valuable nuance: it adjusts the model's parameters as new data arrives, so that the prediction improves on its own over time.

The challenge in the classroom is to ensure that mathematics does not feel like an end in itself. Working with numerical solvers—Runge-Kutta methods are a good example—helps students develop applied intuition that they can then apply to energy or process optimization problems. Thus, what began as abstract theory ultimately becomes a modeling tool at the service of engineering and sustainability.

Table 6. Mathematical Modeling Techniques in Industry 4.0

Technique	Application	Main Advantage	Key Reference
Differential Equations	Thermal and Fluid Dynamics	High physical fidelity	Analuisa-Sánchez (2025)
Monte Carlo simulation	Uncertainty in supply chains	Nonparametric robustness	Zavala Ortiz (2020)
Numerical Optimization	Multiperiod Resource Allocation	Optimal Solutions	Zavala Ortiz (2020)
Bayesian calibration	Real-time parameter tuning	Continuous model learning	Bermúdez (2023)

Note: Prepared by the author based on Analuisa-Sánchez (2025), Zavala Ortiz (2020), and Bermúdez (2023).

3. KEY INDUSTRY 4.0 TECHNOLOGIES

Various technologies associated with Industry 4.0 represent new digital transformation paradigms across different production processes, driven by the integrated use of tools that enhance both efficiency and flexibility, as well as decision-making based on real-time data or historical system performance records. In this context, automation, control, and collaborative robotic systems enable the execution of high-precision, highly reliable tasks. Unlike traditional systems robots programmed for repetitive tasks-collaborative robots (cobots) interact directly with humans, whether through physical contact or without it. Artificial intelligence and data science facilitate the processing of vast amounts of information to derive actionable insights, utilizing machine learning techniques, predictive tools, and statistical methods. Key contributions include failure prediction, process optimization, and improved product quality, alongside the automation of decision-making in complex systems. Furthermore, the Internet of Things (IoT) and industrial connectivity enable the real-time interconnection of various devices and systems; this allows for the instrumentation and monitoring of critical system variables, facilitating decisions that optimize processes and bolster security across different system levels. Additive manufacturing introduces more flexible production models based on layer-by-layer fabrication, waste reduction, and systematic on-demand production. Finally, digital twins enable the simulation and analysis of real-world systems within virtual environments that are updated in real-time using system state instrumentation and model-based observers. Together, these tools and technologies pave the way for smarter, more efficient industrial systems.

3.1 Automation and Collaborative Robotics

Industrial automation is a fundamental component of Industry 4.0, as it enables the execution of production processes with minimal human intervention; to achieve this, it integrates programmable systems, advanced sensor and transducer technologies, and sophisticated, intelligent control systems. In this context, technological evolution has driven the transition toward cyber-physical systems, which integrate the physical and digital worlds, facilitating remote monitoring, data and signal analysis, and real-time decision-making. This development fosters seamless, close interaction between humans and machines, particularly in the field of collaborative robotics (Lee et al., 2015).

Unlike traditional industrial robotics characterized by operation in rigid, highly structured environments collaborative robots are designed to interact directly and safely with humans in shared spaces that are flexible and adaptable. This collaborative capability is achieved through the incorporation of advanced technologies such as motion, force, and torque sensors; high-resolution, responsive actuators; computer vision systems; collision and contact detection algorithms; and real-time adaptive control strategies. Integrating these elements makes production processes more efficient and flexible while also enhancing safety and ergonomics in the workplace (Haddadin et al., 2017; Villani et al., 2018). From a technical standpoint, collaborative robots feature advanced control architectures that establish various operating modes, ensuring safe and efficient human-robot interaction. Impedance control is widely used in haptic and robotic systems involving a human in the control loop, as it allows for the dynamic regulation of the relationship between force and motion (specifically, position and velocity at the point of physical contact). Meanwhile, programming based on haptic or robotic guidance offers an intuitive strategy in which the user manually guides the robot to teach it tasks; this approach reduces programming complexity and enhances flexibility in production environments characterized by uncertainty. Similarly, multimodal perception systems integrate data from vision, haptic, force, and proximity sensors, enabling the robotic system to interpret its environment more robustly and adapt to changing conditions in real time. Recent approaches utilizing brain-computer interfaces in robotics demonstrate how integrating processed neural signals with robotic systems facilitates more direct and adaptive interaction, thereby expanding control and feedback capabilities in complex applications such as neurorehabilitation (Ajoudani et al., 2018; García-Blancas et al., 2025).

Figure 4. Cyber-physical systems and human-robot physical interaction system

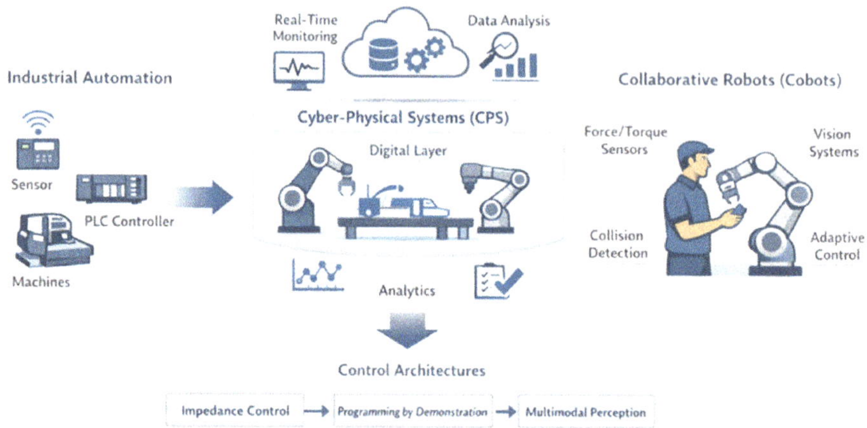

(García-Blancas et al., 2025; Villani et al., 2018)

One of the primary benefits of collaborative robotics lies in significantly improved productivity particularly in high-precision, repetitive tasks that pose risks to workers. These systems operate continuously with highly reliable repeatability, contributing to reduced cycle times and decreased product variability within the production process. Implementation facilitates the reallocation of human labor toward activities requiring greater cognitive value such as supervision, data analysis, and decision-making, thereby increasing system efficiency and fostering safer, more reliable work environments. The integration of collision detection and avoidance algorithms, alongside adaptive control strategies, ensures reliable human-robot interaction in shared workspaces (Lasota et al., 2017; Bicchi et al., 2008). Regarding industrial safety, collaborative robots represent a significant advancement by incorporating principles of safe human-machine interaction directly into their design. Unlike conventional industrial robots, cobots are designed to share workspace with human operators, necessitating compliance with rigorous international safety standards. In this context, standards such as ISO 10218 (Parts 1 and 2) in their most recent versions establish safety requirements for industrial robots and robotic systems, while the technical specification ISO/TS 15066 focuses specifically on safe interaction in collaborative robotics (ISO, 2025, 2016).

Figure 5. Industrial safety standards for collaborative robotics

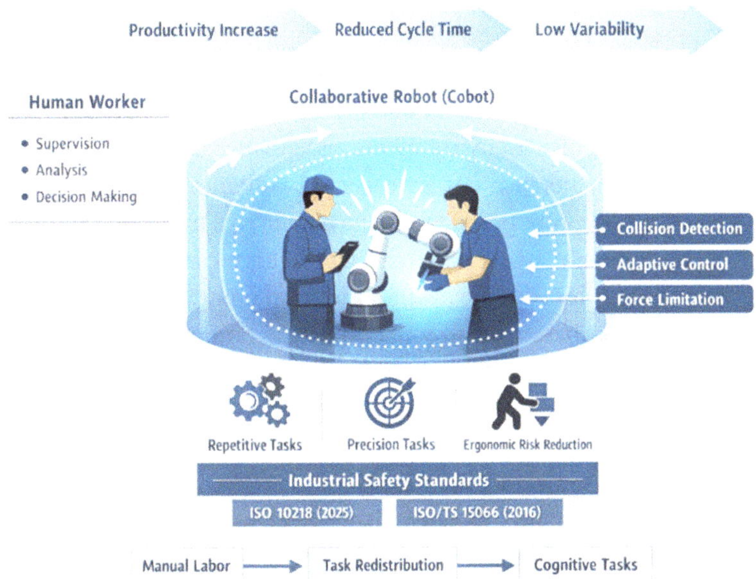

(ISO, 2025, 2016)

These standards address various modes of collaboration, such as safety-rated monitored stops, hand guiding, power and force limiting, and speed and separation monitoring between the robot and the human. To this end, permissible biomechanical limits for force, torque, and energy are established for cases of accidental contact; these limits are based on studies regarding human body tolerance to impact or mechanical contact. Proprioceptive and exteroceptive sensing capabilities are integrated using technologies such as joint torque sensors, force sensors at the end-effector or human-contact areas, collision detection systems, and control algorithms that allow the robot's motion to be stopped or modified within milliseconds in response to any unexpected interaction (Haddadin et al., 2017; Lasota et al., 2017). Thanks to technological advancements and regulations governing the design and operation of human-robot interaction systems, these systems have been successfully implemented in sectors where direct collaboration between humans and machines is essentia, such as flexible manufacturing, the automotive industry, electronics, and precision assembly or manufacturing. In addition to increased productivity, safety and ergonomic conditions in the workplace are improved, thereby reducing the incidence of accidents and facilitating a more natural integration between workers and automated systems (Ajoudani et al., 2018).

Collaborative robotics offers a distinct advantage over traditional automated systems, which entail high costs and significant time requirements for reconfiguration or reprogramming due to its high operational flexibility. Cobots can rapidly adapt to changes in processes, products, or operating conditions thanks to their intuitive programming and reconfigurable architectures. This makes them particularly well-suited for flexible manufacturing environments and small-batch production, where customization and rapid response times are essential (Villani et al., 2018). Through the Internet of Things (IoT), robots can exchange data in real time, facilitating monitoring and predictive maintenance. Artificial intelligence optimizes performance through pattern learning, while deep learning-based computer vision systems enable the recognition of complex objects, thereby allowing for autonomous decision-making in complex, dynamic environments (Ajoudani et al., 2018; Lee et al., 2015). From an economic perspective, although the initial investment in collaborative robots can be substantial, these systems typically offer a favorable return on investment over the medium to long term (Graetz & Michaels, 2018).

The adoption of collaborative robots entails significant challenges that must be addressed comprehensively to ensure successful implementation. Key challenges include the need for workforce training and reskilling, cybersecurity in highly interconnected environments, and integration with legacy systems—factors that can limit interoperability and increase transition costs. The growing connectivity of industrial systems exposes cobots to cyberattack vulnerabilities, highlighting the need for robust cybersecurity and data protection strategies within smart manufacturing environments (Humayed et al., 2017). Additionally, there is a significant social dimension regarding the acceptance of these innovative technologies and the transformation of human roles in the workplace; automation redefines job functions and necessitates the development of new skills focused on supervision, analysis, and decision-making (Acemoglu & Restrepo, 2020). Automation and collaborative robotics not only enhance efficiency, productivity, and safety in industrial processes but also drive a redefinition of human-machine interaction. This shift fosters the creation of smarter, more flexible, and human-centric work environments, where technology acts as an enabler of human performance rather than a substitute, thereby promoting more sustainable and adaptable production models.

3.2 Artificial Intelligence and Data Analytics

Artificial intelligence (AI) is a fundamental pillar of Industry 4.0, enabling the transformation of vast volumes of data and signals into actionable information for strategic and operational decision-making. In digitized industrial environments, the availability of data from sensors, production systems, and interconnected platforms has driven the development of AI-based solutions capable of enhancing organizational efficiency, quality, and competitiveness (Lee et al., 2015). By leveraging machine learning techniques, companies can develop predictive models that identify patterns in historical data and relate them to data analyzed in real time. This makes it possible to anticipate machinery failures through predictive maintenance, optimize operating parameters in production processes, and improve quality control via the early detection of defects or irregularities. The use of advanced algorithms, such as deep neural networks and supervised and unsupervised learning methods, facilitates the analysis of complex systems involving multiple interdependent variables (Goodfellow et al., 2016; Wuest et al., 2016).

Real-time data analytics enables continuous monitoring of industrial system performance, facilitating anomaly detection, bottleneck identification, and the generation of early warnings regarding potential failures. This approach not only improves responsiveness to unexpected events but also contributes to continuous process optimization through the use of predictive analytics techniques. Predictive analytics relies on statistical models and machine learning algorithms that using historical and real-time data allow for estimating the future behavior of critical system variables, anticipating failures, predicting demand, or identifying operational deviations before they occur (Kusiak, 2018).

Figure 6. Functional architecture of artificial intelligence in Industry 4.0

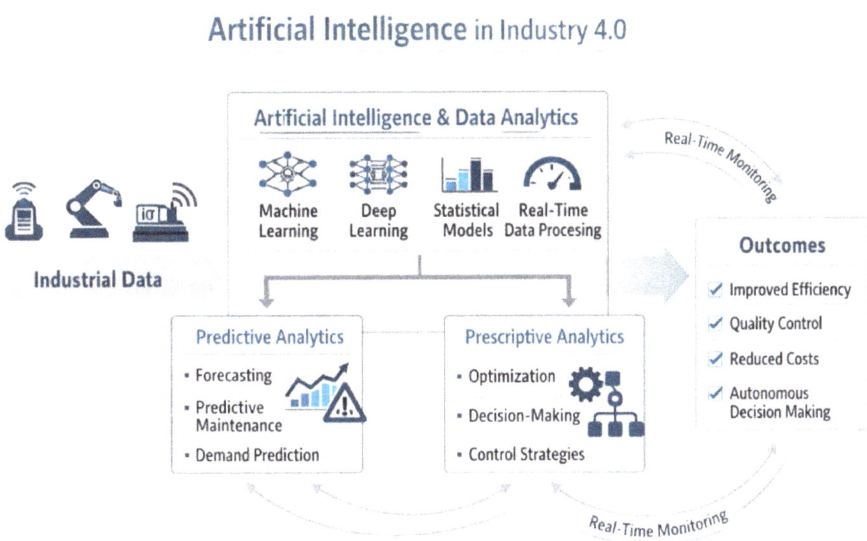

(Kusiak, 2018)

Integrating AI into production systems enables a shift toward automated decision-making, allowing systems to act autonomously based on analyzed data. This significantly reduces reliance on human intervention for routine or highly complex analytical tasks, thereby increasing operational efficiency and minimizing the margin of error. AI facilitates the development of smart factories, where decision-making is data-driven and focused on continuous improvement (Russell & Norvig, 2021; Brynjolfsson & McAfee, 2017). In the medical industry, artificial intelligence and data science have demonstrated a particularly significant impact, especially in applications such as biomedical signal analysis, rehabilitation, and computer-aided diagnosis. Deep learning-based approaches have enabled the development of predictive models for complex diseases like multiple sclerosis, improving diagnostic accuracy and clinical data analysis (Ponce de Leon-Sanchez et al., 2023). The use of synthetic data and machine learning techniques has facilitated the recognition of abnormal gait patterns, such as "crouch gait", contributing to the development of advanced tools for the assessment and motor rehabilitation of human bipedal walking (Gonzalez-Islas et al., 2024). These applications demonstrate how the integration of AI and data analytics enables medical care that is more personalized, predictive, and evidence-based.

The application of artificial intelligence and data analytics not only optimizes industrial processes but also drives the transition toward the smarter, adaptive, and autonomous production systems characteristic of Industry 4.0.

3.3 Internet of Things and Industrial Connectivity

The Industrial Internet of Things (IIoT) is a key technology within the Industry 4.0 paradigm, enabling the interconnection of devices, machines, sensors, and systems via digital networks that facilitate real-time data collection, exchange, and analysis. This digital infrastructure transforms traditional production environments into highly interconnected systems where physical components communicate with one another and with management platforms to enhance operational efficiency and decision-making (Atzori et al., 2010; Lee et al., 2015). IIoT enables the continuous monitoring of critical production process variables, such as temperature, pressure, mechanical vibration, humidity, and energy consumption using sensors distributed throughout the production chain. This capacity for massive data sensing allows not only for remote process control but also for the implementation of strategies for predictive maintenance, energy optimization, and product quality improvement. Consequently, real-time data integration facilitates a faster response to operational deviations and potential failures, thereby reducing downtime and operating costs (Gubbi et al., 2013; Xu et al., 2018).

Recent developments demonstrate the implementation of IoT-based embedded systems integrated with V2X (Vehicle-to-Everything) communication technologies, enabling real-time information transmission among devices, infrastructure, and mobile systems. These architectures extend the scope of IoT to mobility and smart city applications, facilitating distributed decision-making and enhancing the efficiency and safety of complex dynamic systems (Campero-Jurado et al., 2019). Complementarily, proposals focused on environmental monitoring using low-cost IoT platforms based on microcontrollers such as the ESP32 demonstrate the feasibility of implementing accessible solutions for real-time data acquisition, processing, and visualization, thereby strengthening information management in academic and industrial environments (Hernández Arteaga et al., 2025).

Taken together, the IIoT and associated connectivity represent a fundamental element in the evolution toward smart factories, where decision-making is supported by real-time data and signals, as well as advanced analytics.

Figure 7. Architecture of the industrial Internet of Things (IIoT) in Industry 4.0

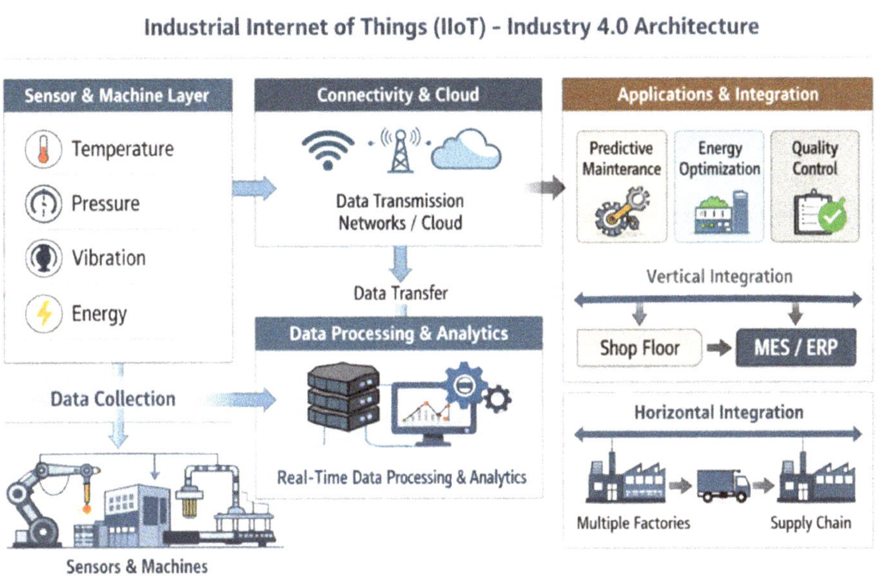

(Lee et al., 2015; Gubbi et al., 2013)

3.4 Additive Manufacturing and New Production Models

Additive manufacturing (3D printing) represents one of the most significant contributions to modern production systems within the framework of Industry 4.0. Unlike traditional subtractive manufacturing methods, in which material is removed to shape a part, additive manufacturing builds objects layer by layer based on 3D models designed on digital platforms; this enables greater design freedom, waste reduction, and optimized material usage (Gibson et al., 2021; Ngo et al., 2018). This capability is particularly relevant for fabricating complex geometric structures that would be difficult or impossible to achieve using conventional subtractive manufacturing techniques. This has had a notable impact on sectors such as medicine, aerospace, and the automotive industry, where the ability to produce unique or highly specialized parts is critical (Attaran, 2017).

Additive manufacturing aligns with circular economy principles by promoting more efficient resource use and minimizing waste generated during production. It enables material reuse and the repair or remanufacture of components, thereby extending their useful life. This approach not only reduces environmental impact but also creates new business opportunities based on more sustainable and decentralized production models (Ford & Despeisse, 2016). Integrating additive manufacturing with conventional processes has led to "hybrid manufacturing," which combines additive and subtractive techniques to leverage the advantages of both approaches. This synergy enhances dimensional accuracy, surface quality, and the mechanical properties of components while optimizing production times and reducing costs. Hybrid manufacturing is particularly valuable for producing high-value-added parts and repairing critical components in advanced industrial sectors (Zhu et al., 2017).

Figure 8. Additive manufacturing process and applications in Industry 4.0

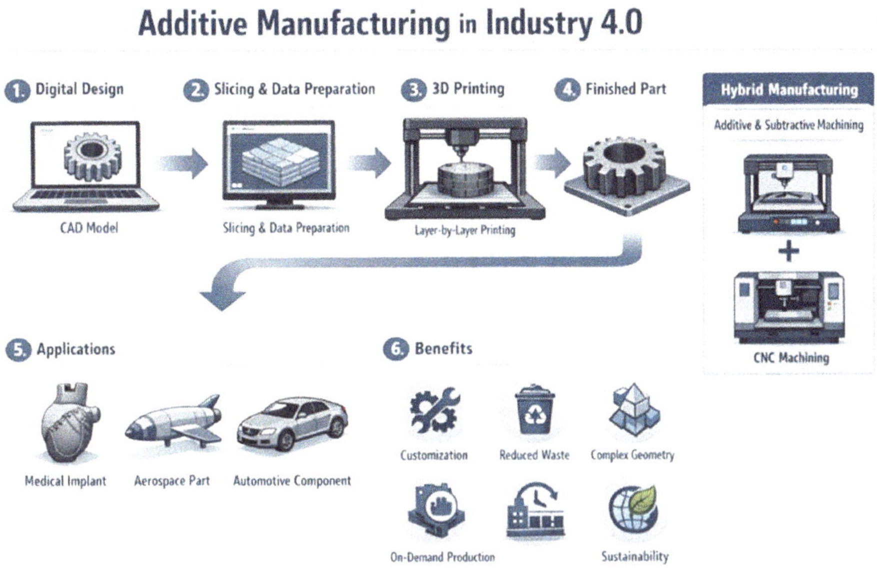

(Gibson et al., 2021; Ngo et al., 2018)

Additive manufacturing not only redefines design and manufacturing processes but also drives new production models based on digitalization, flexibility, and sustainability. Its integration with other Industry 4.0 technologies positions it as a key element in the transition toward smarter, more personalized, and more efficient production systems.

3.5 Digital Twins and Simulation

Digital twins have established themselves as a key technology in Industry 4.0, enabling the creation of dynamic virtual representations of physical systems to simulate, analyze, and optimize their behavior. They are continuously updated using real-time data, accurately reflecting the operating conditions of industrial machines and processes (Tao et al., 2019). This technology relies on the integration of systems such as IoT, cyber-physical systems, and data analytics. To achieve this, signals, including temperature, mechanical vibration, and energy consumption are captured and processed; this not only allows for real-time system monitoring but also enables the generation of predictive models capable of anticipating failures and future behaviors (Kritzinger et al., 2018). One of the primary benefits is advanced simulation, which allows for the evaluation of various scenarios without disrupting actual operations. Consequently, it is possible to optimize processes, analyze configurations, and reduce the risks and costs associated with physical testing (Negri et al., 2017).

Figure 9. Functional architecture of digital twins in Industry 4.0

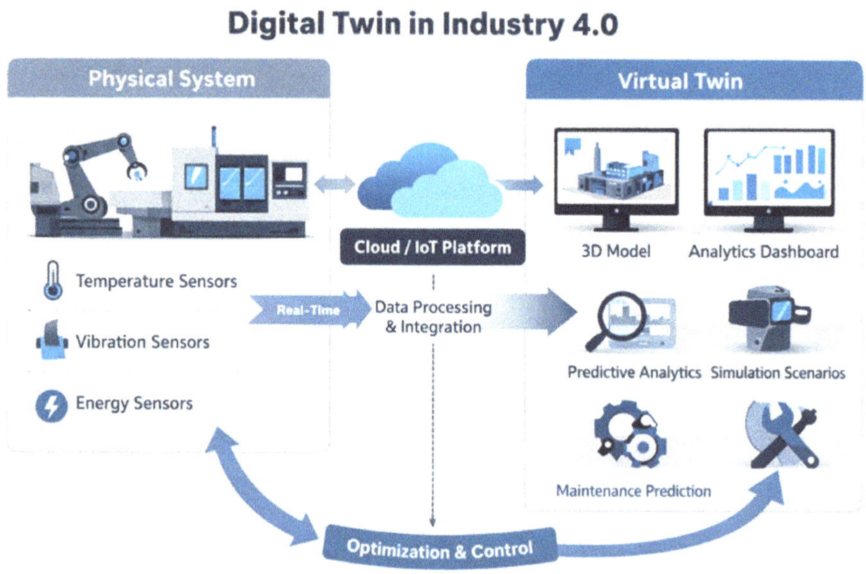

(Tao et al., 2019)

Digital twins facilitate predictive maintenance and continuous improvement, and enable the identification of anomalies. They constitute a fundamental tool for the development of industrial systems that are more efficient, intelligent, and decision-oriented.

4. TRANSITION TO INDUSTRY 5.0: THE HUMAN FACTOR

The transition to Industry 5.0 represents an evolution of the Industry 4.0 paradigm by explicitly incorporating the human factor as a central element of technological development. Unlike Industry 4.0, which focuses on automation, digitalization, and efficiency Industry 5.0 promotes an approach that integrates sustainability, resilience, and human well-being into the production system (European Commission, 2021). This new paradigm does not aim to replace humans; rather, the technology is designed to enhance human capabilities, fostering closer collaboration between people and intelligent systems. The worker shifts from being a passive operator to an active agent who interacts, supervises, and makes decisions with the support of advanced technologies (Nahavandi, 2019). Industry 5.0 emphasizes product customization, adaptation to individual needs, and social responsibility in technological development (Lu et al., 2022). This approach seeks to align technological innovation with sustainable development goals, thereby promoting more efficient processes (Breque et al., 2021). Consequently, the transition from Industry 4.0 to Industry 5.0 entails not only a technological transformation but also a cultural and organizational one, with human capital positioned as a key element (Xu et al., 2021).

Figure 10. Human-centric Industry 5.0 conceptual model

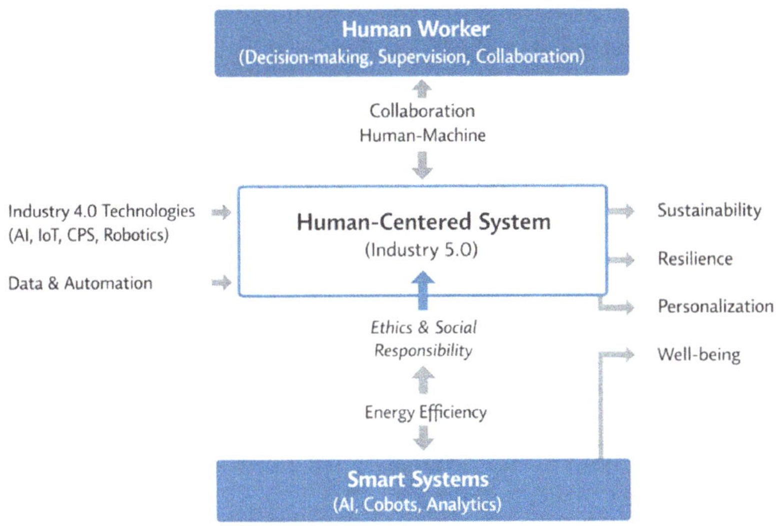

(European Commission, 2021; Nahavandi, 2019).

4.1 Human-Machine Collaboration

Human-machine collaboration is a cornerstone of Industry 5.0, proposing interaction models in which human and technological qualities integrate synergistically to maximize system performance while prioritizing human well-being, autonomy, and development. This paradigm fosters human-centric collaboration, with technology acting as an enabler that amplifies human capabilities rather than replacing them (Villani et al., 2018; European Commission, 2021). In this context, collaborative robots enable safe, direct interaction within shared spaces by incorporating advanced sensors, adaptive control, and perception mechanisms that respond dynamically to human interaction (Haddadin et al., 2017). Industry 5.0 introduces the concept of cognitive and ergonomic safety, designing systems to reduce mental workload, prevent fatigue, and enhance the user experience during interaction; furthermore, the integration of artificial intelligence enables more adaptable, personalized systems capable of learning from an operator's preferences, behaviors, and states. This paves the way for more natural collaborative frameworks, where the machine anticipates needs, adjusts its behavior in real-time, and facilitates assisted decision-making (Ajoudani et al., 2018; Nahavandi, 2019). Consequently, the interaction shifts from being reactive to becoming proactive and context-aware.

The development of intuitive interfaces such as systems based on voice recognition, gestures, augmented reality, and haptic feedback strengthens this relationship by enabling more fluid and accessible communication. These technologies not only reduce operational complexity but also boost user trust and acceptance, which are key factors in advanced industrial environments (Lasota et al., 2017). Furthermore, recent research into human-machine interaction within the healthcare sector demonstrates how collaborative systems can extend beyond industrial settings. In particular, the development of bimanual exergaming platforms for neurorehabilitation shows that integrating interactive interfaces, sensors, and real-time feedback allows for the design of user-centered systems that foster motor recovery and patient engagement. Such solutions reinforce the Industry 5.0 approach by prioritizing personalization, accessibility, and human well-being within advanced technological systems (Juárez Chavero et al., 2026). In Industry 5.0, value lies not merely in automation but also in the ability to intelligently integrate human capabilities with advanced technologies, thereby creating systems that are more resilient, inclusive, and sustainable (Brynjolfsson & McAfee, 2017; Breque et al., 2021).

4.2 Human-Centered Design

Human-centered design is a fundamental principle of Industry 5.0, as it seeks to ensure that technologies adapt to the needs, capabilities, and limitations of users. This approach transcends the traditional view of technical efficiency to incorporate dimensions such as well-being, inclusion, and user experience, integrating ergonomic, cognitive, and emotional aspects from the initial stages of system design (Norman, 2013). The human being is positioned as the central element of the technological system, guiding the development of solutions toward environments that are safer, more accessible, and more satisfying. In accordance with international standards, design must focus on understanding the context of use, user participation, and the iterative evaluation of developed solutions (ISO 9241-210, 2019). Physical and cognitive ergonomics contribute to reducing fatigue, preventing human error, and improving overall worker performance by adapting systems to the user's perceptual and motor capabilities (Salvendy, 2012).

In the context of Industry 5.0, human-centric design incorporates the concept of dynamic adaptability, whereby systems can adjust in real time to user conditions, such as experience level, cognitive load, or physical state. Emerging technologies like augmented reality, haptic interfaces, and intelligent systems enable personalized interaction, providing assistance, instant feedback, and decision-making support (Hollnagel, 2014). By prioritizing human well-being and the user experience, this approach contributes to the development of more resilient, inclusive, and sustainable systems; it fosters the creation of safer, collaborative, and adaptable work environments where technology serves as an ally to human development rather than merely acting as an automation tool.

4.3 Ethics and Technological Responsibility

The rapid advancement of emerging technologies, particularly within the context of Industry 5.0, has intensified the need to address the ethical aspects associated with their development, implementation, and use. Technology ethics focuses on ensuring that these innovations are geared toward human well-being, social equity, and sustainability, while avoiding the negative impacts that can arise from their indiscriminate adoption (Floridi et al., 2018). Responsibility lies not only with technology developers but also with organizations, governments, and society as a whole. One of the key ethical challenges concerns the automation of decision-making based on artificial intelligence systems. Because these systems rely on vast amounts of data and complex algorithms, they can reproduce or even amplify existing biases, leading to unfair or discriminatory decisions if not properly designed. Consequently, concepts such as transparency, explainability, and algorithmic traceability become essential to ensuring the trustworthiness and legitimacy of these systems (Russell & Norvig, 2021).

Another critical aspect is privacy and data protection. In highly digitized environments, where IoT devices and cyber-physical systems collect real-time information, there is a risk of the misuse of personal and sensitive data situations in which user information is exploited for commercial or strategic purposes without adequate oversight (Zuboff, 2019). Consequently, it is essential to establish regulatory frameworks that protect individual rights and ensure the ethical use of information. In the workplace, the automation and robotization of production processes raise questions regarding the future of employment and the transformation of required skills; while these technologies can boost productivity, they may also lead to job displacement or inequalities if appropriate transition policies are not implemented. Various international initiatives have proposed ethical principles, such as fairness, autonomy, and responsibility aimed at guiding the development of trustworthy, human-centric technologies (Jobin et al., 2019). These principles seek to ensure that technology is not only technically efficient but also socially acceptable and morally responsible. Within the framework of Industry 5.0, ethics and technological responsibility take on even greater significance by placing the human being at the center of the production system. This entails designing and implementing technologies that respect human dignity, foster inclusion, and contribute to sustainable development.

4.4 Creativity and Innovation as a Competitive Advantage

Creativity and innovation play a central role as differentiating factors in the face of the growing automation of production processes. While Industry 4.0 focused on digitalization, efficiency, and automation, Industry 5.0 introduces a human-centric vision in which strategic value lies in the ability to integrate technological potential with human cognitive, creative, and social skills (Breque et al., 2021). In this context, creativity is a key competency that enables organizations to adapt to complex, uncertain, and highly dynamic environments. Unlike automated systems, which operate based on rules, historical data, and pre-trained models human creativity is characterized by the ability to generate original ideas, reinterpret problems, and propose innovative solutions in unstructured contexts. This ability is fundamental to processes such as personalized product design, process improvement, and the creation of new business models, where cognitive flexibility and divergent thinking are essential (Amabile, 1996). Thus, creativity not only complements automation but transcends it by enabling disruptive innovation. Far from displacing human creativity, the integration of advanced technologies like artificial intelligence enhances it through human-machine collaboration. This approach, known as augmented creativity, allows users to leverage digital tools to explore multiple scenarios, analyze vast amounts of information, and accelerate creative processes; technology thereby acts as a catalyst for innovation, expanding human capabilities rather than replacing them (Daugherty & Wilson, 2018).

Innovation as a competitive advantage in Industry 5.0 is closely linked to the ability of organizations to foster environments that stimulate creativity. Factors such as organizational culture, participatory leadership, team diversity, and continuous learning directly influence the generation of innovative ideas. Cognitive diversity, in particular, has been shown to improve complex problem-solving by integrating diverse perspectives an essential aspect of interdisciplinary technological environments (Page, 2007). The capacity for innovation impacts not only economic competitiveness but also the creation of social value and the response to global challenges, such as sustainability and human well-being. Creativity becomes a fundamental component in developing production systems that are more resilient, inclusive, and human-centric, aligning with the principles of Industry 5.0 (Florida, 2003; Brynjolfsson & McAfee, 2017).

In conclusion, the transition to Industry 5.0 redefines the role of creativity as a central element in the interaction between humans and advanced technologies. Far from being replaced by automation, human creativity establishes itself as a key competitive advantage that drives innovation, adaptability, and value creation in smart industrial environments.

5. SUSTAINABILITY AND CIRCULAR ECONOMY AS TRAINING AXES

Sustainability has established itself as one of the most relevant cross-cutting themes in contemporary professional education. In a global context marked by the climate crisis, biodiversity loss, and growing social inequality, higher education institutions face the imperative to incorporate the principles of sustainable development into their academic programs (Silva-Hormazábal and Alsina, 2023). The United Nations 2030 Agenda, with its 17 Sustainable Development Goals (SDGs), establishes a framework that calls for the training of professionals capable of generating innovative solutions to today's socio-environmental challenges (Bugallo-Rodríguez and Vega-Marcote, 2020).

At the same time, the circular economy is emerging as a transformative paradigm that challenges the linear model of production and consumption. This approach proposes a regenerative system in which resources remain in use for as long as possible, their maximum value is extracted, and they are recovered and regenerated at the end of their useful life (Nguyen, 2023). Integrating these principles into education not only addresses an ecological need but also prepares students for emerging labor markets that demand skills related to sustainable resource management (Flores Marín and González Castillo, 2024).

This paper examines how the principles of sustainability and the circular economy are integrated as core components of higher education, and how STEAM (Science, Technology, Engineering, Arts, Mathematics) methodologies serve as a key pedagogical tool for developing the necessary competencies within the framework of Industry 4.0 and the transition toward Society 5.0 (Ramírez-Cedillo et al., 2025; Pérez-Domínguez et al., 2023).

Figure 11. Pillars of sustainable development and their relationship to the 20230 Agenda

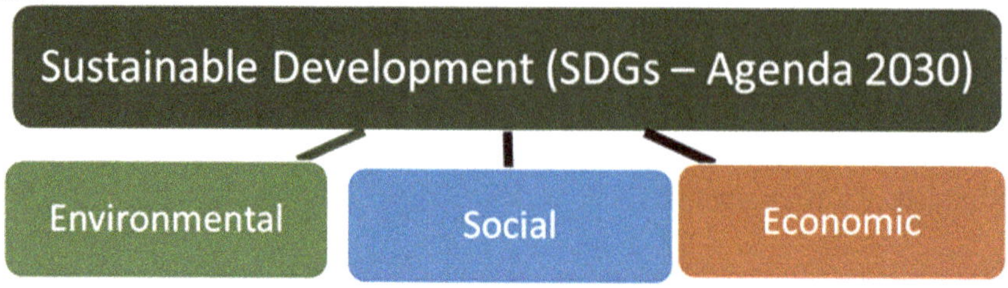

5.1 Principles of Sustainability Applied to Vocational Education

Education for sustainability (EfS) is based on a set of pedagogical principles that go beyond the mere transmission of environmental knowledge. According to Silva-Hormazábal and Alsina (2023), EfS involves the development of cross-cutting competencies that include systems thinking, the anticipation of future consequences, interpersonal collaboration, and the ability to make ethical decisions in contexts of uncertainty. These principles align closely with the key competencies defined by UNESCO for sustainability: systems thinking competency, anticipatory competency, normative competency, strategic competency, and collaborative competency.

In the field of vocational education, a radical change in curricula and programs is required to integrate the principles of sustainability. Abnoulgid et al. (2025) note that the Quality 4.0 paradigm in higher education demands the incorporation of sustainable practices into all academic processes, from curriculum design to the assessment of learning. This approach recognizes that sustainability cannot be an isolated subject but rather an organizing principle for the educational process as a whole.

Sustainability-oriented professional education is structured around three fundamental dimensions: environmental, social, and economic. Núñez-Naranjo (2025) emphasizes that Education 4.0 provides a conducive framework for this integration by promoting the use of digital technologies and active methodologies that enable complex problems to be addressed in an interdisciplinary manner. Students thus develop a holistic understanding of socio-environmental challenges and acquire the tools to propose innovative and viable solutions.

Table 7. Principles of sustainability applied to professional education

Principle	Description	Educational Application
Systems thinking	Understanding the interrelationships among social, economic, and environmental systems	Interdisciplinary projects that address complex issues
Expectation	Ability to anticipate the future consequences of present actions	Scenario analysis and environmental impact simulations
Ethical responsibility	Decision-making that considers collective and planetary well-being	Case studies on ethical dilemmas in industry
Collaboration	Interdisciplinary collaboration among various social actors	Community projects and university-business-society partnerships
Critical thinking	Questioning unsustainable models of production and consumption	Debates and critical analysis of industrial practices

Note: Based on Silva-Hormazábal & Alsina (2023), UNESCO (2017), and Abnoulgid et al. (2025).

5.2 Circular Economy: Key Concepts and Their Integration into the Curriculum

The circular economy is a regenerative economic model that contrasts with the linear "extract, produce, use, and dispose" paradigm. This approach, grounded in the seminal work of the Ellen MacArthur Foundation, proposes three fundamental principles: eliminating waste and pollution by design, keeping products and materials in use, and regenerating natural systems (Nguyen, 2023). In the educational context, the circular economy offers a powerful conceptual framework for training professionals capable of rethinking production and consumption processes.

Integrating the circular economy into the university curriculum requires a multidimensional approach. De Angelis and Ianulardo (2025) argue that education in the circular economy must go beyond theory, incorporating practical experiences that allow students to apply circular principles in real-world contexts. This includes product life-cycle analysis, design for reuse and recycling, and the evaluation of circular business models.

The STEAM Euskadi project, documented in the Funghi Thinking program, is a prime example of how to integrate the circular economy with STEAM education. This project uses mushroom cultivation from coffee waste as the backbone of a learning process that integrates natural sciences, technology, mathematics, and the arts, while bringing the principles of the circular economy to life through a tangible and meaningful experience for students (STEAM Euskadi, 2023).

Figure 12. The circular economy cycle and its main phases

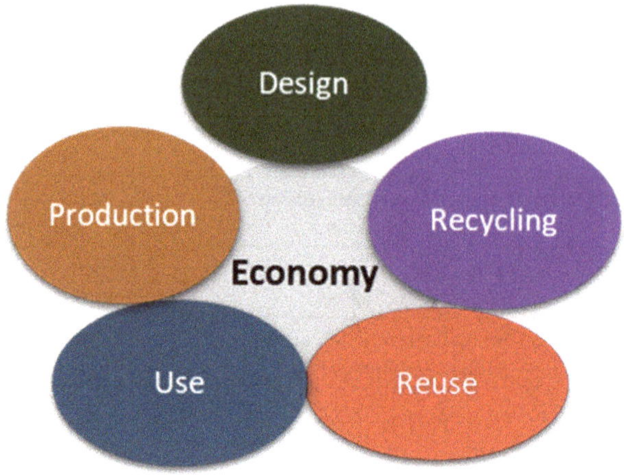

Table 8. Comparison between the linear economic model and the circular economy model

Dimension	Linear model	Circular economy
Resource flow	Extract → Produce → Use → Dispose	Closed loop: reduce, reuse, recycle, regenerate
Product design	Planned obsolescence	Design for durability, repair, and reuse
Waste management	Landfills and incineration	Treating Waste as a Resource
Economic value	Loss of value at the end of its useful life	Value retention and regeneration
Environmental impact	Resource depletion and pollution	Ecosystem regeneration
Educational role	Specialized technical training	Interdisciplinary training with a systems-based approach

Note: Based on Nguyen (2023) and De Angelis & Ianulardo (2025).

5.3 Success Stories and Best Practices in Education for Sustainability

The existing literature provides several successful examples of incorporating sustainability and the circular economy into educational design. It reveals that linking theory to practice, inter-institutional coordination, and proactive approaches are essential for the successful implementation of these efforts. In the Latin American context, Silva-Hormazábal and Alsina (2023) describe a STEAM education program for sustainability in a rural setting in Chile. This study demonstrates how integrating STEAM disciplines with the SDGs enables the simultaneous development of scientific and sustainability competencies, adapting content to local realities and fostering the link between academic knowledge and community needs. The results indicate a significant improvement in students' understanding of environmental concepts and in their motivation. In Europe, STEAM Euskadi's Funghi Thinking program (2023) serves as a good example of incorporating the circular economy into education. Through their project to grow mushrooms from organic waste, students apply the principles of the circular economy and also gain first-hand skills in science, technology, engineering, art, and mathematics. This demonstrates that the program is effective in fostering systems thinking and environmental awareness among young students.

In Europe, STEAM Euskadi's Funghi Thinking program (2023) serves as a model for how the circular economy can be integrated into educational practice. This project, which involves growing mushrooms from organic waste, allows students to directly experience the principles of the circular economy while developing skills in science, technology, engineering, art, and mathematics. The program has proven effective in developing systems thinking and environmental awareness among young students.

In Asia, Ho (2023) analyzes the implementation of STEAM programs in educational institutions in Ho Chi Minh City, Vietnam, highlighting how the integration of sustainability as a cross-cutting theme enhances meaningful learning and real-world problem-solving. The findings underscore that teacher training and the availability of technological resources are key factors for successful implementation.

Likewise, Gueye and Exposito (2020) propose the concept of University 4.0, in which sustainability is integrated as a guiding principle that permeates all university functions: teaching, research, outreach, and institutional management. This model proposes that universities not only teach about sustainability but also actively practice it in their operations and become living laboratories of sustainable practices.

Table 9. Success Stories in Education for Sustainability Using the STEAM Approach

Case/Program	Country	Main Approach	Key Results
Rural STEAM for Sustainability	Chile	STEAM projects integrated into rural schools with a focus on sustainability	Greater engagement, environmental awareness, and interdisciplinary skills
Pensamiento de Setas – STEAM Euskadi	Spain	Circular economy through mycelium biotechnology and STEAM	Thousands of students trained in the circular economy and biotechnology
STEAM Education in HCMC	Vietnam	Analysis of STEAM implementation with a focus on sustainability	Identification of strategies for preparing the green industry
University 4.0 Framework	Multinational	Digital Transformation of Higher Education Institutions with Sustainability Integration	Comprehensive Model for Institutional Transformation
STEM Skills for Industry 4.0	Mexico	Systematic review of STEM skills for the Fourth Industrial Revolution	Competency framework aligned with the demands of Industry 4.0

Note: Based on Silva-Hormazábal & Alsina (2023), STEAM Euskadi (2023), Ho (2023), Gueye & Exposito (2020), and Flores Marín & González Castillo (2024).

6. STEAM LEARNING AND INNOVATION METHODOLOGIES

STEAM methodologies represent an integrative educational approach that seeks to overcome traditional disciplinary fragmentation by integrating science, technology, engineering, the arts, and mathematics into meaningful and contextualized learning experiences. Unlike the STEM approach, the inclusion of the arts in the acronym STEAM recognizes the fundamental role of creativity, divergent thinking, and aesthetic sensitivity in the comprehensive training of professionals (Henriksen, 2017; Domínguez Osuna et al., 2019).

In the context of Education 4.0, STEAM methodologies take on particular relevance as they align with the demands of the Fourth Industrial Revolution and the transition toward Society 5.0. Núñez-Naranjo (2025) emphasizes that the convergence of STEAM competencies with emerging technologies—such as artificial intelligence, the Internet of Things, additive manufacturing, and augmented reality—shapes a new educational paradigm that requires innovative, student-centered pedagogical methodologies focused on solving real-world problems.

The effective implementation of STEAM methodologies requires a paradigm shift in teaching practice. Jiménez León et al. (2021) note that current trends in STEM/STEAM education in higher education point toward the integration of project-based learning, the use of digital technologies, interdisciplinary collaboration, and links with the private sector. These trends are reflected in various specific methodologies, which are analyzed in the following subsections.

Figure 13. Components of the STEAM approach and their interdisciplinary integration

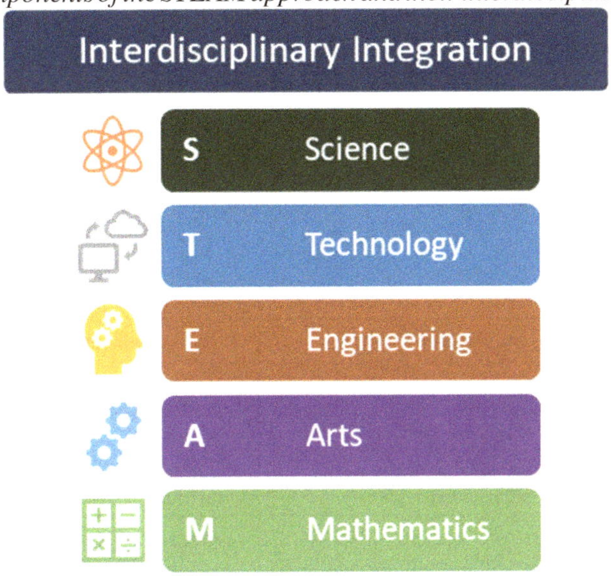

6.1 Foundations of the STEAM Approach in Higher Education

The STEAM approach in higher education is grounded in a theoretical foundation that integrates various pedagogical and epistemological currents. Henriksen (2017) proposes the DT+STEAM framework (Design Thinking integrated with STEAM), which combines design thinking with the STEAM disciplines to foster creativity, innovation, and the resolution of complex problems. This framework recognizes that creativity is not exclusive to the arts but rather a cross-cutting competency that manifests itself in all scientific and technological disciplines.

Domínguez Osuna et al. (2019) analyze the challenges of implementing the STEM+A (STEAM) approach in engineering programs, emphasizing that incorporating the arts is not limited to adding artistic content but involves integrating creative thinking, aesthetics, and visual communication as fundamental competencies in the training of engineers. The authors identify the main challenges as resistance to change in traditional academic cultures, a lack of faculty training in interdisciplinary methodologies, and the need for flexible infrastructure that facilitates collaborative work. Gras and Alí (2023) offer a comprehensive overview of STEM education and its application in various contexts, emphasizing that the success of these approaches depends on coherence between learning objectives, pedagogical strategies, and assessment systems. The authors emphasize that assessment in STEAM contexts must be authentic, performance-based, and aimed at demonstrating students' ability to integrate knowledge from multiple disciplines in solving real-world problems.

Coello Pisco et al. (2021) contribute to this discussion by analyzing the professional STEM skills required for Industry 4.0, identifying a set of technical and cross-disciplinary competencies that educational programs must develop. Among these competencies are computational thinking, digital literacy, data analysis skills, the ability to work in multidisciplinary teams, and adaptability to changing environments.

Table 10. Key Competencies of the STEAM Approach in Higher Education

STEAM Dimension	Key Competencies	Pedagogical Strategies
Science (S)	Scientific inquiry, evidence-based reasoning, environmental literacy	Laboratory research, field studies, data-driven research
Technology (T)	Digital literacy, programming, computational thinking	Programming projects, integration of digital tools, technology-mediated collaboration
Engineering (E)	Design process, systems thinking, problem-solving	Engineering design challenges, prototyping, and optimization projects
Arts (A)	Creativity, visual communication, empathetic design	Design thinking workshops, multimedia production, human-centered design
Mathematics (M)	Quantitative reasoning, statistical analysis, mathematical modeling	Data analysis projects, simulation exercises, mathematical problem-solving

Note: Based on Henriksen (2017), Domínguez Osuna et al. (2019), and Coello Pisco et al. (2021).

6.2 Design Thinking as a Pedagogical Tool for Innovation

Design Thinking (DT) has established itself as one of the most effective methodologies for fostering innovation in educational contexts. Originating in the field of industrial design and popularized by Stanford University and the firm IDEO, DT proposes a human-centered, iterative process consisting of five phases: empathize, define, ideate, prototype, and evaluate (Henriksen, 2017). In its educational application, DT serves as a pedagogical tool that enables students to develop innovation skills through the creative resolution of real-world problems.

The integration of DT with the STEAM approach, as proposed by Henriksen (2017) in his DT+STEAM framework, enhances students' creative abilities by providing a structured process for innovation. In the empathy phase, students use social science and arts skills to understand user needs; in the define phase, they apply scientific analysis to narrow down the problem; in the ideate phase, they use divergent thinking and artistic creativity; in the prototype phase, they integrate engineering and technology; and in the evaluate phase, they use mathematical and scientific methods to measure results.

Ramírez-Cedillo et al. (2025) document the implementation of DT in the Tec21 model at the Tecnológico de Monterrey, where students work in the Smart Factory as a space for experiential learning. In this environment, students apply design thinking to develop solutions to real-world problems in the manufacturing industry, integrating Industry 4.0 competencies with a human-centered approach characteristic of Society 5.0. The results show that combining DT with advanced technologies significantly increases students' capacity for innovation.

Punto Crea, as reported in various educational experiences, proposes a methodology that combines Challenge-Based Learning (CBL) with the STEAM approach and Design Thinking. This proposal integrates the identification of community issues as a starting point, the use of technological tools for research, the prototyping of solutions, and the creative presentation of results. The methodology emphasizes the importance of students developing not only technical skills but also empathy, communication, and leadership skills.

Figure 14. Phases of Design Thinking Applied to the STEAM Approach

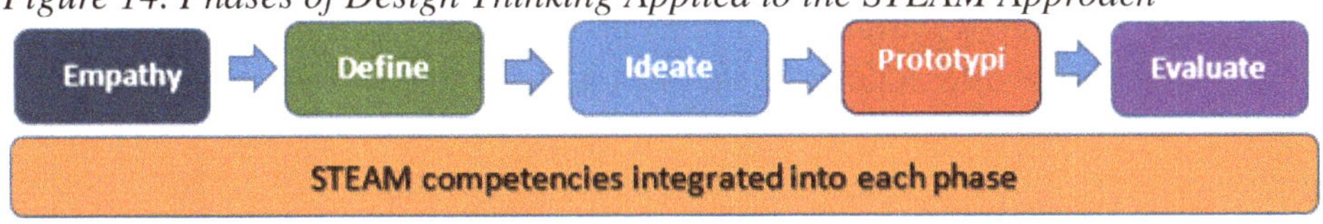

Table 11. Phases of Design Thinking and Their Connection to STEAM Competencies

DT Phase	Description	Associated STEAM Competencies
Empathize	Deep understanding of users, their needs, and context	Arts (empathic observation), Sciences (ethnographic research), Mathematics (data collection)
Define	Synthesizing findings into a clear problem statement	Engineering (problem framing), Science (analytical synthesis), Arts (narrative construction)
Ideate	Divergent generation of creative solutions	Arts (creative thinking), Technology (digital brainstorming tools), Mathematics (feasibility assessment)
Prototype	Rapid construction of tangible representations of solutions	Engineering (manufacturing), Technology (digital tools, 3D printing), Arts (visual design)
Evaluate	Test prototypes with users and iterate based on feedback	Science (experimental testing), Mathematics (quantitative analysis), Technology (data collection tools)

Note: Based on Henriksen (2017) and Ramírez-Cedillo et al. (2025).

6.3 Rapid Prototyping and Experiential Learning

Rapid prototyping is an experiential learning methodology that allows students to turn ideas into tangible models in an agile and iterative manner. In the STEAM context, prototyping integrates engineering, technology, and arts competencies, while requiring the use of mathematical reasoning and scientific principles to validate proposed solutions (Flores Marín and González Castillo, 2024). Industry 4.0 technologies such as 3D printing, laser cutting, programmable electronics, and augmented reality have democratized access to prototyping, making it an accessible pedagogical tool for institutions of various kinds.

Ramírez-Cedillo et al. (2025) describe how the concept of the "Student 5.0" is brought to life at the Tecnológico de Monterrey's Smart Factory, where students use advanced manufacturing technologies to prototype solutions to real-world industrial problems. This learning space integrates collaborative robots, additive manufacturing systems, the Internet of Things (IoT), and digital twins, providing an environment that replicates Industry 4.0 conditions and allows students to develop prototyping skills in an authentic context.

Experiential learning, grounded in Kolb's theory, finds rapid prototyping to be an ideal means of implementation. Núñez-Naranjo (2025) notes that Education 4.0 requires the creation of learning environments that enable active experimentation, critical reflection, and continuous iteration. Prototyping meets these requirements by offering a learning cycle that includes the conceptualization of an idea, its physical or digital realization, the evaluation of its performance, and iterative improvement based on feedback.

Flores Marín and González Castillo (2024) emphasize that prototyping skills are essential for Industry 4.0, as they help reduce product development times, minimize production costs, and foster incremental and disruptive innovation. In the educational context, prototyping also fosters tolerance for error, perseverance, and the ability to learn from failures—social-emotional competencies that are fundamental to professional performance in highly uncertain environments.

Table 6. Rapid prototyping technologies in STEAM educational contexts

Technology	Description	STEAM Educational Application
3D Printing	Additive manufacturing using polymers, resins, or metals	Design visualization, engineering prototypes, artistic sculpture
Laser cutting	Precision cutting and engraving of flat materials	Architectural models, mechanical components, art installations
Arduino/Raspberry Pi	Open-source microcontrollers and single-board computer platforms	IoT projects, sensor-based experiments, interactive art installations

continued on following page

Table 6. Continued

Technology	Description	STEAM Educational Application
Augmented reality	Digital overlay of information onto physical environments	Visualization of scientific phenomena, interactive design review
Digital twins	Virtual replicas of physical systems for simulation and analysis	Process optimization, predictive maintenance training, systems analysis
CAD/CAM software	Computer-aided design and manufacturing tools	Product design, engineering analysis, and manufacturing process planning

Note: Based on Flores Marín & González Castillo (2024) and Ramírez-Cedillo et al. (2025).

6.4 Integration of STEAM With Industry 4.0 and 5.0

The integration of STEAM methodologies with the paradigms of Industry 4.0 and Society 5.0 opens up new horizons for higher education. Pérez-Domínguez et al. (2023) analyze the transition from Industry 4.0—focused on automation and digitization—to Industry 5.0, which places humans back at the center of the production process. This transition calls for " " professionals who not only master digital technologies but also possess humanistic, creative, and ethical competencies that enable them to design technologies that serve social well-being.

Ramírez-Cedillo et al. (2025) introduce the concept of the Student 5.0, which describes the profile of a professional trained at the intersection of STEAM competencies and the requirements of Industry 5.0. This student is characterized by the ability to integrate advanced technical skills—such as collaborative robot programming, big data analysis, and the management of cyber-physical systems—with socio-emotional competencies such as empathy, creativity, collaborative leadership, and social responsibility.

Flores Marín and González Castillo (2024) identify the STEM competencies required by Industry 4.0, including computational thinking, the management of advanced manufacturing technologies, cybersecurity, big data analysis, and artificial intelligence. The authors argue that training in these competencies should be conducted using active methodologies that simulate real-world industrial conditions and allow students to gain practical experience before entering the workforce.

Abnoulgid et al. (2025) present the Quality 4.0 perspective as an integrative framework that links quality management with Industry 4.0 technologies in the context of higher education. This approach proposes that educational institutions adopt data-driven quality practices, automate academic processes, and personalize learning through artificial intelligence, while maintaining a commitment to a humanistic and sustainable education.

Gueye and Exposito (2020) complement this vision with their proposal for University 4.0, which conceives the university as an innovation ecosystem where research, teaching, technology, and social engagement converge. In this model, STEAM methodologies are implemented in digital fabrication labs (FabLabs), coworking spaces, and virtual learning platforms that simulate the productive environments of the Fourth Industrial Revolution.

Table 12.

<table>
<tr><td>Industry 4.0</td><td rowspan="6">Transition →</td><td>(Industry / Society 5.0</td></tr>
<tr><td>Automation and efficiency</td><td>Human-technology collaboration</td></tr>
<tr><td>IoT . AI . Big Data. Cloud</td><td>Cobots – Digital Twins – Custom AI</td></tr>
<tr><td>Technical skills</td><td>Technical + human skills</td></tr>
<tr><td>Resource optimization</td><td>Regenerative and responsible design</td></tr>
<tr><td>Technical Specialist</td><td>Student 5.0: creative and ethical</td></tr>
</table>

The human being returns to the center of the production process (Pérez-Dominguez et al. 2023; Nahavandi, 2019)

Table 13. Comparison between Industry 4.0 and Society 5.0 in the STEAM educational context

Dimension	**Industry 4.0**	**Society/Industry 5.0**
Core Focus	Automation and efficiency	Human-technology collaboration
Key Technologies	IoT, AI, Big Data, Cloud Computing	Cobots, Digital Twins, Custom AI
Educational Objective	Development of technical skills	Holistic skills development (technical + soft skills)
Role of the arts/ humanities	Peripheral or absent	Central to human-centered innovation
Approach to sustainability	Efficiency-oriented resource optimization	Regenerative and socially responsible design
Student Profile	Technically Qualified Specialist	Student 5.0: creative, ethical, interdisciplinary

Note: Based on Pérez-Domínguez et al. (2023) and Ramírez-Cedillo et al. (2025).

Table 14. Integrative Framework: STEAM, Sustainability, and Industry 4.0/5.0

Component	Contribution to education	Example of Application
STEAM methodology	Interdisciplinary integration and creative problem-solving	Design Thinking projects addressing sustainability challenges
Principles of Sustainability	Ethical Framework and Systems Thinking	Life cycle analysis of products and services
Circular economy	Regenerative design and a resource-efficient mindset	Waste recovery projects using biotechnology
Industry 4.0 technologies	Digital tools for prototyping, analysis, and collaboration	IoT-enabled environmental monitoring systems
Society 5.0 Values	A human-centered approach to technological innovation	Inclusive design projects for diverse communities
University Model 4.0	Institutional Framework for Integrated Education	Smart Factory learning environments with industry partnerships

Note: Based on the integrated analysis by Henriksen (2017), Ramírez-Cedillo et al. (2025), Pérez-Domínguez et al. (2023), and Gueye & Exposito (2020).

7. INTEGRATIVE PROJECTS AS A CONSOLIDATION STRATEGY

In today's educational landscape, shaped by the challenges of digital transformation and the transition toward Industry 4.0 and 5.0, there is an increasing need to reconsider traditional teaching strategies. The fragmented delivery of knowledge has proven insufficient for preparing individuals capable of addressing complex problems in real-world contexts. Within this scenario, integrative projects emerge as a relevant strategy to connect different areas of knowledge and promote competency development under the STEAM education framework. Figure 7 illustrates the conceptual model of Industry 5.0, where the human being is placed at the center, a perspective that is closely aligned with the principles of STEAM education.

This section examines integrative projects as a strategy for consolidating learning processes, emphasizing their contribution to skills development, their relationship with societal needs, and the challenges associated with their implementation.

7.1 Definition and Scope of the Challenge

Integrative projects constitute a methodology through which students engage with relevant problems within a particular context. Unlike conventional exercises, these projects are not limited to finding a predefined answer; instead, they require exploration, analysis, and informed decision-making throughout the process.

The development of this strategy begins with the identification of a meaningful problem connected to the surrounding environment, allowing students to recognize its practical relevance. Examples include the design of water collection systems, the optimization of industrial processes, or the creation of technological solutions aimed at supporting vulnerable communities.

Addressing the challenge requires more than simply understanding the problem. Students must examine its variables, constraints, and potential impacts, which encourages critical thinking and strengthens the ability to formulate questions—an essential skill across different fields of knowledge.

7.2 Integration of STEAM Skills

A significant contribution of integrative projects lies in their capacity to connect STEAM competencies in a practical and meaningful way. By bringing together different areas of knowledge, these projects promote a more comprehensive approach to learning.

This integration can be observed through three main dimensions:

- Technical: the scientific and technological knowledge needed to solve the problem.
- Creative: the ability to innovate, design, and propose original solutions.
- Human: social skills, ethics, communication, and teamwork.

This approach moves beyond the traditional separation between disciplines and helps students develop a more holistic understanding of reality. It also promotes meaningful learning by applying knowledge to concrete situations. STEAM integration can be formalized as a vector system of competencies:

$$K = \left(K_s, K_t, K_e, K_a, K_m\right)$$

where each component represents competencies in: science, K_s; technology, K_t; engineering, K_e; art/design, K_a; mathematics, K_a. This integrative approach is based on interdisciplinary educational models (Yakman, 2008; Bybee, 2013).

From the perspective of dynamical systems, it follows that

$$\frac{dK(t)}{dt} = F(K(t), U(t), E(t))$$

where F is a nonlinear vector function that models the interaction between competencies, $U(t)$ represents control inputs (methodologies, tools, educational strategies) and $E(t)$ rcpresents the environment (problem, socio-technical context, constraints).

An expanded form of the system is:

$$\frac{dK_i(t)}{dt} = \sum_{j=1}^{5} \left(a_{ij} \cdot K_j(t) + b_i \cdot U_i(t) + c_i \cdot E_i(t)\right)$$

where a_{ij} represents the link between disciplines, b_i influence of strategies (control inputs) and c_i describes the impact of the environment. The interpretation of the model is as following: If $a_{ij} > 0$ there is synergy between disciplines, If $a_{ij} < 0$ there is conflict or competition for cognitive resources and $a_{ij} = 0$ the disciplines are independent (an undesirable case in STEM).

This model allows us to analyze integration as a problem of stability and convergence, in which the goal is for the system to reach a desired state, K^*.

$$\lim_{t\to\infty} K(t) = K^*$$

The STEM process can be formulated as a dynamic optimization problem:

$$\min J = \int_0^T \left[w_1 P(t) + w_2 C(t) + w_3 I(t) + w_4 R(t)\right] dt$$

where $P(t)$ is the system performance, $C(t)$ represents the cost, $I(t)$ is the impact (social/environmental), $R(t)$ is the risk or uncertainty and w_i represent the project's priority weights.

The entire system can be represented as a control system (Closed-loop STEM):

$$U(t) = G(K(t),\ Y(t))$$

$$Y(t) = H(K(t))$$

where $Y(t)$ are the observable outputs (project results), H is the measurement (evaluation) function and G is the control policy (iteration, redesign, learning).

This creates a feedback loop:

Modeling → Implementation → Evaluation → Adjustment

Interpretation in a STEM context: science and mathematics govern the dynamics of the model (definition of F), technology serves as a means of implementing U(t), engineering optimizes the system's trajectory toward K and art/design influences H(K), that is, how the results are perceived and evaluated. The model incorporates several relevant characteristics, including its behavior as a complex adaptive system, the presence of nonlinear interactions, multidisciplinary coupling, iterative feedback mechanisms, and multi-objective optimization.

Functional Integration Model

Within an integrative project, STEAM competencies are not treated as isolated elements; instead, they operate as an interconnected system of interdependent variables, where their interactions influence the overall performance of the system. This perspective aligns with contemporary STEM education models that highlight the integration of practices, cross-disciplinary concepts, and disciplinary knowledge (National Research Council, 2012).

Considering a systems approach, this functional integration can be described as a multidimensional dynamic system in which each competency, (K_i), represents a subsystem with its own inputs, outputs, and feedback mechanisms. The relationships established among these competencies may be represented through a coupling matrix, (A):

$$K_{out} = A \cdot K_{in}$$

where (K_{in}) denotes the vector of initial competencies, (K_{out}) corresponds to the vector of integrated competencies obtained after the process, and (A) is the interaction matrix that describes the cognitive, methodological, and technological dependencies among them.

Through this representation, it is possible to examine phenomena such as interdisciplinary synergy, critical dependencies, and different levels of coupling strength. At the operational level, this integration is reflected in workflows where scientific modeling, technological development, and engineering design activities take place concurrently rather than following a sequential process.

Additionally, the system exhibits characteristics of iterative feedback:

$$K(t+1) = f(K(t), E, R)$$

where (K(t)) describes the competency state at iteration (t), (E) defines the problem environment, (R) includes the associated constraints and requirements, and (f(·)) denotes an update function based on learning and validation processes.

The functional integration of competencies can be assessed through systemic performance metrics that consider aspects such as interdisciplinary coherence, efficiency in knowledge transfer, and the capacity to converge toward optimal solutions.

Operational Translation in the Project

From a STEM perspective, the operational translation of competencies within a project can be interpreted as the process of transforming disciplinary knowledge into concrete procedures, tools, and system-level implementations. Instead of being treated as separate domains, Science, Technology, Engineering, Art, and Mathematics interact through an integrated workflow, where each area contributes to different levels of abstraction and execution, as described in interdisciplinary STEM frameworks (National Research Council, 2012; Bybee, 2013).

Within this framework, Science provides the theoretical foundation required to describe the behavior of real-world phenomena. This requires the formulation of physical, chemical, or biological principles and their representation through analytical or computational models. Such models may involve differential equations, statistical approaches, or simulation environments that support prediction, hypothesis testing, and the interpretation of system behavior under different conditions. This perspective is consistent with active and inquiry-based learning approaches in science education (Freeman et al., 2014).

Technology serves as the link between theoretical models and their implementation in functional systems. It involves software platforms, embedded systems, sensors, data acquisition devices, and artificial intelligence algorithms that enable scalability, real-time processing, and interaction with the surrounding environment. In this way, technology connects abstract representations with practical applications (OECD, 2018).

Engineering combines scientific principles and technological resources to develop functional solutions through structured design methodologies. Its activities include defining system architectures, selecting components, prototyping, testing, and optimizing designs under specific constraints. These processes commonly involve iterative cycles and multi-objective optimization strategies, where performance, cost, reliability, and sustainability must be considered simultaneously (Dym et al., 2005; ABET, 2019).

The incorporation of Art and Design adds a human-centered perspective to the system, addressing aspects related to usability, accessibility, and the interaction between users and technology. This dimension includes user experience (UX) design, interface development (UI), visual communication, and aesthetic consistency. From a technical perspective, these elements may be represented as an optimization problem focused on user satisfaction and cognitive efficiency, in accordance with STEAM integration models (Yakman, 2008).

Mathematics supports the remaining domains by providing the formal structures required for modeling, analysis, and optimization. Through mathematical methods, it becomes possible to formulate algorithms, analyze data statistically, perform numerical simulations, and solve optimization problems. These structures contribute to the rigor, reproducibility, and scalability of the resulting solutions (Felder & Brent, 2016).

From a systems integration perspective, this operational translation can be represented as a pipeline:

Model → Algorithm → Implementation → System → User Interaction

where each stage is associated with a dominant STEM component while maintaining continuous feedback interactions among them. For instance, information generated by technological systems may contribute to the refinement of scientific models, whereas user interaction can guide engineering redesigns or adjustments in computational approaches. This iterative exchange is consistent with incremental and iterative development models (Larman & Basili, 2003).

The process therefore operates as an adaptive cycle, similar to a closed-loop system in which outputs are continuously assessed through performance metrics and used to improve previous stages. This mechanism supports progressive refinement and convergence toward optimal or near-optimal solutions, following principles commonly applied in engineering design and problem-based learning environments (Prince & Felder, 2006).

Within a STEM framework, operational translation can be understood as more than a simple allocation of roles among disciplines. It represents a coordinated and dynamic process of knowledge transformation that facilitates the resolution of complex problems through structured, efficient, and scalable approaches, while responding to the competencies demanded by the future workforce (World Economic Forum, 2020).

Integration Through Iterative Cycles

The process is structured in Design Thinking + Engineering cycles: problem definition, Ideation, prototyping, validation and iteration. Each cycle involves feedback between disciplines, generating a dynamic learning system.

Integration Indicators

These aspects can be assessed through indicators such as the interdisciplinary index, the level of knowledge transfer reflected in the application of concepts to new contexts, and system complexity, measured by the number of variables and relationships included in the model.

7.3 Communication and Presentation of Solutions

Developing solutions also requires the ability to communicate them effectively. For this reason, integrative projects include the presentation of results as a fundamental stage.

In this phase, students develop skills such as:

- Clear and structured oral expression
- Use of visual aids (graphs, prototypes, models)
- Logical and persuasive reasoning

Effective communication not only allows ideas to be conveyed, but also enables proposals to be defended and an impact to be made. This capability is particularly relevant in professional environments, where ideas need to be clearly communicated and understood by different stakeholders.

8. CONCLUSIONS AND FUTURE PERSPECTIVES

8.1 Key Competencies for the Industrial Future

The transition toward Industry 4.0 and 5.0 has significantly influenced the requirements of the labor market. In this context, companies increasingly seek professionals capable of adapting to changing environments and addressing complex problems.

Key competencies include:

- Critical and analytical thinking
- Creativity and innovation
- Collaborative work
- Adaptability and continuous learning

Integrative projects provide opportunities for students to develop these competencies naturally by engaging them in real-world situations that require decision-making and the ability to manage uncertainty.

8.2 Linkage Between Education, Industry and Society

A relevant aspect of integrative projects is their capacity to establish a connection between education and real-world contexts. Through this relationship, learning processes can generate tangible contributions to society.

The interaction among these three areas results in several benefits, including:

- Practical application of knowledge
- Development of solutions with social impact
- Training of more aware and responsible professionals

It also promotes knowledge transfer and innovation, both of which contribute to economic and social development.

8.3 Challenges and Opportunities of STEAM Training

Although STEAM education offers significant advantages, its implementation still involves several challenges.

The main challenges include:

- Lack of teacher training
- Infrastructure limitations
- Rigid curricula

These challenges also present opportunities for innovation. The incorporation of emerging technologies, including artificial intelligence and simulation tools, can further enrich the educational process. STEAM education may also contribute to preparing students for global challenges by promoting the development of a more sustainable and equitable society.

Integrative projects constitute a relevant pedagogical strategy for consolidating learning within the STEAM education framework. Through the integration of knowledge and the development of key competencies, these projects provide students with opportunities to address future challenges.

Given the increasing complexity and rapid transformation of current environments, education needs to move toward more flexible and interdisciplinary approaches focused on solving real-world problems. Integrative projects contribute to this transition by strengthening the teaching-learning process and supporting the development of individuals capable of generating meaningful changes in their surroundings.

From this perspective, STEM integration can be represented as a controlled dynamic system in which competencies evolve as coupled states, methodologies operate as control signals, assessment mechanisms close the feedback loop, and the overall process converges toward optimal solutions under multiple constraints.

REFERENCES

ABET. (2019). *Criteria for accrediting engineering programs.* ABET Engineering Accreditation Commission.

Abnoulgid, F., Aouhassi, S., Mansouri, K., & Akef, F. (2025). Quality 4.0 in higher education: Integrating Industry 4.0 technologies in higher education quality management practices. *Frontiers in Education, 10,* 1594377. Advance online publication. DOI: 10.3389/feduc.2025.1594377

Abras, C., Maloney-Krichmar, D., & Preece, J. (2004). User-centered design. In Bainbridge, W. S. (Ed.), *Berkshire encyclopedia of human-computer interaction* (Vol. 2, pp. 763–768). Berkshire Publishing Group.

Acemoglu, D., & Restrepo, P. (2020). Robots and jobs: Evidence from US labor markets. *Journal of Political Economy, 128*(6), 2188–2244. DOI: 10.1086/705716

Aheleroff, S., Huang, H., Xu, X., & Zhong, R. Y. (2022). Toward sustainability and resilience with Industry 4.0 and Industry 5.0. *Frontiers in Manufacturing Technology, 2*, 951643. Advance online publication. DOI: 10.3389/fmtec.2022.951643

Ajoudani, A., Zanchettin, A. M., Ivaldi, S., Albu-Schäffer, A., Kosuge, K., & Khatib, O. (2018). Progress and prospects of the human–robot collaboration. *Autonomous Robots, 42*(5), 957–975. DOI: 10.1007/s10514-017-9677-2

Amabile, T. M. (1996). *Creativity in context: Update to The social psychology of creativity.* Westview Press.

Analuisa-Sánchez, J. J., López Chica, J. A., & Macías Loor, C. A. (2025). Las ecuaciones diferenciales como pilar metodológico en la interpretación y representación de sistemas dinámicos dentro de la educación superior: Aplicaciones en el ámbito de la ingeniería y las matemáticas avanzadas. *Revista Social Fronteriza, 5*(4), e833. Advance online publication. DOI: 10.59814/resofro.2025.5(4)833

Attaran, M. (2017). The rise of 3-D printing: The advantages of additive manufacturing over traditional manufacturing. *Business Horizons, 60*(5), 677–688. DOI: 10.1016/j.bushor.2017.05.011

Atzori, L., Iera, A., & Morabito, G. (2010). The Internet of Things: A survey. *Computer Networks, 54*(15), 2787–2805. DOI: 10.1016/j.comnet.2010.05.010

Bermúdez, A. (2023). Modelos matemáticos en la industria. Universidad de La Laguna. https://imarrero.webs.ull.es/sctm03.v2/modulo3/ABermudez.pdf

Bicchi, A., Peshkin, M., & Colgate, J. E. (2008). Safety for physical human–robot interaction. In Siciliano, B., & Khatib, O. (Eds.), *Springer handbook of robotics* (pp. 1335–1348). Springer., DOI: 10.1007/978-3-540-30301-5_58

Breque, M., De Nul, L., & Petridis, A. (2021). Industry 5.0: Towards a sustainable, human-centric and resilient European industry. European Commission. https://data.europa.eu/doi/10.2777/308407

Brynjolfsson, E., & McAfee, A. (2017). *Machine, platform, crowd: Harnessing our digital future*. W. W. Norton & Company.

Bugallo-Rodríguez, Á., & Vega-Marcote, P. (2020). Circular economy, sustainability and teacher training in a higher education institution. *International Journal of Sustainability in Higher Education, 21*(7), 1351–1366. DOI: 10.1108/IJSHE-02-2020-0049

Bybee, R. W. (2013). *The case for STEM education: Challenges and opportunities*. NSTA Press.

C3 UNAM. (2022). Sistemas complejos. Centro de Ciencias de la Complejidad, Universidad Nacional Autónoma de México. https://www.c3.unam.mx/noticias/noticia222.html

Campero-Jurado, I., Quintanar Gomez, J., Vargas-Buitrón, O. D., Trejo-Macotela, F. R., Robles-Camarillo, D., & Simancas-Acevedo, E. (2019). Embedded system based on IoT and V2X for smart cities. *International Journal of Combinatorial Optimization Problems and Informatics, 10*(3), 50–58. https://ijcopi.org/ojs/article/view/128

Castillo-Castillo, M. (2025). Adaptación y aplicación de la metodología STEAM en entornos educativos con recursos limitados. *Episteme Koinonía, 8*(16), 437–459. DOI: 10.35381/e.k.v8i16.4641

Coello Pisco, S., Rodríguez Gómez, B., González Cañizalez, Y., & Hidalgo Crespo, J. (2021). Habilidades profesionales STEM e industria 4.0 para estudiantes de Física Aplicada en proyectos disciplinarios I+D+i. Revista de Investigación, Formación y Desarrollo. *Generando Productividad Institucional, 9*(3), 1–18.

Daugherty, P. R., & Wilson, H. J. (2018). *Human + machine: Reimagining work in the age of AI*. Harvard Business Review Press.

Davis, F. D. (1989). Perceived usefulness, perceived ease of use, and user acceptance of information technology. *Management Information Systems Quarterly, 13*(3), 319–340. DOI: 10.2307/249008

De Angelis, R., & Ianulardo, G. (2025). Walking the talk on education for sustainable development: The value of circular economy education in the age of complexity. *Circular Economy and Sustainability*, *5*(4), 3305–3316. DOI: 10.1007/s43615-025-00577-5

Dintén, R., López Martínez, P., & Zorrilla, M. (2021). Arquitectura de referencia para el diseño y desarrollo de aplicaciones para la Industria 4.0. *Revista Iberoamericana de Automática e Informática Industrial*, *18*(3), 300–311. DOI: 10.4995/riai.2021.14532

Domínguez Osuna, P. M., Olivares Carmona, K. M., Rodríguez Elías, O. M., & Gutiérrez Franco, E. (2019). Retos de ingeniería: Enfoque educativo STEM+A en la revolución industrial 4.0. *Innovación Educativa (México, D.F.)*, *19*(80), 15–32.

Dym, C. L., Agogino, A. M., Eris, O., Frey, D. D., & Leifer, L. J. (2005). Engineering design thinking, teaching, and learning. *Journal of Engineering Education*, *94*(1), 103–120. DOI: 10.1002/j.2168-9830.2005.tb00832.x

European Commission, Directorate-General for Research and Innovation. (2021). Industry 5.0, a transformative vision for Europe: Governing systemic transformations towards a sustainable industry. Publications Office of the European Union. https://data.europa.eu/doi/10.2777/17322

Euskadi, S. T. E. A. M. (2023). *Funghi Thinking: Programa de economía circular y STEAM*. Departamento de Educación del Gobierno Vasco.

Felder, R. M., & Brent, R. (2016). *Teaching and learning STEM: A practical guide*. Jossey-Bass.

Flores Marín, J. A., & González Castillo, S. (2024). Competencias STEM para la Industria 4.0: Una revisión sistemática. *Congreso Internacional de Investigación Academia Journals*, *638*, 1–10.

Florida, R. (2002). *The rise of the creative class: And how it's transforming work, leisure, community and everyday life*. Basic Books.

Floridi, L., Cowls, J., Beltrametti, M., Chatila, R., Chazerand, P., Dignum, V., Luetge, C., Madelin, R., Pagallo, U., Rossi, F., Schafer, B., Valcke, P., & Vayena, E. (2018). AI4People—An ethical framework for a good AI society: Opportunities, risks, principles, and recommendations. *Minds and Machines*, *28*(4), 689–707. DOI: 10.1007/s11023-018-9482-5 PMID: 30930541

Fogaça, D. R., Grijalvo, M., & Sacomano Neto, M. (2025). What are Industry 4.0 and Industry 5.0 all about? An integrative institutional model for the new industrial paradigms. *Administrative Sciences*, *15*(4), 118. Advance online publication. DOI: 10.3390/admsci15040118

Ford, S., & Despeisse, M. (2016). Additive manufacturing and sustainability: An exploratory study of the advantages and challenges. *Journal of Cleaner Production, 137*, 1573–1587. DOI: 10.1016/j.jclepro.2016.04.150

Freeman, S., Eddy, S. L., McDonough, M., Smith, M. K., Okoroafor, N., Jordt, H., & Wenderoth, M. P. (2014). Active learning increases student performance in science, engineering, and mathematics. *Proceedings of the National Academy of Sciences of the United States of America, 111*(23), 8410–8415. DOI: 10.1073/pnas.1319030111 PMID: 24821756

García-Blancas, J., Domínguez-Ramírez, O. A., Rodríguez-Torres, E. E., Ramirez-Zamora, J. D., & Rodriguez-Hernandez, E. (2025). A technological proposal for a robot brain computer interface for neurorehabilitation purposes. *The European Physical Journal. Special Topics, 234*(1), 195–223. DOI: 10.1140/epjs/s11734-024-01463-1

Gibson, I., Rosen, D., & Stucker, B. (2021). *Additive manufacturing technologies* (3rd ed.). Springer., DOI: 10.1007/978-3-030-56127-7

Gonzalez-Islas, J.-C., Dominguez-Ramirez, O. A., Lopez-Ortega, O., & Pena Ramirez, J. (2024). Crouch gait recognition in the anatomical space using synthetic gait data. *Applied Sciences (Basel, Switzerland), 14*(22), 10574. Advance online publication. DOI: 10.3390/app142210574

Goodfellow, I., Bengio, Y., & Courville, A. (2016). *Deep learning*. MIT Press.

Graetz, G., & Michaels, G. (2018). Robots at work. *The Review of Economics and Statistics, 100*(5), 753–768. DOI: 10.1162/rest_a_00754

Gras, A., & Alí, L. (2023). *Educación STEM y su aplicación*. Editorial Académica.

Grybauskas, A., Stefanini, A., & Ghobakhloo, M. (2022). Social sustainability in the age of digitalization: A systematic literature review on the social implications of Industry 4.0. *Technology in Society, 70*, 101997. Advance online publication. DOI: 10.1016/j.techsoc.2022.101997

Gubbi, J., Buyya, R., Marusic, S., & Palaniswami, M. (2013). Internet of Things: A vision, architectural elements, and future directions. *Future Generation Computer Systems, 29*(7), 1645–1660. DOI: 10.1016/j.future.2013.01.010

Gueye, B., & Exposito, E. (2020). Universidad 4.0: El paradigma de la industria 4.0 aplicado a la educación. In *Proceedings of CONTE 2020* (pp. 1–6). ACM. https://doi.org/DOI: 10.1145/3434780.3436620

Haddadin, S., De Luca, A., & Albu-Schäffer, A. (2017). Robot collisions: A survey on detection, isolation, and identification. *IEEE Transactions on Robotics, 33*(6), 1292–1312. DOI: 10.1109/TRO.2017.2723903

Henriksen, D. (2017). Creating STEAM with design thinking: Beyond STEM and arts integration. *The STEAM Journal, 3*(1), 11. Advance online publication. DOI: 10.5642/steam.20170301.11

Hernández Arteaga, R., Téllez Vargas, L. N., Ramírez Zamora, J. D., & Domínguez Ramírez, O. A. (2025). Diseño e implementación de una estación de monitoreo ambiental basada en ESP32 para laboratorios académicos. Ibero Ciencias. *Revista Científica y Académica, 4*(4), 418–446. DOI: 10.63371/ic.v4.n4.a389

Hollnagel, E. (2014). *Safety-I and Safety-II: The past and future of safety management.* CRC Press., DOI: 10.1201/9781315607511

Humayed, A., Lin, J., Li, F., & Luo, B. (2017). Cyber-physical systems security—A survey. *IEEE Internet of Things Journal, 4*(6), 1802–1831. DOI: 10.1109/JIOT.2017.2703172

International Organization for Standardization. (2016). ISO/TS 15066:2016 robots and robotic devices—Collaborative robots. https://www.iso.org/standard/62996.html

International Organization for Standardization. (2019). ISO 9241-210:2019 ergonomics of human-system interaction—Part 210: Human-centred design for interactive systems. https://www.iso.org/standard/77520.html

International Organization for Standardization. (2025). ISO 10218-1:2025 robotics—Safety requirements—Part 1: Industrial robots. https://www.iso.org/standard/73933.html

International Organization for Standardization. (2025). ISO 10218-2:2025 robotics—Safety requirements—Part 2: Industrial robot applications and robot cells. https://www.iso.org/standard/73934.html

Ivanov, D., & Dolgui, A. (2020). Viability of intertwined supply networks: Extending the supply chain resilience angles towards survivability. A position paper motivated by COVID-19 outbreak. *International Journal of Production Research, 58*(10), 2904–2915. DOI: 10.1080/00207543.2020.1750727

Jobin, A., Ienca, M., & Vayena, E. (2019). The global landscape of AI ethics guidelines. *Nature Machine Intelligence, 1*(9), 389–399. DOI: 10.1038/s42256-019-0088-2

Juárez Chavero, M. I., Rodríguez Hernández, E., Domínguez-Ramírez, O. A., Villafuerte Segura, R., & Jarillo Silva, A. (2026). Prueba piloto de una plataforma exergaming bimanual para tareas de neurorehabilitación. Pädi Boletín Científico de Ciencias Básicas e Ingenierías del ICBI, 14(Especial), 46–58. https://doi.org/DOI: 10.29057/icbi.v14iEspecial.15496

Kaihara, T., Nishino, N., Ueda, K., Tseng, M., Váncza, J., Schönsleben, P., Teti, R., & Takenaka, T. (2018). Value creation in production: Reconsideration from interdisciplinary approaches. *CIRP Annals*, *67*(2), 791–813. DOI: 10.1016/j.cirp.2018.05.002

Kritzinger, W., Karner, M., Traar, G., Henjes, J., & Sihn, W. (2018). Digital twin in manufacturing: A categorical literature review and classification. *IFAC-PapersOnLine*, *51*(11), 1016–1022. DOI: 10.1016/j.ifacol.2018.08.474

Kusiak, A. (2018). Smart manufacturing. *International Journal of Production Research*, *56*(1–2), 508–517. DOI: 10.1080/00207543.2017.1351644

Larman, C., & Basili, V. R. (2003). Iterative and incremental development: A brief history. *Computer*, *36*(6), 47–56. DOI: 10.1109/MC.2003.1204375

Lasi, H., Fettke, P., Kemper, H.-G., Feld, T., & Hoffmann, M. (2014). Industry 4.0. *Business & Information Systems Engineering*, *6*(4), 239–242. DOI: 10.1007/s12599-014-0334-4

Lasota, P. A., Fong, T., & Shah, J. A. (2017). A survey of methods for safe human–robot interaction. *Foundations and Trends in Robotics*, *5*(4), 261–349. DOI: 10.1561/2300000052

Lee, E. A. (2008). Cyber physical systems: Design challenges. In 2008 11th IEEE International Symposium on Object and Component-Oriented Real-Time Distributed Computing (ISORC) (pp. 363–369). IEEE. https://doi.org/DOI: 10.1109/ISORC.2008.25

Lee, J., Bagheri, B., & Kao, H.-A. (2015). A cyber-physical systems architecture for Industry 4.0-based manufacturing systems. *Manufacturing Letters*, *3*, 18–23. DOI: 10.1016/j.mfglet.2014.12.001

Lu, Y., Zheng, H., Chand, S., Xia, W., Liu, Z., Xu, X., Wang, L., Qin, Z., & Bao, J. (2022). Outlook on human-centric manufacturing towards Industry 5.0. *Journal of Manufacturing Systems*, *62*, 612–627. DOI: 10.1016/j.jmsy.2022.02.001

Miah, M. T., Erdei-Gally, S., Dancs, A., & Fekete-Farkas, M. (2024). A systematic review of Industry 4.0 technology on workforce employability and skills: Driving success factors and challenges in South Asia. *Economies (Basel)*, *12*(2), 35. Advance online publication. DOI: 10.3390/economies12020035

Nahavandi, S. (2019). Industry 5.0—A human-centric solution. *Sustainability (Basel), 11*(16), 4371. Advance online publication. DOI: 10.3390/su11164371

National Research Council. (2012). *A framework for K–12 science education: Practices, crosscutting concepts, and core ideas*. National Academies Press., DOI: 10.17226/13165

Negri, E., Fumagalli, L., & Macchi, M. (2017). A review of the roles of digital twin in CPS-based production systems. *Procedia Manufacturing, 11*, 939–948. DOI: 10.1016/j.promfg.2017.07.198

Ngo, T. D., Kashani, A., Imbalzano, G., Nguyen, K. T., & Hui, D. (2018). Additive manufacturing: 3D printing. A review of materials, methods, applications and challenges. *Composites. Part B, Engineering, 143*, 172–196. DOI: 10.1016/j.compositesb.2018.02.012

Norman, D. A. (2013). The design of everyday things (Rev. and expanded ed.). Basic Books.

Núñez-Naranjo, A. F. (2025). *Educación 4.0 y competencias STEAM: Nuevas estrategias para la enseñanza del futuro*. Editorial Universidad Tecnológica Indoamérica.

OECD. (2018). The future of education and skills [OECD Publishing.]. *Education*, •••, 2030.

Page, S. E. (2007). *The difference: How the power of diversity creates better groups, firms, schools, and societies*. Princeton University Press.

Pérez-Domínguez, L. A., López García, J. C., & Aguilar Molina, R. (2023). Industria 4.0 vs. 5.0: Contexto, fundamentos y una revisión de la literatura. *Mundo FESC, 13*(S1), 1–20.

Perignat, E., & Katz-Buonincontro, J. (2018). STEAM in practice and research: An integrative literature review. *Thinking Skills and Creativity, 31*, 31–43. DOI: 10.1016/j.tsc.2018.10.002

Ponce de Leon-Sanchez, E. R., Dominguez-Ramirez, O. A., Herrera-Navarro, A. M., Rodriguez-Resendiz, J., Paredes-Orta, C., & Mendiola-Santibañez, J. D. (2023). A deep learning approach for predicting multiple sclerosis. *Micromachines, 14*(4), 749. Advance online publication. DOI: 10.3390/mi14040749 PMID: 37420982

Prince, M., & Felder, R. (2006). Inductive teaching and learning methods: Definitions, comparisons, and research bases. *Journal of Engineering Education, 95*(2), 123–138. DOI: 10.1002/j.2168-9830.2006.tb00884.x

Ramírez-Cedillo, E., Armendáriz-Rodríguez, M., García-Ávila, J., Quintero-Sánchez, D., Ortiz-Espinoza, A. A., & Vargas-Martínez, A. (2025). Student 5.0: Immersive learning in next-gen Automation of Manufacturing Systems courses for the Industry 5.0 era. *Frontiers in Education, 10*, 1416761. Advance online publication. DOI: 10.3389/feduc.2025.1416761

Russell, S., & Norvig, P. (2021). *Artificial intelligence: A modern approach* (4th ed.). Pearson.

Salvendy, G. (Ed.). (2012). *Handbook of human factors and ergonomics* (4th ed.). Wiley., DOI: 10.1002/9781118131350

Schwab, K. (2017). *The fourth industrial revolution*. Currency.

Silva-Hormazábal, M., & Alsina, Á. (2023). Educación STEAM para la sostenibilidad en un contexto rural: Una experiencia integradora. *Revista Iberoamericana de Educación, 25*(39), 188–210. DOI: 10.35362/rie2539188

Soori, M., Dastres, R., Arezoo, B., & Jough, F. K. G. (2024). Intelligent robotic systems in Industry 4.0: A review. *Journal of Advanced Manufacturing Science and Technology, 4*(3), 2024007. Advance online publication. DOI: 10.51393/j.jamst.2024007

Tao, F., Zhang, H., Liu, A., & Nee, A. Y. C. (2019). Digital twin in industry: State-of-the-art. *IEEE Transactions on Industrial Informatics, 15*(4), 2405–2415. DOI: 10.1109/TII.2018.2873186

UNESCO. (2017). *Educación para los objetivos de desarrollo sostenible: Objetivos de aprendizaje*. UNESCO., DOI: 10.54675/CZBA9153

Uniminuto Virtual. (2024, August 15). La educación STEAM logra capacitar profesionales integrales. Corporación Universitaria Minuto de Dios. https://virtual.uniminuto.edu/blog/la-educacion-steam-logra-capacitar-profesionales-integrales/

Van Laar, E., Van Deursen, A. J., Van Dijk, J. A., & De Haan, J. (2017). The relation between 21st-century skills and digital skills: A systematic literature review. *Computers in Human Behavior, 72*, 577–588. DOI: 10.1016/j.chb.2017.03.010

Villani, V., Pini, F., Leali, F., & Secchi, C. (2018). Survey on human–robot collaboration in industrial settings: Safety, intuitive interfaces and applications. *Mechatronics, 55*, 248–266. DOI: 10.1016/j.mechatronics.2018.02.009

Wamba, S. F., Gunasekaran, A., Akter, S., Ren, S. J., Dubey, R., & Childe, S. J. (2017). Big data analytics and firm performance: Effects of dynamic capabilities. *Journal of Business Research, 70*, 356–365. DOI: 10.1016/j.jbusres.2016.08.009

Wan, J., Tang, S., Shu, Z., Li, D., Wang, S., Imran, M., & Vasilakos, A. V. (2016). Software-defined industrial Internet of Things in the context of Industry 4.0. *IEEE Sensors Journal, 16*(20), 7373–7380. DOI: 10.1109/JSEN.2016.2565621

World Economic Forum. (2020). The future of jobs report 2020. https://www.weforum.org/reports/the-future-of-jobs-report-2020/

World Economic Forum. (2023). The future of jobs report 2023. https://www.weforum.org/publications/the-future-of-jobs-report-2023/

Wuest, T., Weimer, D., Irgens, C., & Thoben, K.-D. (2016). Machine learning in manufacturing: Advantages, challenges, and applications. *Production & Manufacturing Research, 4*(1), 23–45. DOI: 10.1080/21693277.2016.1192517

Xu, L. D., Xu, E. L., & Li, L. (2018). Industry 4.0: State of the art and future trends. *International Journal of Production Research, 56*(8), 2941–2962. DOI: 10.1080/00207543.2018.1444806

Xu, X., Lu, Y., Vogel-Heuser, B., & Wang, L. (2021). Industry 4.0 and Industry 5.0—Inception, conception and perception. *Journal of Manufacturing Systems, 61*, 530–535. DOI: 10.1016/j.jmsy.2021.10.006

Yakman, G. (2008). STEAM education: An overview of creating a model of integrative education. *Purdue University Conference Proceedings.*

Zavala Ortiz, S. A. (2020). Modelado matemático. Tecnológico Nacional de México. https://rinacional.tecnm.mx/bitstream/TecNM/5627/1/LIBRO_ModeladoMat_SAUL%20ZAVALA%20%281%29.pdf

Zhang, C., Chen, Y., Chen, H., & Chong, D. (2021). Industry 4.0 and its implementation: A review. *Information Systems Frontiers, 26*(5), 1773–1783. DOI: 10.1007/s10796-021-10153-5

Zhu, Z., Dhokia, V., Nassehi, A., & Newman, S. T. (2017). A review of hybrid manufacturing processes—State of the art and future perspectives. *International Journal of Computer Integrated Manufacturing, 30*(4–5), 349–371. DOI: 10.1080/0951192X.2012.749530

Zuboff, S. (2019). *The age of surveillance capitalism: The fight for a human future at the new frontier of power.* PublicAffairs.

Chapter 4

STEAM Skills to Meet Social and Productive Needs

Erika Cervantes Juárez
http://orcid.org/0000-0001-9974-228X
Instituto Politécnico Nacional, Puebla, Mexico

Daniel Sánchez Guzmán
Instituto Politécnico Nacional, Mexico

ABSTRACT

Current needs in both industry and academia require highly trained personnel capable of implementing and developing activities that involve the use of modern technologies, enabling efficient responses to everyday problems. Among the key skills required are critical, creative, and computational thinking, as well as problem-solving abilities, collaboration, and interdisciplinary work—competencies that can be effectively developed within a STEAM-oriented educational framework. The present work aims to demonstrate, from a STEAM perspective, how social problems can be adapted and solved according to the demands of a contemporary and highly productive environment. Additionally, a model for the integration of technologies based on a practical example with a specific implementation in engineering programs, through the incorporation of the LSEESC methodology as an example of the use of spreadsheets and active learning sequences in STEAM-oriented education.

DOI: 10.4018/979-8-2600-3658-7.ch004

1 INTRODUCTION

In recent years, globalization has reshaped not only industrial and economic systems but also the structure and purpose of educational processes. Within this context, education faces the challenge of evolving traditional content-based approaches toward models that emphasize the development of integrated competencies (Durlak et al., 2011)). These require rethinking how knowledge is constructed, applied, and transferred in learning environments increasingly influenced by technological advances and interdisciplinary demands (Durlak et al., 2011; Bayer, 1996).

Rather than focusing exclusively on technical proficiency, current educational approaches emphasize fostering social skills that enable students to engage with complex and dynamic scenarios. These competencies are not isolated; in fact, they are progressively developed through structured learning experiences that connect theory with practice. As an example, we can analyze the formation of engineers, who must therefore consider the development of social skills such as adaptability, collaboration, and problem-solving in real-world contexts (Bayer, 1996; Lavasani et al., 2011). In this regard, it is important to incorporate active teaching methodologies aligned with STEM or STEAM principles, referring to Science, Technology, Engineering, and Mathematics, even with the recent incorporation of arts-based abilities (Dost, 2024; Mulvey et al., 2022; Yusufjanovna, 2026; Suherman et al., 2025). There are many ways to achieve effective results in teaching; however, active learning sequences and problem-oriented activities can create educational scenarios that promote both conceptual understanding and applied reasoning. This approach contributes to the development of competencies aligned with contemporary educational and professional demands, reinforcing the role of professional education in addressing current and emerging challenges (Hake, 1998).

In particular, the use of structured methodologies becomes essential to guide this integration in a coherent and replicable manner, it is important to support the design of learning environments where students actively participate in the construction of solutions, integrating tools, data analysis, and modeling processes, because visual information is usually retained better than textual or numerical information. Students are more likely to remember and understand the material when data are presented as graphs, which provide a clear, concise way to communicate complex information (Mackinlay, 1987). So, this can create social conditions that make participation safer, more inclusive, and more relational. The evidence is promising, but much of it is descriptive rather than causal, and several of the most relevant papers are recent enough that the field still looks unsettled. In this sense, the academic dimension is essential, as university programs are the primary spaces where these competencies must be intentionally developed in early educational stages (Yusufjanovna, 2026; Brennan & Resnick, 2012). Therefore, it can be argued that, in response to globalization, education needs to evolve toward more integrative, active, and contextualized learning models providing a meaningful and relevant framework and can be justified as effective in developing social skills because of its emphasis on active, collaborative, and problem-oriented learning.

By engaging students in real-world challenges that require interdisciplinary perspectives, STEAM environments promote interaction, communication, and teamwork. In this context, students are not only required to apply technical knowledge but also to negotiate ideas, share responsibilities, and construct solutions collectively. Previous studies as realized by Jeannette M. Wing; Shuchi Grover and Roy Pea (Wing, 2006, Grover & Pea, 2013) have highlighted that the integration of computational thinking and interdisciplinary practices fosters and collaborative problem-solving and critical thinking skills among students. Furthermore, research in science and engineering education has demonstrated that active learning methodologies significantly enhance student interaction and engagement, contributing to the development of communication and teamwork skills (Hake, 1998). In addition, frameworks for computational thinking emphasize the importance of collaborative and creative practices as essential components of learning processes (Brennan & Resnick, 2012). Therefore, STEAM education can create social conditions that make participation safer, more inclusive, and more relational and not only supports the acquisition of disciplinary knowledge but also, promotes essential soft skills such as communication, adaptability, and collaborative problem-solving, which are fundamental in both academic and professional contexts (Yusufjanovna, 2026; Suherman et al., 2025; Brennan & Resnick, 2012).

From this perspective, a clear example is engineering education, which is closely linked to this approach because it not only promotes disciplinary knowledge but also fosters key transversal skills required in a global context, such as critical thinking, creativity, collaborative work, problem solving, modeling, data analysis, and the effective use of technology. In this context, and based on the information compiled and previous work, we have identified the importance of the relationship between the STEAM approach and the development of social skills and a possible way to integrate these lines is to use data visualization and computational thinking as drivers of social interaction. Pointing out that these lines focus on collaborative and interdisciplinary environments and technology-mediated problem-solving (Yusufjanovna, 2026; (Brennan & Resnick, 2012).

In different contexts, education has had to evolve, and computational skills have been shown to be highly necessary, for example, in:

1. Experimental Data Analysis: Students can enter experimental data into a spreadsheet and use formulas to analyze it.

2. Simulation: By using functions and graphs, students can simulate physical phenomena and observe their behavior
3. Problem Solving: Spreadsheets can help students solve complex mathematical problems related to physics
4. Visualization of Abstract Concepts: Graphs and diagrams can help students understand abstract physical concepts more tangibly.

When it is necessary to develop Computational Thinking (CT) in the early stages of students' education, it is difficult to start with programming, and a spreadsheet is an effective tool widely used for data organization, as it allows the structured organization of large amounts of data. In addition, they are helpful for performing calculations, as they allow the use of formulas and functions to perform complex computations and represent data visually. It is also possible to create iterations, such as increments and intervals, which are obtained from basic calculations (Shute et al., 2017). Specifically, spreadsheet software, such as Microsoft Excel, has been used primarily for data organization, manipulation, and graphing, a role it has had since the 1980s (Obaid,1989). The most recent versions can be worked on online and enable real-time synchronization, making them a valuable tool for STEAM education and promoting collaborative work (Cervantes-Juarez & Sanchez-Guzman, 2022)

Spreadsheets are potent and effective tools in teaching, not only for facilitating the learning of complex concepts but also for developing students' critical skills. Most studies reported significant improvements in conceptual understanding of physics when using spreadsheets (Weintrop et al., 2016) and facilitated the visualization of data and abstract concepts, allowing students to experiment with variables and observe immediate results (Weintrop et al., 2016; Tariq et al., 2025). There was variability in the magnitude of the impact, influenced by factors such as intervention design and educational context (Peng et al., 2025). The exact sciences, such as mathematics, physics, and chemistry, often involve abstract concepts that can be difficult to understand through verbal descriptions or mathematical equations (Yeni, 2024). Graphs allow students to visualize relationships between variables, such as how one variable changes in response to another. This helps transform abstract concepts into more concrete and understandable visual representations, allowing students to identify patterns, trends, and anomalies in the data (Suherman et al., 2025). By interpreting graphs, students develop critical thinking skills, such as analyzing, evaluating, and drawing conclusions based on empirical evidence (Yeni, 2024).

Accordingly, this chapter proposes a set of active learning methodologies framed within the STEAM approach to promote the development of both social and technical competencies. The proposed strategies include the Learning Science and Engineering with Electronic Spreadsheets Cycle (LSEESC), interactive simulations, data manipulation and visualization, and collaborative engineering activities.

Through these examples, the chapter demonstrates how computational thinking, interdisciplinary collaboration, and technology-enhanced learning can prepare future engineers, for example, to address the social and productive challenges of the century. This chapter is organized as follows: Section 1 reviews the importance of the relationship between STEAM education and society and engineering 4.0, and the second section is focused on data visualization as an effective driver of productive and social development. Section 3 describes the proposed LSEESC methodology as a foundation of STEAM education and its pedagogical principles, followed by a fourth section with an example of application in a collaborative activity that relates the theoretical and computational thinking by illustrative applications in engineering education, followed by a discussion of their educational implications. Finally, the chapter concludes with the main findings and future research directions.

2 STEAM EDUCATION, COMPUTATIONAL THINKING, ENGINEERING 4.0 AND SOCIETY

The transformation of society today is driven by digital technologies, automation, artificial intelligence, and data analysis, which have redefined the competencies expected of future professionals, and it is not possibly continuing to focus exclusively on disciplinary knowledge; it is necessary to prepare professionals capable of solving complex real-world problems through interdisciplinary collaboration, creativity, critical thinking, and social responsibility. Within this context, the STEAM (Science, Technology, Engineering, Arts, and Mathematics) educational approach has emerged as a pedagogical framework that integrates technical knowledge with creativity, innovation, communication, and human-centered problem solving and, as a consequence, contributes to developing social competencies that are increasingly recognized as essential for engineering practice. Teamwork, communication, leadership, creativity, and ethical decision-making have become indispensable skills in Industry 4.0 environments characterized by multidisciplinary teams and continuous technological innovation. The implementation of collaborative projects within STEAM environments has been shown to strengthen these competencies while simultaneously improving academic motivation (Lavasani et al., 2011; Yusufjanovna, 2026). Moreover, social and emotional competencies constitute a fundamental component of successful engineering education. Research has consistently demonstrated that educational interventions explicitly designed to promote collaboration, empathy, communication, and self-regulation significantly improve both academic achievement and interpersonal relationships among students (Durlak et al., 2011). Likewise, the development of social competence facilitates effective participation in collaborative engineering projects and promotes professional skills required in modern workplaces (Bayer, 1996).

A relevant example of this kind of social need is the importance of developing Computational thinking (CT) as a key competency, given its ability to support systematic problem-solving across multiple scientific and technological disciplines. Originally introduced by Wing (2006), CT extends beyond computer programming by incorporating cognitive processes such as abstraction, decomposition, algorithmic thinking, pattern recognition, and generalization that enable individuals to formulate and solve complex problems efficiently. Recent research has expanded this concept by highlighting computational thinking as a universal problem-solving methodology applicable across science, engineering, and mathematics education (Grover and Pea, 2013) and rather than teaching programming languages exclusively, CT focuses on developing reasoning skills that allow students to analyze problems, organize information, construct models, evaluate solutions, and communicate results effectively.

"Computational thinking is a fundamental skill for everyone, not just for computer scientists. To reading, writing, and arithmetic, we should add computational thinking to every child's analytical ability." (Wing, 2006)

The stages of computational thinking development can be listed as follows (Grover & Pea, 2013; Mackinlay, 1987; Weintrop et al., 2016; Yeni, 2024; Suherman et al., 2025).

1. Decomposition: Breaking down a complex problem into smaller, more manageable parts to identify the individual components of a problem so that they can be addressed independently.
2. Pattern Recognition: Identify similarities and patterns in data or problems to look for regularities and trends that can simplify problem-solving.
3. Abstraction: Focusing on the relevant information and discarding unnecessary details allows the generalization of problems and solutions to similar situations.
4. Algorithm Design: Creating a step-by-step sequence to solve the problem will enable the student to design systematic procedures to reach a solution.
5. Evaluation and Debugging: Test and adjust the solutions to ensure they work properly, and debug until the best version is obtained.
6. Automation: Enables implementing solutions that can be executed automatically using tools and technologies to perform repetitive tasks efficiently.

The development of computational thinking is crucial not only for computer science and the exact sciences but also for cross-cutting skills that benefit multiple disciplines and everyday life (Peng et al., 2025; Yeni, 2024). The process of discretization involves transforming continuous variables into discrete ones and is fundamental in many areas of science and engineering, as it enables the analysis and simulation of continuous systems using computational tools (Yeni, 2024). For a student to understand the concept of discretization, it is necessary to cover the following aspects:

- **Basic mathematics:** Understanding of concepts such as intervals, functions, and graphs.
- **Calculation:** Familiarity with continuous functions, derivatives, and integrals.
- **Physics:** Knowledge of continuous phenomena that can be modeled through discretization.
- **Continuous vs. Discrete Variables:** Understanding the difference between variables that can take any value within a range and those that can only take specific values.
- **Intervals and Sampling Points:** Understanding how to divide a continuum into intervals and select sampling points.
- **Approximation Errors:** Discussion of how discretization can introduce errors and how to minimize them.
- **Technical Skills and Software Use:** Basic familiarity with spreadsheets or other computational tools.
- **Data Analysis:** Ability to enter, manipulate, and analyze data in a spreadsheet.

Brennan and Resnick (2012) proposed one of the most influential frameworks for studying computational thinking by distinguishing computational concepts, practices, and perspectives. This framework emphasizes that students should not only acquire technical knowledge but also develop reflective and collaborative approaches to solving engineering problems. Within engineering education, CT has become closely associated with scientific modeling, mathematical representation, data analysis, and visualization. Weintrop et al. (2016) proposed a computational thinking taxonomy specifically designed for mathematics and science classrooms, identifying data practices, modeling and simulation, computational problem solving, and systems thinking as essential dimensions of STEM learning. Recent systematic reviews confirm that integrating CT into STEM curricula significantly improves students' analytical reasoning, creativity, and collaborative learning outcomes (Tariq et al., 2025; Peng et al., 2025; Yeni, 2024). Furthermore, integrating computational thinking into STEAM environments promotes interdisciplinary learning by allowing students to connect scientific concepts with engineering design, mathematical reasoning, and technological tools (Juandi et al., 2024; Kristanto et al., 2023).

Collaborative learning also plays a significant role in the development of computational thinking. For example, Lai et al. (2023) proposed that the social cognitive factors—including communication, peer interaction, and shared problem solving—

positively influence students' CT performance. Similarly to Rojas-Noguera et al. (2026) concluded that collaborative activities substantially improve students' ability to construct computational solutions while strengthening teamwork and communication skills. Spreadsheet environments naturally support several computational thinking practices, including algorithmic reasoning, abstraction, decomposition, iterative calculations, and data visualization. Students can immediately observe the effects of modifying variables, facilitating conceptual understanding through interactive experimentation. Mackinlay (1987) demonstrated the importance of effective graphical representation in improving information interpretation and decision-making. These visualization principles remain highly relevant in engineering education, where graphical analysis frequently complements mathematical modeling and experimental validation. Similarly, Uddin (2017) reported that Microsoft Excel significantly improves students' understanding of physics concepts by enabling numerical simulations, graphical visualization, and interactive analysis of experimental data. Spreadsheet-based instruction facilitates the transition from theoretical equations to observable physical behavior, strengthening conceptual learning.

Spreadsheet activities can also be integrated naturally with interactive educational technologies such as digital simulations, as the PhET Interactive Simulations project (PhET Interactive Simulations, n.d.), or as the Tracker as an open-source video analysis and modeling tool for physics education (Brown et al., 2026), which allows students to compare theoretical models with simulated phenomena, reinforcing scientific reasoning through experimentation. When combined with conceptual assessment instruments, for example, in physics, such as the Force Concept Inventory (Hestenes et al., 1992), spreadsheet activities provide opportunities to evaluate conceptual understanding while promoting evidence-based learning. Furthermore, spreadsheet-based methodologies support the development of competencies aligned with Industry 4.0 by integrating data analysis, digital literacy, visualization, collaborative work, and computational reasoning into authentic engineering contexts. An example is the LSEESC, which is a pedagogical approach that integrates spreadsheet-based learning with the development of computational thinking. Previous implementations have shown that engineering students improve conceptual understanding, computational reasoning, and collaborative problem-solving skills when scientific phenomena are modeled through spreadsheet activities (Cervantes and Sánchez, 2022) that had demonstrated that spreadsheet-supported instructional strategies effectively foster computational thinking among engineering students while promoting active learning.

These competencies are consistent with recent recommendations to CT as a fundamental element of engineering curricula (Barr and Stephenson, 2011). Consequently, electronic spreadsheets should not be considered merely office software but rather educational environments that promote computational thinking, scientific reasoning, collaborative learning, and interdisciplinary problem-solving. Their accessibility, flexibility, and compatibility with simulation tools make them particularly appropriate for introductory engineering education, where students are beginning to acquire the analytical competencies required for professional practice.

3 DATA VISUALIZATION AS A DRIVER FOR MEETING SOCIAL AND PRODUCTIVE NEEDS

The discretization process represents a key link between theoretical knowledge and practical application within a STEAM framework. From a scientific perspective, it enables the analysis of continuous phenomena; mathematically, it allows the transformation of functions into discrete representations using intervals and sampling points. In the technological domain, discretization is implemented using computational tools such as spreadsheets, facilitating data analysis and visualization (Weintrop et al., 2016; Suherman et al., 2025). From this perspective, it supports modeling and solving real-world problems through numerical methods, while in the artistic dimension, it contributes to the effective representation and interpretation of data. Therefore, discretization can be understood as an integrative process that embodies the interdisciplinary nature of STEAM education. This approach not only reinforces the mathematical concept of rate of change but also supports the development of computational thinking and modeling skills within a STEAM framework (Peng et al., 2025; Juandi et al., 2024; Kristanto et al., 2023).

Figure 1. Examples of possible integration of the STEAM approach through the discretization process

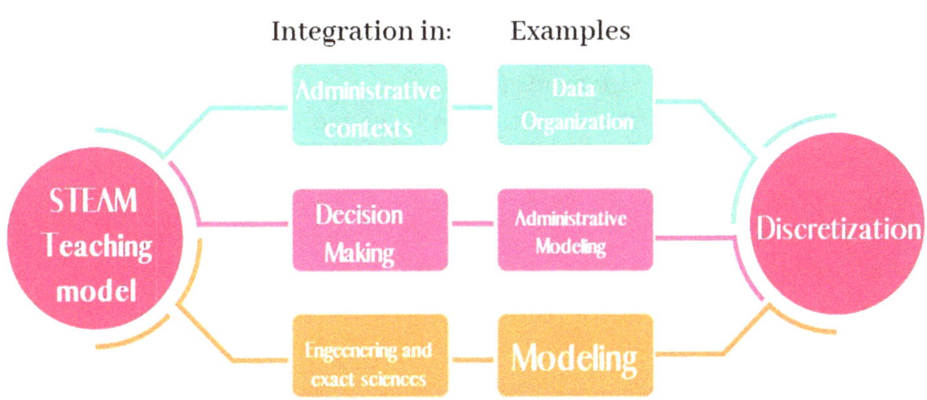

The Figure **1** illustrates a few examples of how a real-world continuous phenomenon is transformed into a discretized representation through scientific modeling and mathematical formulation, enabling its implementation using technological tools, supporting engineering problem-solving, and enhancing data visualization.

In the exact sciences, mistakes are common when calculating or interpreting data, so graphs allow students to quickly identify discrepancies between experimental results and theoretical expectations, helping them correct errors and improve the accuracy of their calculations (Weintrop et al., 2016). Data visualization and graphical representation play a fundamental role within the STEAM framework, as they enable the integration of scientific understanding, mathematical modeling, technological tools, and engineering applications through meaningful visual communication. In science and engineering education, graphs serve as essential cognitive tools that facilitate the interpretation of complex phenomena and the identification of patterns and relationships (Tariq et al., 2025). From a mathematical perspective, graphical representations bridge symbolic expressions and conceptual understanding, allowing students to better comprehend functions and variations. Furthermore, the use of technological tools such as spreadsheets enhances students' ability to generate, analyze, and interpret data in real time. Visualization also incorporates an artistic dimension, as effective graph design requires clarity, structure, and aesthetic considerations to communicate information accurately. Previous studies have highlighted that well-designed visual representations significantly improve students' understanding and problem-solving abilities, particularly in data-driven learning environments as mentioned by Jock D. Mackinlay (Mackinlay, 1987). Therefore, data visualization can be understood as a central component of STEAM education, supporting both analytical reasoning and communication skills because the use of graphs in teaching promotes more active and participatory learning because the students do not only receive information passively, it is neccesary to interact with the data, create their graphs, experiment with different variables, and observe the effects which helps them to internalize knowledge more effectively.

In administrative contexts, discretization is the process of transforming organizational information into a manageable form for analysis and decision-making. Applications such as inventory control, productivity monitoring, financial projections, and dashboard design illustrate how discretization supports data organization and problem-solving. Within a STEAM framework, these activities integrate mathematical modeling, technological tools, visualization, and engineering reasoning while promoting collaborative and analytical skills. Let us examine the simple case of a linear equation and use it to illustrate the discretization process. In this sense, an example of using spreadsheets to create graphs and visualize how a continuous function is transformed into a series of discrete points. In comparison, these expressions can clearly show the difference and correlation with an expression of a linear expression as:

$$y = mx + b$$

Which includes parameters as m and b and, x and y are the independent and dependent values respectively which can be used to compute discrete values. The discretized form of the linear equation transforms a continuous relationship into a step-by-step computational process, and expresses the model as:

$$y_{i+1} = y_i + m\Delta x$$

As can be observed in this simple example, students can iteratively construct solutions using discrete intervals, which facilitates implementation in technological tools such as spreadsheets, where a continuous function can be approximated with discrete steps to model processes that change over time, such as discretized differential equations [9]. It is also possible to calculate and analyze errors between discrete and continuous values, exploring how reducing the interval size affects discretization accuracy [5]. The above can be calculated in the spreadsheets using standard mathematical formulas. Each spreadsheet consists of cells organized into rows and columns, where data, formulas, and functions can be entered. Spreadsheets are versatile tools used for a wide range of applications, from accounting and finance to scientific data analysis and project management (Suherman et al., 2025). An example of how the computational thinking model can be applied in the teaching of exact sciences is the solution of exercises. In this way, several methodologies can reinforce these processes by structuring collaborative and technology-mediated learning environments. On the other hand, computational thinking is a fundamental skill in the digital era that involves solving problems logically and systematically, much like a computer would. This type of thinking develops through several stages that help to decompose complex problems, recognize patterns, abstract, and create algorithms (Juandi et al., 2024; Tariq et al., 2025). The emergence of the digital era and Industry 4.0 has prompted a rethink of traditional teaching practices and the development of educational models that integrate digital technologies with interdisciplinary learning and teachers have recognized that incorporating a variety of active teaching strategies promotes student learning, which is crucial for developing computational thinking. Teachers can use various strategies and tools, such as:

- Use of Software and Digital Tools Incorporate programs such as spreadsheets, programming languages, and simulators

- Problem-Based Projects To pose real problems requiring decomposition, pattern recognition, and algorithm design.
- Programming Activities To teach basic concepts of programming and computer logic.
- Simulations and Models Use simulations to visualize abstract concepts and experiment with different scenarios.

4 LSEESC METHODOLOGY AS A STEAM PERSPECTIVE

In the exact sciences, mistakes are common when calculating or interpreting data. Graphs allow students to quickly identify results that do not make sense or are inconsistent with theoretical expectations, helping them correct errors and improve the accuracy of their calculations. In this sense, using spreadsheets to create graphs, visualize how a continuous function is transformed into a series of discrete points, and present data in tabular format can clearly show discrete values (Uddin, 2017).

STEAM serves as the overarching educational framework, and globalization provides the context that justifies the development of new competencies. On the other hand, the LSEESC (Cervantes-Juarez & Sanchez-Guzman, 2022). Methodology represents a concrete pedagogical pathway for developing these competencies in the classroom and is presented as a teaching strategy that enables the practical implementation of the STEAM approach in engineering education. According to this, the main objectives of this purpose are:

- Active learning sequences
- The use of spreadsheets
- Modeling
- Analysis of phenomena
- Problem solving
- Student participation
- The connection between concepts and their application

The LSEESC uses graphs to promote more active and participatory learning. Students not only receive information passively but also interact with the data, create their graphs, experiment with different variables, and observe the effects (Cervantes-Juarez & Sanchez-Guzman, 2022). This helps them to internalize knowledge more effectively because the visual information is retained better than textual or numerical information. Students are more likely to remember and understand the material when data are presented as graphs. Graphics provide a clear and concise way to communicate complex information. These characteristics demonstrate that

LSEESC operationalizes the STEAM approach, particularly in the area of exact sciences within engineering education (Cervantes-Juarez & Sanchez-Guzman, 2023). This strategy can be implemented in several phases; in general, it can be as follows:

Phase 1. Problem Identification and Conceptual Analysis

The implementation process begins by presenting students with a real or simulated problem. During this stage, students identify the variables involved, establish the model's assumptions, and define the learning objectives.

Phase 2. Mathematical Modeling and Spreadsheet Construction

Once the problem has been analyzed conceptually, students develop its mathematical representation using an electronic spreadsheet. A protocol will be designed to guide the implementation. It is necessary to define the time, number of sessions, and activities for each one.

Phase 3. Data Visualization, Simulation, and Validation

After constructing the numerical model, students generate graphical representations of the calculated data. Scatter plots allow students to compare the theoretical linear relationship between position and time with experimental data obtained through video analysis using Tracker or interactive simulations such as PhET (PhET Interactive Simulations, n.d.; Brown et al., 2024).

Students analyze discrepancies or similarities between theoretical predictions and experimental observations, discuss possible sources of measurement uncertainty, and validate the mathematical model through graphical interpretation. This stage promotes CT practices, including data organization, visualization, pattern recognition, and model evaluation.

Phase 4. Data analysis

The selected studies will be analyzed using both quantitative and qualitative methods to extract patterns, trends, and conclusions regarding the use of spreadsheets in teaching. Clear criteria will be established to determine which studies are relevant to the investigation, based on factors such as the educational context, students' level, and the nature of spreadsheet use.

Each team discusses whether the mathematical model adequately represents the observed phenomenon, explains the physical meaning of the graph's slope, and evaluates the limitations of the assumptions used. The activity concludes with a classroom discussion in which students compare different modeling strategies, justify their conclusions, and reflect on the applicability of spreadsheet-based modeling to more complex engineering problems. This final phase reinforces communication skills, collaborative learning, critical thinking, and scientific argumentation, while consolidating the computational thinking competencies developed throughout the learning cycle.

For example, in a Uniform Rectilinear Motion (URM) activity, students analyze the movement of a vehicle traveling at constant velocity along a straight path. After observing a short experimental video or a PhET simulation, they identify the independent variable (time), the dependent variable (position), and the constant parameter (velocity). Students are encouraged to discuss the physical meaning of each variable and formulate predictions about the system's expected behavior (see Table 1).

Table 1. Illustrative example of the LSEESC methodology applied to Uniform Rectilinear Motion (URM)

LSEESC Stage	Example in Uniform Rectilinear Motion (URM)
1. Problem Identification and Conceptual Analysis	Students observe the motion of an object using a PhET simulation or a video analyzed with Tracker. They identify the physical variables involved (position, time, and velocity), discuss the characteristics of uniform rectilinear motion, formulate hypotheses, and establish the learning objectives.
2. Mathematical Modeling and Spreadsheet Construction	Students implement the mathematical model $x = x_0 + vt$ in Microsoft Excel. They create a spreadsheet containing discrete time values, calculate positions using formulas, organize numerical data, and learn to use cell references and automatic calculations while developing algorithmic thinking.
3. Data Visualization, Simulation and Validation	The calculated data are represented using scatter plots. Students compare the theoretical model with experimental measurements obtained from Tracker or simulated data from PhET. Differences between experimental and theoretical results are analyzed to validate the mathematical model and identify possible measurement errors.
4. Interpretation, Collaboration, and Reflection	Students interpret the graphical results, explain the physical meaning of the slope as constant velocity, discuss the validity of the mathematical model, and present their conclusions collaboratively. Reflection focuses on computational thinking, teamwork, scientific communication, and the applicability of spreadsheet-based modeling to engineering problems.

Overall, this implementation illustrates how the LSEESC methodology simultaneously develops technical competencies—including computational thinking, mathematical modeling, spreadsheet programming, scientific reasoning, and data analysis—as well as social and professional skills such as collaboration, communication, negotiation, shared decision-making, leadership, and interdisciplinary reasoning. Consequently, the methodology aligns with the objectives of STEAM education by integrating technical knowledge with the social and productive competencies required in contemporary engineering practice (see Figure 2).

Figure 2. Simple comparison of how basic scientific models can support the development of competencies aligned with globalization and emerging industrial demands

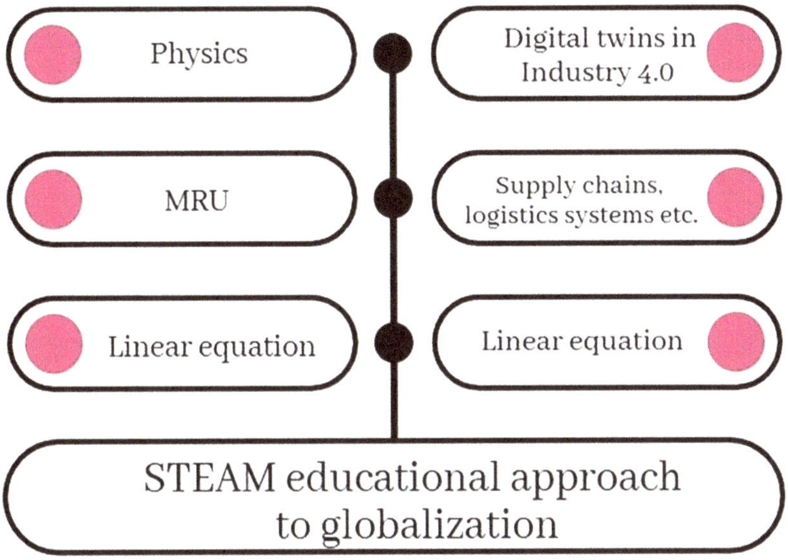

So, the LSEESC methodology facilitates the integration of these elements by structuring learning sequences that promote active participation, collaborative work, and problem-solving. Through this approach, students not only understand the physical and mathematical foundations of motion but also develop key STEAM competencies, including data analysis, computational thinking, and effective communication of results. Within the STEAM framework, the integration of data visualization and discretization processes can be effectively illustrated, for example, through classic examples in physics and math. In this case, the LSEESC was implemented as a collaborative STEAM activity in which students worked in teams of four to five members. Each team assigned complementary roles, including a coordinator, spreadsheet developer, data analyst, experimental analyst, and presenter. This organization encouraged communication, collaboration, shared decision-making, and responsibility, while promoting interdisciplinary learning by integrating mathematics, physics, computational thinking, and engineering.

Table 2. STEAM competencies fostered through the proposed learning activity.

Learning Stage	**Technical Competencies**	**STEAM Social Competencies**
Role assignment and activity planning	Project organization	Collaboration, communication, shared decision-making
Spreadsheet model development	Computational thinking, mathematical modelling	Teamwork, interdisciplinary reasoning
Model validation and debugging	Analytical thinking, problem solving	Negotiation, peer feedback, collaborative problem solving
Data visualization and graph interpretation	Data analysis, scientific reasoning	Critical discussion, evidence-based communication
Presentation of engineering solutions	Engineering analysis, interpretation of results	Oral communication, teamwork, reflection, interdisciplinary collaboration

5 ILLUSTRATIVE APPLICATION OF THE LSEESC METHODOLOGY IN A COLLABORATIVE STEAM ACTIVITY

Let us propose an example of STEAM activity based on discretization by using *Simulator and Spreadsheets*. This structure allows for a complete and meticulous approach to the research, ensuring that all relevant variables are considered and that the results are robust and applicable to a variety of educational contexts (**18?**). In this case, the learning objective is for students to relate the linear equation to the uniform motion model through discretization, graphical analysis, and technological tools such as PhET simulations and spreadsheets. As shown in Figure **5**, the graphical representation of position as a function of time allows students to identify the linear nature of motion under constant velocity. The equivalence between linear equations and uniform motion provides a powerful framework for integrating mathematical abstraction with physical interpretation through discretization and technological tools. This corresponds to a digital model created as an exact replica of a real thing.

The example of activity began with an analysis of a simple linear equation to help students understand the relationships among mathematical expressions, numerical data, and graphical representations. Students first predicted the function's behavior and then implemented the equation in an electronic spreadsheet by discretizing the independent variable into equally spaced time intervals. Using spreadsheet formulas, they generated numerical data and constructed both continuous and discrete graphical representations. During this process, students discussed the effects of discretization on computational modeling and interpreted the differences between analytical and numerical representations. This physical phenomenon, described by continuous variables such as position and velocity over time, is transformed into a discrete representation that enables its analysis using technological tools. From a scientific perspective, MRU provides a model for describing motion under constant acceleration, in which variables such as time, velocity, and position are interrelated. This function can be discretized into intervals and sampling points, allowing the construction of numerical representations. Through this discretization process, continuous behavior is approximated using finite data sets, facilitating computational analysis. On the other hand, the technological component is incorporated through the use of spreadsheets, where students organize data, apply formulas, and generate graphical representations. This process enables real-time visualization of motion, allowing students to identify patterns such as linear and quadratic relationships between variables. It also supports the modeling and validation of physical systems, as students can compare theoretical predictions with discretized data.

$y = mx + b$

Then, the students must solve tasks such as:

1. Create data table
2. Generate graph
3. Compare continuous vs discrete model
4. Analyze slope as velocity

Furthermore, data visualization plays a crucial role by transforming numerical results into graphical representations that enhance interpretation and communication. As highlighted by J. D. Mackinlay (Mackinlay, 1987), effective graphical representations improve understanding of relationships in data, thereby supporting analytical reasoning. In this sense, the design and interpretation of graphs also incorporate an artistic dimension, emphasizing clarity, structure, and visual communication because it is necessary to improve readability, compare representations, and communicate results, promoting:

- Critical thinking
- Computational thinking
- Collaboration
- Data analysis
- Problem solving
- Scientific communication

This model of linear equation can be extended beyond physics to represent administrative processes, for example, in constant rates, such as sales growth, inventory accumulation, or productivity. In this sense, it becomes a general model for discretization and data organization across engineering and management contexts for example:

$$Physics{:}x(t) \;=\; x_0 + vt$$

$$Administration{:}Sales(t) \;=\; Sales_0 + rt$$

The proposed activity can be implemented as a collaborative STEAM learning experience. Students work in small teams, assuming complementary roles, including data collection, spreadsheet programming, model validation, graphical interpretation, and presentation of results. This organization encouraged communication, collaborative problem-solving, shared decision-making, and peer learning while integrating concepts from physics, mathematics, engineering, and computational thinking.

Spreadsheet-based modeling is widely used in engineering, logistics, industrial management, quality control, manufacturing, and business decision-making. Therefore, the activity develops digital competencies directly transferable to productive environments (Uddin, 2017). Beyond technical competencies, engineers increasingly require teamwork, communication, collaborative problem-solving, negotiation, and evidence-based decision-making. The proposed activity promotes these competencies because students jointly construct the computational model, discuss discrepancies, validate assumptions, and communicate engineering conclusions supported by data visualization. The proposed methodology contributes simultaneously to three dimensions of STEAM education: technical competencies (computational thinking, spreadsheet modelling, physics); professional competencies (problem-solving, data analysis, engineering reasoning) and social competencies (collaboration, communication, peer learning, and shared decision-making).

Collaborative learning environments have consistently demonstrated positive effects on communication, social competence, teamwork, and students' sense of belonging in STEM education (Bayer, 1996; Yusufjanovna, 2026). Students worked in teams of three to five members. Each team organized the activity by assigning complementary roles such as project coordinator, spreadsheet developer, data analyst, and presenter. This distribution encouraged responsibility, communication, and collaborative planning. Team members jointly developed the spreadsheet model using the equations of uniformly accelerated motion. During this stage, students discussed mathematical assumptions, verified formulas, and collaboratively debugged calculation errors. Figure 3, shows an example of the graphs generated by the students in the example of URM.

Figure 3. Example of a lineal graph with the model in a URM and comparison with discretization

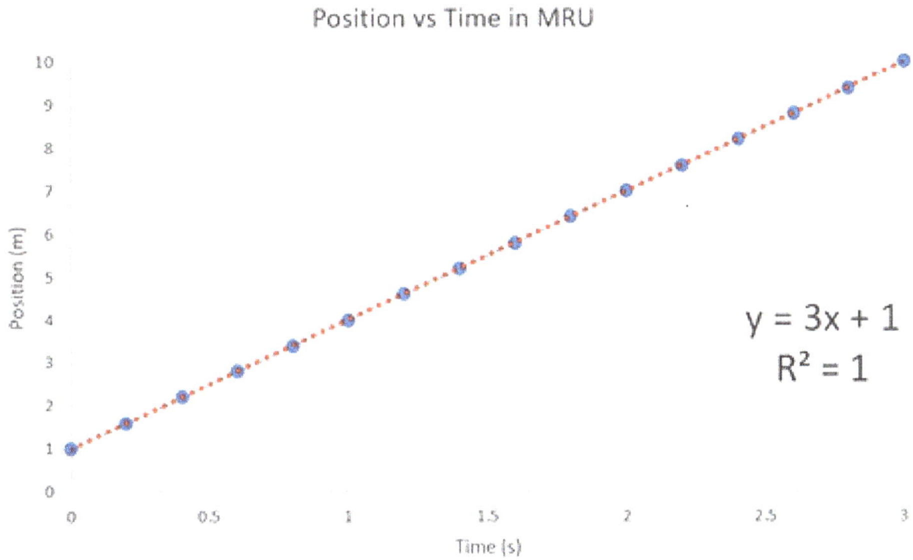

Teams compared analytical calculations, spreadsheet outputs, and PhET simulations (see Figure 4). Differences between the results were discussed until a consensus was reached on the model's validity. Students interpreted displacement, velocity, and acceleration graphs to explain engineering scenarios such as vehicle motion, industrial transport systems, or production processes. Finally, each team presented its computational model and justified its engineering decisions with graphical evidence. Class discussions promoted critical thinking and interdisciplinary reasoning.

Figure 4. Example of the use of Phet simulator in URM (PhET Interactive Simulations)

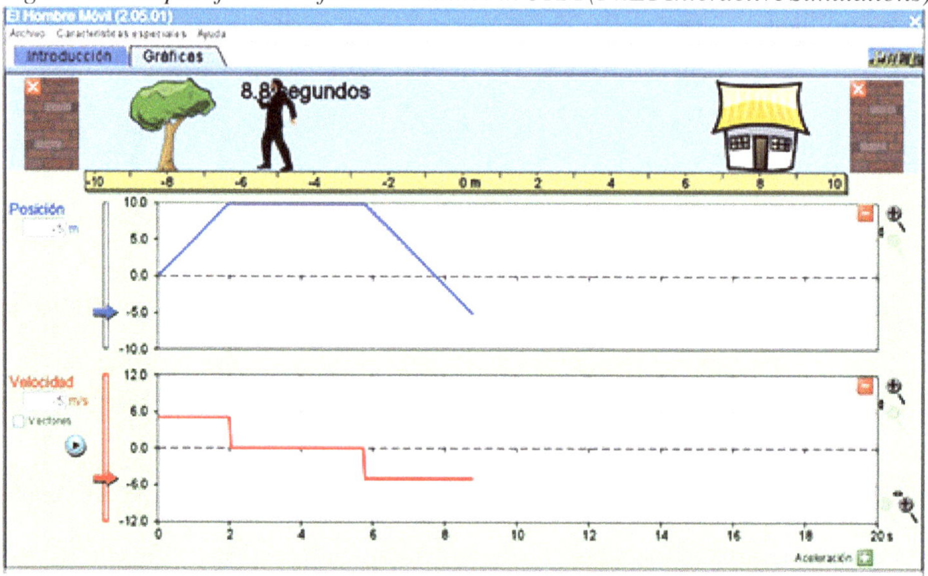

This comparison illustrates how a common mathematical structure can be transferred across disciplinary contexts, from abstract mathematical representation to physical modeling and data-driven industrial applications through discretization. Within a STEAM framework, this progression highlights how foundational concepts can support the development of analytical, computational, and technological competencies while fostering interdisciplinary problem solving. Moreover, the incorporation of technological tools such as spreadsheets, simulations, and digital twin concepts reinforces the connection between academic training and contemporary productive needs, showing how simple models can serve as entry points to more complex Industry 4.0 applications (Lai et al., 2023; Rojas-Noguera et al., 2026). In this sense, discretization is not only a numerical strategy, but also an integrative educational mechanism that links scientific reasoning, technological implementation, and social and productive skill development, and methodologies such as LSEESC provide a practical pathway for operationalizing these connections in engineering education.

After analyzing the linear model, students extended the strategy to the equations describing uniformly accelerated motion (UAM). Working collaboratively, they programmed the equations of position and velocity, generated numerical simulations, and analyzed the resulting graphs. Team members continuously compare their results, discuss discrepancies, and refine their spreadsheet models until a consensus is reached regarding the correctness of the implementation.

To connect computational modeling with real-world observations, students analyzed a free-fall video using Tracker Video Analysis software (Brown et al.,

2024). The software allowed them to obtain experimental position and time data, which were subsequently compared with the spreadsheet simulation. This comparison encouraged students to validate their computational models, identify potential experimental errors, and discuss differences between theoretical predictions and measured data (see Figure 5). Students analyze uniformly accelerated rectilinear motion (UARM) by recording the motion with Tracker, extracting position–time data, constructing a spreadsheet model in Microsoft Excel, generating graphical representations, and validating the mathematical model through comparison with theoretical predictions. The activity promotes computational thinking, data visualization, scientific reasoning, and collaborative problem-solving.

Figure 5. Example of use of Tracker video analysis

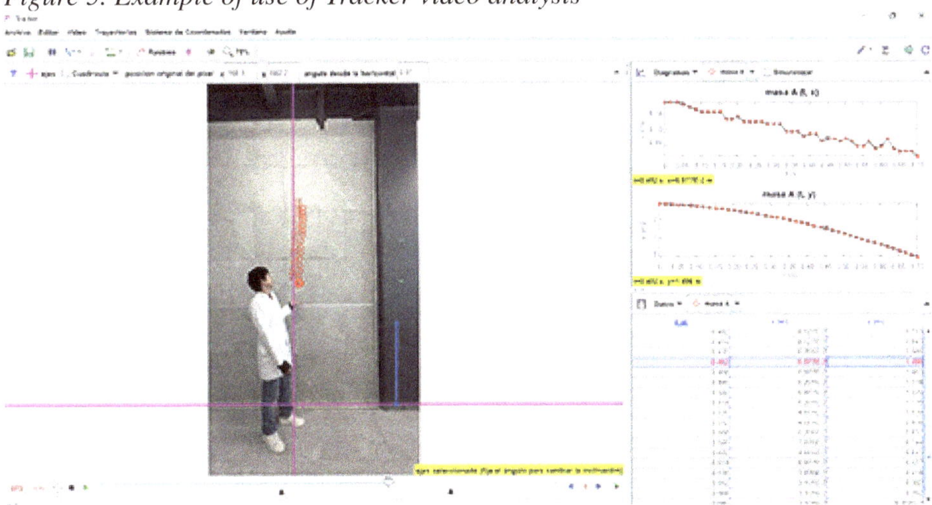

(Brown et al., 2024)

One of the most valuable conceptual discussions emerged when students compared the object's trajectory with its position-time graph. Initially, many students assumed that because the object moved along a straight path, the corresponding position graph should also be linear. However, by contrasting the Tracker data with the spreadsheet model, they recognized that although the trajectory is rectilinear, the position varies quadratically with time under constant acceleration. This comparison promoted conceptual change through evidence-based reasoning and collaborative discussion. Finally, each team presented its computational model, graphical analysis, and interpretation of the physical phenomenon to the rest of the class. During the presentations, students justified their conclusions using mathematical models, experimental evidence, and graphical representations while responding to questions from their peers. This stage strengthened scientific communication, collaborative problem-solving, critical thinking, and the ability to transfer knowledge to engineering contexts.

Figure 6. Example of using Excel for regression with a second-degree polynomial in relation of data collected from Tracker video analysis

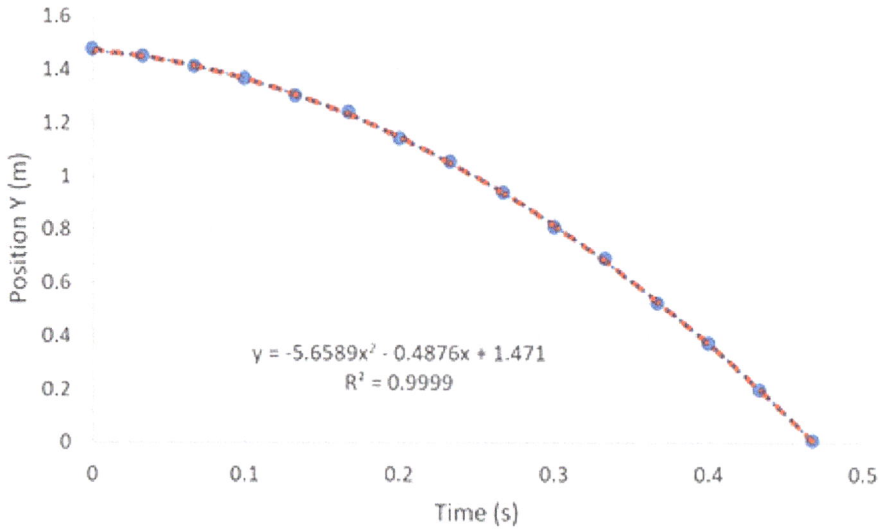

6 CONCLUSIONS

Spreadsheets have demonstrated a significant positive impact on conceptual understanding, particularly in areas involving data management, information visualization, modeling, and scenario simulation. By providing an interactive environment where students can manipulate variables and observe outcomes in real time, spreadsheets facilitate understanding of abstract and complex concepts while strengthening the connection between mathematical representation and practical application. Their use allows students to construct graphs, generate dynamic tables, and develop models that represent real-world situations, promoting a deeper understanding of how variables interact and evolve.

In disciplines such as mathematics, physics, economics, and engineering, spreadsheets support the simulation of phenomena and the exploration of multiple scenarios, enabling students to experiment, analyze behaviors, and evaluate the effect of changing parameters. This process not only enhances conceptual understanding, but also promotes logical reasoning, problem decomposition, and analytical thinking—competencies closely aligned with STEAM education.

Moreover, when integrated with pedagogical strategies such as problem-based learning, collaborative learning, gamification, and flipped classroom models, spreadsheets become more than computational tools; they function as mediating technologies for active and socially situated learning. These approaches foster collaboration, communication, shared decision-making, and collective problem solving, reinforcing the development of both technical and social skills. In this sense, the educational value of spreadsheets extends beyond numerical analysis, supporting environments where students learn through interaction, experimentation, and interdisciplinary inquiry.

Within the framework, this chapter illustrates how these capabilities can evolve from simple linear models and motion representations toward more complex applications associated with smart logistics and digital twin models. This progression highlights how discretization and spreadsheet-based modeling can serve as foundational pathways to Industry 4.0 concepts, in which data-driven systems, simulation, and cyber-physical models are increasingly relevant. Thus, what begins as the discrete study of uniform motion can be extended to modeling principles used in intelligent supply chains, predictive systems, and digital twins, demonstrating how basic STEAM learning experiences can scale to meet contemporary productive and industrial needs.

From this perspective, discretization is not only a numerical strategy, but also an integrative educational mechanism that links conceptual understanding, technological implementation, collaborative learning, and emerging Industry 4.0 competencies. Methodologies such as LSEESC provide a practical pathway for operationalizing these connections in engineering education, bridging foundational scientific models with the skills required in increasingly digital, interconnected, and data-driven professional environments.

In this context, the LSEESC Methodology can be used as an implementation strategy to enhance learning of concepts in physics, science, and engineering through electronic spreadsheets. This approach fosters students' conceptual understanding, critical thinking, and physical reasoning by engaging them in activities such as programming dynamic systems, modeling their mathematical evolution, generating and analyzing graphs, and explaining physical phenomena. It also promotes deep comprehension and knowledge transfer, enabling students to identify how these concepts apply in professional contexts through real-life examples or simulations.

REFERENCES

Barr, V., & Stephenson, C. (2011). Bringing computational thinking to K–12. *ACM Inroads.*

Bayer, J. K. (1996). Social competence and social skills training for children and adolescents: A literature review. *Australian Journal of Guidance & Counselling, 6*(S1), 1–14.

Brennan, K., & Resnick, M. (2012). New frameworks for studying and assessing the development of computational thinking. In *Proceedings of the 2012 Annual Meeting of the American Educational Research Association.* AERA., Available https://scratched.gse.harvard.edu/ct/files/AERA2012.pdf

Brown, D., Hanson, R., & Christian, W. (2024). Tracker Video Analysis and Modeling Tool (Version 6.3) [Computer software]. Open Source Physics. https://opensourcephysics.github.io/tracker-website

Cervantes-Juarez, E., & Sanchez-Guzman, D. (2022). Developing computational thinking in engineering students. In *IEEE Frontiers in Education Conference (FIE).*

Dost, G. (2024). Students' perspectives on the "STEM belonging" concept at A-level, undergraduate, and postgraduate levels: An examination of gender and ethnicity in student descriptions. *International Journal of STEM Education, 11*(1), 12. DOI: 10.1186/s40594-024-00472-9

Durlak, J. A., Weissberg, R. P., Dymnicki, A. B., Taylor, R. D., & Schellinger, K. B. (2011). The impact of enhancing students' social and emotional learning: A meta-analysis of school-based universal interventions. *Child Development, 82*(1), 405–432. DOI: 10.1111/j.1467-8624.2010.01564.x PMID: 21291449

Grover, S., & Pea, R. (2013). Computational thinking in K–12: A review of the state of the field. *Educational Researcher, 42*(1), 38–43. DOI: 10.3102/0013189X12463051

Hake, R. R. (1998). Interactive-engagement versus traditional methods: A six-thousand-student survey of mechanics test data. *American Journal of Physics, 66*(1), 64–74. DOI: 10.1119/1.18809

Hestenes, D., Wells, M., & Swackhamer, G. (1992). Force Concept Inventory. *The Physics Teacher, 30*(3), 141–158. DOI: 10.1119/1.2343497

Juandi, D.. (2024). Computational thinking in mathematics instruction integrated with STEAM education. *Journal of Physics: Conference Series.*

Kristanto, Y. D.. (2023). Integrating STEAM education and computational thinking. *Journal of Physics: Conference Series*.

Lai, X., Ye, J., & Wong, G. K. W. (2023). Effectiveness of collaboration in developing computational thinking skills: A systematic review of social cognitive factors. *Journal of Computer Assisted Learning*, *39*(5), 1418–1435. DOI: 10.1111/jcal.12845

Lavasani, M. G., Afzali, L., & Afzali, F. (2011). Cooperative learning and social skills. *Cypriot Journal of Educational Sciences*, *6*(4), 186–193.

Mackinlay, J. D. (1987). Automating the design of graphical presentations of relational information. *Communications of the ACM*, *30*(6), 902–910.

Mulvey, K. L.. (2022). The role of inclusion, discrimination, and belonging for adolescent STEM engagement. *Journal of Research in Science Teaching*, *59*(8), 1447–1464. DOI: 10.1002/tea.21762

Obaid, A., & Alak, G. (1989). Application of spreadsheet programs in the learning of numerical methods. *Computers & Education*, *13*(1), 25–31. DOI: 10.1016/0360-1315(89)90035-3

Peng, J.. (2025). Cultivating computational thinking in STEM courses. *Education and Information Technologies*. Advance online publication. DOI: 10.1007/s10639-025-13716-0

PhET Interactive Simulations. (n.d.). *The Moving Man*. University of Colorado Boulder. https://phet.colorado.edu

Rojas-Noguera, E., Revelo-Sánchez, O., & Jiménez-Toledo, J. A. (2026). Exploring computational thinking through collaborative work in secondary education: A systematic literature review. *TecnoLógicas*, *29*(65), e3537. DOI: 10.22430/22565337.3537

Shute, V. J., Sun, C., & Asbell-Clarke, J. (2017). Demystifying computational thinking. *Educational Research Review*, *22*, 142–158. DOI: 10.1016/j.edurev.2017.09.003

Suherman, S.. (2025). The role of STEM teaching in enhancing creativity and computational thinking. *Computers*.

Tariq, R.. (2025). Computational thinking in STEM education: A systematic review of pedagogical approaches. *Frontiers of Computer Science*.

Uddin, Z. (2017). Teaching physics using Microsoft Excel. *Physics Education*, •••, 52.

Weintrop, D., Beheshti, E., Horn, M., Orton, K., Jona, K., Trouille, L., & Wilensky, U. (2016). Defining computational thinking for mathematics and science classrooms. *Journal of Science Education and Technology*, *25*(1), 127–147. DOI: 10.1007/s10956-015-9581-5

Wing, J. M. (2006). Computational thinking. *Communications of the ACM*, *49*(3), 33–35. DOI: 10.1145/1118178.1118215

Yeni, S. (2024). Computational thinking integrated in school subjects. *Computers and Education Open*.

Yusufjanovna, T. Z. (2026). Creating a socially beneficial product within STEAM clubs and its educational effectiveness. *International Journal of Pedagogics*, *6*(1), 123–128. DOI: 10.37547/ijp/Volume06Issue01-27

Chapter 5
STEAM as a Strategy in Education and the Workplace for Integrating Emerging Technologies

Patricia Vázquez-Villegas
http://orcid.org/0000-0003-1568-4954
Tecnologico de Monterrey, Mexico

Juan-Carlos Rojas
http://orcid.org/0000-0001-7718-4555
Tecnologico de Monterrey, Mexico

Martha Patricia Robles Gutiérrez
http://orcid.org/0009-0000-3143-9831
Universidad Politécnica de Pachuca, Mexico

ABSTRACT

This chapter examines the STEAM movement as an interdisciplinary, human-centered framework for integrating emerging digital technologies, such as artificial intelligence, augmented and virtual reality, the Internet of Things, robotics, and 3D printing, into higher education and lifelong learning. The STEAM approach provides a coherent conceptual foundation for articulating scientific, technological, artistic, and humanistic knowledge, enabling learners and professionals to navigate the accelerated processes of digital transformation in an ethical, creative, and contextualized way. The chapter analyzes five theoretical frameworks that conceptualize STEAM as a central integrative axis: 1) STEAM to address complex societal challenges, especially the climate emergency; 2) STEAM as a path to social inclusion and inter-

DOI: 10.4018/979-8-2600-3658-7.ch005

cultural cohesion, with the arts acting as mediators of meaning and expression; 3) STEAM as an analytical framework for informed decision-making on the adoption and pedagogical use of emerging technologies; 4) STEAM and ethical enactivism, which integrates systems thinking, cognition, and value-oriented design for smart and inclusive learning ecosystems; and 5) STEAM as a sustainable ethical model for integrating AI in line with the principles of Society 5.0. The analysis shows how these frameworks collectively promote interdisciplinary learning, authentic problem-solving, equity, and university–industry collaboration. It also identifies persistent challenges in Latin America (digital divides, infrastructure constraints, and institutional resistance to change) alongside opportunities to strengthen innovation ecosystems through inclusive pedagogies and multisectoral partnerships. The chapter concludes that the value of these technologies lies less in the tools themselves than in the pedagogical and ethical design surrounding them, and it derives differentiated implications for teachers, universities, industry, and policymakers seeking responsible, inclusive, and effective STEAM education.

1. INTRODUCTION

The rapid digital transformation is redefining education and work globally. To catch up, thousands of students and professionals are looking for more effective ways to learn new skills in areas such as artificial intelligence (AI), machine learning, quantum computing, the Internet of Things (IoT), data science, business intelligence, cybersecurity, or green energy, to increase their income (Li, 2024). This makes it necessary to adopt a more integrated and renewed perspective on the relationship between productive development, technology, innovation, education, skills, employment and employability (Đorđević et al., 2025). In some countries, this leads to challenges, including infrastructure and regulatory constraints and gaps in digital literacy, as well as opportunities such as personalized learning pathways and better workforce preparation (Acevedo Carrillo et al., 2026). To address uncertainty, it is important that labor market strategies prioritize closing the digital divide and strengthening human capital through targeted programs to update and retrain professional skills (Weller, 2020).

The STEAM (science, technology, engineering, arts and mathematics) integrated curriculum, whose holistic approach is gaining momentum globally, effectively responds to these and other challenges of the 21st century, and has been classified as "inspiration for innovation" and "transformative approach" (Belbase et al., 2022, p. 2920). The STEAM movement aims to encourage innovative thinking and develop skills such as creativity, critical thinking, communication, and collaboration, with benefits including female empowerment and increased student engagement and motivation (Pedrosa de Souza and Sivini Ferreira, 2025; Salas-Pilco, 2024). Globally, it is seen as an interdisciplinary approach that can revolutionize educational strategies by equipping students with the skills and capabilities needed to succeed in today's industries and markets (Belbase et al., 2022). On the other hand, it contributes to achieving educational diversity and its objectives, as well as to sustainable development, by developing the necessary skills to face current challenges and prepare communities for the future (Belbase et al., 2022; Gavari-Starkie et al., 2024).

In Mexico and throughout Latin America, the current moment to adopt STEAM is particularly opportune for closing gaps in technological literacy and fostering inclusive development (Bascopé et al., 2020). The approach promotes a global vision of education in which science, technology, and the arts do not operate independently, thereby transforming theory into models applicable to real-world contexts, a shift that has been especially relevant in rural settings (Gavari-Starkie et al., 2024). However, research-based interventions that adopt a STEAM approach remain limited, and there is little systematic evidence on their outcomes in these countries. In addition, the shortage of people with the necessary skills to fill vacancies in technology sectors, coupled with persistent digital literacy gaps in the region, raises the need for interdisciplinary approaches at all levels of education, from childhood to vocational training, to foster the creativity and innovation that national development demands (Oliveros Ruiz, 2021).

On the other hand, although STEAM education and emerging technologies have been extensively studied separately, the literature offers a set of scattered theoretical frameworks that rarely articulate with each other and tend to remain at the conceptual level (Basilotta-Gómez-Pablos et al., 2022; Leavy et al., 2023). This offers limited guidance on how to operationalize the ethical and contextualized integration of technologies in authentic educational and professional environments. This gap is especially pronounced in resource-limited settings, where systematic evidence on STEAM interventions remains scarce (Belbase et al., 2022; Gavari-Starkie et al., 2024). Also, most studies focus on a single level of education rather than encompassing higher education, continuing education, and the work environment (Oberländer et al., 2020). Accordingly, this chapter addresses this gap by consolidating five complementary STEAM frameworks and demonstrating how each can guide the ethical, interdisciplinary, and contextual integration of emerging technologies across the lifespan.

With the above in mind, this chapter examines STEAM as a strategy for integrating emerging technologies into university and continuing education and explores how it can drive adaptive systems that promote creativity, equity, and innovation. In doing so, it responds to the critical need to align educational strategies with rapid technological change, ensuring that students of all ages acquire relevant competencies for an ever-evolving workforce, with particular attention to the Latin

American context. To this end, the chapter offers clear theoretical frameworks, practical examples, ethical guidance, and contextual analyses to support informed decision-making, project design, skills development, and the creation of inclusive, innovative learning and innovation environments that engage with a wide range of emerging technologies.

2. BACKGROUND

Multiple forms of inequality persist globally, especially in areas such as literacy, wealth distribution, and access to opportunities, which manifest differently across groups defined by age, race, and gender (Shabalala, 2025). These disparities have been associated, to a large extent, with accelerated technological progress coupled with insufficient acquisition of skills that would allow people to improve their living conditions and participate fully in increasingly digitized environments (Goedhart et al., 2022). Against this backdrop of persistent inequalities linked to technological progress and limitations in skills development, investing in skills from an early age and across the lifespan becomes an urgent priority.

Meeting this challenge involves considering a wide range of contextual factors, including the age, literacy level, and socio-cultural conditions of the target populations, as well as the availability of services and infrastructure that allow their full participation in society. Added to this is the importance of emotional resilience and socio-emotional skills, essential components of a comprehensive education. However, in this chapter, we will focus specifically on job skills related to the effective and efficient use of digital technology, given its critical role in inclusion, productivity, and the improvement of living conditions in highly digitalized environments. In this regard, recent studies have shown that students approaching graduation from higher education increasingly require more digital skills to access employment (Torbaghan et al., 2023).

2.1. Digital Skills and the Skills Gap in the Workforce

In a study conducted in Mexico, we found that information and data skills were most needed by employers, while teachers and employers also identified skills in cyber protection and security, as well as in the digital environment, as necessary (Robles Gutiérrez et al., 2024). Subsequently, we define these competencies across six key dimensions to strengthen students' graduation profiles in the industrial field. These competencies were designed by integrating students' real digital skills, teachers' criteria for effective learning, and employers' labor market needs; that is, a proposal that combines education, practice, and labor demand. This strengthens students' professional profiles, improves their employability, and offers a replicable and adaptable framework that must be further developed through continuous academic dialogue (Gutiérrez et al., 2025).

Although various initiatives of this type have been developed in many universities and countries to identify and define this competence, both digital and non-digital, these advances tend to remain at the conceptual level (Basilotta-Gómez-Pablos et al., 2022). Significant challenges remain in their effective implementation: how to translate these competencies into concrete pedagogical practices? How to articulate them in school and work environments? What sequence of actions is necessary for students to develop them in an authentic and sustained way? (Barnes et al., 2024; Forcael et al., 2022). In many cases, educational institutions lack operational guidelines that enable them to incorporate these into the classroom or align them with the real demands of contemporary work.

In response to these limitations, we propose STEAM-based educational frameworks that allow not only the introduction, but also the contextualized adaptation of emerging technologies in training processes and work environments. This comprehensive approach of interdisciplinary experiences that link theoretically defined competencies with real situations of creation, problem-solving, and innovation favors a more effective transition between learning and its professional application.

2.2. The Evolution of STEM to STEAM

STEM education (without the integration of the arts) has traditionally emphasized technical and scientific skills, with increasingly evident limitations to foster creativity. The incorporation of creativity in STEM approaches has been widely recognized in the literature, given the need to integrate novel elements and innovative pedagogical strategies that foster more effective student participation (Pollard et al., 2018). Empirical evidence indicates a positive correlation between STEM education and the development of creativity, suggesting that sustained exposure to and meaningful involvement in these disciplines can strengthen students' creative abilities (Borg Preca et al., 2023). However, the stories of innovators underscore that technical knowledge alone is not enough: creativity arises when that knowledge is combined with imagination and dialogue (Mishra et al., 2013). It is precisely this dimension that traditional STEM disciplines tend to leave aside, and that the arts are well positioned to contribute. For this reason, the "A" of the arts is incorporated into the framework: the STEAM approach integrates artistic creation and expression to activate the imagination and creativity that preparation for future challenges demands, without which technical development is incomplete (Decorte & Vlieghe, 2024) (Figure 1)

Figure 1. Evolution from STEM to STEAM as an Integrative Educational Framework

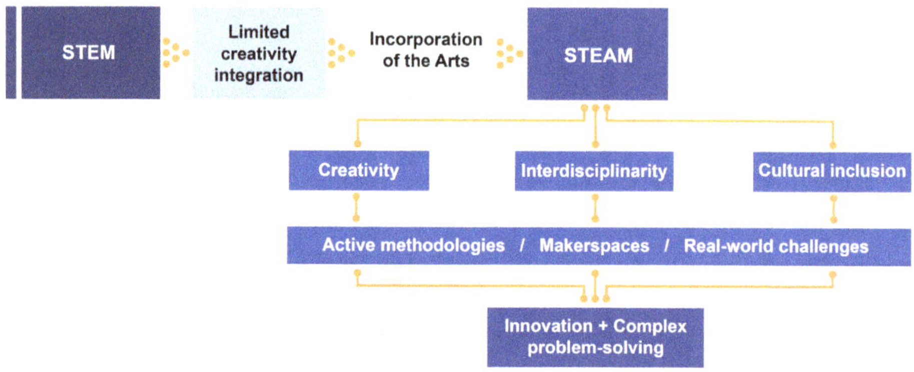

Figure 1 schematically illustrates how integrating the Arts into traditional STEM frameworks significantly enriches the learning experience, even embracing cultural inclusion. These essential elements are brought to life through dynamic, active methodologies and engagement with real-world challenges. This approach not only stimulates innovation but also improves complex problem-solving skills. These examples represent just a selection of the various strategies that STEAM education encompasses.

The inclusion of the Arts is therefore a strategic response to the growing need for design thinking and creative problem-solving in complex scenarios, fostering collaborative creativity and interdisciplinary dialogue (Guyotte et al., 2015). The latter has been evidenced by significant improvements in creative skills and self-efficacy among university students participating in STEAM-based training courses (Gu et al., 2023). In addition, integrating the Arts can foster cognitive and socio-emotional skills, promoting a holistic learning experience that transcends the traditional boundaries of the subjects in question (Johnson-Green et al., 2020).

It has been said that STEAM is underpinned by pillars such as creativity, inclusion, and emerging technologies, which are necessary to address global challenges and foster sustainable innovation (Aguayo et al., 2023). But, despite these benefits, its effective integration remains a challenge, with risks of diluting both Arts and STEM components if not carefully balanced (Johnson-Green et al., 2020). As such, educators are encouraged to adopt transdisciplinary approaches that maintain the integrity of both domains, ensuring that the Arts contribute equally to learning outcomes alongside STEM subjects (Costantino, 2018). This balanced integration not only enriches the educational experience, but also equips students with the skills needed to function and innovate in a complex and rapidly evolving world (Perignat & Katz-Buonincontro, 2018).

Especially in culturally diverse regions, the STEAM curriculum has been observed to improve relevance and engagement with learning. This approach is supported by the integration of culturally relevant pedagogy, which has been shown to improve motivation among underrepresented and minority students (Serrano Corkin et al., 2020). Arts inclusion provides a culture-focused engagement tool that engages underrepresented and underserved students by incorporating cultural cues and making student learning experiences more accessible (Cummings et al., 2018). In these cases, the integration of the arts fosters an intercultural and inclusive environment, creating cooperation and a common language in education, crucial for the internationalization and inclusion of diverse student populations (Nieto-Miguel et al., 2023). The use of storytelling, a cultural practice, in informal STEM learning activities has also been shown to increase student engagement and learning opportunities, highlighting the importance of integrating cultural elements into educational practices (Acosta & Haden, 2023).

In this sense, "makerspaces" (defined as spaces for the implementation of solutions by students, either individually or through collaborative work, aimed at development, prototyping and validation of their proposals) are a promising approach to enhance creativity in STEAM education, providing practical experiences that encourage creative thinking throughout the different educational levels (Soomro et al., 2023). However, studies have also emphasized the importance of pedagogical methodologies, teacher training and support (Chappell et al., 2025; García-Aranda et al., 2020). For example, strategies such as problem-based learning and challenge-based learning have been shown to foster students' creativity and the value of integrating STEM problem-solving with creative expression (Weng et al., 2023). Real challenges incorporated into curricula have also boosted students' creativity and content knowledge, as evidenced by projects that address community service challenges (B. Huang et al., 2025).

The evolution towards holistic educational models that prepare students for interdisciplinary innovation reflects a significant shift in educational paradigms from various fields. This shift is driven by the need to integrate diverse disciplines to effectively address complex and real-world problems. In the face of this conceptual evolution, the STEAM framework becomes relevant by offering a structure that not only articulates different disciplines but also connects knowledge to meaningful, situated practices. It is established as an approach that addresses interdisciplinary challenges ethically, innovatively, and in a contextualized way, breaking down traditional academic silos and promoting a more integrated and collaborative approach to learning and problem-solving.

2.3. Emerging Technologies and Integrating AI Into Education and Work

Emerging technologies are profoundly transforming social functions (education, work and cultural interactions) and pose both opportunities and challenges. This transformation spans multiple industries and, in a transversal way, demands the development of new interdisciplinary skills.

In the field of education, the integration of information and communication technologies (ICT) has revolutionized teaching and learning methodologies, promoting student autonomy and improving digital communication skills (Jora & Basnet, 2025). On this basis, AI and immersive technologies, such as AR, offer personalized and interactive learning experiences that improve student engagement and motivation and encourage practical skill development through real-world simulations (Garg et al., 2025; Wang & Huang, 2025). Along the same lines, innovations such as autonomous robots and extended reality make it possible to enrich users' experiences and expand the inclusion of groups with specific needs across different educational and cultural environments (Kotis et al., 2025).

In the workplace, technologies such as AI, drones, and digital platforms are reshaping job roles and organizational structures. Although this change is positive, it requires a strategic response that mitigates the potential negative consequences for workers and society, ensuring that technological development and implementation involve diverse actors to foster positive social outcomes (Bailey, 2022; Le Blanc et al., 2024). Its scope, however, goes beyond employment; In some fields, these technologies only add value if they solve fundamental challenges (accuracy, accessibility and ethics of the data), without which the information generated loses reliability; once these obstacles are overcome, they open up new opportunities to collect and analyze data that support decision-making and communication (Schirpke et al., 2023). Therefore, its social implications highlight the need for solid governance frameworks that balance risks and benefits and are underpinned by social integration and adaptive risk management (Trump et al., 2018). And while technology has notably boosted economic development, innovation, and social connectivity, its transformative potential can only be realized with careful support and policies capable of responding to the complexity of its effects (Groen & Walsh, 2013; Oh et al., 2020).

On the other hand, the convergence of these technologies in smart education is crucial to prepare people for an ever-evolving industrial landscape, especially as the world moves from Industry 4.0 to Industry 5.0, with an emphasis on human-machine collaboration (Adel, 2024); hence the importance of promoting lifelong learning, adaptability and reskilling. Responding to this demand requires agile human resource development strategies that emphasize digital literacy and interdisciplinary training (Nnadi et al., 2025), as well as AI literacy frameworks that promote a deep understanding of these systems, their implications, and collaboration between people and AI (Allen & Kendeou, 2024). Interdisciplinary educational models demonstrate the effectiveness of integrating AI into curricula to strengthen critical thinking and problem-solving, especially in fields such as health (Zhang et al., 2026). Thus, as universities and industries collaborate to close skills gaps, it is essential to develop curricula that respond to the needs of the sector and prepare students for the demands of modern technologies (Paśko et al., 2022).

2.3.1 The Case of Mexico: Industry 4.0 and the Digital Economy

In Mexico, the adoption of advanced technologies in sectors such as manufacturing, education, and health is increasingly driven by the principles of Industry 4.0 and the digital economy. In manufacturing, Industry 4.0 technologies, including AI, the Internet of Things (IoT), and cyber-physical systems, are transforming production processes by enabling smart manufacturing systems that improve efficiency, adaptability, and productivity, while promoting sustainability through waste reduction and optimized use of resources (Ryalat et al., 2024; Singh et al., 2023). The integration of advanced mechatronic systems further supports this transformation, facilitating real-time data sharing and automation and enabling the development of intelligent and interconnected manufacturing environments (Ryalat et al., 2024).

In the education sector, these technologies increase student engagement, simulate real-world scenarios, and develop essential soft skills, although their use is largely limited to universities and manufacturing-related courses (Moraes et al., 2023). Meanwhile, in the healthcare sector, the digital economy plays a critical role in improving healthcare standards in Mexico by optimizing infrastructure, increasing service efficiency, and ensuring a more equitable allocation of resources (Haoran, 2025).

This digital transformation is part of a broader trend in which Industry 4.0 technologies are seen as key drivers of innovation, sustainability and competitiveness in sectors such as health and education, enabling digital transformation and fostering inter-institutional collaboration (Romano et al., 2025; Yaqub & Alsabban, 2023). Despite these advances, challenges remain in the widespread adoption and implementation of these technologies, which requires strategic frameworks to overcome barriers and fully realize the potential of Industry 4.0 in Mexico (Yaqub & Alsabban, 2023; C. Zhang et al., 2024).

2.4. The Digital Divide and Equitable Access

Addressing the digital divide and promoting equitable access to digital technologies requires a comprehensive approach that takes into account socio-economic, cultural and infrastructural factors. The COVID-19 pandemic has highlighted the urgent need to close this gap in diverse settings where lower socioeconomic groups, culturally diverse communities, and people with disabilities face significant barriers to access. A multi-stakeholder approach involving improvements in digital literacy, workforce training, and the co-design of culturally appropriate and financially sustainable models is essential (Gallegos-Rejas et al., 2023). Digital inequality is not simply a matter of access, but is deeply intertwined with offline socioeconomic disparities, as seen in the experiences of people from low socioeconomic backgrounds who face challenges compounded by intersectional factors such as gender, ethnicity, and age (Goedhart et al., 2022). These disparities in infrastructure, frequently observed in Latin American countries, where digital infrastructure is unevenly distributed, further exacerbate these inequalities and underscore the need for equitable access as a democratic right (Correa et al., 2023). The pandemic intensified these challenges globally, revealing the complexity of the digital divide and the need for strategies that address underlying social structures to promote inclusion (Ji & She, 2026).

Research indicates that closing digital divides is critical for sustainable digital societies, as it requires scaling existing models to incorporate new variables and critically examine the effects of the intervention (Vassilakopoulou & Hustad, 2023). In some contexts, infrastructural barriers and limited government support highlight the need for resilience practices that empower communities to develop their digital systems, despite external and internal challenges (Korostelina & Barrett, 2023). In others, digital inclusion has improved, but a significant portion of the population remains excluded, with gender, age, education, and socioeconomic status being critical determinants of access to digital inclusion (Bokhari & Awuni, 2024). Overall, a multifaceted strategy that integrates socio-economic, cultural and infrastructural considerations is essential to effectively address the digital divide and promote equitable access to digital technologies.

2.5. Ethics and the Challenge of Meaningful Integration

The effective adoption of STEAM tools and new technologies depends on integrating technical knowledge with creativity and ethical considerations, as highlighted by multiple studies. In this vein, ethical activism in STEAM education emphasizes a values-based approach that integrates creativity, inclusion, and emerging technologies, ensuring that all citizens are prepared to use digital technologies ethically and critically (Aguayo et al., 2023).

This ethical emphasis is especially relevant when considering emerging technologies such as generative AI, as its incorporation into education further underscores the importance of articulating technological knowledge and ethical understanding, as students often recognize its creative potential but lack awareness of its ethical implications (Z. Huang et al., 2025). In a complementary way, the development of a sustainable learning model for Society 5.0 also emphasizes the ethical integration of advanced technologies, thus enhancing citizenship and ecological literacy, and positioning higher education as a cornerstone for achieving sustainability goals (Torres-Rivera et al., 2025).

Thus, the challenge lies not only in incorporating new technologies into STEAM environments, but in ensuring that their use is articulated in a coherent way with interdisciplinary pedagogical processes that promote deep, creative, contextualized, meaningful and personally relevant learning (Engelman et al., 2017; Juškevičienė et al., 2021; Leavy et al., 2023).

3. STEAM THEORETICAL FRAMEWORKS AS INTEGRATORS

Given the difficulties identified in the adoption of emerging technologies, it is necessary to have models that guide pedagogical and technological decision-making. Below are five STEAM theoretical frameworks that articulate the use of technologies in an interdisciplinary and ethical way and are aligned with real needs. We will begin this section by defining what a theoretical framework encompasses. According to (Myburgh & Tammaro, 2013), a framework explains what and how certain topics or information are, how they work, how they relate to other disciplines or professions, and their purpose:

"A theoretical framework is a basic, hypothetical, logical, conceptual structure or description of a complex entity or process, which can be used to develop theory by classifying and organizing complex information and providing a unified and coherent view. A theoretical framework comprises a set of concepts (ontology), and a description of the interrelationships (propositions or principles) between entities and/or phenomena (taxonomy)." (p. 133)

For its part, Calder et al. (2023) He mentions that:

"Theoretical frameworks build on the insight provided by granular, effect-specific explanations. Because frameworks facilitate the integration of different paradigm-specific variable explanations, they offer a path to making progress towards building a cumulative and more general understanding of behavior." (p. 2)

Based on these definitions, a theoretical framework, by offering a coherent conceptual structure and an organized set of ideas and relationships, can allow us to understand the STEAM educational approach as a strategy capable of integrating emerging technologies, since it helps to classify and connect scientific, technological, artistic and mathematical knowledge, facilitating the understanding of complex phenomena and the articulation of multiple paradigms. Thus, the approach provides a basis for designing educational and work experiences in which technology is incorporated in an interdisciplinary, creative and context-adapted way (which is very important), guiding informed decision-making and promoting a cumulative and adaptable understanding of how people learn, create and innovate with new tools.

Since the emerging technology adoption ecosystem is complex, a STEAM framework acts as an organizational structure that helps tidy up this chaos and provides a foundation for technology decision-making (Figure 2).

Figure 2. The STEAM framework addresses complex issues in the integration of emerging technologies

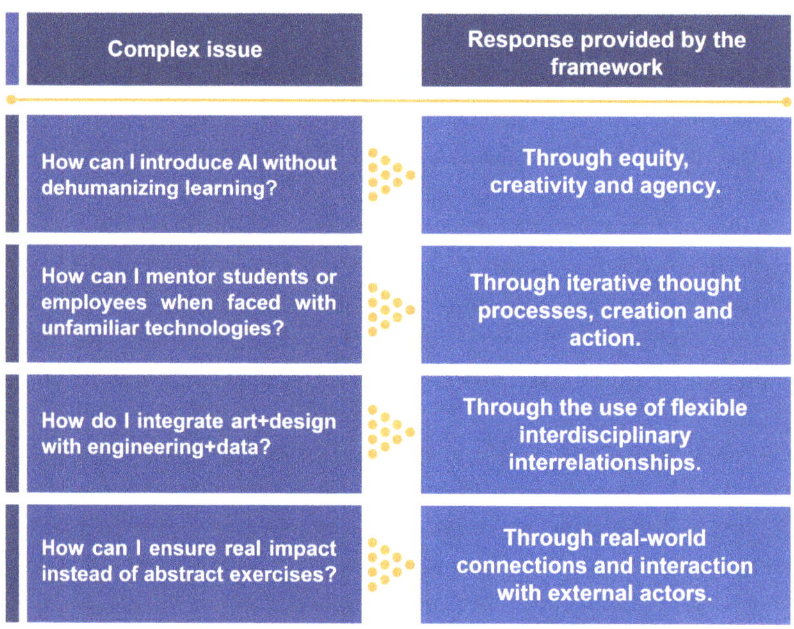

Figure 2 illustrates how a STEAM-based theoretical framework addresses recurring complex problems that arise when integrating emerging technologies into educational and professional contexts. The left-hand column presents representative challenges, including the ethical incorporation of AI without dehumanizing learning, mentoring students and professionals facing unfamiliar technologies, integrating art and design with engineering and data-driven practices, and ensuring real impact beyond abstract or isolated exercises. The right-hand column shows how the STEAM framework responds to these challenges through fairness, creativity, and learner agency; iterative thought processes–creation–action; flexible interdisciplinary interrelationships; and authentic, real-world connections with external stakeholders. These responses position STEAM as a human-centered, ethical, and action-oriented framework that supports informed decision-making, interdisciplinary collaboration, and the meaningful integration of emerging technologies into education and work.

Due to its disciplinary nature, STEAM merges scientific thinking, engineering and design, artistic practices, technology, creativity, social dimension and ethics, integrating technology not as a fragment but as part of a coherent system. Based on the above, 5 theoretical frameworks that can help the reader integrate the STEAM strategy into education and work with emerging technologies are described below.

3.1. STEAM for the Climate Emergency

There is limited understanding of the cultural dynamics that influence learning processes. In addition, there is still little research on the intersection between secondary and higher education, which hinders the continuity of training in interdisciplinary approaches. Added to this is a weak articulation between STEAM initiatives and open science approaches, which limits the potential for broad and collaborative participation. These limitations restrict social participation in solving real problems and strengthening scientific citizenship. For this reason, the researchers Chappell et al. (2025) analysed European research, reports and projects to identify the key characteristics of effective STEAM education. Seven key features emerged from this review and are shown in Figure 3.

Figure 3. Key dimensions of STEAM education, according to Chappell et al. (2025), which can be measured before and after an educational intervention. The data are representative

This comparative visualization of the key dimensions of effective STEAM education illustrates the expected changes observed before and after the implementation of a structured STEAM framework. The radar graph represents seven main dimensions identified by the authors. The "before" profile reflects a fragmented or uneven integration of these dimensions, while the "after" profile illustrates a more balanced and coherent configuration. The figure illustrates how the systematic implementation of STEAM principles can strengthen interdisciplinarity, learning agency, equity, and authentic engagement with real challenges, and support the ethical and inclusive integration of emerging technologies in educational and professional contexts.

More explicitly, each dimension can be explained as follows:

1. Equity: An ethical and fair stance that runs through the entire design and evaluation of STEAM, seeking to flatten hierarchies between disciplines and redistribute voice, time, and resources among diverse students.
2. Disciplinary interrelatedness: using and integrating knowledge (multi/inter/transdisciplinary) from science, technology, arts, and humanities as required by the problem, with A as the catalyst for connections and meanings

3. Collaboration: establishing contacts between students, teachers, fellow teachers, external actors (community, NGOs, industry, cultural institutions) and, in a post-human key, with the material and environmental environment.
4. Real-World Connections: Poses authentic challenges (e.g., climate, city, health), with civic purpose and links to local policies and contexts, so that students see impact and identity in what they do.
5. Think-do-do: intertwine critical and creative thinking with practical thinking and prototyping (physical and/or digital), to understand, experiment and intervene in complex problems
6. Creativity: treating creativity not only as a skill, but also as an engine of social change, linked to play, design, arts and technology, to generate original and relevant responses to real challenges.
7. Inclusion, empowerment, and personalization: Inclusion and personalization: opening participation, strengthening self-efficacy and autonomy, and enabling personalized trajectories that connect students' interests, identities, and life contexts.

These features constitute the conceptual framework that the authors called Road-STEAMer, designed to guide STEAM educational policies and practices in Europe. These authors present the application of the framework in two specific cases. The first shows how primary and secondary students work on real ocean problems through a combination of science, arts and digital technologies, especially collaborative virtual reality, which favors *thinking-doing and doing*, creativity and collaboration between schools, aquariums and universities, although with a still limited disciplinary integration and an equity that is more implicit than explicit.

The second case exemplifies a transdisciplinary implementation in higher education, where participants from arts, sciences, entrepreneurship, and design co-create innovative responses to climate challenges based on creative pedagogies, design thinking, and collaboration with community actors, excelling in creativity, real-world connections, and teamwork, albeit with tensions between individual agency and group dynamics. In the case of the school-work ecosystem in Latin America, this framework could be applied with great creativity. STEAM as a framework for the ethical integration of emerging technologies in education and industry: a review of Chappell's framework. et al. (2025).

Table 1. STEAM as a framework for the ethical integration of emerging technologies in education and industry. Adapted from the framework of Chappell et al. (2025).

Frame Feature	**Short Description**	**Application for technology integration in industry**
Real-world connections	It uses authentic problems and real actors from the social, scientific and political ecosystems.	Connect educational projects with real technological challenges in the industry (automation, traceability, AI, advanced manufacturing), involving companies to define case studies, provide data or co-supervise processes.
Disciplinary Inter-relationship	Integrate arts, sciences, technology and design according to the needs of the challenge, with methodological flexibility.	Create mixed teams (engineering, design, UX, data, industrial operations) to prototype technological solutions; for example, integrating artistic visualization and data analysis to improve industrial interfaces or production processes.
Thinking-Making-Doing	Iterative cycles in which students think, create, and act through physical or digital prototypes.	It uses agile methodologies and industrial makerspaces to quickly prototype solutions (sensors, control panels, AR/VR simulations), and validate them in real environments, integrating learning with continuous improvement processes.
Creativity	It conceives creativity as a driver of innovation and social change, expressed through play, design and the arts.	Promote industrial innovation laboratories that combine artistic techniques (storyboarding, performance, visual thinking) and digital tools (digital twins, generative AI) to devise more efficient products or processes.
Equity + Inclusion/ Empowerment/ Personalization	It fosters access, diversity, autonomy, and personalized learning and participation paths.	Design programs in which diverse teams (gender, fields, seniority) collaborate using accessible technology; they enable customized specialization pathways (e.g., robotics, sustainability) based on industry roles.
Collaboration	Collaborative work between students, educators, external actors and material/digital environments.	Build university and industrial networks in which mixed teams co-develop technological solutions (e.g., predictive maintenance, automation), using collaborative tools (Mural, IoT platforms, multi-user VR).

These features of the framework illustrate how STEAM functions not only as a curricular integration of disciplines, but also as a coherent design logic for the ethical and situated integration of emerging technologies in education and industry. The applications described demonstrate that technology integration is most meaningful when it is integrated into authentic challenges, co-designed with diverse actors, and oriented towards continuous improvement and inclusion. In this sense, the framework provides practical guidance to connect education and industry, supporting innovation that is not only technically effective, but also socially responsible, context-aware and sustainable throughout life.

3.2. STEAM as a Path to Inclusion and Social Cohesion

In the face of the growth of increasingly multicultural university environments and the persistent disconnect between students from different backgrounds, and in a social context that fosters individuality and hinders collective development, Higher Education faces significant challenges related to inclusion, social cohesion and the construction of shared meanings. Added to this is the limited number of studies on integrated STEAM education at the university level, especially in teacher training, despite its potential to address real social problems, promote the integration of knowledge and foster inclusive experiences.

In this context, the authors Nieto-Miguel et al. (2023) developed a conceptual framework that highlights the relevance of integrated STEAM education, with special emphasis on the role of art as an intercultural mediator and as a tool to promote dialogue, contextualized expression, critical reflection, and understanding of sociocultural diversity. This approach conceives art as a fundamental component to generate shared narratives, stimulate divergent thinking, democratize participation and promote intercultural creativity that contributes to equality, tolerance and social justice in teacher education.

Based on this reflection, focused on the training of future teachers, the authors argue that integrated STEAM, when it incorporates a rigorous artistic dimension, can become a key axis for internationalization, inclusion and social cohesion in the university, offering teachers experiences that they will be able to transfer to their own classrooms in increasingly diverse contexts. In the future, access to technologies such as AI will not be a factor of disparity, but the ability of their teachers to integrate it pedagogically into teaching.

3.3. Criteria for Informed Decision-Making

In view of the rapid expansion of emerging technologies in educational contexts, Leavy et al. (2023) propose an analytical framework that organizes the evidence from 43 studies and allows characterizing, comparing, and designing STEAM experiences: it identifies which technologies are used, how the arts are integrated, what level of disciplinary integration is achieved, what methodologies are used to assess learning, and what pedagogical motivations guide the interventions. This framework provides clear criteria for making informed decisions when incorporating AI, AR/VR, robotics, makerspaces, and other technologies into training and work scenarios. The five criteria identified are:

1. Emerging technologies used: AR/VR/MR; programming and robotics; *maker movement* (digital manufacturing, textiles, 3D printing); and other technological applications (applications, simulations).
2. Integrated arts: 3D and multimedia, visual arts, performing arts, music and literature (storytelling).
3. Interdisciplinary integration: classification of experiences ranging from technology and art to the integration of the five STEAM areas, distinguishing between multidisciplinary, interdisciplinary and transdisciplinary approaches.
4. Assessment methodologies: quantitative, qualitative and mixed studies, with special attention to attitudes and beliefs, experiences, intervention outcomes and disciplinary learning.
5. Pedagogical motivations: solving real problems; develop 21st century skills; promote equity and access; and improve attitudes towards STEAM disciplines and careers.

Table 2. Guidelines for decision-making in STEAM-based technology integration. Adapted from Leavy et al. (2023).

Frame Axis	Guiding Questions (Design and Decision Making)	Application in education	Work/Industry Application
Emerging technologies	Which technology best responds to the problem, desired outcome, and available resources? (AR/VR, robotics, AI, makerspaces, apps)	Select, for example, AR/VR for immersive visualization in science education or textiles for creative electronics projects.	Choose IoT + analytics for traceability, digital twins/ VR for safe training, and collaborative robots to improve processes.
Integrated Arts	Which art form enhances understanding, communication, and inclusion in this context? (visual, performative, musical, 3D, narrative)	Use digital storytelling or music and programming (e.g., EarSketch) to teach programming with cultural and creative meaning.	It incorporates UX design, visual thinking, and multimedia media to create accessible interfaces and communicate data to non-technical audiences.
Interdisciplinary Integration	Does it authentically integrate science, technology, engineering, arts, and math activity around a real challenge?	Design transdisciplinary projects (e.g., perceiving a local problem, modeling it mathematically, and communicating it through art).	Form mixed teams (data, engineering, operations, design) that co-define requirements and prototype end-to-end solutions.

continued on following page

Table 2. Continued

Frame Axis	Guiding Questions (Design and Decision Making)	Application in education	Work/Industry Application
Assessment methodologies	How will learning, outcomes, and user experience be evaluated? (pre- and post-evaluations, rubrics, validated instruments, mixed methods)	It combines content testing with creative evidence (portfolios, prototypes, magazines) and with measures of perception or attitudes.	Assesses operational KPIs (time, quality, safety), technology adoption, and competencies (collaboration, creativity) using mixed methods.
Pedagogical motivations	What is the purpose behind integration? (solving a real problem, 21st century skills, equity, career guidance)	Develop community challenges (in the environment and mobility) to activate agency, creativity and interest in STEAM pathways.	Align with operational needs (efficiency, safety, sustainability) and upskill diverse teams for inclusive adoption of technology.

The analysis of Leavy et al. (2023) offers a clear understanding of how emerging technologies shape the current landscape of STEAM education, identifying patterns, gaps, and opportunities to move towards more integrated, creative, and equitable practices. Its analytical framework provides a basis for designing and researching interventions that effectively integrate technology, art, and STEM disciplines around authentic problems, offering valuable guidance for educators and practitioners alike interested in empowering innovation and skills development in the 21st century.

3.4. Ethical Activism for the Design of Smart and Inclusive STEAM Learning

The work of Aguayo et al. (2023) proposes a theoretical design framework to create intelligent, dynamic and inclusive STEAM learning systems and contexts, integrating emerging technologies (XR/VR/AR, IoT, robotics, maker and big data) with principles of activist ethics and systems thinking. The central premise is that, in order to respond to the challenges of the 2030 Agenda and education 4.0, it is not enough to introduce technology: it is necessary to design based on values (care for life, inclusion, cultural equity), with 4E approaches to cognition (incorporated, active, integrated, extended) and with situated participatory processes, to turn project-based learning and immersive experiences into ethical ecosystems. The 4 bases of the framework are:

1. Systems Thinking and Complexity Theory

It conceives educational contexts as dynamic and non-linear systems in which results arise from socio-material relationships, conditions and couplings (not from isolated pieces). It proposes designing environments that favor interactivity, diversity, mutual influence and decentralized control, with special attention to the sociocultural context. Instead of "adding technology", the ecosystem (actors, flows, rules, spaces, data) is modeled and the conditions are orchestrated for meaningful learning to emerge (e.g., autonomous work cells, collaboration rules, iterations with real feedback).

2. 4E Cognition (Embedded, Inactive, Embedded, Extended)

It situates cognition as bodily, situated, active, and extended by artifacts and environments (including technologies). Learning is not about representing the world "in your head", but about perceiving it and acting with it, incorporating the qualities it offers. It favors immersive and haptic experiences (XR/VR/AR/MR), tangible prototypes (maker, textiles, 3D printing), IoT sensorization and work with digital twins, so that students think with their bodies and with tools that expand their action and perception.

3. Ethical Activism (Ethics of Care and Co-Participation)

He proposes an ethics based on the care of life as a moral foundation (one's own, that of others and of the planet) and on second-person interaction (mutuality, shared sense). It transfers the ethics of discourse to design architecture (values, norms, inclusion criteria) and practices (co-design, community validation). Design with explicit values (equity, access, reciprocity), co-define problems with communities (indigenous, underrepresented), iterate prototypes with situated feedback, and socially validate the transfer (social license).

4. STEAM and Pillars (Creativity, Inclusion, Citizenship, Emerging Technologies)

It reinterprets STEAM as a synergistic curriculum that integrates disciplines with 21st century skills (critical and creative thinking, intellectual openness, responsible innovation, computational thinking) and anchors technology in authentic challenges with cultural and civic relevance. Integrate XR/VR/AR, IoT/robotics/big data, and create not as ornaments, but as smart tools to address real local problems (environment, heritage, mobility) with public participation and results of social and planetary value.

This work illustrates the implementation through a case generator in early childhood education (co-design with the community, XR/3D/printing, validation and transfer around the "guanaco" as local heritage) and exemplifies how the four bases are articulated in a flow of consultation, ethnography, prototyping and validation.

Below, we present an example of how the four bases of the theoretical framework of Aguayo et al. (2023) could be applied to integrate technology in education and work (Table 3).

Table 3. Examples of how to operationalize the 4 bases in education and work. With information from Aguayo et al. (2023).

Theoretical basis	Design Questions	Application in education	Work/Industry Application
Systems Thinking/ Complexity	What actors, relationships, flows and conditions sustain (or hinder) learning/ innovation?	Map the ecosystem (school–family–community) and establish conditions such as role diversity, distributed decision-making, and short iteration cycles.	Mapping the value chain and "truth data points"; Create autonomous, cross-sectional cells with continuous field-based feedback.
4E Cognition	How can learning be embodied, situated, and extended through technologies or artifacts?	Which technological combination offers relevant advantages for the real challenge?	It uses digital twins and mixed reality for safety and ergonomics training; Deploy haptic interfaces for job maintenance.
Ethical Activism	What values guide decisions (care, fairness, reciprocity)? Who is excluded and how can they be included?	Co-design with families/ communities; use social/ environmental impact rubrics; ensure community validation and transfer.	Apply ESG criteria and data ethics in AI/ IoT; creating user committees for risk and capital supervision; have a secured social license to scale.
STEAM (Pillars) + Emerging Technologies	Which technological combination offers relevant advantages for the real challenge?	Use AR for local heritage; robotics for computational thinking; School-level Big Data for civic research.	Deploy IoT and analytics for traceability and energy; collaborative robots for flexible cells; XR for remote expert support.

Table 3 shows how the four theoretical bases act as a coherent scaffolding that turns STEAM into a situated ethical design: systems thinking defines the field and conditions; 4E cognition dictates the type of experiences (bodily, immersive, extended); ethical activism is fundamental in the values and processes of co-participation;

and the pillars of STEAM guide the meaningful integration of emerging technologies in authentic challenges with cultural and civic relevance.

Thus, technology ceases to be merely instrumental and becomes an integral means to learn with others and take care of life in real contexts.

This framework articulates values, systems, and technology to move from mere instrumental adoption to an ethical design of STEAM ecosystems: immersive and creative experiences that embody learning, connect with communities, and care for life and the environment. By offering clear axes (activist ethics, complexity, 4E, smart technologies, inclusion, and co-design) and a practical eight-step sequence, Aguayo et al. (2023) provide guidance to educational institutions and organizations seeking to integrate emerging technologies in ways that retain meaning, equity, and contextual relevance.

3.5. Sustainable Ethical Model for the Integration of AI and STEAM Pedagogies for Higher Education in Society 5.0

The article by Torres-Rivera et al. (2025) proposes a comprehensive educational model to guide Higher Education Institutions towards the principles of Society 5.0, in which technology, especially AI, is articulated with ethics, sustainability and social justice as transformative axes. The model is structured around five theoretical bases (education as a common good, STEAM, ethics in AI, sustainability, human capabilities and educational innovation) and is operationalized through three pillars: multidisciplinary learning, project-based learning (PBL) for sustainability and the society-industry relationship. Its validation was carried out through interviews with specialists, a demonstration case ("Sustainable Classroom") and a comparative analysis of international experiences.

Table 4. Fundamental principles for ethical, sustainable and human-centered STEAM ecosystems, based on Torres-Rivera et al. (2025).

Theoretical basis	Key Principles / Description
1. Education as a common good	Education must transcend technocratic logic and function as a space for ethical deliberation, social justice, and sustainability. In Society 5.0, technology only makes sense when it serves human well-being, equity and intergenerational responsibility.
2. STEAM as an integrating framework	STEAM operates as a transdisciplinary paradigm that brings together science, technology, arts, and humanities to address socio-environmental complexity. It fosters creativity, critical thinking, ethics, and civic agency in the face of real challenges.
3. AI ethics and technology governance	AI integration must adhere to principles of transparency, algorithmic fairness, inclusion, and accountability. The role of the educator involves acting as an ethical mediator, not simply as a technological user.
4. Sustainability and the human capabilities approach	Learning expands freedoms and agency, strengthening social-emotional, ecological, and collaborative competencies. Sustainability is a cross-cutting axis: students must be prepared to act with social and environmental responsibility.
5. Educational and institutional innovation	Transformation requires flexible governance, the involvement of internal and external stakeholders, and experimental spaces such as "living labs." Digitalization only makes sense when it is articulated with democratic and sustainable pedagogical processes.

The basic theories are: Education as a common good, STEAM as an integrating framework, AI ethics and technology governance, Sustainability and the human capabilities approach and Educational and institutional innovation.

Based on the above, strategies could be implemented to integrate emerging technologies (AI, IoT, XR) in schools and work environments. Two examples (A and B) of how this framework could be applied in educational and work contexts are described in Figures 4 and 5.

Figure 4. Example of the application of the framework of Torres-Rivera et al. (2025) to integrate technology in higher education

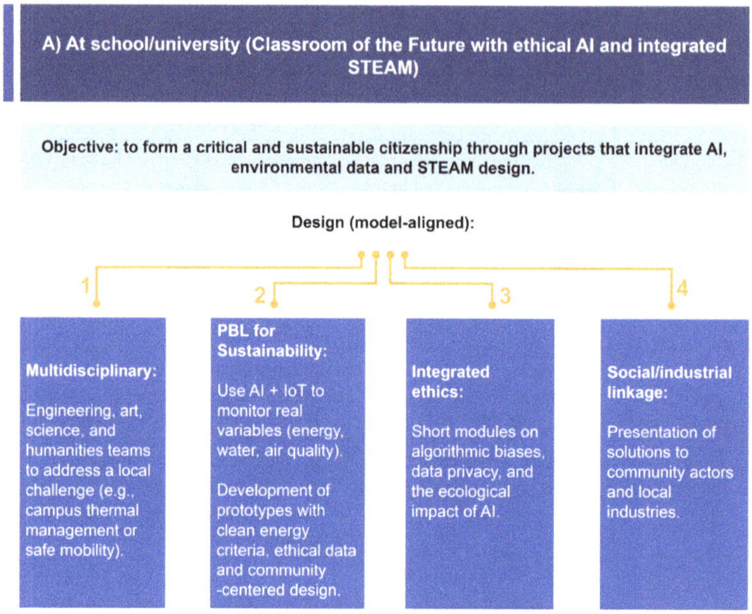

In Figure 4, we illustrate how an ethical and integrated STEAM framework can be operated in school and university contexts by designing a "Classroom of the Future". The model is aimed at promoting critical, responsible and sustainable citizenship, involving students in projects that integrate AI, environmental data and STEAM-based design. The central objective is achieved through an instructional design aligned with models that articulates four complementary components. Together, these components exemplify how ethical AI and STEAM pedagogies can be coherently aligned to create learning ecosystems that connect technological competence, civic responsibility, and sustainability in authentic educational contexts.

Figure 5. Example of the application of the framework of Torres-Rivera et al. (2025) to integrate technology into the work

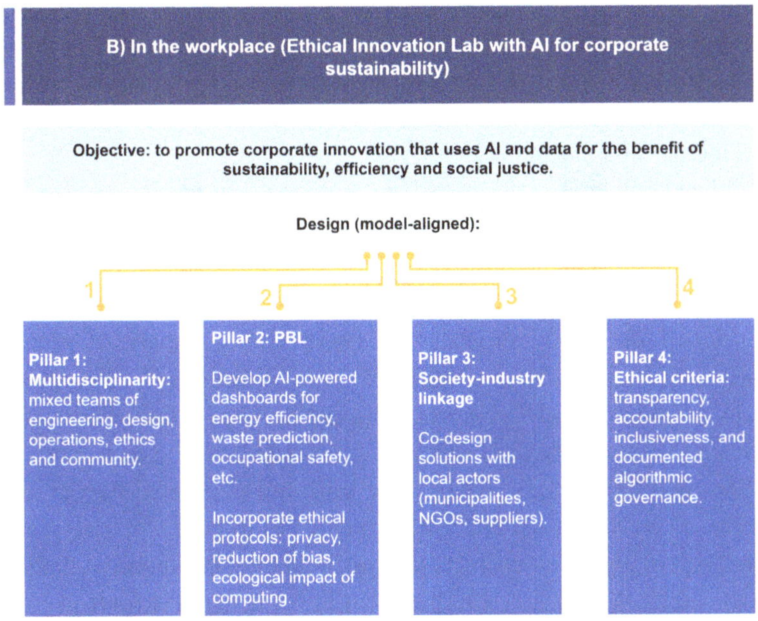

Similarly, Figure 5 presents an AI-based workplace Ethical Innovation Lab designed to support corporate sustainability through a model-aligned approach. Its main objective would be to promote innovation that leverages AI and data to improve sustainability, efficiency and social justice, and to be structured around the four interconnected pillars of the framework.

Torres-Rivera et al. (2025) demonstrate that the integration of AI and STEAM only makes sense when it is based on ethics, sustainability, and human agency. Its five theoretical bases and three operational pillars offer a replicable guide for schools, universities and organizations to move towards the principles of Society 5.0, in which technological innovation is oriented towards the common good, social justice and ecological transformation. This approach displaces instrumental digitalization and proposes an education focused on values, participation and shared responsibility.

4. AI AND EMERGING TECHNOLOGIES IN STEAM LEARNING AND WORK ENVIRONMENTS

The five theoretical frameworks examined in the previous section have the potential to be applied throughout life. The integration of emerging technologies can range from introducing a child to AI to using a plant worker to prevent waste and support factory restructuring, to an older person adopting a digital system for their healthcare. Frameworks function as design logics whose value only becomes fully apparent when tracked in practice. In this section, we exemplify documented applications reported in the literature to show how specific emerging technologies take shape in real STEAM learning and working environments, both in the educational and industrial spheres.

In school and university settings, AI and immersive technologies have been used to deliver personalized, interactive learning experiences that enhance engagement and motivation, while encouraging hands-on skill development through real-world simulations (Garg et al., 2025; Wang & Huang, 2025). These applications materialize the *think-do-do* and dimensions of customization emphasized by the frames. Makerspaces and digital fabrication, including 3D printing, offer a complementary pathway: by providing hands-on prototyping experiences across educational levels, they cultivate the creativity that various frameworks position as a driver of social change (Soomro et al., 2023). When these tools are integrated into problem- and challenge-based learning, evidence shows advances in both creativity and content knowledge, especially when projects address authentic community challenges (B. Huang et al., 2025; Weng et al., 2023), so that the dimension of *Real-world connections* A clear example is the use of collaborative virtual reality by elementary and middle school students to address authentic ocean-related problems by combining science, arts, and digital technologies, connecting schools, aquariums, and universities (Chappell et al., 2025).

These applications are not limited to resource-intensive environments; they are also emerging throughout Latin America, where cultural relevance and equity become central design criteria. Culturally grounded digital storytelling in informal STEM activities has been shown to increase Latino students' engagement and learning opportunities (Acosta & Haden, 2023), while community co-design with XR, IoT, and 3D printing exemplifies how emerging technologies can be anchored in local identity, ethical activism, and social transfer (Aguayo et al., 2023).

In our own institutional contexts in Mexico, comparable efforts have been documented: at Tecnológico de Monterrey, a dialogic STEAM intervention with high school students from marginalized communities in Monterrey fostered critical thinking while explicitly addressing equitable access to quality education during the pandemic (Fernández-Cárdenas & Santillán-Rosas, 2025), and STEAM has been examined as a framework for lifelong learning and complex problem-solving within Latin American open educational resource communities (Ramírez-Montoya et al., 2025).

At the university level, AI has also been used as an analytical tool to support competency-based education: a data-driven study at the same institution applied explainable machine learning to more than 300,000 assessments to predict the achievement of sustainability competencies in bioengineering programs, finding that academic and course-related variables were the strongest predictors, thus reinforcing the equity of the approach (Quintana-Zaez et al., 2025). This case illustrates how AI can inform pedagogical decision-making in higher education.

In professional and industrial settings, the same families of technologies are increasingly being employed in workforce training, simulation, and operational improvement. In Mexican manufacturing plants, the integration of machine learning and digital twins has produced measurable gains, including a 28.6% increase in production throughput and a 35.4% reduction in scrap rates, illustrating how data-driven tools transform real production environments (Flores Ramírez et al., 2026). Virtual reality frameworks, combined with AI, are also employed to create advanced simulation and training environments that support operational competitiveness and nearshoring opportunities (Ponce et al., 2024).

In the educational field, the Tec21 challenge-based learning model at Tecnológico de Monterrey engages students in real industry problems with companies acting as educational partners, and the introduction of 3D printing as a teaching tool exemplifies how emerging technologies are incorporated into engineering curricula to bridge the gap between training and the competencies demanded by Industry 4.0 (Lara-Prieto, Ruiz-Cantisani, et al., 2023; Monroy-Peláez et al., 2025). These cases show that the integration of emerging technologies spans the spectrum from the classroom to the plant, reinforcing the lifelong learning perspective developed in this chapter.

These examples are directly related to the development of job skills. The articulation of digital competencies for the Mexican industrial sector, structured in six key dimensions that integrate students' actual skills, teachers' pedagogical criteria, and employers' labor needs, illustrates how STEAM-informed frameworks can guide the transition from learning to professional application (Robles Gutiérrez et al., 2024, 2025). In these cases, the value of emerging technologies lies less in the tools themselves than in the pedagogical and ethical design that surrounds them, and they produce their greatest educational and professional impact not when they are adopted as ends in themselves, but when they are integrated into authentic challenges, co-designed with diverse actors and oriented towards relevance and equity in the real world.

5. COMPARISON OF THE STEAM APPROACH WITH OTHER SCHOOLS OF THOUGHT

In order to situate the STEAM approach in the contemporary theoretical landscape and justify its relevance to integrate emerging technologies, it is necessary to contrast it with other currents of thought that address the relationship between technology, learning and society. This comparison allows us to identify the conceptual and methodological particularities of STEAM and to delimit its contributions in relation to perspectives that privilege critical analysis, the production of digital knowledge or the socio-technical reorganization of work. It also provides an interpretive framework that clarifies why STEAM is a particularly well-suited approach for articulating creativity, interdisciplinarity, scientific rigor, and ethical considerations in educational and professional contexts.

There are conceptual alternatives to the STEAM approach, including the Digital Humanities framework. According to Coeckelbergh (2024), this perspective argues that technological development should be guided by humanistic principles and focus on valuing human dignity, capabilities, and agency. From this perspective, certain technological practices, especially those based on predictive algorithms and intensive automation, can displace human judgment, generate dynamics of technological dependency and produce undesirable social effects, such as the reproduction of biases or the risk of structural unemployment. It is also argued that digital representations of people and the social reorganization derived from algorithmic systems require critical review and regulatory reevaluation. Consequently, proponents of digital humanism propose regulating emerging technologies, revising curricula, and, in some cases, carrying out broader institutional transformations to ensure that technological practices align with democratic values and with the protection of human rights.

Although STEAM and Digital Humanities share an interest in the relationship between technology and culture, they respond to different traditions. STEAM expands the STEM framework by incorporating the arts to enhance creativity, design and interdisciplinary problem-solving, privileging prototyping as a means of linking knowledge with practice. Its main objective is to prepare students and professionals to face complex challenges through the balanced integration of scientific, technical, artistic and ethical skills.

Digital Humanities, on the other hand, focus on critically examining the sociocultural, political, and epistemological effects of the digital. In this approach, technology is not only used as a tool for creation, but also analyzed as an object of study, addressing issues such as algorithmic representation, data circulation, biases, cultural memory, and the formation of subjectivities in digitized environments. In this way, while STEAM promotes applied innovation, Digital Humanities offer analytical frameworks that allow us to understand and problematize the way in which technology transforms social practices.

Both approaches can be considered complementary. STEAM promotes creativity, design and interdisciplinary production, while Digital Humanities offers critical and ethical analyses that allow the social and cultural implications of such innovations to be assessed. The combination of both perspectives allows professionals to be trained capable of developing innovative technological solutions, while reflecting on their impacts, risks and regulatory dimensions.

While there are other relevant educational approaches, such as constructivism, critical pedagogies of technology, and socio-technical approaches to work, the STEAM framework is particularly relevant in today's technological landscape. Its strength lies in the integration of creativity, scientific rigour, problem-solving, critical thinking and a situated understanding of the human dimension. In addition, it articulates both technical adoption and ethical analysis through contextualized projects, interdisciplinary collaboration, and design processes, thus aligning technological innovation with social values, ethical considerations, and sustainability criteria.

5.1. Theoretical and Practical Implications of Integrating Emerging Technologies Using STEAM Frameworks

The integration of emerging technologies into STEAM frameworks not only transforms educational and professional practices, but also reconfigures the theoretical foundations that underpin teaching and learning in the digital age. After reviewing how STEAM frameworks enable the structured, ethical, contextualized, and interdisciplinary integration of technologies such as AI, AR, and digital fabrication, it is pertinent to examine the theoretical and practical implications of their application in real-world contexts. Therefore, this subsection synthesizes the available evidence showing how the adoption of emerging technologies in STEAM approaches influences contemporary theories of learning, modifies pedagogical dynamics, and poses operational demands for their effective implementation in education and work.

The literature shows that the integration of emerging technologies within STEAM frameworks has profound implications for both learning theory and its application in educational and work contexts. These frameworks reinforce and extend constructivist and inquiry theories, promoting interdisciplinary, project-based, and highly personalized environments that foster creativity, critical thinking, and problem-solving (Alkhatib, 2025; Brahimi & Sarirete, 2024). This evidence confirms the transition from a traditional STEM approach to a STEAM one, in which the arts act as catalysts for innovation in technical disciplines.

From a cognitivist perspective, Suresh Babu et al. (2025) y Leavy et al. (2023) indicate that environments powered by AI and immersive technology enable deeper conceptual understanding through student-centered adaptive experiences, supporting the development of personalized learning models based on intelligent digital tools. However, several studies also warn that the introduction of AI, AR, or other emerging technologies into STEAM frameworks poses new ethical and equity demands, highlighting the need to incorporate digital inclusion criteria and considerations on algorithmic bias (Castillo Galicia & Barajas Zúñiga, 2024). Torres-Rivera et al. (2025) They stress that sustainability and socio-technical perspectives should be explicitly incorporated into the design of these ecosystems, extending traditional theoretical frameworks towards human-centered models.

In pedagogical terms, Doss et al. (2024) demonstrate that the interdisciplinary and transdisciplinary nature of STEAM aligns with theories of situated learning, especially when projects are linked to real problems and implemented through cross-sectoral collaboration. This strengthens communities of practice and socially engaged learning. At the methodological level, advances in research-based, challenge-based and project-based approaches reflect a shift towards learner-centred methodologies, considered fundamental to the competencies required in the fourth and fifth industrial revolutions (Birdthistle et al., 2022; Mukuni, 2023; Tsarkos, 2024). Within this panorama, some STEAM frameworks constitute integrated models that articulate technology, pedagogy and ethics to create sustainable and scalable ecosystems.

In higher education, STEAM frameworks facilitate the incorporation of technology through interdisciplinary curricula and active learning strategies that reinforce creativity, employability, and relevance to the demands of emerging industries (Muslim, 2024). However, the practical implementation of these technologies comes with significant challenges. Some studies document that the adoption of STEAM requires sustained investment in infrastructure, teacher development and technical support, especially to close gaps in digital literacy and ensure adequate pedagogical preparation (Ferrada Ferrada & Márquez Triviño, 2025; Ulbrich et al., 2024). In a complementary way, alliances between industry and education are key to linking learning with real work needs and developing innovation and complex problem-solving skills (Doss et al., 2024; Julio et al., 2024)

Regarding regulatory considerations, the importance of establishing ethical frameworks and institutional policies that govern the responsible use of AI and other technologies and ensure transparency, equity and inclusion as conditions for sustainable adoption in education and work is underlined (Castillo Galicia & Barajas Zúñiga, 2024; Torres-Rivera et al., 2025). Technologies such as immersive and mixed reality improve motivation and interdisciplinary collaboration, although they require iterative processes to ensure contextual fit (Soroko, 2024). Similarly, digital and microlearning models, including ARs and MOOCs, can expand educational access and flexibility, offering scalable solutions in resource-limited contexts (Jatnkoon et al., 2025; Pandey, 2025).

Overall, the literature demonstrates that the integration of emerging technologies into STEAM frameworks not only expands pedagogical and methodological possibilities, but also requires a critical reconsideration of the theoretical, ethical, and operational models that underpin training processes. Technologies enable interdisciplinary, personalized, project- or challenge-based learning, but their incorporation requires infrastructure, ethical policies, teacher professional development, and active collaboration with industry. These implications confirm that STEAM constitutes a robust approach to articulate creativity, technical rigour and social responsibility in educational and work environments, and underline its coherence and orientation towards sustainable, contextualized and human-centered adoption.

5.2. Challenges and Opportunities of the STEAM Framework

The implementation of STEAM in Latin America faces structural and conceptual challenges that limit its adoption and sustainability. In addition to digital divides, lack of resources and educational inequalities, especially visible in rural areas, where access to technological infrastructure and teacher training is limited, there is still resistance to change in institutions that maintain traditional structures and are wary of interdisciplinary pedagogical approaches. These obstacles coincide with those pointed out by Belbase et al. (2022), who highlight that STEAM integration also faces criticism derived from conceptual, pedagogical and institutional limitations: lack of clarity on what and how to integrate, curricular confusion, epistemological tensions between disciplines and poor teacher preparation to design and implement transdisciplinary experiences. Logistical challenges also persist, such as lack of resources, insufficient space and limited time for collaboration between teaching teams, as well as divergent perceptions about the role of the arts in relation to STEM disciplines. Although there is general recognition of the formative potential of STEAM, empirical evidence of its impact remains limited, raising doubts about its efficacy and the risk of weakening mathematical and scientific rigor when integration is not properly implemented. This highlights the need for profound transformations in teacher education, institutional cultures, and support systems to implement STEAM in a coherent and sustainable manner.

Despite this panorama, relevant opportunities are also emerging. STEAM has the potential to become an engine of inclusion, equity, and skills development for the future, equipping students and workers with the capabilities to participate in economies driven by AI, automation, and social innovation. Its interdisciplinary approach promotes creativity, critical thinking and complex problem-solving, essential skills for Education 4.0 and Industry 5.0. Similarly, the articulation of public policies, public-private partnerships, collaboration with the productive sector, and new models of teacher training can accelerate their adoption and strengthen more sustainable learning ecosystems. In this context, strategies such as frugal innovation offer additional opportunities: when implemented in disadvantaged or underrepresented communities, they allow for the development of relevant and accessible technological solutions, helping to close historical gaps and integrate emerging technologies more equitably.

Reducing these inequalities requires deliberate institutional strategies rather than the mere acquisition of advanced technologies. In contexts with limited resources, a first lever is shared infrastructure: sharing access to expensive equipment through university labs, public research centers, and community makerspaces allows students and small organizations to interact with technologies they could not afford individually (Soomro et al., 2023). Adopting open, interoperable architectures and low-cost or offline tools that are able to connect offline further lowers barriers to entry and prevents technology lock-in, while microlearning formats, MOOCs, and mixed reality resources can expand access and educational flexibility where connectivity and budgets are limited (Jatnkoon et al., 2025; Pandey, 2025). Crucially, equitable access should be treated as a democratic right and incorporated into design from the outset through culturally appropriate and sustainably funded models, co-designed with diverse actors, rather than being subsequently adapted (Correa et al., 2023; Gallegos-Rejas et al., 2023).

Equally important is investing in the humane and collaborative conditions that enable equitable adoption of technology. Sustained professional development of teachers (including scalable and low-cost models, such as asynchronous train-the-trainer programs) is essential to prevent advanced tools from widening the gap between resourced and under-resourced institutions (Ferrada Ferrada & Márquez Triviño, 2025; Ulbrich et al., 2024). Public-private partnerships, dual learning schemes and multi-sector alliances can spread the costs and risks of implementation, link learning to real labour needs and strengthen regional innovation ecosystems. Well-resourced institutions can also invest directly in those who lack such capacity, collaborating with underserved and underrepresented sectors (older adults, rural schools, and peri-urban communities) and treating them as collaborative case studies that generate situated and mutually beneficial knowledge, rather than offering one-way help. In parallel, education can be delivered through widely accessible technologies and social media platforms, as illustrated by science communication initiatives, which extend learning opportunities beyond the walls of formal institutions at minimal cost to students. Through these mechanisms, institutions can move from simply introducing advanced technologies to integrating them in ways that actively reduce, rather than reproduce, existing inequalities.

6. CONCLUSION

The research underscores STEAM as a compelling and effective framework for integrating emerging technologies (such as AI, AR/VR, and 3D printing) into higher education and lifelong learning. Across a variety of disciplines, STEAM approaches employ interdisciplinary, project-based, and inquiry-based pedagogies that foster 21st-century skills such as creativity, critical thinking, collaboration, and problem-solving, while AI and immersive technologies bring transformative potential for adaptive and personalized learning that supports inclusion and motivation. However, it also reveals persistent barriers to equitable implementation: insufficient teacher training; infrastructure and resource constraints that deepen digital divides; ethical considerations on AI, algorithmic bias, data privacy and transparency, which remain insufficiently operationalized; and curricula marked by congestion and weak standardization. Collaboration across industry, an important factor in aligning learning with workforce needs, remains uneven and often implicit, and robust longitudinal evidence of sustained impacts on employability and career readiness remains scarce.

In essence, STEAM integration is best understood as the cultivation of an ecosystem of digital competencies whose returns are simultaneously educational, social, and economic: as a Perales and Aróstegui (2024) They argue, the STEAM movement is inseparable from preparing citizens for the knowledge economy and the digital revolution. For these returns to be equitable rather than concentrated, this ecosystem must deliberately reach underrepresented and underserved communities (technical workers, older adults, indigenous populations, women in engineering and other STEM fields, and rural or depopulated areas, among them) so that digital capacity becomes a shared asset and not a new axis of exclusion.

Place-based STEAM approaches that link learning to local territory and identity have proven effective in engaging rural and historically disadvantaged communities, helping to counter inequalities such as teacher shortages and gender gaps (Gavari-Starkie et al., 2022); some initiatives show how project-based STEAM, tailored to the needs of each community, can reach urban, rural, border and indigenous populations throughout Latin America (Avendano-Uribe et al., 2022); and evidence from Mexico indicates that integrating STEAM models and visible female role models in engineering schools can help expand women's enrollment and retention in fields where they remain underrepresented (Oliveros, 2019).

For teachers, the priority is to move beyond the adoption of tools towards sustained professional development focused on interdisciplinary and ethically grounded STEAM pedagogies; Scalable, low-cost models, asynchronous trainer training schemes, and shared open resources can build this capability even when budgets are limited (Ferrada Ferrada & Márquez Triviño, 2025; Ulbrich et al., 2024). Above all, teachers need a genuine understanding of these frameworks for AI to be integrated through the pedagogical dimension of teaching, woven into interdisciplinary and meaningful learning experiences, rather than added as a technical add-on.

Relatedly, the five frameworks described in this chapter are not prescriptive templates to be applied uniformly: teachers can use their descriptions to adapt them to the specific context in which they work, combine elements with each other, or design an entirely new framework tailored to their students, disciplines, and local realities. Systematic evidence on prevailing pedagogical approaches, teaching practices, and resources already used in the country can further inform these decisions (Veytia Bucheli & Contreras Fuentes, 2025).

For universities, the frameworks aim at a curricular redesign that reduces congestion and standardizes STEAM competencies, institutionalizing industry partnerships as explicit and structured collaborations rather than informal contacts, as in challenge-based models where companies act as educational partners (Lara-Prieto, Prieto-Hinojosa, et al., 2023; Monroy-Peláez et al., 2025), bundling expensive infrastructure through shared labs and community makermaker spaces to expand access (Soomro et al., 2023), and the use of STEAM and female models in engineering schools to close persistent gender gaps (Ortiz-Martínez et al., 2023).

For industry and employers, investing in the continuous improvement and retraining of the workforce, including technical staff and workers from disadvantaged sectors, is not only a matter of inclusion, but also a strong competitiveness strategy, as stronger digital and interdisciplinary skills translate directly into productivity, adaptability and capacity for innovation within companies. For policymakers, the analysis makes the case for treating equitable connectivity and infrastructure as a democratic right built in from the ground up (Correa et al., 2023; Gallegos-Rejas et al., 2023), for funding multi-sectoral partnerships, place-based programs, and frugal innovation strategies that reach rural, depopulated, and underrepresented communities (Avendano-Uribe et al., 2022; Gavari-Starkie et al., 2022), and for establishing operational ethical frameworks governing algorithmic bias, data privacy, and transparency in educational AI (Castillo Galicia & Barajas Zúñiga, 2024; Torres-Rivera et al., 2025).

Through these actors, inter-institutional collaboration becomes a lever. Promoting open inter-institutional meetings, convening public and private initiatives around shared STEAM and digital skills agendas can demonstrate that the region, and Mexico in particular, has the collective capacity to design winning and internationally competitive proposals together, rather than isolation; The multi-actor, public-private, and diaspora networks behind the programs illustrate the scope of this type of articulation (Avendano-Uribe et al., 2022). These decisions, in turn, should be informed by future large-scale longitudinal studies assessing the effectiveness and scalability of technology-rich STEAM frameworks, with particular attention to ethics, equity, and accessibility.

In summary, STEAM transcends the methodological field and consolidates itself as a comprehensive strategy for digital transformation in education and work, integrating science, technology, engineering, arts and mathematics around innovation and human dimensions. Its interdisciplinary nature allows for the ethical, creative and effective integration of emerging technologies, as well as the development of skills to face the economic, social and environmental challenges of the 21st century. For this potential to be realized, educational institutions, the productive sector, and governments must strengthen collaboration through the policies, partnerships, and ecosystems described above. Thus proposed, STEAM represents a unique opportunity to build more inclusive, innovative and sustainable societies in Latin America, capable of taking advantage of digitalization not only to grow, but also to transform their future with equity and responsibility.

REFERENCES

Acevedo Carrillo, M., Cabezas Torres, N. M., La Serna La Rosa, P. A., & Araujo Rossel, S. A. (2026). Desafíos y oportunidades de la inteligencia artificial en la educación superior latinoamericana: Una revisión sistemática de la literatura. *Revista InveCom*, *6*(1). Advance online publication. DOI: 10.5281/zenodo.15508755

Acosta, D. I., & Haden, C. A. (2023). Supporting Latine children's informal engineering learning through tinkering and oral storytelling. *Developmental Psychology*, *59*(12), 2342–2355. DOI: 10.1037/dev0001648

Adel, A. (2024). The convergence of intelligent tutoring, robotics, and IoT in smart education for the transition from Industry 4.0 to 5.0. *Smart Cities*, *7*(1), 325–369. DOI: 10.3390/smartcities7010014

Aguayo, C., Videla, R., López-Cortés, F., Rossel, S., & Ibacache, C. (2023). Ethical enactivism for smart and inclusive STEAM learning design. *Heliyon*, *9*(9), e19205. DOI: 10.1016/j.heliyon.2023.e19205

Alkhatib, O. J. (2025). STEAM integration and engineering: Lessons from transformative approaches. In Behera, S. K., Sorayyaei Azar, A., Curle, S., & Dials, J. G. (Eds.), *Transformative approaches to STEAM integration in modern education* (pp. 345–374). IGI Global., DOI: 10.4018/979-8-3693-7408-5.ch015

Allen, L. K., & Kendeou, P. (2024). ED-AI Lit: An Interdisciplinary Framework for AI Literacy in Education. *Policy Insights from the Behavioral and Brain Sciences*, *11*(1), 3–10. DOI: 10.1177/23727322231220339

Avendano-Uribe, B. E., Lombana-Bermudez, A., Flórez, L. V., Chaparro, E., Hernandez-Morales, A. C., Archbold, J., Buitrago-Casas, J. C., & Porras, A. M. (2022). Engaging Scientific Diasporas in STEAM Education: The Case of Science Clubs Colombia. *Frontiers in Research Metrics and Analytics*, *7*, 898167. Advance online publication. DOI: 10.3389/frma.2022.898167

Bailey, D. E. (2022). Emerging Technologies at Work: Policy Ideas to Address Negative Consequences for Work, Workers, and Society. *Industrial & Labor Relations Review*, *75*(3), 527–551. DOI: 10.1177/00197939221076747

Barnes, M., Lafferty, K., & Li, B. (2024). Assessing twenty-first century competencies: Can students lead and facilitate the co-construction process? *Educational Review*, *76*(4), 691–709. DOI: 10.1080/00131911.2022.2142524

Bascopé, M., Reiss, K., Morales, M., Robles, C., Reyes, P., Duque, M. I., & Andrade, J. C. (2020). Latin American STEM policy: A review of recent initiatives on STEM education in four Latin American countries. In Johnson, C. C., Mohr-Schroeder, N. J., Moore, T. J., & English, L. D. (Eds.), *Handbook of research on STEM education* (pp. 443–458). Routledge., https://doi.org/https://doi.org/10.4324/9780429021381-41 DOI: 10.4324/9780429021381-41

Basilotta-Gómez-Pablos, V., Matarranz, M., Casado-Aranda, L.-A., & Otto, A. (2022). Teachers' digital competencies in higher education: A systematic literature review. *International Journal of Educational Technology in Higher Education, 19*(1), 8. DOI: 10.1186/s41239-021-00312-8

Belbase, S., Mainali, B. R., Kasemsukpipat, W., Tairab, H., Gochoo, M., & Jarrah, A. (2022). At the dawn of science, technology, engineering, arts, and mathematics (STEAM) education: Prospects, priorities, processes, and problems. *International Journal of Mathematical Education in Science and Technology, 53*(11), 2919–2955. DOI: 10.1080/0020739X.2021.1922943

Birdthistle, N., Riverola, C., Boorer, L., & Ekberg, S. (2022). Empowering STEAM academics to adopt enterprise pedagogies. In Henry, C., Gabriel, B. F. C. C., Sailer, K., Bernadó-Mansilla, E., & Lahikainen, K. (Eds.), *Strategies for the creation and maintenance of entrepreneurial universities* (pp. 142–167). IGI Global., DOI: 10.4018/978-1-7998-7456-0.ch007

Bokhari, H., & Awuni, E. T. (2024). Digital inequalities in North Africa: Examining employment and socioeconomic well-being in Morocco and Tunisia. *Convergence (London), 30*(3), 1149–1169. DOI: 10.1177/13548565231209673

Borg Preca, C., Baldacchino, L., Briguglio, M., & Mangion, M. (2023). Are STEM Students Creative Thinkers? *Journal of Intelligence, 11*(6), 106. DOI: 10.3390/jintelligence11060106

Brahimi, T., & Sarirete, A. (2024). Transforming learning in STEAM: How AI tools and language models catalyze educational advancement. In Baroudi, S., & Lytras, M. D. (Eds.), *Transformative leadership and sustainable innovation in education: Interdisciplinary perspectives* (pp. 39–58). Emerald Publishing Limited., DOI: 10.1108/978-1-83753-536-120241004

Calder, B. J., He, S., & Sternthal, B. (2023). Using theoretical frameworks in behavioral research. *Journal of Business Research, 161*, 113758. DOI: 10.1016/j.jbusres.2023.113758

Castillo Galicia, A. M., & Barajas Zúñiga, Z. (2024). Integrando inteligencia artificial en la capacitación técnica para la empresa ART. *DIDAC*, (84), 75–83. DOI: 10.48102/didac.2024..84_JUL-DIC.214

Chappell, K., Hetherington, L., Juillard, S., Aguirre, C., & Duca, E. (2025). A framework for effective STEAM education: Pedagogy for responding to wicked problems. *International Journal of Educational Research Open*, *9*, 100474. DOI: 10.1016/j.ijedro.2025.100474

Coeckelbergh, M. (2024). What is digital humanism? A conceptual analysis and an argument for a more critical and political digital (post)humanism. *Journal of Responsible Technology*, *17*, 100073. DOI: 10.1016/j.jrt.2023.100073

Correa, J., Ulloa-Leon, F., Vergara-Perucich, F., Aguirre-Nuñez, C., & Truffello, R. (2023). Infrastructural inequality: Exploring the emergence of digital classes in the Metropolitan Area of Santiago, Chile. *Bulletin of Geography. Socio-Economic Series*, (62), 107–122. DOI: 10.12775/bgss-2023-0037

Costantino, T. (2018). STEAM by another name: Transdisciplinary practice in art and design education. *Arts Education Policy Review*, *119*(2), 100–106. DOI: 10.1080/10632913.2017.1292973

Cummings, D., Cheeks, L., & Robinson, R. (2018). Culturally-Centric Outreach and Engagement for Underserved Groups in STEM. *Proceedings of the 49th ACM Technical Symposium on Computer Science Education, SIGCSE '18*, 447–452. DOI: 10.1145/3159450.3159565

Decorte, B., & Vlieghe, J. (2024). Towards a pedagogical conception of imagination in STEAM education. *Ethics and Education*, *19*(2), 218–232. DOI: 10.1080/17449642.2024.2361560

Đorđević, B., Zbiljić, S. M., & Radosavljević, M. (2025). Impact of the digital skills on employability: Cross-sectional analysis. *Economies (Basel)*, *13*(7), 196. Advance online publication. DOI: 10.3390/economies13070196

Doss, T. P., Poursharif, G., Price, H., & Buck, L. (2024). Education for Industry 5.0 and ESD: Co-creation of engineering design challenges with industry. In *2024 IEEE Global Engineering Education Conference (EDUCON)* (pp. 1–6). IEEE. DOI: 10.1109/EDUCON60312.2024.10578850

Engelman, S., Magerko, B., McKlin, T., Miller, M., Edwards, D., & Freeman, J. (2017). Creativity in authentic STEAM education with EarSketch. In *Proceedings of the 2017 ACM SIGCSE Technical Symposium on Computer Science Education* (pp. 183–188). Association for Computing Machinery. DOI: 10.1145/3017680.3017763

Fernández-Cárdenas, J. M., & Santillán-Rosas, I. M. (2025). Learning Critical Thinking Through Dialogic STEAM Educational Activities: A Case of High School Students in Northeastern Mexico During Pandemic Times. *SAGE Open, 15*(4), 21582440251388756. DOI: 10.1177/21582440251388756

Ferrada Ferrada, C., & Márquez Triviño, C. (2025). Explorando el impacto de las tecnologías emergentes en la educación STE(A)M: Un análisis bibliométrico de las publicaciones en la base de datos Scopus. *Ducere: Revista de Investigación Educativa, 4*(1), e202503. DOI: 10.61303/2735668X.v4i1.73

Flores Ramírez, A., Bradley, R., Andrade Flores, L., Guerrero Carrillo, A., González-Escamilla, A., Ponce, P., Ramírez-Cedillo, E., & Anthony, B. W. (2026). Immersive cognitive factory twin: Optimizing industry 5.0 with an integrated VR, ML, and LLM framework. In *Production and Manufacturing Research* (Vol. 14, Issue 1). DOI: 10.1080/21693277.2026.2664909

Forcael, E., Garcés, G., & Orozco, F. (2022). Relationship Between Professional Competencies Required by Engineering Students According to ABET and CDIO and Teaching–Learning Techniques. *IEEE Transactions on Education, 65*(1), 46–55. DOI: 10.1109/TE.2021.3086766

Gallegos-Rejas, V. M., Thomas, E. E., Kelly, J. T., & Smith, A. C. (2023). A multi-stakeholder approach is needed to reduce the digital divide and encourage equitable access to telehealth. *Journal of Telemedicine and Telecare, 29*(1), 73–78. DOI: 10.1177/1357633X221107995

García-Aranda, C., Molina-García, A., & Balsera, M. del C. M., Martínez-Cuevas, S., Hurtado, E. R., Rodríguez, J. P., Rodríguez-Chueca, J., Fungairiño, Y. T., Hernández, M. R., Miquel, M. G., Moreno, F. I. D., Gómez, E. J. G., García-Soto, M. del M. de la F., Giannakis, S., González, I. del C., Núñez, M. M., Contreras, F. B., & García, P. C. I. (2020). Creativity and innovation skills in university STEM education: The CHET Project approach. In *Sixth International Conference on Higher Education Advances* (pp. 679–687). Universitat Politècnica de València. DOI: 10.4995/HEAd20.2020.11127

Garg, N., Kaur, A., Ahmad, F., & Dutta, R. (2025). Augmenting Education: The Transformative Power of AR, AI, and Emerging Technologies. *Human Behavior and Emerging Technologies, 2025*(1), 5681184. DOI: 10.1155/hbe2/5681184

Gavari-Starkie, E., Espinosa-Gutiérrez, P.-T., & Lucini-Baquero, C. (2022). Sustainability through STEM and STEAM Education Creating Links with the Land for the Improvement of the Rural World. *Land (Basel), 11*(10), 1869. DOI: 10.3390/land11101869

Gavari-Starkie, E., Espinosa-Gutiérrez, P.-T., Lucini-Baquero, C., & Pastrana-Huguet, J. (2024). Importance of STEM and STEAM Education for Improvement of the Land in the RURAL Environment: Examples in Latin America. *Land (Basel)*, *13*(3), 274. DOI: 10.3390/land13030274

Goedhart, N. S., Verdonk, P., & Dedding, C. (2022). "Never good enough." A situated understanding of the impact of digitalization on citizens living in a low socioeconomic position. *Policy and Internet*, *14*(4), 824–844. DOI: 10.1002/poi3.315

Groen, A. J., & Walsh, S. T. (2013). Introduction to the Field of Emerging Technology Management. *Creativity and Innovation Management*, *22*(1), 1–5. DOI: 10.1111/caim.12019

Gu, X., Tong, D., Shi, P., Zou, Y., Yuan, H., Chen, C., & Zhao, G. (2023). Incorporating STEAM activities into creativity training in higher education. *Thinking Skills and Creativity*, *50*, 101395. DOI: 10.1016/j.tsc.2023.101395

Guyotte, K., Sochacka, N., Costantino, T., Kellam, N., & Walther, J. (2015). Collaborative Creativity in STEAM: Narratives of Art Education Students' Experiences in Transdisciplinary Spaces. *International Journal of Education & the Arts*, *16*(15), 1–38. DOI: 10.59236/ijea16n15

Haoran, Z. (2025). Bridging Digital Divide: How the Digital Economy Affects Health Care in Developed and Developing Nations. *World Medical & Health Policy*, *17*(4), 767–774. DOI: 10.1002/wmh3.70040

Huang, B., Jong, M. S.-Y., Tsai, C.-C., & Shang, J. (2025). Unlocking students' creative potential in designing technological-enriched design solutions. *Journal of Research on Technology in Education*, *57*(5), 1044–1060. DOI: 10.1080/15391523.2024.2342915

Huang, Z., Fu, X., & Zhao, J. (2025). Research on AIGC-Integrated Design Education for Sustainable Teaching: An Empirical Analysis Based on the TAM and TPACK Models. *Sustainability (Basel)*, *17*(12), 5497. DOI: 10.3390/su17125497

Jatnkoon, T., Jantakun, K., Jantakun, T., & Pasmala, R. (2025). STEAM Microlearning Model based on Massive Open Online Courses with Augmented Reality Technology to enhance Creativity and Innovation. *Higher Education Studies*, *15*(2), 321. DOI: 10.5539/hes.v15n2p321

Ji, D., & She, H. (2026). Digital divide revisited during and beyond COVID-19. *Media Culture & Society*, *48*(1), 191–207. DOI: 10.1177/01634437251363779

Johnson-Green, E., Lee, C., & Flannery, M. (2020). A Musical Perspective on STEM: Evaluating the EcoSonic Playground Project from a Co-Equal STEAM Integration Standpoint. *International Journal of Education & the Arts, 21*(14). https://doi.org/doi.org/10.26209/ijea21n14

Jora, M. B., & Basnet, H. B. (2025). ICT Integration in the 21st Century's Classroom Teaching and Learning. *Rupantaran: A Multidisciplinary Journal, 9*, 9–20. (Education). DOI: 10.3126/rupantaran.v9i01.89333

Julio, Y. R., Viloria-Núñez, C., Galindo-Jaramillo, J.-F., Mangones, A. P., & Correa, C. C. R. (2024). Innovation Strategies for Training Management with STEAM, IoT, and AI through Design Thinking. *2024 IEEE Eighth Ecuador Technical Chapters Meeting (ETCM)*, 1–6. DOI: 10.1109/ETCM63562.2024.10746011

Juškevičienė, A., Dagienė, V., & Dolgopolovas, V. (2021). Integrated activities in STEM environment: Methodology and implementation practice. *Computer Applications in Engineering Education, 29*(1), 209–228. DOI: 10.1002/cae.22324

Korostelina, K. V., & Barrett, J. (2023). Bridging the digital divide for Native American tribes: Roadblocks to broadband and community resilience. *Policy and Internet, 15*(3), 306–326. DOI: 10.1002/poi3.339

Kotis, K., Angoura, E., & Lyngri, E.-I. (2025). Emerging Technologies in Smart Libraries for Visually Impaired People: Challenges and Design Considerations. *Journal on Computing and Cultural Heritage, 18*(3), 1–37. DOI: 10.1145/3727965

Lara-Prieto, V., Prieto-Hinojosa, A. I., Galindo-Cota, E., Galvan, J. A., & Swain-Oropeza, R. (2023). Challenge-Based Learning and the Industry Liaison as Educational Partners. In *2023 IEEE IFEES World Engineering Education Forum and Global Engineering Deans Council: Convergence for a Better World: A Call to Action, WEEF-GEDC 2023—Proceedings*. DOI: 10.1109/WEEF-GEDC59520.2023.10344279

Lara-Prieto, V., Ruiz-Cantisani, M. I., Arrambide-Leal, E. J., de la Cruz-Hinojosa, J., Mojica, M., Rivas-Pimentel, J. R., & Membrillo-Hernández, J. (2023). Challenge-Based Learning Strategies Using Technological Innovations in Industrial, Mechanical and Mechatronics Engineering Programs. *International Journal of Instruction, 16*(1), 1. DOI: 10.29333/iji.2023.16115a

Le Blanc, P., Ulfert, A.-S., Peeters, M., Rispens, S., & Scherer, S. (2024). How emerging technologies shape the future of work. *European Journal of Work and Organizational Psychology, 33*(2), 115–119. DOI: 10.1080/1359432X.2024.2324937

Leavy, A., Dick, L., Meletiou-Mavrotheris, M., Paparistodemou, E., & Stylianou, E. (2023). The prevalence and use of emerging technologies in STEAM education: A systematic review of the literature. *Journal of Computer Assisted Learning*, *39*(4), 1061–1082. DOI: 10.1111/jcal.12806

Li, L. (2024). Reskilling and Upskilling the Future-ready Workforce for Industry 4.0 and Beyond. *Information Systems Frontiers*, *26*(5), 1697–1712. DOI: 10.1007/s10796-022-10308-y

Mishra, P., Terry, C. A., & Henriksen, D.Deep-Play Research Group. (2013). Square Peg, Round Hole, Good Engineering. *TechTrends*, *57*(2), 22–25. DOI: 10.1007/s11528-013-0641-5

Monroy-Peláez, Á. R., Juarez-Acosta, I., Miralrio, A., & Montes de Oca, S. (2025). Implementation of 3D printing as a didactic tool for problem solving of engineering systems and devices. In *Frontiers in Education* (Vol. 10). DOI: 10.3389/feduc.2025.1541586

Moraes, E. B., Kipper, L. M., Hackenhaar Kellermann, A. C., Austria, L., Leivas, P., Moraes, J. A. R., & Witczak, M. (2023). Integration of Industry 4.0 technologies with Education 4.0: Advantages for improvements in learning. *Interactive Technology and Smart Education*, *20*(2), 271–287. DOI: 10.1108/ITSE-11-2021-0201

Mukuni, J. (2023). Behold the Fourth Industrial Revolution and How to Keep Pace with Workplace Competencies in an Ever-Changing World of Work! In El-Farr, H. (Ed.), *The Changing Landscape of Workplace and Workforce*. IntechOpen., DOI: 10.5772/intechopen.1002648

Muslim, R. (2024). STEAM-Based Learning for Mechanical Engineering. *Journal of Mathematics and Mathematics Education*, *13*(2), 221. DOI: 10.20961/jmme.v13i2.91848

Myburgh, S., & Tammaro, A. M. (2013). Constructing a theoretical framework. In *Exploring Education for Digital Librarians* (pp. 133–172). Chandos Publishing., DOI: 10.1016/B978-1-84334-659-3.50007-4

Nieto-Miguel, I., Sanz-Camarero, R., Ortiz-Revilla, J., & Greca, I. M. (2023). La Potencialidad de la Educación STEAM Integrada y el Papel del Arte para la Internacionalización de la Formación Docente. *Journal of International Students*, *13*(S1). Advance online publication. DOI: 10.32674/jis.v13iS1.6600

Nnadi, L. C., Ding, D., Godwin-Ojukwu, E. D., Watanobe, Y., & Naruse, K. (2025). Strategic Human Resource Development for Emerging Technologies: A Scoping Review in ICT, Robotics, Data Science, and CPS. *IEEE Access : Practical Innovations, Open Solutions, 13*, 133994–134013. DOI: 10.1109/ACCESS.2025.3592301

Oberländer, M., Beinicke, A., & Bipp, T. (2020). Digital competencies: A review of the literature and applications in the workplace. *Computers & Education, 146*, 103752. DOI: 10.1016/j.compedu.2019.103752

Oh, S., PhD, DiNitto, D. M., PhD, & Powers, D. A., PhD. (. (2020). Spillover Effects of Job Skills Training on Substance Misuse Among Low-Income Youths With Employment Barriers: A Longitudinal Cohort Study. *American Journal of Public Health, 110*(6), 900–906. *ProQuest One Academic*, (2404088206). Advance online publication. DOI: 10.2105/AJPH.2020.305631

Oliveros, M. A. (2019). STEAM como herramienta para fomentar los estudios de ingeniería. *Revista Científica (Maracaibo), 35*(2), 158–166.

Oliveros Ruiz, M. A. (2021). Panorama of teaching in higher education institutions under science, technology, engineering and mathematics (STEM) programs. *Revista Científica (Maracaibo), 40*(1), 2–12. DOI: 10.14483/23448350.16764

Ortiz-Martínez, G., Vázquez-Villegas, P., Ruiz-Cantisani, M. I., Delgado-Fabián, M., Conejo-Márquez, D. A., & Membrillo-Hernández, J. (2023). Analysis of the retention of women in higher education STEM programs. *Humanities & Social Sciences Communications, 10*(1), 101. DOI: 10.1057/s41599-023-01588-z

Pandey, P. (2025). Role of Digital Technology for Advancing STEAM Learning. In Behera, S. K., Sorayyaei Azar, A., Curle, S., & Dials, J. G. (Eds.), (pp. 159–182). Advances in Educational Technologies and Instructional Design. IGI Global., DOI: 10.4018/979-8-3693-7408-5.ch007

Paśko, Ł., Mądziel, M., Stadnicka, D., Dec, G., Carreras-Coch, A., Solé-Beteta, X., Pappa, L., Stylios, C., Mazzei, D., & Atzeni, D. (2022). Plan and Develop Advanced Knowledge and Skills for Future Industrial Employees in the Field of Artificial Intelligence, Internet of Things and Edge Computing. *Sustainability (Basel), 14*(6), 3312. DOI: 10.3390/su14063312

Pedrosa de Souza, D., & Sivini Ferreira, H. (2025). Potentials of the Science, Technology, Engineering, Arts and Mathematics (STEAM) education for gender inclusion in science: A systematic literature review. *Revista Electrónica de Enseñanza de las Ciencias, 24*(1), 186.

Perales, F. J., & Aróstegui, J. L. (2024). The STEAM approach: Implementation and educational, social and economic consequences. *Arts Education Policy Review, 125*(2), 59–67. DOI: 10.1080/10632913.2021.1974997

Perignat, E., & Katz-Buonincontro, J. (2018). From STEM to STEAM: Using Brain-Compatible Strategies to Integrate the Arts: by David A. Sousa and Tom Pilecki. (2013). Thousand Oaks, CA: Sage. 280 pp. *Arts Education Policy Review, 119*(2), 107–110. DOI: 10.1080/10632913.2017.1300970

Pollard, V., Hains-Wesson, R., & Young, K. (2018). Creative teaching in STEM. *Teaching in Higher Education, 23*(2), 178–193. DOI: 10.1080/13562517.2017.1379487

Ponce, P., Anthony, B., Bradley, R., Maldonado-Romo, J., Méndez, J. I., Montesinos, L., & Molina, A. (2024). Developing a virtual reality and AI-based framework for advanced digital manufacturing and nearshoring opportunities in Mexico. *Scientific Reports, 14*(1), 11214. DOI: 10.1038/s41598-024-61514-4

Quintana-Zaez, J. C., Vázquez-Villegas, P., & Valdes-Ramirez, D. (2025). Identifying Key Predictors of Students' Competency Achievement Using Machine Learning Models: A Bioengineering Case Study. *IEEE Access : Practical Innovations, Open Solutions, 13*, 168855–168877. DOI: 10.1109/ACCESS.2025.3613250

Ramírez-Montoya, M.-S., Zavala, G., Patiño, A., & Ibarra-Vázquez, G. (2025). STEAM Education of the Future in the Framework of Complexity: Case of Good Practice in OER LATAM Community. *Academic Journal of Interdisciplinary Studies, 14*(4), 7. DOI: 10.36941/ajis-2025-0054

Robles Gutiérrez, M. P., Mendoza Diaz, N. V., Del Razo Robles, L. E., Dominguez-Ramirez, O. A., & Guerrero Azpeitia, L. A. G. (2025). *Identification of Digital Competencies to Strengthen the Graduation Profile of Students Close to Graduation From a Polytechnic University in Central Mexico*. 1–8. DOI: 10.1109/FIE63693.2025.11328313

Robles Gutiérrez, M. P., Mendoza Diaz, N. V., Del Razo Robles, L. E., & Maria Jimenez Romero, A. (2024). WIP:Perceptions of Use and Requirements for Digital Competencies of Engineers According to Employers in Central Mexico. *2024 IEEE Frontiers in Education Conference (FIE)*, 1–8. DOI: 10.1109/FIE61694.2024.10893060

Romano, A. L., Henrique Dos Santos, C., Koch, C., Lourenço Ubeda, C., Rorato Fogaça, D., César Almada Santos, F., & Freitas, V. (2025). Startups in the Era of Industry 4.0 and 5.0: Technologies, Decisions, Framing, and Competences. *IEEE Access : Practical Innovations, Open Solutions, 13*, 187042–187057. DOI: 10.1109/ACCESS.2025.3627113

Ryalat, M., Franco, E., Elmoaqet, H., Almtireen, N., & Al-Refai, G. (2024). The Integration of Advanced Mechatronic Systems into Industry 4.0 for Smart Manufacturing. *Sustainability (Basel), 16*(19), 8504. DOI: 10.3390/su16198504

Salas-Pilco, S. Z. (2024). K-12 STEAM Education in Latin America: A Systematic Review. *2024 IEEE World Engineering Education Conference (EDUNINE)*, 1–6. DOI: 10.1109/EDUNINE60625.2024.10500534

Schirpke, U., Ghermandi, A., Sinclair, M., Van Berkel, D., Fox, N., Vargas, L., & Willemen, L. (2023). Emerging technologies for assessing ecosystem services: A synthesis of opportunities and challenges. *Ecosystem Services*, *63*, 101558. DOI: 10.1016/j.ecoser.2023.101558

Serrano Corkin, D. M., Ekmekci, A., & Fisher, A. (2020). Integrating Culture, Art, Geometry, and Coding to Enhance Computer Science Motivation Among Underrepresented Minoritized High School Students. *The Urban Review*, *52*(5), 950–969. DOI: 10.1007/s11256-020-00586-8

Shabalala, N. P. (2025). Global citizenship education as a strategy for social, justice and identity: Achieving balance for meaningful social impact. *Globalisation, Societies and Education*, *0*(0), 1–13. DOI: 10.1080/14767724.2025.2537371

Singh, A., Madaan, G., Hr, S., & Kumar, A. (2023). Smart manufacturing systems: A futuristics roadmap towards application of industry 4.0 technologies. *International Journal of Computer Integrated Manufacturing*, *36*(3), 411–428. DOI: 10.1080/0951192X.2022.2090607

Soomro, S. A., Casakin, H., Nanjappan, V., & Georgiev, G. V. (2023). Makerspaces Fostering Creativity: A Systematic Literature Review. *Journal of Science Education and Technology*, *32*(4), 530–548. DOI: 10.1007/s10956-023-10041-4

Soroko, N. (2024). Features of organizing steam educational projects using immersive technologies. *Physical and Mathematical Education*, *39*(2), 51–59. DOI: 10.31110/fmo2024.v39i2-07

Suresh Babu, C. V., Nithika Scree, R., & Varshini, R. (2025). The role of artificial intelligence in personalized STEAM education: Enhancing student-centered learning. In Son, N. D. (Ed.), *Integrating personalized learning methods into STEAM education* (pp. 169–188). IGI Global., DOI: 10.4018/979-8-3693-7718-5.ch008

Torbaghan, M. E., Sasidharan, M., Jefferson, I., & Watkins, J. (2023). Preparing Students for a Digitized Future. *IEEE Transactions on Education*, *66*(1), 20–29. DOI: 10.1109/TE.2022.3174263

Torres-Rivera, A. D., Rendón Peña, A. A., Díaz-Torres, S. T., & Díaz-Torres, L. A. (2025). Ethical Integration of AI and STEAM Pedagogies in Higher Education: A Sustainable Learning Model for Society 5.0. *Sustainability (Basel)*, *17*(19), 8525. DOI: 10.3390/su17198525

Trump, B. D., Hristozov, D., & Linkov, I. (2018). An introduction to Environment Systems and Decisions' Special Issue on Emerging Technologies. *Environment Systems & Decisions*, *38*(2), 161–162. DOI: 10.1007/s10669-018-9689-2

Tsarkos, A. (2024). Navigating Change in Education 5.0: A Model for Successful Digital Transformation. In Chemsi, G., Elimadi, I., Sadiq, M., & Radid, M. (Eds.), (pp. 265–290). Advances in Educational Marketing, Administration, and Leadership. IGI Global., DOI: 10.4018/979-8-3693-3045-6.ch015

Ulbrich, E., Da Cruz, M., Anđić, B., Tejera, M., Dana-Picard, N. T., & Lavicza, Z. (2024). Cross-cultural examination of 3D modelling and 3D printing in STEAM education: Comparing results from teachers in Montenegro and Austria. *London Review of Education*, *22*(1). Advance online publication. DOI: 10.14324/LRE.22.1.12

Vassilakopoulou, P., & Hustad, E. (2023). Bridging Digital Divides: A Literature Review and Research Agenda for Information Systems Research. *Information Systems Frontiers*, *25*(3), 955–969. DOI: 10.1007/s10796-020-10096-3

Veytia Bucheli, M. G., & Contreras Fuentes, Y. B. (2025). Tendencias investigativas acerca del método STEAM en México: Mapeo sistemático de la literatura. *Transdigital*, *6*(11), e422–e422. DOI: 10.56162/transdigital422

Wang, D., & Huang, X. (2025). Transforming education through artificial intelligence and immersive technologies: Enhancing learning experiences. *Interactive Learning Environments*, *33*(7), 4546–4565. DOI: 10.1080/10494820.2025.2465451

Weller, J. (2020). Las transformaciones tecnológicas y el empleo en América Latina: Oportunidades y desafíos. *Revista de la CEPAL*, *2020*(130), 7–27. DOI: 10.18356/ce83a6d1-es

Weng, X., Ng, O.-L., Cui, Z., & Leung, S. (2023). Creativity Development With Problem-Based Digital Making and Block-Based Programming for Science, Technology, Engineering, Arts, and Mathematics Learning in Middle School Contexts. *Journal of Educational Computing Research*, *61*(2), 304–328. DOI: 10.1177/07356331221115661

Yaqub, M. Z., & Alsabban, A. (2023). Industry-4.0-Enabled Digital Transformation: Prospects, Instruments, Challenges, and Implications for Business Strategies. *Sustainability (Basel)*, *15*(11), 8553. DOI: 10.3390/su15118553

Zhang, C., Chen, Y., Chen, H., & Chong, D. (2024). Industry 4.0 and its Implementation: A Review. *Information Systems Frontiers*, *26*(5), 1773–1783. DOI: 10.1007/s10796-021-10153-5

Zhang, X. M., Li, B., & Huang, L. (2026). 'Brain + X': Interdisciplinary health professions education for the AI era. *Medical Teacher*, *48*(3), 434–443. DOI: 10.1080/0142159X.2025.2560570

Chapter 6

Educational Strategies to Unleash Creativity and Soft Skills:

Creativity, Social Skills, and Evidence-Based Educational Strategies in Competency-Based Approaches

Luis Arturo Guerrero Azpeitia
http://orcid.org/0000-0002-8905-7243
Polytechnic University of Pachuca, Mexico

Mario Alejandro Vega Navarrete
http://orcid.org/0000-0003-2739-8840
Metropolitan Polytechnic University of Hidalgo, Mexico

Pedro José Argumedo Teuffer
https://orcid.org/0000-0003-3264-7442
Metropolitan Polytechnic University of Hidalgo, Mexico

Alma Delia Paz Gómez
Metropolitan Polytechnic University of Hidalgo, Mexico

ABSTRACT

This chapter presents an analysis of the relationship between creativity and soft skills within the contemporary educational context, highlighting their fundamental role in the training of agents capable of addressing the challenges of a society character-

DOI: 10.4018/979-8-2600-3658-7.ch006

ized by constant transformation, digitalization and the complexity of professional environments. The cognitive process is conceived from a sociocultural perspective, soft skills from a socioemotional, subjective and transversal perspective and the psychological perspective of the social agent as a trigger for autonomy, self-efficacy, self-sufficiency, self-regulation and metacognition, all of which together directly influences the agent's ability to manage learning, make decisions and adapt to different personal and professional situations. Based on this conceptual framework, various constructivist educational strategies are discussed to promote and develop creativity and interpersonal skills based on their explicit and structural integration in the curricular design.

INTRODUCTION

This section presents a comprehensive analysis of the relationship between creativity and soft skills within the contemporary educational context, highlighting their fundamental role in shaping individuals capable of addressing the challenges of a society characterized by constant transformation, digitalization, and the complexity of professional environments. Creativity is approached as a cognitive process of a social and cultural nature, which does not emerge in isolation within the individual but is constructed through interaction with other agents and developed through language, experience, and symbolic mediation, allowing for its internalization and subsequent externalization in a continuous cycle of knowledge construction. Creativity is emphasized not as a static individual trait, but as a dynamic, participatory, and distributed process in which ideas evolve through the collaboration of multiple actors, highlighting principles such as originality, exploration of alternatives, intrinsic motivation, and the ability to question established frameworks in order to generate innovation. The chapter delves into the concept of soft skills, distinguishing them from hard skills by emphasizing their socio-emotional, subjective, and transversal nature, linked to competencies such as communication, teamwork, decision-making, critical thinking, and emotional management, all of which are essential for effective performance in diverse personal and professional contexts. Their classification into interpersonal, cognitive, and emotional regulation dimensions, as well as their impact on employability, psychosocial well-being, and social cohesion, demonstrating the need to structurally integrate them into educational processes. A close relationship between creativity and soft skills is established, indicating that creativity requires these competencies to fully develop, particularly in collaborative environments where innovation emerges from interaction, effective communication, and problem-solving. The chapter also examines psychological and cognitive factors such as autonomy, self-efficacy, self-sufficiency, self-regulation, and metacognition, which directly influence an individual's ability to manage learning, make decisions, and adapt to different situations, highlighting theoretical models that describe these processes as dynamic cycles of planning, execution, and reflection. The complementarity between divergent and convergent thinking is presented as a foundation for problem-solving, where the former enables the generation of multiple creative alternatives and the latter facilitates the selection of the most appropriate solution, underscoring the importance of integrating both approaches in education to foster balanced thinking. The chapter introduces various proof related to educational strategies that promote the growth of creativity and soft skills, such as hackathons, cooperative learning, gamification, project-based learning, design thinking, the use of prototypes, and interdisciplinary environments, all of which encourage active participation, meaningful learning, real-world problem-solving, and the collective construction of knowledge. These strategies are grounded in constructivist and student-centered approaches, where social interaction, collaboration, and the use of technology play a key role in generating relevant learning experiences. The importance of proof related to educational strategies is highlighted as a systematic process that involves formulating questions, searching for and critically analyzing information, applying findings, and evaluating their impact on learning, thereby enabling continuous improvement in teaching practice. Regarding curriculum design, the authors emphasize the need to explicitly and structurally integrate creativity and soft skills through vertical, transversal, or mixed approaches within competency-based education models, allowing for their progressive advancement throughout academic training, supported by tools such as curriculum mapping to avoid gaps or redundancies.

1. FUNDAMENTALS OF CREATIVITY AND SOFT SKILLS

a. Creativity

Creativity can be understood as "the cognitive process of information is manifested through the production and generation of situations, ideas or objects with a certain degree of originality; this style of mind aims in some way to impact or transform the present reality of the individual" (López & Recio, 1998, p. 29).

In this sense, starting from the premise that creativity, as a cognitive process, demands a social and cultural construction, initially appearing on an interpersonal level and subsequently being internalized by the social agent (Vygotsky, 1978). Furthermore, if considered as a dialectical process, creativity is externalized for mediation, either symbolically or physically, before being internalized again, thus continuing the virtuous cycle.

For this purpose, language is a cognitive tool with a mediating and constitutive function of thought—and consequently of learning—transforming mental functions into higher functions such as self-regulation and abstract thought. However, these functions are not generated individually but rather in an eminently social process in which an agent's potential is fostered through guided interaction (Vygotsky, 1979/1995).

Thus, by considering creativity as a process with a more social than individual construction, the participation of diverse social agents is required in its configuration and reconfiguration, in its conception and in its evolution. In this context, creativity as a participatory process conceives of six fundamental principles (Clapp, 2018, p. 55):

1. Individuals are not creative; ideas are creative.
2. Ideas function as plots or storylines that are embodied in a succession of artifacts that evolve over time.
3. The advancement of a creative idea is distributed among a diverse and dynamic set of actors, known as the group of contributing participants.
4. The growth of creative ideas is useful work.
5. There is no single way to be creative, but rather multiple ways in which a variety of individuals participate in the expansion of creative ideas.
6. Individuals play distinct roles when participating in creativity, but these roles are neither fixed nor one-dimensional.

Under these principles, It is possible to consider that creativity is a higher psychological function that does not arise spontaneously, out of nowhere, but is a process of construction — and deconstruction — mediated and regulated by social experience, language, culture and, of course, by oriented interaction.

Regarding the general principles that in some way determine creativity, we have (López & Recio, 1998, pp. 30-31):

a) It is characterized by its originality and the search for concepts with greater scope and impact.
b) It depends on attention to both purposes and results.
c) It explores as many alternatives as possible regarding objectives and approaches to the problem.
d) It relies more on mobility than on fluidity.
e) It works more at the boundaries than at the center of thought.
f) It depends on being both objective and subjective.
g) It relies more on intrinsic than extrinsic motivation.

These principles, at least in part, reflect the consideration of somewhat disruptive actions, demanding not only the merge of known or unknown elements in novel ways, but also the questioning and transformation of referential, conceptual, or dominant frameworks, as the case may be. In this way, creativity can generate innovation that can clearly alter paradigms and, consequently, change ways of thinking, seeing, or modifying the social and individual reality of the agents involved. The types of creativity are: plastic, fluent, philosophical, scientific, inventive, and social (see Table 1).

Table 1. Types of creativity

Plastic	Fluent	Philosophical	Scientific	Inventiveness	Social
It manifests itself in visual arts: architecture, writing, and painting.	Associated with feelings, affections, and attitudes	Generalization of knowledge and interpretation of the world	Applied to ingenuity and talent in research	Applied to solving everyday problems	Ass wit rela

b. Soft Skills

The term "competencies" is known to be polysemous, but for the purposes of this topic, we can conceptualize them as the set of knowledge, skills, abilities, and attitudes that a person articulates and mobilizes to perform a specific function in a given context. In this sense, two of its components can be highlighted: Hard skills correspond to technical and specific competencies, while soft skills are linked to interpersonal and socio-emotional capabilities.

Hard skills are the objective component of competencies and are acquired through academic training, specific instruction, or experience; they can also be measured and/or certified. In contrast, soft skills are subjective and are conceptualized as the set of non-technical competencies linked to socio-emotional, behavioral, and relational dimensions that influence people's effective performance in various contexts (see Table 2).

Table 2. Comparison between hard and soft skills shows their main differences in order to understand their complementarity

Criteria	Hard skills	Soft skills
Nature	Technical and scientific skills	Emotional skills
Acquisition	Formal education and technical training	Social experience, personal progress, and training
Evaluation	Exams, certifications, technical tests	Observation, performance, 360° evaluation
Applicability	Specific to a function or profession	Multiple contexts
Orientation	Objective	Subjective
Development	Specific	Transversal skills

Source: Prepared by the author based on information from Ramírez and Manjarrez (2022).

While it is true that, based on the concept of competence presented here, an articulation between hard and soft skills is required, it is relatively common in the educational system to have a tendency to privilege the former over the latter.

Particularly in the case of soft skills, although there is no consensus on their classification, three categories can be considered:

1) Interpersonal; 2) Cognitive and; 3) Emotional control, (see Table 3).

Table 3. Classification of soft skills and their main characteristics

Criteria	Characteristic
Interpersonal skills	Assertive communication Empathy Trust Negotiation Cooperation
Cognitive skills	Decision-making Teamwork Problem-solving Critical thinking Self-assessment Analysis Understanding consequences
Emotional control	Emotional management and recognition in stressful situations Intense feelings

Source: (Garavito et al., 2024, p. 6).

With reference to the importance of soft skills in different areas of people's lives, various organizations, government entities, educational institutions and productive sectors, among others, agree that they favor and promote employability, psychosocial well-being, public health, economic competitiveness and social cohesion, to mention just a few aspects.

Regarding the relationship between creativity and soft skills, empirical evidence identifies a connection between teamwork skills in students and motivation for learning (languages). A positive correlation has been found between motivational profiles, creative level, and type of teamwork skills (Calero et al., 2024).

Regarding strategies for developing soft skills, the implementation of hackathons has proven to be an alternative for future engineering professionals, improving employability and preparation for the labor market (Araújo et al., 2025).

While it is true that, nowadays, people are valued not only for what they know but also for what they do with it, an important point is to establish that the theoretical and conceptual approach to soft skills will depend on various components associated with disciplines or areas of knowledge. It will also depend on the sociocultural environment in a broad sense (Arce, 2024); therefore, a social perspective is reinforced in its construction and maturation.

In this way, it can be identified that creativity is not an isolated skill, but rather requires its interaction with a set of soft skills, predominantly — and without detriment to hard skills — by reinforcing innovation, communication, collaborative work in a social environment for its improvement through social interaction, problem-solving and autonomy, among other components.

2. PSYCHOLOGICAL AND COGNITIVE FACTORS

a. Self-Sufficiency and Metacognition

Autonomy, etymologically, is made up of autos ("oneself" or "by oneself") and nomos ("norm", "law" or "government"), therefore, it can be interpreted as "giving oneself the law" or "governing oneself by one's own rules", so it can be considered as the ability of a person to make decisions without external influence, regulations or some other type of influence, that is, to act independently.

Regarding self-efficacy, Bandura (1977), cited by Rodríguez et al. (2020, p. 75), states that self-efficacy beliefs are defined as "beliefs in one's own ability to organize and execute the actions required to manage future situations." Therefore, for a social agent, these beliefs influence their behavior more significantly than their past actions. In addition, the sources of self-efficacy are: 1) previous experiences of success or failure; 2) vicarious experiences; 3) verbal persuasion; and 4) physiological states experienced when performing different tasks (Rodríguez et al., 2020, p. 76).

The Royal Spanish Academy (n.d., definition 1) defines self-sufficiency as "the state or condition of someone who is self-sufficient." Clearly, it can have various facets, such as the spiritual, emotional, cognitive, and material, to name just a few. In this sense, self-sufficiency involves resolving situations and making decisions independently, developing self-acceptance, and feeling happy with oneself. Furthermore, self-sufficiency provides perspective and guidance in various aspects of daily life and, consequently, in academic life.

Regarding self-regulation, it is composed of the Greek roots auto ("by oneself") and regulate ("to measure," "to adjust," "rule"), as well as the suffixion (action and effect). Therefore, it can be understood as the capacity of a person (or entity) to establish their own rules and adhere to them of their own volition without external intervention. Particularly in the case of students, self-regulation can be understood as the control they have over their motivations, emotions, behavior, and, of course, their cognition. Specifically, and according to Simmerman and Moylan (2009, cited by Panadero and Alonso-Tapia, 2014), the phases and processes of self-regulation are identified in Figure 1.

Figure 1. Phases and processes of self-regulation according to Zimmerman and Moylan that allow us to understand how the construction mechanisms

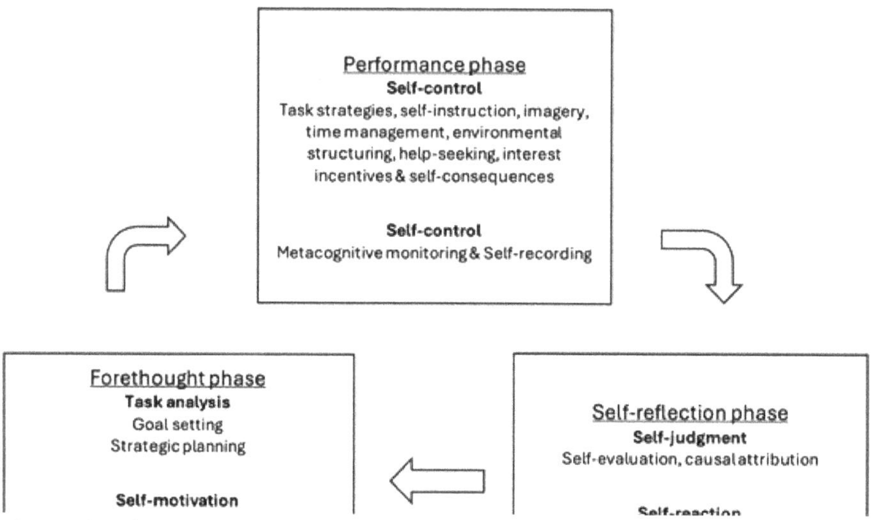

Source: (Panadero y Alonso -Tapia, 2014, p. 452).

In this cyclical model, it can be identified that the established phases demand specific processes, such as task analysis and self-motivation in the planning phase; self-observation and self-control in the execution phase; and, finally, self-judgment and self-reaction in the self-reflection phase.

Metacognition refers to the knowledge that an agent has of their own cognitive processes and products, and inherently involves their active monitoring, regulation, and organization in relation to the cognitive data involved in the accomplishment of specific tasks (Gandini, 2018). In this conception, two clearly defined processes can be identified: 1) the first associated with metacognitive knowledge and 2) metacognitive control. To establish the relationship within each process and its interrelation with the other, this is presented in Figure 2.

Figure 2. Main components of metacognition allow us to understand the dialectical process between metacognitive control and knowledge

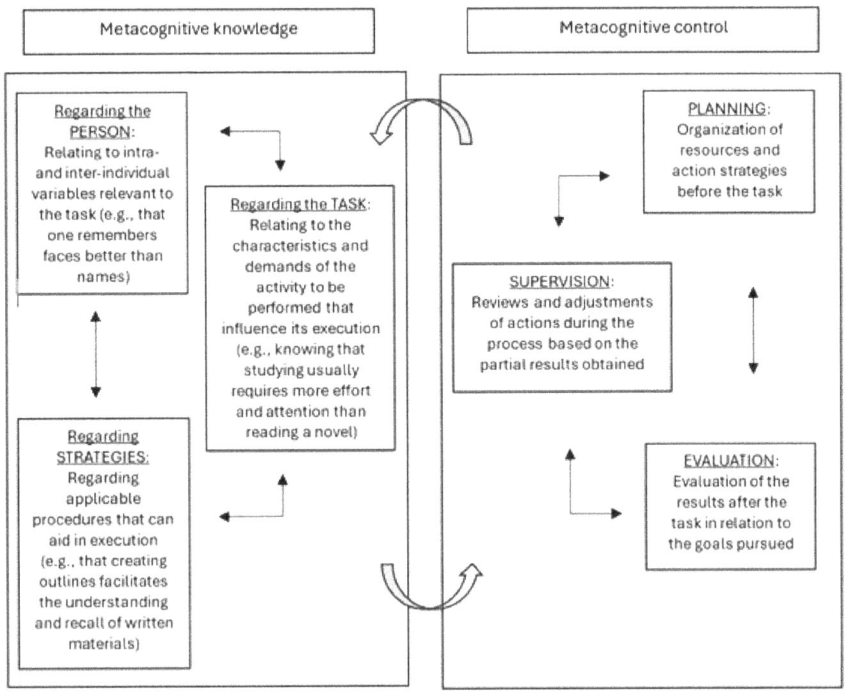

Source: García et al. (2002), citado por (Gandini, 2018, p. 56).

Under this construct, the agent is aware not only of his own cognitive processes and his individual limitations in relation to a task or function, but also takes actions to mitigate or correct his limitations; in this way, the cycle is complemented and presents a constant configuration and reconfiguration in a virtuous manner.

In accordance with the above, it can be established that, to execute a specific task, there is a close relationship between: autonomy, with motivational bases by demanding a voluntary decision to execute it; self-efficacy, based on the belief of possessing competence(s) to develop it; self-regulation, which demands a strategic management of the behavior related to it; metacognition, which is a reflective exercise of the thought involved; and self-sufficiency, which demands an integrated functional result to perform competently in a broad sense by developing the ability to think about how to solve the task.

b. Divergent Thinking vs. Convergent Thinking

Divergent thinking, as a process that values multiple facts and different points of view to approach situations from various angles in order to propose new alternatives and ways of interpreting, explaining, or intervening, requires the fulfillment of three conditions: a) information about the aspects that define and influence a given situation; b) the willingness and courage to question established rules; and c) the ability to apply new approaches to the original situation. Convergent thinking, on the other hand, requires the formulation of a proposal based on the evaluation of various options or alternative solutions to the situation in which one wishes to intervene or act (see Table 4).

Table 4. The comparison between divergent and convergent thinking allows not only to visualize their differences but to a certain extent their complementarity

Criteria	Divergent thinking	Convergent thinking
Fundamental concept	Generating possibilities or alternative solutions	Evaluation and specification of possibilities or alternative solutions
Type of tests	Valuative	Objectives
Associated risks	Dispersion or lack of concreteness	Rigidity or limitation of alternatives
Intentionality	Various responses to a situation	Finding the most suitable answer
Implicit skills	Fluency, flexibility, originality, elaboration	Order, logic, sequential structure, cause and effect
Dominant type of intelligence	Creativity, lateral thinking	Logical-mathematical intelligence

Source: Prepared by the author based on Gilhooly et al., (2007).

It is necessary to establish that by its very nature convergent thinking tends inherently to generate a thought that can be considered orthodox, in contrast divergent thinking fosters variability, each under certain processes according to Cropley, (2006) (see Table 5).

Table 5. Example of convergent and divergent thinking that shows its applicability and concreteness in various actions of the social subject

Kind of Thinking	Convergent	Divergent
Typical Processes	- Being logical - Recognizing the familiar - Combining what "belongs" together - Homing in on the single best answer - Reapplying set techniques - Preserving the already known - Achieving accuracy and correctness - Playing it safe - Sticking to a narrow range of obviously relevant information - Making associations from adjacent fields only	- Being unconventional - Seeing the known in a new light - Combining the disparate - Producing multiple answers - Shifting perspective - Transforming the known - Seeing new possibilities - Taking risks - Retrieving a broad range of existing knowledge - Associating ideas from remote fields
Typical Results for the Individual	- Greater familiarity with what already exists - Better grasp of the facts - A quick, "correct" answer - Completion of a high level of skill - Closure on an issue - A feeling of security and safety	- Alternative or multiple solutions - Deviation from the usual - A surprising answer - New lines of attack or ways of doing things - Exciting or risky possibilities - A feeling of uncertainty or excitement

Source: Cropley (2006).

While divergent and convergent thinking have their differences, it's important to note that they complement each other and are therefore highly recommended for problem-solving and decision-making, as these processes often require choosing one solution from several alternatives to a problematic situation. In short, convergent thinking promotes description and a focus on analyzing the causes of a problem through the systematization of information. Divergent thinking, on the other hand, fosters imagination to establish diverse perspectives using novel and creative techniques. Both perspectives contribute to problem-solving.

3. PROOF RELATED TO EDUCATIONAL STRATEGIES

According to Harden (1999), Evidence-Based Education (EBE) is the administration, by teachers in their practice, of educational methods and approaches based on the best available evidence. This definition can be found in different types of strategies related to this field. A representative example of the steps to follow when developing an EBE process is shown in Figure 3.

Figure 3. Evidence-based assessment

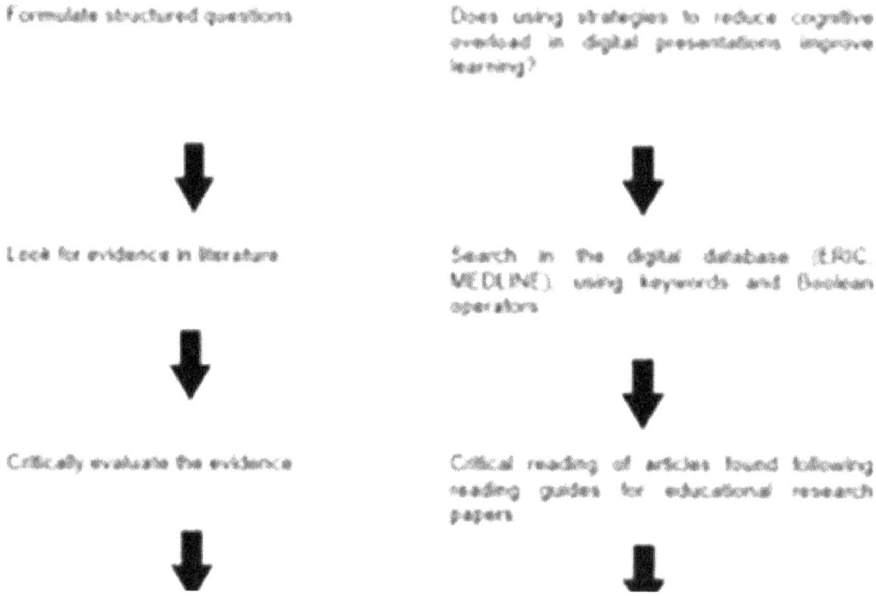

Fuente: (Sánchez et al., 2020).

Strategies related to the EBE:

a. Hackathons

In the educational field, a Hackathon is defined by Reyes et al. (2025) as an activity in which students and teachers collaborate for a short period to solve challenges or problems through flexible and interconnected networking. Their actions are geared towards sharing and documenting existing knowledge or co-producing new knowledge, materials, or any type of product valued by that community. The term "Hack" comes from the word "hacker," which refers to groups of software programmers who work together to solve a specific problem in the field of computing.

The Hackathon is considered a didactic strategy that directly impacts the teaching-learning process, resulting in dynamics with greater group participation, collaboration, and meaningful learning. This strategy is based on the constructivist paradigm of collective learning, where interaction among participants is crucial for sharing perspectives and reflections on the problem at hand, as well as integrating concepts derived from these exercises that would make a significant contribution to educational practice, such as Project-Based Learning (PBL), case studies, and others. This strategy fosters connections between theory, practice, and collective learning.

The particular characteristics of this strategy prioritize the collaboration of a network of interconnected people, collaborating horizontally in work teams. Another characteristic is defining the activity to be carried out focused on overcoming a challenge or solving a problem. Also important is the tangible and measurable final product or result that contributes to the solution of the problem or challenge, along with the use of digital platforms for the interconnection of the members, applying it to research, co-production and reporting of results.

The objectives of this strategy are collaborative, networked learning, aimed at both students and teachers. One objective is to develop digital competencies related to information technologies; another is to define and document different teaching strategies for teaching and learning digital technologies, and to promote the ability to teach using digital technology, where individuals are familiar with digital technologies for sharing knowledge and addressing problems, among other aspects of information.

b. Cooperative Learning in Active Environments

According to Johnson et al. (1994), cooperative learning is summarized as a teaching method in which a small group of individuals or students work together to achieve common goals and maximize individual and collective learning.

Cooperative learning can be classified into three types of learning groups: formal cooperative learning groups, informal learning groups, and cooperative-based groups. These three types of groups differ in how the teaching method is applied and the duration of each type of learning.

1) Characteristics of formal cooperative learning: The teacher specifies the objectives of the class, makes a series of decisions prior to teaching, explains the task, monitors student learning and their interdependence, and subsequently reviews the learning in a cooperative manner, evaluating the effectiveness of the method for the group's learning. Formal cooperative learning groups operate over a period ranging from one hour to several weeks of class time.

2) Characteristics of informal cooperative learning: The teacher can use direct instruction or instructional resources, such as videos, lectures, or demonstrations, to focus students' attention on a specific topic for analysis, fostering a climate conducive to cooperative learning. This type of learning encourages students to form small groups to discuss a topic for two or three minutes before and after the main lesson. Similar to formal learning groups, these groups engage in intellectual work, organizing, analyzing, explaining, and integrating the concepts presented during direct instruction. This process can last from a few minutes to an hour.

3) Characteristics of Cooperative Learning Groups: These are heterogeneous learning groups with permanent members whose objective is to enable their mem-

bers to support one another in achieving good academic performance through group encouragement and assistance. The goal of these groups is to progress in meeting academic goals, such as learning theoretical and practical knowledge, completing assigned tasks, and attending classes. Writing reports and giving presentations contributes to cooperative learning. This learning approach typically operates for at least twelve months.

Cooperative learning consists of five basic elements, these are:

The first is the interdependence of the members that make up the work group; the second element is the individual and group responsibility of all members of the work group; the third is the stimulating interaction among the members of the work group, that is, helping and supporting each other in the learning process; the fourth is teaching the work group essential interpersonal and group practices, such as leading the progress of a topic, making decisions, creating a climate of trust, communicating and managing conflicts, among others; the fifth and final element is group evaluation, that is, the members of the group analyze whether they are achieving the proposed goals or not, maintaining a positive working relationship, making decisions about which actions or behaviors should be maintained or, if necessary, modified.

This teaching method basically comprises different stages in its execution: preliminary decisions, task execution and teamwork, cooperative learning, and post-class activities. Below is a basic structure of the method and the participants involved in each stage:

a) The preliminary decisions:
    - The selection of teaching materials and objectives. (Teacher)
    - The formation of groups. (Teacher)
    - The classroom layout. (Teacher)
    - The assignment of roles. (Teacher)

b) Task execution (Teamwork):
    - Explanation of the academic task. (Teacher and student)
    - Positive interdependence. (Teacher and student)
    - Desirable behaviors. (Teacher and students)

c) The cooperative class:
    - Implementing the cooperative learning model. (Teacher and students)
    - Monitoring student behavior. (Teacher)
    - Closing the class. (Students)

d) Post-class activities:
    - Evaluating the quality and quantity of learning. (Teacher and student)
    - Assessing group effectiveness. (Teacher)

c. Gamified Environments

The Polytechnic University of Madrid (2020) defines gamification as the use of certain game characteristics in an educational setting, with the aim of increasing student engagement in achieving objectives. This allows for fun and learning from mistakes, while simultaneously motivating change in students: attitudinal, conceptual, unfolding of new skills, among others.

The authors (Werbach and Hunter, 2013) identify three characteristics of the gamification method: Dynamics, Mechanics, and Components.

1) Dynamics

The dynamic element within gamification encompasses five types: constraints, which limit both the environment and each player; emotions, such as surprise, curiosity, and enjoyment; narrative, the story surrounding the game that connects all events to establish the objectives of an assigned mission; progression, the identification of achievements and progress perceived by each player within the game; and finally, relationships, the interactions between players, such as cooperation and competition. These dynamics focus on achieving objectives and utilize what are known as game mechanics.

2) Mechanics

The mechanics of the game (Cortizo, 2011) are defined as a series of rules that attempt to generate games that can be enjoyed with a certain addiction and commitment from the players by providing them with challenges through a video game or other application.

Some of the mechanisms used in gamification include the challenges players face, the opportunities presented to them within the game, competition where players are divided into winners and losers, and cooperation to achieve in-game objectives. Rewards, incentives, or prizes are also considered in recognition of the effort invested in the game's activities.

3) Components

Another element considered within gamification is what is known as components, which are more concrete elements that will appear or interact in the event of gamification involved with the dynamics and mechanics of the game.

The components identified by Harranz and Colomo (2012) include the achievements of objectives as they are reached. These include avatars, which are visual representations of the players within the gamification system; badges, which recognize achievements in the game; opportunities to share resources with others, known as gifts; and the establishment of levels within the game that mark the participants' progress. Finally, the players are assigned teams within the game.

d. Prototypes

According to Sánchez et al. (2018), "a prototype refers to a sample or first mold in which a figure or other object is manufactured, any type of machine under test conditions, designed for demonstration." In other words, the prototype is a substantial part of research projects, seeking to promote ideas from different perspectives that involve a significant number of variables. The characteristics of a prototype are scientific and innovative ideas. For Helm et al. (2019), prototypes strengthen academic knowledge and student training through the design of products that encourage the construction of their knowledge, seeking the feasibility of their production and commercialization.

After a rigorous process of scientific and theoretical research, the objective of designing and building a prototype is to evaluate all the parameters and variables of a process in order to understand their response and develop a product or service. To achieve this objective, Pinilla (2014) emphasizes that the characteristics of the assumptions first emerge, from which individual sub-problems framed within these assumptions are deduced and represented through sketches and models.

Next, the proposals are studied, and the process moves to the analysis stage of the models' characteristics. These models are then transformed into prototypes when they are suitable for evaluating aspects relevant to the intended use of the object. Finally, a final phase begins where, based on the prototypes, the specifications are defined to confirm the requirements of the product being developed.

Pinilla et al. (2011) argue that the construction of a process involves transitions that enhance the improvement of a prototype through revisions and actions that contribute to understanding reality and its nature (see Figure 4).

Figure 4. Development and testing of prototypes

Source: Product Prototype: Definition, Types, and Examples in Design & Benefits, Varun Saharawat | October 30, 2025. URL: https://pwskills.com/blog/product-prototype/

4. COGNITIVE AND DESIGN METHODS

Derived from the relationship established by a student or subject, it is inferred that interacting with a design or object of study, visually or otherwise, leads to an interaction process. According to Morales and del Moral (2022, 2023), when information is generated, it must be processed to be considered knowledge, creating possibilities for interpretation—that is, the emergence of cognitive processes. Morin (1992) states that all knowledge, whatever its nature, presupposes a knowing mind, whose possibilities and limitations are those of the human brain, as well as linguistic and informational aspects derived from a given culture, from a specific society.

a. PBL

Project-Based Learning (PBL) "consists of learning experiences centered on students' interests and needs, organized around a challenge, linking learning objectives with real-world problems" (Sotomayor et al., 2021). PBL makes it possible to articulate essential objectives, considered necessary for advancing to new learning, with integrated and meaningful social challenges and opportunities for connection across different fields of knowledge within a single project.

PBL consists of five phases. The first phase is the Challenge, where students engage with a project problem. The second is a Question, characterized by being authentic, meaningful, and motivating, which initiates rigorous learning in the third phase, Research. This phase seeks answers to a problem from diverse and multiple sources, formulating hypotheses, investigating, consulting experts, and acquiring the necessary data to find the desired answer. Subsequently, students proceed to the Creation phase, producing tangible or intangible products such as diagrams, reports, explanations, narrative texts, models, and so on. Finally, the Communication phase involves students demonstrating their learning by organizing the various products (see Figure 5).

Figure 5. PBL Learning Path Phase.

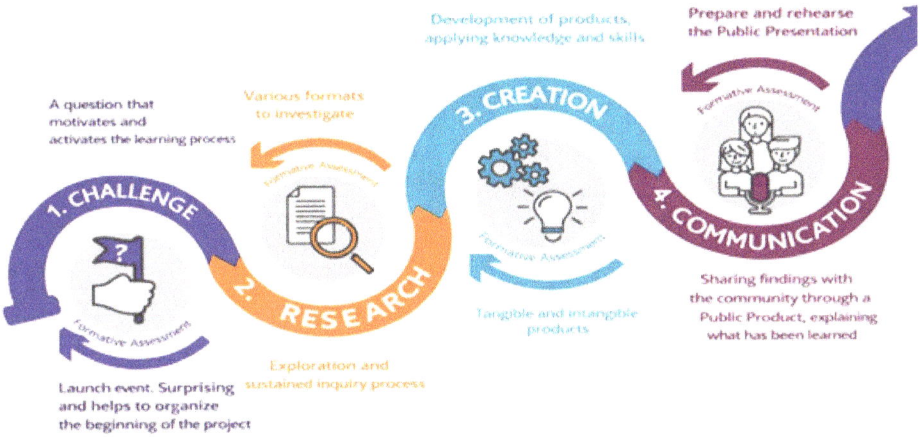

Source: PBL Learning Pathway. Innovation Center of the Ministry of Education of Santiago, Chile, (2021).

b. Design Thinking

Design thinking is a human-centered methodology that allows for the resolution of complex problems and fosters innovation. According to Brown (2008), it is a discipline that leverages the sensitivity and methods of designers to find a convergence between people's needs and market opportunities from a viable business perspective.

The stages involved in applying the Design Thinking discipline to a specific topic involve a phase that must be carefully structured to reach a solution to a specific problem (see Table 6).

Table 6. Summary of the stages of Design Thinking

Stage	Objective	Tools	Classroom Application
Empathize	Identify the needs of users and their environment.	Surveys, interviews, empathy maps, or personal profiles.	"What, how and why"
Define	Create a user profile for whom the solution or product is designed.	Visual analysis tools such as mood boards. Porters diagram, or value curves.	Problem tree.
Ideate	Develop creative solutions based on innovative ideas fostering teamwork.	Idea selection, customer journey maps, discussion groups, or idea matrices.	Brainstorming.
Prototype	Turn idesa and concepts into tangible outputs through creation of real prototypes.	Rough prototypes, infographics, or mock-ups.	Prototype.
Test/Evaluate	Test prototypes to identify prototype potential weaknesses or gaps and implement improvements.	Constructive feedback, experience evaluation, or green/red cards.	The session concludes by asking students to create their own CV.

Source: (Izquierdo et al., 2022).

c. Interdisciplinary Environments

Interdisciplinarity is the communion between disciplines. As Klein (2021) points out, it is the collaboration between two or more disciplines that come together to study, evaluate, and address a specific situation from different perspectives, generating activities that promote holistic evolution and avoid isolated and repetitive work that is often exhausting (see Figure 6).

Interdisciplinarity fosters holistic learning. In this regard, Klein (2021) emphasizes the generation of meaningful learning through the application of science to everyday life, creating greater potential for discernment, a better interpretation of reality, and the ability to develop criteria for changing that reality.

Interdisciplinarity has a significant impact on the understanding of learning, is included in education improvement policies, and various strategies are designed to facilitate curriculum application; this allows for the determination of achievements and difficulties, both technical and didactic.

Interdisciplinarity develops in the student different competencies to perform professional or work activities, based on the combination of knowledge, skills, attitudes and values, required for a specific objective.

Figure 6. Interdisciplinary Dynamic example.

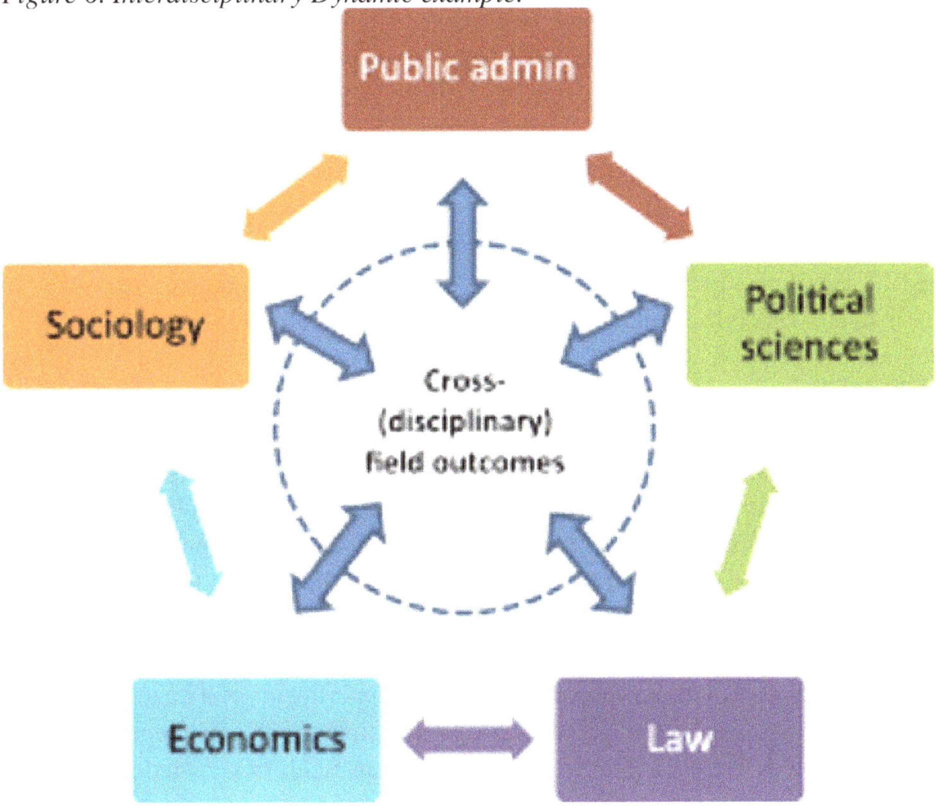

Source: Public administration teaching and interdisciplinarity: considering the consequences - Gerrit van der Waldt, 2014, volume 32, issue 2. https://doi.org/10.1177/0144739414523285

Interdisciplinarity is strengthened if it has a theoretical foundation, showing its practical functionality.

Another perspective on interdisciplinarity is given by Fiallo (2001), which demands serious work on the part of academic and research groups, and requires the adoption of positions that favor flexibility between disciplines and the search for communicators.

According to Fiallo, (2001) and Udina and Atabekova, (2012), some of the advantages of interdisciplinarity are the following:

- Ensuring the active use of information and communication technologies and their transformation into learning technologies.
- Comprehensive study of new content and enriching opportunities for its application to real life.
- Optimizing time management by avoiding unnecessary repetition of content.
- Promoting the preparation of future professionals for teamwork.
- The opportunity to collaborate on finding solutions to new problems through contributions from different disciplines.
- The richness of an interdisciplinary approach, which is more comprehensive in content and scope than a purely disciplinary approach.

However, there are some challenges to consider regarding the transition from disciplinary to interdisciplinary teaching. According to Udina and Atabekova (2012), this transition is complex and slow, and universities and other professional training institutions are undertaking significant work toward achieving their objectives. There are few materials related to this topic, as well as few didactic proposals that pursue this purpose. Other authors, such as Llano et al. (2016), mention that interdisciplinarity is a necessity in today's world and implies a multidimensional approach that cannot be carried out from isolated disciplines. This requires curricular and methodological work by teachers across the different departments of a degree program.

Based on the above, it is understood that interdisciplinary environments are spaces that integrate different disciplines, as well as various fields of knowledge and areas of science, for the deployment of different technologies and projects that seek to solve a specific problem in academia, society, business or government.

5. CURRICULUM INTEGRATION AND ASSESSMENT

The interest in integrating creativity and soft skills into the curriculum requires a profound restructuring of the curriculum. The mere application of teaching methodologies does not, and will not, resolve current problems. This restructuring must define the fundamental elements of professional training. This involves modifying not only the usual curriculum design processes but also the assessment methods, considering creativity and soft skills as a focal point that depends on the context, the student's academic life, and the self-perception in their training. Assessment becomes the mechanism to articulate the curriculum, creativity, and soft skills in a quantifiable manner. Some empirical studies suggest reliability coefficients above 0.80 in validated creativity assessment instruments, indicating that these constructs can be measured in a consistent and comparable way (Akdemir-Beveridge et al., 2026).

a. Explicit Integration Into Curricula

Currently, for curriculum incorporation and assessment, the inclusion of creativity and soft skills is pedagogically necessary, unlike conventional practice where this aspect is optional for teachers. Digitalization, process automation, and the knowledge-based economy have revolutionized professional profiles. Professionals trained solely in technical competencies will be less qualified to meet today's demand for professionals (World Economic Forum, 2020; OECD, 2020). For this reason, new trends in curriculum growth place these skills as a structural part of curricula at different educational levels. However, it is important to note that their inclusion must be considered and based on a consolidated plan that can be systematically evaluated in accordance with the guidelines governing each institution's educational model (UNESCO, 2021; OECD, 2020).

Various educational systems have proposed incorporating creativity and soft skills in a structural way, which are widely reported in various scientific dissemination forums. Meta-analytic evidence suggests moderate effect sizes ($d \approx 0.40$–0.50) in the improvement of soft skills when STEM-based approaches are implemented across different educational contexts (Rizakhojayeva et al., 2025).

This structural incorporation requires the definition of clear curricular mechanisms that specify how these competencies are distributed across programs, how they progress over time, and how they are aligned with disciplinary content (Biggs et al., 2022; OECD, 2020). Without such mechanisms, their assimilation risks remaining at a declarative level rather than being effectively implemented in teaching practice. Experimental results suggest that structured interventions, such as the use of full-scale models, can produce measurable increases in creativity scores compared to traditional instruction, with reported improvements above 15% in design performance (Elaby et al., 2023).

These proposals can be classified under two approaches:

The cross-curricular approach assumes that these competencies will be addressed in all subjects, where they are assessed. The vertical approach considers specific subjects within the curriculum to assess these competencies.

The transversal approach makes professional training more solid, however, it could be ambiguous as it depends on the teacher's interpretation to work on these competencies; and the vertical approach may contribute to the improvement of competencies (OECD, 2020; European Commission, 2022).

From a curricular perspective, this approach requires coordination among subjects to ensure that competencies are not only addressed but also progressively developed. This implies the need for shared planning criteria, common learning outcomes, and articulated assessment strategies across courses (Biggs et al., 2022; Harden et al., 1999).

They propose ensuring the growth of these competencies through the accomplishment of mixed approaches. According to Holcombe et al. (2022), the vertical approach creates spaces within the curriculum for the development of competencies. Subsequently, the transversal approach leverages the teacher's experience to progressively develop competencies, in conjunction with technical training.

In practice, this combination demands an explicit curricular design in which each course has a defined role in the evolution of these competencies, avoiding both redundancy and fragmentation (OECD, 2020). This also facilitates the monitoring of student progression throughout the program.

An opportunity for incorporating these competencies lies in their realization within the Competency-Based Education (CBE) model. This model appears to encourage the improvement of theoretical and practical knowledge through real-world environments or contexts. Empirical applications in engineering education show increases in students' self-efficacy levels, with reported gains above 20% after implementing competency-based frameworks in controlled settings (Ahmad et al., 2026). It may facilitate students to demonstrate their competency progress in observable and accessible ways using a specific rubric, thus avoiding subjective evaluations based on abstract teacher definitions. Biggs and Tang (2022) state that, in the competency-based model, it is essential to generate clear learning criteria that produce explicit and quantifiable results, which must be validated throughout teaching, learning, and assessment.

Within higher education institutions with a competency-based educational model, engineering programs present a challenge for implementing creativity and soft skills. This is because their curriculum is technical and their faculty were typically trained under models that did not always consider these competencies or lacked pedagogical training to apply them (ABET, 2025).

This challenge is also curricular in nature, as it requires redefining the structure of engineering programs to incorporate these competencies without compromising technical content (European Commission, 2022). This may involve redistributing course content, introducing interdisciplinary modules, or integrating project-based components that connect multiple subject areas (Bell et al., 2022; Llano et al., 2016).

The carrying out of these blended learning approaches must be planned to determine the best way to integrate them into a specific curriculum. Curriculum mapping is a key tool in this process, allowing the curriculum to be structured into introductory, innovative, and consolidation courses for these competencies, thus avoiding duplication or gaps in competency development (OECD, 2020; European Commission, 2022). Curriculum mapping enables the identification of specific points where these competencies are introduced, reinforced, and mastered, providing a clear visualization of their progression (OECD, 2020; Kuh et al., 2006). This systematic organization supports decision-making regarding course design and ensures alignment between learning outcomes, teaching activities, and assessment methods.

Competencies such as creativity, which require continuous improvement based on personal experience, cannot be developed in a single course. According to Kuh et al. (2006), enabling planning across three different stages. It serves as a strategic tool for planning curricular content that develops these competencies using a blended learning approach.

The curriculum has been reviewed and the subjects for the three different blocks defined, it is necessary to determine how to implement creativity and soft skills within each subject. One way to ensure they meet the desired criteria is to integrate them through learning outcomes. These outcomes should clearly and analyze the extent of the student's competencies (OECD, 2020; European Commission, 2022).

This process also requires the explicit definition of the level of achievement expected at each stage, ensuring that learning outcomes are scaffolded and coherent throughout the curriculum (Biggs et al., 2022). Such alignment facilitates both teaching practice and the evaluation of student progression.

These competencies are addressed in introductory courses, starting from their theoretical foundations. Biggs and Tang (2022) emphasize that the competency is not being formally developed, but rather the necessary knowledge is being provided so that the student can develop them in subsequent courses and demonstrate them practically in consolidation courses.

It is possible to integrate the different approaches depending on the curricular stage that is developed, associating it with the type of subject, teaching and evaluation strategies, which allow curricular merge (see Table 7).

This adaptability highlights the need for flexible curricular structures that can accommodate different pedagogical strategies while maintaining coherence in the accomplishment of competencies (OECD, 2020; UNESCO, 2021).

Table 7. Integration of creativity and soft skills into the curriculum

Curriculum stage	Approach	Type of subjects	Teaching strategies	Evaluation strategies
Introduction	Vertical	Basic / theoretical courses	Case studies, debates, guided reflection	Conceptual questionnaires, self-assessment
Development	Mixed	Intermediate courses	Problem-based learning, collaborative work	Analytical rubrics, digital portfolios
Consolidation	Cross	Integrative projects / internships	Real projects, professional simulations	Performance evaluation, peer evaluation

Source: Prepared by the author based on OECD (2020), Biggs and Tang (2022) and UNESCO (2021).

This table presents how creativity and soft skills are incorporated into the different stages of the curriculum (introduction, development and consolidation), including the approaches, types of subjects, teaching strategies and assessment methods used at each stage.

b. Authentic Evaluation

Soft skills and creativity are not effective if they are not developed by students. (Darling-Hammond et al., 2020) state that if, during this process, there is a lack of an assessment strategy that allows students to determine their strengths and areas for improvement, soft skills will not be effective.

This introduces the fundamental principle of authentic assessment, which aims to establish tasks that promote the improvement of knowledge, cognitive skills, and socio-emotional competencies in an integrated manner within the student's real-world context or, failing that, in simulated environments. The student will consider the activity itself and its outcome, integrating mental tools, making decisions, and planning strategies based on their creativity to solve problems, generating learning and developing skills (UNESCO, 2021; OECD, 2020).

This is intended to support that authentic assessment may contribute to that creativity is genuine learning. To verify this, key dimensions must be considered; Guilford (1977) defined them as the originality, flexibility, fluency, and relevance of the solutions.

It is necessary to define assessment instruments that are focused on evaluating creative processes, and that allow the student to actively regulate their creativity Brookhart, (2010).

Assessment tools such as analytical rubrics and digital portfolios are useful. Rubric-based assessment models grounded in creativity theory have demonstrated improvements in inter-rater agreement, increasing the objectivity of evaluation processes (Damayanti et al., 2024). According to Yang et al. (2017) and Shavelson et al. (2010), implementing assessment strategies that go beyond and provide feedback on students' strengths, may contribute to the possibility of critical self-management of learning.

Defining a suitable methodology for evaluating soft skills remains challenging, given that they are intangible skills that change significantly depending on the context. Empirical studies with training professionals report considerable variability in the interpretation and assessment of soft skills across institutional contexts, highlighting the need for standardized criteria (Saira Banu & Kalai Lakshmi, 2025). The instruments designed for their assessment must be defined according to the specific criteria for these skills. The OECD (2020) and UNESCO (2021) highlight structured observation, self-assessment, and peer assessment as key strategies, allowing for a comparison between the teacher's and peer evaluators' perceptions and the students. There is a selection of different assessment instruments, as well as potential evidence to evaluate some of the social skills commonly mentioned in the literature (see Table 8).

Table 8. Proposed assessment tools for essential soft skills

Competence	Evaluation instrument	Evidence
Creativity	Analytical rubric	Creative product, process
Communication	Co-evaluation	Oral presentations
Teamwork	Structured observation	Role registration
Critical thinking	Digital portfolio	Written reflections

Source: Prepared by the author based on OECD (2020), Biggs and Tang (2022) and UNESCO (2021).

The key competencies—creativity, communication, teamwork, and critical thinking—are presented along with the assessment tools used and the types of evidence recommended for each competency..

There has been a growing interest in developing effective rubrics and establishing records associated with strategies that improve student feedback. Ritter et al. (2017) point out the need for greater objectivity in assessing soft skills evolution, demonstrating that evaluation is possible but requires the design of methodological strategies based on the student's context.

One strategy that can be used is performance-based assessment, by focusing on the students' actions and decision-making in solving problems within their context or in simulated real-world environments, allowing for the integrated evaluation of creativity and soft skills. This strategy often involves forming teams to carry out projects or case studies in which students not only acquire technical knowledge but also develop their competencies in proposing and implementing solutions relevant to those they will encounter in their professional lives. According to Darling-Hammond et al. (2020), this may be interpreted as an interconnection between curriculum, learning, and industry because it may promote learning environments based on professional needs without sacrificing relevance in educational training.

Technology is currently an ally for evaluating creativity and soft skills, as it offers learning management and collaborative activity management platforms that support the structuring of problem-solving processes while simultaneously collecting evidence of the improvement and participation of each team member. According to the authors (Viberg et al., 2018; Ifenthaler and Yim-Kim Yau, 2020), this information becomes crucial for teachers, as it enables them to monitor each student's learning in the different competencies being assessed.

Technological tools are not only an instrument but a tool that may promote and contribute to the authentic assessment of skills.

The unification and evaluation of these vertical and transversal strategies within the curriculum presents contradictions beyond the methodologies themselves. In practice, the new competency-based educational models implemented by educational institutions present a content load in a short period. Resistance persists among teachers due to the workload that their design and planning represent compared to more traditional methodologies. Fullan (2020) highlights that there is also a lack of institutional policies that ensure authentic assessment, or that the criteria established within them are not precise.

The biggest obstacles to authentic assessment are not strictly methodological but related to teacher resistance and institutional policies.

6. PRACTICAL RECOMMENDATIONS FOR ITS ACCOMPLISHMENT

The curricular combination of creativity and soft skills cannot and should not be considered as isolated elements; rather, they must be addressed through an approach that considers proper articulation within the curriculum, the institution, and academia. Figure 7 illustrates that these dimensions are not isolated, but rather interrelated, forming an ecosystem around these competencies in which any change in one dimension will have repercussions.

Figure 7. Ecosystem model for the expansion of creativity and soft skills

The diagram illustrates how institutional, pedagogical, and curricular dimensions come together to foster creativity and soft skills, highlighting elements within each dimension.

Source: Created by the author using Canva.

a. Activity Design

To develop a workforce capable of addressing real-world industry challenges,The workforce must be creative and possess the necessary soft skills to collaborate effectively within their teams. This requires activities promoting assimilation, progress, and evaluation to adhere to the principles of authentic assessment (Darling-Hammond et al., 2020). Effective teamwork and clear communication are crucial for solving real-world problems, ensuring that all involved parties have an understanding of the issue and that decision-making is holistic.

Boud et al. (1985) establish that this can be achieved through the performance of interdisciplinary projects and challenges as an essential strategy in the improvement of soft skills and the consolidation of creativity. Students, far from simply applying theoretical topics, are expected to propose solutions based on real-world problem contexts. Empirical evidence from STEM-based learning environments shows improvements in collaborative and problem-solving performance when students engage in interdisciplinary activities (Rizakhojayeva et al., 2025). They will also need to develop the ability to integrate additional knowledge to ensure a solution from different perspectives of the problem. Interaction with diverse groups of people associated with multiple areas of work on the solution develops and consolidates essential skills such as communication, negotiation, and leadership, which are highly valued in the professional and labor sectors.

b. Teaching Methodologies

These strategies for integrating and evaluating activities related to creativity and soft skills can be aligned with a competency-based education approach. These strategies should be explicitly considered as one of the expected competencies in vocational training. Biggs and Tang (2022) specify that aligning the expected outcomes in the curriculum with their respective completion and evaluation activities within this approach may support the pedagogical coherence and effectiveness of the educational model.

Priority should be given to integrative activities that connect students' knowledge with their cognitive skills and attitudes. This is not possible if the curriculum does not clearly define the learning outcomes, the competencies to be developed, and their importance in students' professional careers.

The fusion and application of these activities in the curriculum does not end with their execution; it is necessary to provide students with metacognitive and reflective time in which they learn to develop their own learning methods. This is achieved when students are not only aware of what they know, but also of their strengths and areas for improvement; and based on this awareness, adapt their study methods to maximize their strengths and mitigate their weaknesses. The student becomes a key factor in their own learning. Shavelson (2010) emphasizes that students are aware of their learning process and, based on their experience, foster meaningful learning alongside the improvement of their creativity and soft skills in a cross-curricular manner.

All the designed teaching activities and methodologies would be ineffective without institutional support. The institution is responsible for defining and implementing internal policies that create an environment conducive to the inclusion and administration of the curriculum changes described above. This will depend directly on academic leadership and the administrative organization of institutional authorities. Holcombe et al. (2021) suggest implementing an institutional policy that encourages teaching innovation within the context of integrating soft skills and creativity through the accomplishment of training programs supported by regulatory frameworks.

While innovation depends directly on each teacher, it will be the institution that consolidates it as a policy and appears to support for its continuity in both the transversal and vertical approaches.

The institution must develop these policies within the framework of international regulations. There is a need to integrate creativity and soft skills into the curriculum.

The labor market is influenced by automation and trends from organizations such as: the World Economic Forum, (2020), European Commission, (2022) and the OECD, (2020); which identify them as a strategic axis of vocational training.

The practical recommendations presented help to find application in educational approaches based on STEAM (Science, Technology, Engineering, Arts, and Mathematics), which integrate interdisciplinarity, emerging technologies, and the emergence of transversal skills. The chapter delves into the role of the STEAM approach as an educational and professional strategy, as a framework for addressing social and productive needs, and as a pathway for training in the contexts of Industry 4.0 and 5.0.

By way of conclusion, Figure 8 represents a model of incorporation of white skills, cognitive and psychological factors, convergent and divergent thinking, as well as proof related to educational strategies, all as fundamental elements to be known and recognized in curriculum merge. Of course, these components refer to a sine qua non condition, where the sociocultural context is predominant in their formation.

Figure 8. Integrative model of strategies for the growth of creativity and soft skills

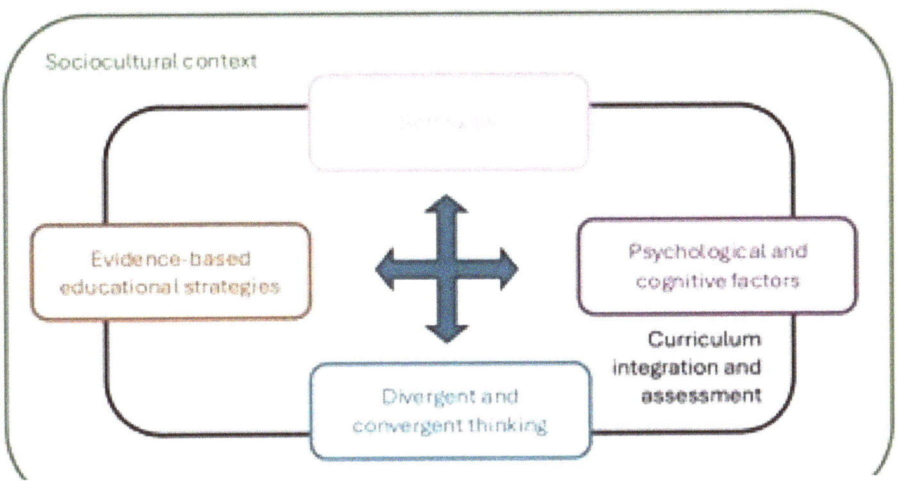

Source: Created by the author.

REFERENCES

ABET. (2025). *Criteria for accrediting engineering programs, 2025–2026*. https://www.abet.org/accreditation/accreditation-criteria/criteria-for-accrediting-engineering-programs-2025-2026/

Ahmad, A., Amry, D., Chen, Z., & Hu, Y. (2026). Building entrepreneurial self-efficacy in engineering students: Towards a new methodological framework. *Entrepreneurship Education*, *9*(1), 21–56. DOI: 10.1007/s41959-025-00156-7

Akdemir-Beveridge, Z. G., & Zaghi, A. E. (2026). ECAT as a contextualized TTCT: Evidence of convergent validity in engineering creativity assessment. *Frontiers in Education*, *11*, 1705312. Advance online publication. DOI: 10.3389/feduc.2026.1705312

Araújo, A. A., Kalinowski, M., & Baldassarre, M. T. (2025). Embracing experiential learning: Hackathons as an educational strategy for shaping soft skills in software engineering. In *2025 IEEE Conference on Software Engineering Education and Training (CSEE&T)* (pp. 319–324). IEEE. DOI: 10.1109/CSEET66350.2025.00040

Arce Rangel, L. M. (2024). Habilidades blandas en la gestión cultural: nuevos retos [Soft skills in cultural management: New challenges]. *Córima. Revista de Investigación en Gestión Cultural*, *9*(17), 1–27. Advance online publication. DOI: 10.32870/cor.a9n17.7472

Bandura, A. (1977). Self-efficacy: Toward a unifying theory of behavioral change. *Psychological Review*, *84*(2), 191–215. DOI: 10.1037/0033-295X.84.2.191 PMID: 847061

Biggs, J., Tang, C., & Kennedy, G. (2022). *Teaching for quality learning at university* (5th ed.). McGraw-Hill Education.

Boud, D., Keogh, R., & Walker, D. (Eds.). (1985). *Reflection: Turning experience into learning*. Kogan Page.

Brookhart, S. M. (2010). *How to assess higher-order thinking skills in your classroom*. ASCD.

Brown, T. (2008). Design thinking. *Harvard Business Review*, *86*(6), 84–92. https://hbr.org/2008/06/design-thinking PMID: 18605031

Calero López, I., González-Peiteado, M., & Rodríguez-López, B. (2024). Are creativity, L2 motivation and soft skills related? A study in VET students. *Education Sciences*, *14*(3), 214. Advance online publication. DOI: 10.3390/educsci14030214

Clapp, E. P. (2018). *La creatividad como proceso participativo y distribuido: Implicación en las aulas*. Narcea.

Cortizo Pérez, J. C., Carrero García, F. M., Monsalve Piqueras, B., Velasco Collado, A., Díaz del Dedo, L. I., & Pérez Martín, J. (2011). Gamificación y docencia: Lo que la universidad tiene que aprender de los videojuegos. In *VIII Jornadas Internacionales de Innovación Universitaria: Retos y oportunidades del desarrollo de los nuevos títulos en educación superior*. Universidad Europea de Madrid. http://hdl.handle.net/11268/1750

Cropley, A. J. (2006). In praise of convergent thinking. *Creativity Research Journal, 18*(3), 391–404. DOI: 10.1207/s15326934crj1803_13

Damayanti, N. A., Yus, A., & Mahya, V. A. (2024). Assessment rubric based on Guilford's creativity theory. In *Proceedings of the 2nd International Conference on Chemistry & Chemical Education (ICCCE)*. https://journal.ar-raniry.ac.id/index.php/ICCCE/article/view/5372

Darling-Hammond, L., Schachner, A., & Edgerton, A. K. (with Badrinarayan, A., Cardichon, J., Cookson, P. W., Jr., Griffith, M., Klevan, S., Maier, A., Martinez, M., Melnick, H., Truong, N., & Wojcikiewicz, S.). (2020). *Restarting and reinventing school: Learning in the time of COVID and beyond*. Learning Policy Institute. https://learningpolicyinstitute.org/product/restarting-reinventing-school-covid

Elaby, M., Mohamed, H., Wafa, M., & Sweilam, S. (2023). Impact of full-scale models on students' creativity in basic design course. *Creativity Studies, 16*(2), 411–432. DOI: 10.3846/cs.2023.15718

European Commission. (2022). *Communication from the Commission to the European Parliament, the Council, the European Economic and Social Committee and the Committee of the Regions on a European strategy for universities* (COM(2022) 16 final). https://eur-lex.europa.eu/legal-content/EN/TXT/?uri=CELEX:52022DC0016

Fiallo Rodríguez, J. (2001). *La interdisciplinariedad en la escuela: Un reto para la calidad de la educación*. Pueblo y Educación.

Fullan, M. (2020). *Liderar en una cultura de cambio* (J. G. Ross, Trans.). Ediciones Morata. https://edmorata.es/producto/liderar-en-una-cultura-de-cambio/

Fundación Chile. (2021). *Aprendizaje basado en proyectos: Un enfoque pedagógico para potenciar aprendizajes*. Educarchile. https://www.educarchile.cl/sites/default/files/2021-09/ABP-un-enfoque-pedagogico-para-potenciar-aprendizajes.pdf

Gandini, F. (2018). Metacognición y aprendizaje. In A. M. Palacios, M. A. Pedragosa, & M. Querejeta (Coords.), *Encuentro en la encrucijada: Psicología, cultura y educación*. EDULP. https://www.memoria.fahce.unlp.edu.ar/libros/pm.4860/pm.4860.pdf

Garavito-Hernández, Y., Villamizar-Mancilla, A. F., & Castañeda-Villamizar, L. P. (2024). Importancia de las habilidades blandas en el contexto laboral: Una revisión de la literatura académica. *Innova Research Journal*, *9*(3), 1–24. DOI: 10.33890/innova.v9.n3.2024.2531

Gilhooly, K. J., Fioratou, E., Anthony, S. H., & Wynn, V. (2007). Divergent thinking: Strategies and executive involvement in generating novel uses for familiar objects. *British Journal of Psychology*, *98*(4), 611–625. DOI: 10.1111/j.2044-8295.2007.tb00467.x PMID: 17535464

Gutiérrez Martínez, F., & Mateos Sanz, M. M. (2006). El desarrollo de los conocimientos y habilidades metacognitivas. In F. Gutiérrez Martínez, J. A. García Madruga, & N. Carriedo López (Coords.), *Psicología evolutiva II: Desarrollo cognitivo y lingüístico* (Vol. 2, pp. 93–128). Universidad Nacional de Educación a Distancia.

Harden, R. M., Grant, J., Buckley, G., & Hart, I. R. (1999). BEME Guide No. 1: Best evidence medical education. *Medical Teacher*, *21*(6), 553–562. DOI: 10.1080/01421599978960 PMID: 21281174

Helm-Stevens, R., Hanshaw, G. O., & Kim, J. (2019). The Hanshaw Helm-Stevens rapid prototype instructional design model: Examining the dimensions of structure and dialogue within the framework of higher education. *American Journal of Economics and Business Administration*, *11*(1), 35–46. DOI: 10.3844/ajebasp.2019.35.46

Herranz Sánchez, E., & Colomo-Palacios, R. (2012). La gamificación como agente de cambio en la ingeniería del software. *Revista de Procesos y Métricas*, *9*(2), 30–56.

Holcombe, E. M., Kezar, A. J., Elrod, S., & Ramaley, J. A. (Eds.). (2023). *Shared leadership in higher education: A framework and models for responding to a changing world*. Routledge., DOI: 10.4324/9781003446965

Ifenthaler, D., & Yau, J. Y.-K. (2020). Utilising learning analytics to support study success in higher education: A systematic review. *Educational Technology Research and Development*, *68*(4), 1961–1990. DOI: 10.1007/s11423-020-09788-z

Izquierdo Izquierdo, M., Gómez Calero, C., & García Lázaro, D. (2022). Design thinking, una metodología para fomentar el aprendizaje significativo. *Revista Ingeniería Industrial*, *21*, 1–20. DOI: 10.22320/S07179103/2022.01

Johnson, D. W., Johnson, R. T., & Johnson Holubec, E. (1999). *El aprendizaje cooperativo en el aula*. Paidós.

Klein, J. T. (2021). *Beyond interdisciplinarity: Boundary work, communication, and collaboration*. Oxford University Press., DOI: 10.1093/oso/9780197571149.001.0001

Kuh, G. D., Kinzie, J. L., Buckley, J. A., Bridges, B. K., & Hayek, J. C. (2006). *What matters to student success: A review of the literature*. National Postsecondary Education Cooperative.

Llano Arana, L., Gutiérrez Escobar, M., Stable Rodríguez, A., Núñez Martínez, M. C., Masó Rivero, R. M., & Rojas Rivero, B. (2016). La interdisciplinariedad: Una necesidad contemporánea para favorecer el proceso de enseñanza aprendizaje. *Medisur, 14*(3), 320–327. https://medisur.sld.cu/index.php/medisur/article/view/3233

López, B. S., & Recio, H. (1998). *Creatividad y pensamiento crítico* (1.ª ed.). Trillas.

Morales González, E., & Del Moral Zamudio, Y. A. (2022). Los objetos de diseño desde una mirada cognitiva. *Cuadernos del Centro de Estudios en Diseño y Comunicación. Ensayos, 172*(172). Advance online publication. DOI: 10.18682/cdc.vi172.7122

Morin, E. (1992). *El método IV: Las ideas: Su hábitat, su vida, sus costumbres, su organización* (Sánchez, A., Trans.). Cátedra.

OECD. (2020). *Curriculum (re)design: A series of thematic reports from the OECD Education 2030 project—Overview brochure*. OECD. https://www.oecd.org/education/2030-project/contact/Curriculum_Redesign_Thematic_Reports.pdf

Panadero, E., & Alonso-Tapia, J. (2014). ¿Cómo autorregulan nuestros alumnos?: Modelo de Zimmerman sobre autorregulación del aprendizaje. *Anales de Psicología, 30*(2), 450–462. DOI: 10.6018/analesps.30.2.167221

Pinilla, M. A., Parra, C., & Rojas, E. (2011). El prototipo en el diseño: Actitud creativa de cambio. *Dearq, 8*, 18–31. https://www.redalyc.org/articulo.oa?id=341630317004

Pinilla Gamboa, M. A. (2014). Dar sentido a las posibilidades: Síntesis y prototipo en diseño. *Iconofacto, 10*(15), 22–34. https://dialnet.unirioja.es/servlet/articulo?codigo=5204359

Ramírez Chávez, M. A., & Manjarrez Fuentes, N. N. (2022). Habilidades blandas y habilidades duras, clave para la formación profesional integral. *Revista de Ciencias Sociales y Económicas, 6*(2), 27–37. DOI: 10.18779/csye.v6i2.590

Real Academia Española. (n.d.). Autosuficiencia. In *Diccionario de la lengua española*. Retrieved February 10, 2026, from https://dle.rae.es/autosuficiencia

Reyes-Angona, S., Pattier Bocos, D., & López Moreno, I. (2025). *Guía didáctica hackathon educativo*. Universidad Complutense de Madrid. https://docta.ucm.es/entities/publication/b20d9225-f299-4150-bef7-ec77cfb3d4ea

Ritter, B. A., Small, E. E., Mortimer, J. W., & Doll, J. L. (2018). Designing management curriculum for workplace readiness: Developing students' soft skills. *Journal of Management Education*, *42*(1), 80–103. DOI: 10.1177/1052562917703679

Rizakhojayeva, G., Ramankulov, S., Akeshova, M., Nurizinova, M., Tuyakov, Y., & Abdrakhmanov, R. (2025). STEM-based approaches to soft skills development: A synthesis of meta-analytic findings and empirical evidence. *Frontiers in Education*, *10*, 1663155. Advance online publication. DOI: 10.3389/feduc.2025.1663155

Rodríguez-Rey, R., & Cantero-García, M. (2020). Albert Bandura: Impacto en la educación de la teoría cognitiva social del aprendizaje. *Padres y Maestros*, *384*(384), 72–76. DOI: 10.14422/pym.i384.y2020.011

Saira Banu, K. A., & Kalai Lakshmi, T. R. (2025). Bridging the gap: Aligning soft skills with industry demands for enhanced employability: Challenges and insights from training professionals in engineering colleges of Ernakulam, Kerala. *TPM. Testing, Psychometrics, Methodology in Applied Psychology*, *32*(S6), 1186–1195. https://tpmap.org/submission/index.php/tpm/article/view/1955

Sánchez Carlessi, H. H., Reyes Romero, C. A., & Mejía Sáenz, K. B. (2018). *Manual de términos en investigación científica, tecnológica y humanística*. Universidad Ricardo Palma. https://www.urp.edu.pe/pdf/id/13350/n/libro-manual-de-terminos-en-investigacion.pdf

Sánchez Mendiola, M., & Martínez González, A. (Eds.). (2020). *Evaluación del y para el aprendizaje: Instrumentos y estrategias*. Universidad Nacional Autónoma de México, Coordinación de Desarrollo Educativo e Innovación Curricular. https://cuaed.unam.mx/descargas/investigacion/Evaluacion_del_y_para_el_aprendizaje.pdf

Servicio de Innovación Educativa de la Universidad Politécnica de Madrid. (2020). *Gamificación en el aula*. Universidad Politécnica de Madrid. https://innovacioneducativa.upm.es/sites/default/files/guias/Guia-Gamificaci%C3%B3n.pdf

Shavelson, R. J. (2010). On the measurement of competency. *Empirical Research in Vocational Education and Training*, *2*(1), 41–63. DOI: 10.1007/BF03546488

Sotomayor, C., Vaccaro, C., & Téllez, A. (2021). *Aprendizaje basado en proyectos: Un enfoque pedagógico para potenciar aprendizajes*. Fundación Chile. https://fch.cl/wp-content/uploads/2021/10/ABP-un-enfoque-pedagogico-para-potenciar-aprendizajes.pdf

Udina, N. N., & Atabekova, A. A. (2012). Interdisciplinary approach to teaching language for specific purposes. *RUDN Journal of Law*, *16*(1), 226–229.

UNESCO. (2021). *Reimagining our futures together: A new social contract for education*. UNESCO., DOI: 10.54675/ASRB4722

Viberg, O., Hatakka, M., Bälter, O., & Mavroudi, A. (2018). The current landscape of learning analytics in higher education. *Computers in Human Behavior*, *89*, 98–110. DOI: 10.1016/j.chb.2018.07.027

Vygotski, L. S. (1979). *El desarrollo de los procesos psicológicos superiores*. Crítica. (Original work published 1978)

Vygotsky, L. S. (1995). *Pensamiento y lenguaje* (Kozulin, A., Ed.). Paidós.

Werbach, K., & Hunter, D. (2014). *Gamificación: Revoluciona tu negocio con las técnicas de los juegos* (Educación, P., Trans.). Vuelapluma. (Original work published 2012)

World Economic Forum. (2020). *The future of jobs report 2020*. https://www.weforum.org/publications/the-future-of-jobs-report-2020/

Yang, M., Wang, T., & Lim, C. P. (2017). E-portfolios as digital assessment tools in higher education. In Spector, M. J., Lockee, B. B., & Childress, M. D. (Eds.), *Learning, design, and technology: An international compendium of theory, research, practice, and policy*. Springer., DOI: 10.1007/978-3-319-17727-4_83-1

Chapter 7
Generative AI and Large Language Models in Smart Education for Metaverse-Based Learning

Khalil Omar
http://orcid.org/0000-0002-5328-5762
University of Petra, Jordan

Hussam Fakhouri
Al-Balqa Applied University, Jordan

Faten F. Hamad
http://orcid.org/0000-0001-7548-0529
Sultan Qaboos University, Oman & University of Jordan, Jordan

ABSTRACT

The intertwining of generative artificial intelligence, large language models, and the Metaverse are transforming the realm of smart education. This chapter discusses that convergence by a mixed-methods design comprising of systematic literature review, a reference architecture of GenAI-driven Metaverse classrooms, and a real empirical study on the Open University Learning Analytics Dataset (OULAD). There are four predictive models to the detection of at-risk learners, and XGBoost is tested on four predictive models under stratified cross-validation with predictions of 93.08% and 0.9785 AUC-ROC. It also tests a hybrid model where tabular features are augmented with DistilBERT embeddings, with results offering subtle insights

DOI: 10.4018/979-8-2600-3658-7.ch007

to guide the decision to use the LLM representations to add any educational value. This chapter incorporates these findings into a six-principle ethical framework of bias, hallucination, privacy and academic integrity and suggests concrete research directions of the next generation of immersive, AI-enhanced learning environments.

INTRODUCTION

Over the last three years, there has been an unprecedented rapid advancement in artificial intelligence, with generative models like GPT-4, Claude, and LLaMA showing fluent natural-language understanding, multimodal reasoning, and scale-generated, creatively produced content (Brown et al., 2020; Touvron et al., 2023). Simultaneously, the Metaverse, a persistent three-dimensional virtual ecosystem, a combination of virtual reality, augmented reality and Web 3.0 infrastructures, has become a serious contender of the next pedagogical frontier (Mystakidis, 2022; Wang et al., 2022). When these two trajectories meet within the context of smart education they pose some urgent questions regarding how the design, delivery, assessment and governance of learning will be delivered in the years ahead. In this chapter, the intersection is considered.

There is a lot at stake economically. The USD 7.3 trillion education market has a highly dynamic segment in EdTech, which is one of the main areas of emerging-technology investment (HolonIQ, 2022). Empirical evidence related to immersive learning has also been accruing: According to an enterprise study of virtual-reality soft-skills training by PwC, VR learners completed training up to four times faster than peers in the classroom, were 3.75 times more emotionally engaged with the content, and demonstrated 275 percent more confidence in applying the new skills (PwC, 2020). In parallel, generative AI has augmented the set of tools that an educator can use, including large language models that can be used to scaffold one-to-one tutoring, as well as generate adaptive practice materials and converse with learners in a natural, high-quality language (Kasneci et al., 2023; Lee and Wu, 2025).

Although this is gaining traction, the combination of generative AI and large language models with the Metaverse-based smart education has not been theorized or tested. According to recent systematic reviews, the vast majority of current scholarship is either conceptual or descriptive or only conducted on a small scale during pilot demonstrations (Alfaisal et al., 2024; Tlili et al., 2022). Of consequence are three gaps that are mainly consequential. To begin with, the literature on the use of individual technologies in isolation without considering their combined application in immersive smart-education environments is fragmented and has no unifying conceptual framework on how the technologies can be deployed together in immersive smart-education settings. Second, anecdotal case reports tend to support claims related to pedagogical effectiveness, and thus it is not easy to cross-study compare and contrast. Third, ethical and infrastructural issues are usually addressed as an appendix to technical proposals as opposed to being considered as design constraints that are addressed at the very beginning. Algorithms bias (Bender et al., 2021), model hallucination (Ji et al., 2023), and biometric and behavioral surveillance in immersive environments (Falchuk et al., 2018) interplay in some subtle ways within a classroom of the Metaverse, especially when underage students are involved.

In order to overcome these difficulties, this chapter has four contributions, which interlock. It will first synthesize the recent literature on generative AI, large language models, the Metaverse, and smart education to come up with a coherent picture of the converging landscape. Second, it suggests a 4-layer pedagogical framework, and a complementary reference system framework that map the functional roles of generative AI and LLMs throughout the immersive Metaverse classroom. Third, it presents a real empirical study of OULAD (Kuzilek et al., 2017) in which classical machine-learning baselines and a hybrid model based on tabular features and semantic embeddings of DistilBERT are evaluated to early detect at-risk learners - a core capability of any AI-augmented immersive classroom. Fourth, it summarizes the ethical, legal, and pedagogical risks of the convergence into a six-principle mitigation framework that can be directly adapted by researchers, educators and platform designers.

The chapter is methodologically based on a mixed method design. The conceptual foundation is created by a systematic review of peer-reviewed articles in 2019-2025 based on IEEE Xplore, ACM Digital Library, ERIC, and Scopus. A quantitative empirical component reports actual results of an experiment at OULAD under stratified cross-validation, five-fold cross-validation, of actual results of an experiment. Three classical baselines (logistic regression, random forest, gradient-boosted trees) are considered along with a hybrid model that adds DistilBERT embeddings to the tabular features, allowing principled analysis of when the use of the LLM representations can be used to predict education. The framework is based on observable practice as a qualitative analysis of representative case implementations forms the framework.

The chapter will be divided in the following way. The following section is a review of the literature in the background in four streams. The Main Focus section then elaborates the pedagogical framework, introduces the reference system architecture, presents the empirical study and discusses main issues and ethical concerns and provides concrete mitigations. Six open questions are identified by a Future Research Directions section and the Conclusion summarizes the contributions of the chapter.

BACKGROUND

An integrated treatment of generative AI and large language models in smart education based on the Metaverse and immersive learning requires foundations across four overlapping research streams: generative AI and large language models; the Metaverse and immersive learning; smart education and learning analytics; and the explicitly hybrid systems in which language models provide pedagogical content and dialog, immersive environments provide embodied context, and learning analytics provide closed-loop feedback. This section reviews each of the streams and then a review of the recent literature that has been engaging in the convergence of these streams and which forms the shared vocabulary and evidentiary base out of which the framework, architecture, and empirical study of the chapter proceed.

Generative AI and Large Language Models

Generative artificial intelligence is a type of machine-learning system that can generate new content - text, images, audio, video or code - through learning the statistical structure of training data and sampling the learned distribution (Brown et al., 2020). Among the models of large language models (LLMs) are placed in a specific pedagogical focus. LLMs are deep neural networks with their architecture based on the Transformer architecture proposed by Vaswani and others (2017) and trained on very large text corpora using self-supervised tasks like masked language modeling and next-token prediction. The contribution that was made by the Transformer was the self-attention mechanism, which enables each token within a sequence to selectively attend to every other token.

The history of modern LLMs is traced back to BERT and the GPT family, to more recent open foundation models like LLaMA. It was demonstrated that the transferable representations to a variety of downstream tasks could be acquired through bidirectional pretraining of unlabeled text using BERT (Devlin et al., 2019). Scaling the autoregressive generation to hundreds of billions of parameters and exposing unexpected emergent abilities in few-shot learning, the GPT family (Brown et al., 2020) scaled. The introduction of open weights and competitive ability in LLaMA (Touvron et al., 2023) has made available to the wider research community. The tasks an LLM can accomplish without or with minimal task specific training, such as translation, summarization, question answering, code generation and increasingly fluent multi turn dialogue are all expanded with each generation.

To be used in education, the salient attribute of modern LLMs is that they can be used on-demand to generate contextually-appropriate natural-language output which makes them suitable substrates of the explanatory dialogue, formative feedback, content adaptation, and assessment scaffold (Kasneci et al., 2023). Emergent capabilities also exist in large-scale models, i.e., capabilities like multi-step arithmetic, analogical reasoning and teaching which emerge as large-scale models become sufficiently large. The properties extend applicability to educational situations, although the abilities that manifest themselves without being explicitly specified may also manifest themselves without being explicitly indicated.

Some of the engineering paradigms have developed to adapt general-purpose LLMs to specific domains: supervised fine-tuning on domain-specific curated corpora, instruction tuning to make outputs more aligned with human preferences, and retrieval-augmented generation, which trains a frozen LLM on a background knowledge store to ground responses in current, verifiable, or institution-specific information without retraining. In educational use cases, retrieval augmentation is becoming more popular, because it enables curricular content to be authoritative and up to date, reduces the tendency of the model to fabricate information, and it allows institutional knowledge to be incorporated, without exposing it to the training process.

The scale which makes it possible to do these things also has some practical limitations. Latency of the inference process, memory requirement, and power consumption have inspired distillation methods. Sanh and colleagues (2019) presented DistilBERT, a compressed version of BERT that retains about ninety-seven percent of the language-understanding capability of its teacher with forty percent of the number of parameters and running about sixty times faster. Distillation is not only an optimization of efficiency but an enabler of deployment in environments that are constrained by bandwidth and necessitate the use of head-mounted devices, learning portals that run on the browser, and classrooms that are limited by bandwidth.

The Metaverse and Immersive Learning

As a research object, the Metaverse dates back several decades to crystallize into a manageable scholarly object since the beginning of the 2020s. The definition of the Metaverse as a constant, ever-present, multiuser space integrating physical reality with digital virtuality, using immersive technologies like virtual reality, augmented reality and mixed reality is one of the most cited contemporary definitions. Park and Kim (2022) further develop it into a wider taxonomy that breaks down the Metaverse into hardware, software and content elements and identifying application domains that range across entertainment, commerce, healthcare and education. Lee and colleagues (2021) give a detailed technical treatment of the Metaverse stack to include the underlying networking, computing and interaction technologies that the application-level taxonomies that the authors assume are based on.

The empirical history of the pedagogical relevance of immersive technology is longer. In a systematic review of the virtual-reality application in higher education, Radianti and colleagues (2020) reported the design patterns and outcomes in 38 published studies, and found consistent evidence of positive effects on engagement, motivation and procedural skill acquisition and persistent gaps in pedagogical theory and learning-science grounding. Wang and others (2022) generalized these results to the era of the Metaverse with an Edu-Metaverse ecosystem framework describing the stratified relationships among learners, educators, virtual classrooms, content engines, and analytics infrastructures. In a combined content and bibliometric analysis, Tlili and colleagues (2022) have noted that early Metaverse-education scholarship was disproportionately optimistic and that the empirical evaluation of pedagogical assertions was lagged behind by technical demonstrations.

There are three strands of immersive-learning evidence which are relevant here. The former is embodied cognition: immersive activities enable students to practice procedures (laboratory work, surgical training, language interaction) as opposed to merely watching them, and embodied practice is linked to better transfer to real-world performance. An increase in reported presence is associated with increased involvement and better memory of procedural information, especially tasks that are well served by spatial reasoning, or fine-motor training. The second strand is related to affective engagement: A study of enterprise learning by PwC (2020) has found that VR learners were 3.75 times more emotionally engaged with content and 4 times more focused than their counterparts in similar e-learning settings. An affective engagement is a functional contributor as engaged learners devote more time to task and persist through the productive frustration that comes along with non-trivial learning gains. The third thread is access: well-designed Metaverse classrooms compress geographic and physical-resource constraints and enable distributed laboratory experiences to learners who would otherwise be unreachable due to geographic or physical-resource constraints. This trend is reported by Mystakidis and colleagues (2022), in their systematic mapping of AR overlays to STEM higher education, where AR overlays provide visualizations in laboratories to ordinary classrooms at a fraction of the cost of physical replication.

Smart Education and Learning Analytics

Smart education is an umbrella term to describe educational systems that incorporate intelligent technologies such as artificial intelligence, learning analytics, the Internet of Things and connected platforms to provide adaptive and personalized, evidence-informed instruction. The construct builds on previous research on intelligent tutoring systems and adaptive learning by focusing on data-driven adaptation in continuous closed loops: the activity of a learner is instrumented, analyzed and used to re-calibrate the process of delivering instructions to a learner in near real time. The intellectual lineage is through early intelligent-tutoring systems of the 1980s, to cognitive tutors which used cognitive-task analysis, to modern data-driven systems, which learn pedagogical strategies using large-scale instructional traces. COVID-19 accelerated the topicality of this paradigm by causing abrupt transitions to remote and online learning; the case studies of higher education report that despite the need to make urgent changes, the issues of engagement, assessment integrity, and support of students have remained an unsolved problem.

One of the sub-streams has become predictive learning analytics i.e. the use of statistical and machine-learning models to predict learner outcomes. Mubarak and colleagues (2021) showed the use of deep neural networks to the MOOC interaction data to early predict the dropout. The Open University Learning Analytics Dataset, which was publicly released by Kuzilek and colleagues (2017) has become de facto benchmark, which provides demographic, behavioral and assessment information about over thirty-two thousand learners across twenty-two module presentations of seven distance-learning courses. The strengths of the dataset are that it has a combination of scale, richness and ecological validity: the data were collected in the reality of real instruction at a large open-enrollment university, and the variables span the entire pipeline of registration through final outcome. Later research has investigated predictive targets as far as final examination results up to assessment-by-assessment performance to the binary at-risk classification that is used here (Hlosta et al., 2017; Patel and Amin, 2024).

The pedagogical promise of smart education is directly, and closely, related to the quality and timeliness of analytic feedback. In a controlled study of pre-service teachers, Sailer and colleagues (2023) demonstrated that adaptive feedback provided by artificial neural networks had a significant positive effect on the quality of diagnostic justifications made in written assignments but did not significantly impact the quality of diagnostic-accuracy outcomes - a finding that highlights both the potential and the calibrated scope of the adaptive support provided by artificial neural networks. Findings of this kind set a quality standard: the usefulness of making predictions depends on whether the predictions are used to make actual pedagogical action, whether the learner is in control of acting upon the predictions, and whether the very process of making a measurement is done in an ethically and transparently oriented fashion.

The Convergence: GenAI, LLMs, the Metaverse, and Smart Education

There is a very small but fast expanding literature, which deals with convergence of these four streams. Based on the previous conceptualization of the role of artificial intelligence in the educational Metaverse as proposed by Zhang and others (2022), Hwang and Chien (2022) suggest conceptual scaffolding of the role of artificial intelligence in the educational Metaverse, distinguishing between three modes: AI as content generator, AI as embodied tutor, and AI as analytic instrument. Fan and colleagues (2024) discuss the infrastructural turn, which was introduced by Web 3.0, which consists of decentralized identity, verifiable credentials, and tokenized incentive structures. The field is organized around five sub-domains (immersive content, intelligent agents, analytics, governance, and interoperability) and the integration of LLMs and embodied virtual agents is one of the frontiers with the highest impact.

Experimental demonstrations are coming out at an increased pace than analyses that are being synthesized. More recently, it has been investigated how conversational LLMs can be integrated with immersive virtual worlds to provide intelligent tutoring in the form of embodied non-player characters that can converse with learners in a conversational way (Ackermann et al., 2025). Anthropomorphic agents of Embodied LLM in virtual classrooms have been shown to have quantifiable effects on the learner levels of attention, cognitive engagement and willingness to ask clarifying questions, with the strongest effects observed when the anthropomorphic features of the agent are tuned to the disciplinary social norms instead of being maximized indiscriminately. Close work has explored the data-literacy training of virtual reality, language-learning role-play of conversational tutors, and procedural simulation of both clinical and engineering fields. The pattern is that in these studies, an immersive environment is used to provide embodied context to practice; a large language model can be used to provide on-demand pedagogical interaction; and a learning-analytics layer can be used to collect evidence about the performance of learners and adapt the experience.

Holmes and colleagues (2022) offer a much needed ethical contrapunt, stating community-wide principles of the responsible development and deployment of AI in education that would apply with redoubled force when AI is coupled with immersive surveillance affordances. A blend of biometric instrumentation that is inherent to head-mounted displays gaze, head pose, hand position, voice and the inferential power of modern LLMs, results in a category of learner-modeling capabilities that has no apparent historical precedent in traditional schooling. Falchuk and colleagues (2018) expected this issue when they early treated the issue of social-Metaverse privacy, identifying the categories of personal data that immersive systems are almost incidentally being used to gather data about, and that the traditional educational data-protection regimes were not designed to regulate. Surveying the body of adoption studies, Alfaisal and colleagues (2024) conclude that infrastructural preparedness, preparation of instructors, and evidence-based design templates are the major pragmatic bottlenecks that slows wide-scale implementation. Empirical research in the context of a particular country has contributed to strengthening this image: Omar, Abu-Aishah, and colleagues (2024) report that the higher education instructors in Jordan express interest in using the Metaverse to educate students but indicate that concrete measures, such as institutional preparedness, training, and pedagogical guidance, need to be taken into account, and the adoption barriers are not universal but region-specific, and require region-specific interventions.

There are two patterns that should be highlighted. The most common mode of methodology is, first, conceptual or descriptive: published frameworks often outnumber published empirical evaluations, and the empirical evaluations that do exist are often of small scale, short duration and idiosyncratic outcome measures. Second, the literature in both ethical and infrastructural literature has increased more rapidly than the technical literature, perhaps because risks have been shown easier to foresee in the abstract than benefits have been shown to deliver in practice. The current chapter has taken both of the above into consideration: it provides a conceptual model based on the literature, an architecture that can be subjected to an engineering implementation, and an empirical assessment on a known public test-run, as it works on the development of the ethical analysis as a design constraint.

MAIN FOCUS OF THE CHAPTER

The literature reviewed in the section above establishes that the generative AI, large language models, the Metaverse, and smart education are converging, but it leaves three operational questions unanswered: how the components fit together in a pedagogical way, how the components fit together in an architectural way, and whether the resulting systems deliver quantifiable improvements in the learning analytics tasks that lie at the core of their operation. Each of these is dealt with in this Main Focus. It initially suggests a four-layer pedagogical model of the functional roles of generative AI and LLMs in the immersive Metaverse classroom; and then translates that model into a reference system architecture; and then reports a real empirical study on the Open University Learning Analytics Dataset of the classical baselines and a hybrid LLM-augmented model to detect early at-risk learners; and then closes with a structured analysis of issues, ethical concerns, and mitigations.

Pedagogical Framework: Generative AI and LLMs in the Metaverse Classroom

An educational framework based on GenAI-driven Metaverse education must meet three criteria: it must be pedagogically grounded, as opposed to being simply technical, it must organize elements by educational purpose, as opposed to engineering implementation, it must be modular, so that institutions can adopt elements in a piecemeal fashion, and it must be honest about the boundary between what the technology provides and what the human educator still provides. The framework presented here is based on the previous work to formalize the concepts of Learning ecosystems based on the Metaverse (Omar and Gomez, 2025) and extends this concept to include the generative AI and large language models as first-class architectural entities and not as secondary additions. The framework is designed in such a way that it comprises of the four interacting layers namely the Learner Layer, the Pedagogy Layer, the AI Engine Layer and the Immersive Layer and the cross-cutting Governance Layer that constrains all the four. The structure of the framework is shown in figure 1.

Figure 1. Four-layer pedagogical framework with the cross-cutting Governance Layer.

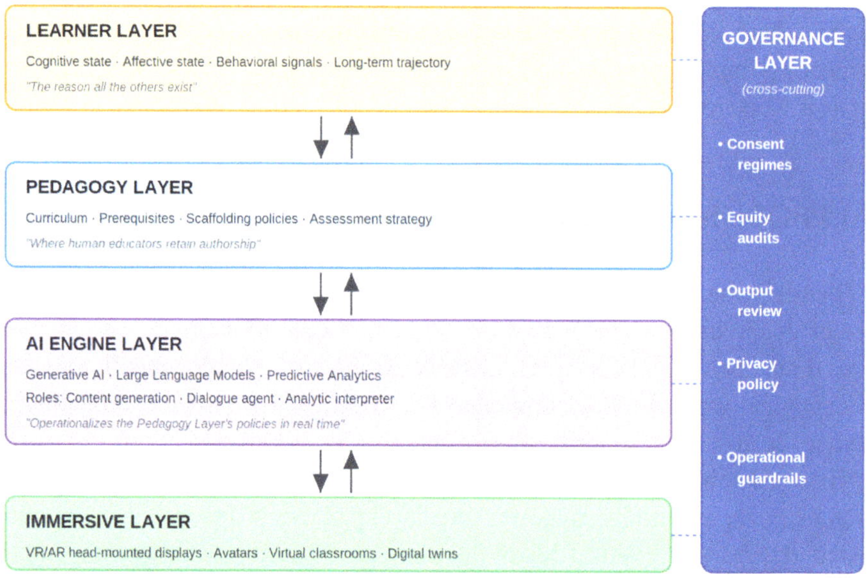

The uppermost layer is the Learner Layer, and the explanation of the existence of all the other layers. It includes cognitive state of the individual learner (prior knowledge, current understanding, misconceptions), affective state of the individual learner (engagement, motivation, confidence, frustration), behavioral signals of the individual learner (attention, response patterns, interaction sequences), and the longer-term trajectory of connecting the current session to agreed learning goals. These cues are both partially instrumented in a Metaverse classroom gaze, response latency, task choices, conversational content and partially inferred. The framework considers the Learner Layer as the source of power of the system: the other layers are its servants.

The Pedagogy Layer describes the instructional design that transforms the current state of the learner to the next pedagogical action. It codes the curriculum, structure of prerequisites, formative-assessment plan, scaffold policy and the long-term pedagogical sequence. Human educators still have the most explicit authorship in the pedagogy layer, which includes what to teach, in what order, with what evidence of mastery must have been met to be promoted, and with what type of support to be given struggling learners. The structure of the Pedagogy Layer should and remains the prerogative of qualified educators, although populating the Pedagogy Layer with candidate content can be done through generative AI.

The operationalization of the policies of the Pedagogy Layer is operationalized in real time by the AI Engine Layer. In this layer, huge language models play a variety of functions. The content generation role generates explanatory text, examples, problems and feedback based on the current state of the learner, and leverages retrieval-augmented generation to base its outputs on curricular content that is vetted. The role of dialogue agent engages conversational tutoring, fielding questions, eliciting reasoning and the provision of Socratic prompts that develop the thinking of the learner, rather than replace it. The role of the analytic interpreter is to transform raw indicators of analytic state in the Learner Layer, into pedagogically meaningful descriptions: instead of telling you that in the last twenty minutes the learner has clicked seventy times, the interpreter will tell you that the learner seems to be flitting between resources without really having to delve into the content, indicating that the learner is probably confused about the structure of the subject matter, rather than its content. All roles are in principle amenable to classical methods, but due to the breadth and the responsiveness of contemporary LLMs to context, they are appealing substrates in the event that costs and risks are appropriately managed.

The medium that the outputs of the framework are delivered to the learner is the Immersive Layer: the head-mounted display, the avatar, the virtual classroom, the digital twin of a laboratory apparatus, the spatial-audio voice of an embodied tutor. The Immersive Layer is what makes a Metaverse classroom look like a advanced web application - the Immersive Layer is what makes the actions of the Pedagogy Layer experienced. The framework considers it to be a presentation medium with high affordances to embodied practice and low affordances to unguided exploration, the temptation to think of immersion as inherently educational is one the framework explicitly discourages.

The Governance Layer is a cross-cutting of the other four. It includes institutional, ethical and legal constraints within which the system is to operate: consent regimes, data-handling policies, model-output review procedures, equity audits, the operational guardrails within which the AI Engine is to operate. The design intuition that ethical deployment is not retrofittable is expressed by treating governance as a cross-cutting issue, and not the final step compliance checklist.

There are three properties to be highlighted. First, the pedagogy-led framework: AI Engine and the Immersive Layer serve the Pedagogy Layer, thus technology decisions are made based on pedagogical decisions made first. Second, it is evidence-conscious: the contribution of each layer is treated as a hypothesis, which can be empirically tested, hence the extent of space devoted to a real-life test of one of the predictive functions of the AI Engine on a publicly available benchmark is quite large. Third, it is boundary-honest: it does not take over all the educational functions into the technological substrate, but rather acknowledges that human educators still have a role to play in designing the curriculum, assessing it as valid, and the moral aspects of teaching.

Reference System Architecture

There are a number of different technical architectures which can be used to realize the pedagogical framework. The reference architecture suggested in this paper is representative, but not prescriptive - one defensible decomposition that can be customized to local constraints by engineers and instructional designers. It has five major components, namely, the Immersive Client, the Avatar and NPC Layer, the Generative Content Engine, the Analytics Engine, and the Privacy and Compliance Layer. Components interact via clearly defined interfaces, and may be deployed in any of the on-premises, cloud, hybrid, and edge configurations. The architecture, and the key data flows are shown in figure 2.

Figure 2. Reference system architecture: five components plus the Privacy and Compliance Layer.

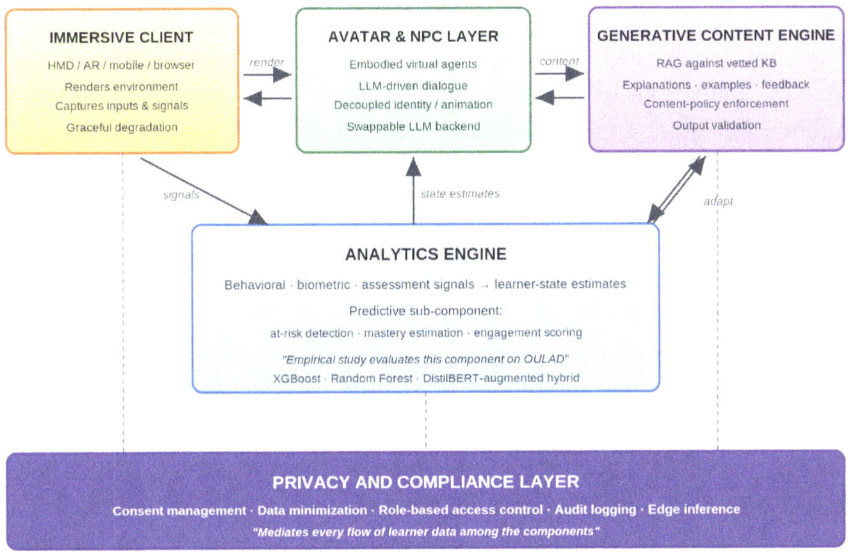

The Immersive Client is the component of the system that runs on the head-mounted display, AR glasses, mobile device or browser. Its duties are to render the virtual environment, receive input provided by the controllers and sensors, provide outputs of the other parts. The client must also work gracefully in degraded conditions - limited bandwidth, intermittent connectivity, lower-end devices - due to educational implementations seldom enjoying uniform infrastructure across all participating learners.

The Avatar and NPC Layer includes the embodied virtual agents, the learner interacts with: peers, tutors, instructors and ambient characters. The main path through which large language models can find their way to the learner in a conversational way is these agents. The architecture considers the issues of avatar identity, dialogue management, and animation to be independent concerns: a single LLM can be used to drive multiple avatars with different personas via prompt-level configuration, and body language and facial expression are generated by special animation models conditioned on the text generated by the underlying LLM. This decoupling permits the upgrading, replacement or constraining of the LLM without re-engineering the avatar system.

Generative Content Engine puts together the curricular content presented via the Immersive Client. Its inputs are the Pedagogy Layer curriculum specification, the current state of the learner accessed via retrieval-augmented generation, and the Analytics Engine providing the current state of the learner. Its outputs are explanatory passages, worked examples, practice problems, formative-feedback messages and remedial materials which are triggered when the Analytics Engine detects difficulty. The engine runs on a content policy which is implemented at prompt-level constraints, and at an output-validation layer, which checks the content generated before it reaches the learner.

The Analytics Engine consumes the behavioral, biometric and assessment cues generated by the Immersive Client and the assessment subsystems, processes them into estimates of the learner-state, and supplies the estimates to the Generative Content Engine and the Avatar Layer, to drive adaptation. Its predictive sub-component has the following functions: early-identifying at-risk learners, estimating mastery, scoring engagement, and inferring emotional-state. This sub-component is assessed in the empirical study reported in the next subsection, against a known public standard.

The Privacy and Compliance Layer mediates all the flows of learner data between the other components, and implements the governance policies that are set at the institutional level. It is the technical implementation of cross-cutting Governance Layer. Among its responsibilities are consent management, data minimization, role-based access control, audit logging and retention enforcement and the technical implementation of legally required protections such as those of minors. In situations where possible, sensitive computations are done on-device or through federated-learning protocols which keep raw data about learners within the perimeter of the institution.

This break down can be subjected to gradual implementation. A typical example of an institution starting with a traditional learning-management system enhanced with LLM-powered dialogue tutors, overlaid with an immersive client over the same back-end services, and finally (but not the least) with a predictive analytics engine, and progressive overlaying governance controls. There are a couple of architectural choices which should be briefly justified. Allowing the operator to change models as the field changes and to audit the conversational behavior of each persona separately, is made possible by decoupling between avatar identity and underlying language model. By running the Generative Content Engine on a vetted knowledge base through retrieval-augmented generation, the issues of hallucinations that were identified above are addressed and the institutions have a direct control over the corpus. Carrying out analytics inference at the edge where possible minimizes the latency as well as the privacy surface area of the system. Lastly, the fact that the Privacy and Compliance Layer is being elevated to the first-class architectural status, indicates 20 years of experience, in which retrofitted compliance has been proven more costly and less efficient than compliance designed in the first place.

Empirical Study: At-Risk Learner Prediction on OULAD with DistilBERT-Augmented Features

The framework and architecture above will bind the chapter to a specific evidentiary position: the usefulness of integrating an engine of generative-AI-driven pedagogy with the predictive analytics engine must be empirically tested, rather than asserted per se. In this subsection a report is given of such a test. It assesses whether adding semantic embeddings based on a distilled large language model to classical machine-learning features enhances the ability to detect at-risk learners early - a core analytic capability of any AI-augmented immersive classroom since the ability to identify at-risk learners early is a precondition to identifying them early.

Research Questions

The study is guided by two research questions:

- **RQ1.** Can DistilBERT-augmented features improve predictive accuracy for at-risk learner detection over classical tabular baselines on a recognized public benchmark?
- **RQ2.** Do any observed gains justify the additional computational cost of running an LLM in an educational analytics pipeline?

When the gains are large, the additional compute and complexity should be used in functions where the contribution of the LLM is more clearly material. When the gains are small or absent, the extra compute and complexity should be used in functions where the contribution of the LLM is more clearly material.

Dataset and Preprocessing

The study is based on the Open University Learning Analytics Dataset (Kuzilek et al., 2017), an anonymized data on 32,593 learners across 22 module presentations in seven distance-learning courses offered by the Open University in the United Kingdom in 2013 and 2014. The data is made available under an open license via the portal of the Knowledge Media Institute at the Open University as well as on the platform Kaggle. It contains seven relational tables, which include studentInfo (demographics and final outcome), studentRegistration, studentVle (daily clickstream), studentAssessment and three reference tables that define courses, assessments, and VLE resources.

The target variable is a binary indicator of at-risk status, based on the final outcome field (final result) of the studentInfo table: a learner is considered to be at-risk when the final outcome is Withdrawn or Fail, and not-at-risk when the final outcome is Pass or Distinction. This is a standard formulation in the OULAD literature, and is equivalent to the educationally significant question of whether one of the learners is on a path to successful completion. The distribution of the classes is moderately unbalanced with the at-risk minority slightly less than half a population.

Three streams were merged in the feature engineering. StudentInfo was used to extract demographic information (gender, age band, region, prior education, IMD deprivation band, disability, prior attempts, credits studied) which were coded into categorical variables. The studentVle clickstream was summarized into per-learner summaries total clicks, number of active days, number of distinct resources accessed, and the span of engagement between first and last interaction. StudentAssessment was aggregated into academic features, the number of assessments completed and the average score of assessment. Missing values in behavioral and assessment features - which usually occur when the learner withdrew before the behavioral and assessment records could be generated - were imputed with a value of zero where the count features are concerned and with the median where the score features are concerned, on the principle that the absence of engagement is in itself a strong predictive signal of withdrawal.

Methodology

We trained three classical baseline models on the tabular feature matrix: a linear baseline model (logistic regression), non-linear ensemble (random forest, Breiman, 2001), and stronger ensemble (gradient-boosted trees, XGBoost library, Chen & Guestrin, 2016). The DistilBERT encoder was obtained via the Hugging Face Transformers library (Wolf et al., 2020), while classical models were developed using scikit-learn (Pedregosa et al., 2011), and XGBoost using the XGBoost Python package. The fourth model, a hybrid approach, added semantic embeddings from a frozen DistilBERT encoder (Sanh et al., 2019), to the standardized tabular features. A tabular profile for each learner was initially written as a short natural-language trajectory description (a few sentences describing learner's demographic band, prior education, engagement metrics and assessment summary) and the written description was fed into DistilBERT to get a 768-dimensional [CLS] embedding. This embedding was then combined with the tabular features that were standardized and given as an input vector of dimension 781 to an XGBoost meta-classifier. The frozen-encoder design helped to prevent fine-tuning expenses and maintain the reproducibility of the LLM while also ensuring that the LLM's pretrained semantic knowledge was added.

The cross validation was performed using a stratified five fold scheme with the class proportions kept the same in each fold. The results presented in terms of accuracy (with cross-fold standard deviation), precision, recall, F1-macro and area under the receiver operating characteristic curve (AUC-ROC). A random seed of 42 was used for all the models. The entire pipeline is given as a companion Jupyter notebook that can be executed on Google Colaboratory or Kaggle with automatic downloading of the data sets.

The OULAD data is available publicly under Creative Commons Attribution 4.0 International (CC BY 4.0) license at https://analyse.kmi.open.ac.uk/open_dataset and also via mirrors at the UCI Machine Learning Repository (10.24432/C5KK69) and figshare (10.6084/m9.figshare.5081998.v1). Companion notebook to experiment is available as a supplement to aid in reproducibility.

Results

The overall performance of the four models is given in the Table 1. The results of all four significantly outperform the previously published results on similar OULAD prediction formulations (Patel & Amin, 2024), which range between seventy-eight and eighty-seven percent. The XGBoost baseline is the best standalone model, with an accuracy of 0.9308 and an AUC-ROC of 0.9785, while logistic regression, a simple model, achieves 0.9157 accuracy, indicating that the engineered features contain a strong signal for the task even without using a powerful non-linear model.

Table 1. Five-fold cross-validation performance on OULAD

Model	Accuracy	Precision	Recall	F1 (macro)	AUC-ROC
Logistic Regression	0.9157 ± 0.0020	0.9518	0.8852	0.9157	0.9708
Random Forest	0.9296 ± 0.0022	0.9647	0.8996	0.9296	0.9785
XGBoost	0.9308 ± 0.0026	0.9601	0.9067	0.9308	0.9785
Hybrid (XGB + DistilBERT)	0.9276 ± 0.0040	0.9634	0.8970	0.9276	0.9764

Best value per column in bold.

The results show that the hybrid model (the main experimental condition based on the chapter's model) is not better than the pure XGBoost baseline model. In terms of the difference, it is small across all five reported metrics, with a difference of ~0.3 percentage points on accuracy and F1-macro, and ~0.0021 on AUC-ROC. The standard deviation of the accuracy of the folds is slightly higher for the hybrid model (0.0040) than the model trained only on the original features (0.0026), suggesting that the additional features derived from the LLM did not decrease the variance in accuracy. A paired two sided t-test of the per-fold accuracies as computed by the companion notebook shows that the differences between XGBoost and the hybrid model is not statistically significant at the conventional 0.05 level, meaning that the two models are statistically equivalent on this benchmark. The ROC curves of all four models have been plotted in figure 3, which shows the same closeness of the top three models in the upper left part of the ROC space.

Figure 3. ROC curves for at-risk learner detection on OULAD across the four evaluated models.

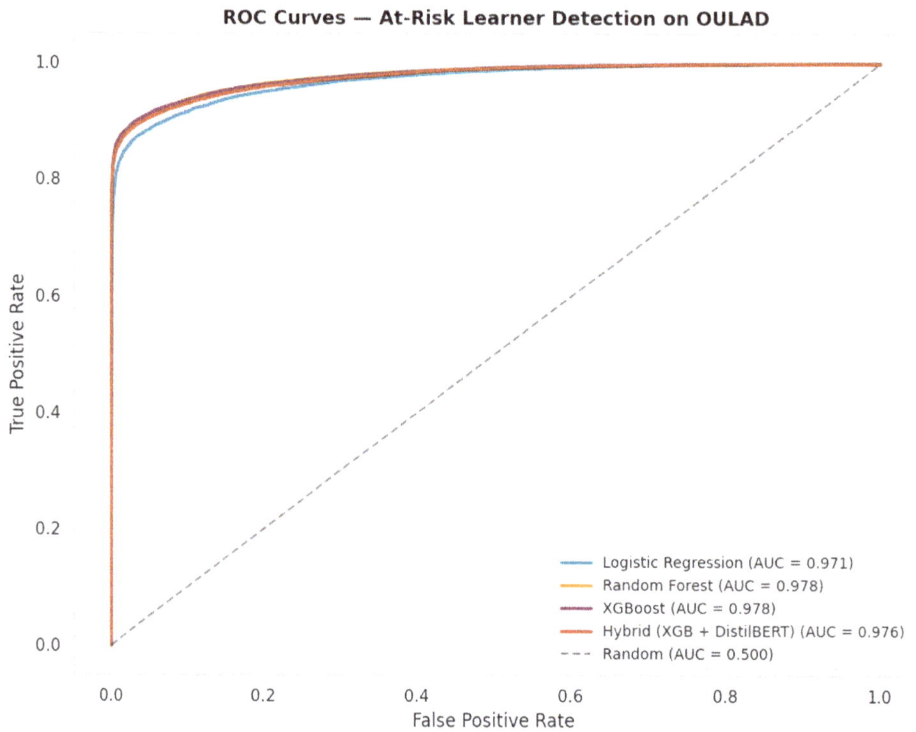

Analysis

The most informative result from the empirical study is that the hybrid model did not outperform the XGBoost baseline model; careful interpretation must be done to explain this result. It's not a condemnation of the use of large language models in educational analytics; it's a clarification of the when and how of LLM-representations adding value. The following three considerations are a context for this interpretation.

Firstly, the OULAD tabular features are very special. The clickstream of the dataset contains fine-grained behavioral data, the demographic data have predictive value, and the assessment scores are direct measures of academic performance. Such features are likely to be well suited to being exploited by tree-based ensembles like XGBoost, leaving little room to gain an additional representation. This is illustrated in Figure 4, where the engagement-related features (engagement span, number assessments submitted, mean score of assessments) collectively make up the vast majority of XGBoost's predictive importance and the demographic features only contribute a small amount. In the domains with a sparser signal, or a noisier signal, the headroom would be more and the contribution of the LLM would be more apparent.

Figure 4. XGBoost feature importances on the OULAD tabular features

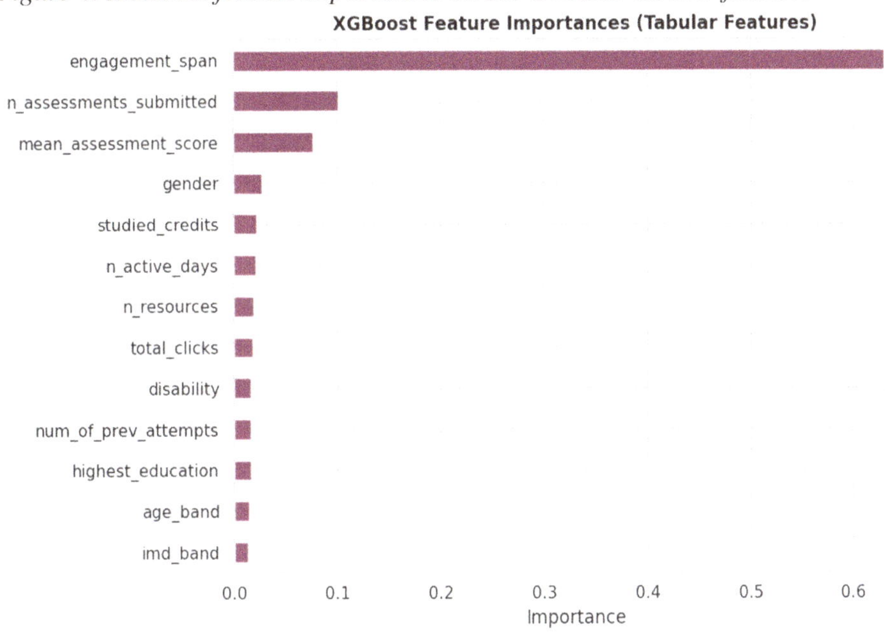

Secondly, the textual trajectory descriptions were combined from the same tabular features that were already provided to the baseline models. Though there is some lexical variation in the synthesis and pretrained semantic knowledge in DistilBERT, the information is limited by the tabular source. Where text is the natural input, e.g. free-response reflections, forum discussions, dialogue logs, open-ended problem solutions, the LLM encoder would be able to access information which is not available in any tabular alternative, and the contribution would be measurable. This finding provides evidence for a nuanced thesis: LLM-derived representations provide benefit when the text is a learner's primary mode of expression, but provide comparatively little benefit when the text is restating features known to the baseline.

Thirdly, the outcome is directly relevant to the reference architecture. The Analytics Engine should selectively use the LLM-derived representations: For prediction tasks where the high-quality tabular signal dominates the LLM-derived embeddings are not competitive and the added compute is not worth it; for prediction tasks where the free-text learner expression dominates, the LLM-derived embeddings offer tangible benefits and the extra compute is warranted. This is a selective attitude in line with the general engineering rule that the components of a system should be selected to do the job that they do best.

This can be confirmed in comparison with previous literature. The accuracy of XGBoost on a similar OULAD is about 0.87 (Patel and Amin, 2024), which is lower than 0.9308 achieved here, plausibly due to feature-engineering choices such as the engagement-span feature, the at-risk binarization and principled treatment of missing data for early-withdrawing learners. Hlosta et al. (2017), at the same institution, also demonstrated that with careful design of features, classical methods can also be used to achieve good predictive performance, for early identification.

There is a need for a scoping clarification. The empirical study checks one feature of the Analytics Engine (early at-risk learner detection) on the OULAD distance-learning data only, and not the complete Metaverse classroom. Conclusions regarding predictive performance thus hold true for similar distance-learning analytics use cases in the first place, as well as by extrapolation for immersive Metaverse classrooms, but not by demonstration. The experiment provides concrete evidence regarding the predictive aspect and methodologically principled evidence of when LLM derived representations add material value to educational analytics, while the chapter provides the framework and the architecture, and the ethical analysis.

Limitations

The empirical results had three limitations that affect their generalizability. Firstly, dataset specificity: OULAD is a collection of distance-learning courses from a single institution, in one time period, and the strong tabular signal documented here might not be applicable to other datasets from other institutions, modalities or time periods. Second, the hybrid-model design: the use of a frozen DistilBERT encoder and synthesized trajectory text is reasonable, but not the most liberal one: other integrations, such as fine-tuning the encoder on educational text or even giving it real textual data from forum or assessment data, might lead to different results. Third, the binary outcome variable: It is common practice to dichotomise the four-way outcomes (Distinction, Pass, Fail, Withdrawn) to a binary at-risk indicator, which loses differences that may have pedagogical interest. All point towards fruitful avenues for future empirical research.

Issues, Ethics, and Mitigation

The responsible deployment of the above framework and architecture requires the additional empirical study. With the integration of generative AI, large language models, and the Metaverse in smart education, ethical, legal, and pedagogical concerns emerge, which need to be taken into account as design constraints right from the beginning. This subsection presents concerns in algorithmic bias and fairness, hallucination in LLM-based tutors, privacy in immersive settings, and academic integrity, and introduces a six-principal framework to mitigate these concerns.

Algorithmic Bias and Fairness

The statistical patterns of the corpora that LLMs are trained on are transferred to the LLMs, which may include patterns that are the result of past and structural inequalities (Bender et al., 2021). In the educational context, such biases can surface in the form of differential service quality among language groups, by using explanations or examples that are predominantly from the majority culture, or by having differential rates of error when the language model talks back to learners whose language patterns are not the same as those in the model's training distribution. There is a similar danger with the predictive analytics components: If they consistently mispredict at-risk status for certain demographic groups, they will turn into a tool for differential treatment for struggling learners. Mitigation involves intentional fairness auditing by protected attributes, adjusting for equalised treatment across groups, and keeping a record of the human pedagogical decision-making process for interventions that are triggered by automated forecasts.

Hallucination in LLM-Driven Tutors

This is a well-known behavior of contemporary large language models, who are known to generate grammatically correct but factually inaccurate content, as surveyed by Ji et al. (2023). In a tutoring situation, hallucination is not a trivial annoyance: a knowledgeable-sounding virtual tutor giving a confident assertion that is a factually incorrect is likely to create misconceptions that will be hard to rectify. There are two types of mitigations: technical and pedagogical. Retrieval-augmented generation makes model output rooted in vetted curricular content, and is best as a first-line defense against fabricated content. Output validation, based on a content policy, is a second line of defense. Pedagogically, it should be made sure that when the learner thinks that the AI tutor is wrong he always has a way to go to a human tutor, and that there are institutional mechanisms for collecting, investigating and correcting the errors he reports.

Privacy in Immersive Environments

HMDs and the rest of the Metaverse infrastructure collect types of learner data that traditional learning platforms cannot: gaze direction, dwell time, head pose, body movements, voice, and conversational content, and optionally, biometric signals from peripherals. Prior to the current commercial wave of head-mounted displays, Falchuk and colleagues (2018) predicted the privacy risks of these types of data. If learners are minors, the legal and ethical considerations are significant, as there are laws and guidance like the United States' Children's Online Privacy Protection Act and the United Kingdom's age-appropriate-design code that provide protection, and the European Union's General Data Protection Regulation has strict requirements, irrespective of age. The data minimization, data residency (where possible, processing biometric signals on the device or within the institutional perimeter) and transparent consent regimes are essential for the mitigation.

Academic Integrity

The power of Generative AI to generate fluent, plausible written works on demand has again raised questions of academic integrity, which the traditional plagiarism-detection regimes are unable to address. Detection alone is not a sufficient response to the challenge; what is more needed is assessment redesign to facilitate assessment of process product(s) (drafts, reflections, oral defenses), context-bound performance, and competencies that cannot be replicated by fluent text generation. The Metaverse classroom provides tangible affordances to redesign, as invigilated assessment, embodied performance and rich interactive demonstration is hard to replicate using text generation only.

A Six-Principle Mitigation Framework

Combining the above, we can come up with the following six design principles that institutions must not consider as optional in any seriousness of using GenAI-driven Metaverse education. Table 2 lists the six principles, the major risk they respectively tackle and a specific operational lever to implement them.

Table 2. Six-principle mitigation framework for responsible deployment of GenAI-driven Metaverse education.

#	Principle	Primary Risk Addressed	Operational Lever
1	Human pedagogical authority preserved at every layer	Over-delegation of educational decisions to AI	Educators retain explicit authorship of curriculum, assessment validity, and the moral dimensions of teaching
2	Continuous bias and fairness auditing across content, dialogue, and predictive analytics	Differential service quality across demographic groups	Scheduled equity audits with documented thresholds for action; auditing extended to predictive components, not confined to language outputs
3	Generated content grounded in vetted sources via retrieval-augmented generation	Hallucination and propagation of misinformation	RAG pipeline plus output validation against a content policy and a path for human review
4	Privacy enforced at the architectural level: minimization, edge or institutional residency, retention limits	Biometric and behavioral surveillance, especially of minors	First-class Privacy and Compliance Layer in the architecture rather than retrofitted compliance
5	Assessment redesigned to leverage Metaverse affordances for invigilated, embodied, process-rich evaluation	Erosion of academic integrity by text-generation tools	Tasks that emphasize process artifacts, embodied performance, and integration of evidence and judgment
6	Adoption decisions made on representative-population evidence	Premature scaling of unvalidated tools	Pilot evaluation on representative learners and tasks before institutional rollout

The use of these six principles does not remove the risks of the convergence, but rather limit them to be contained within an envelope which can be managed by responsible practice.

All the data used in the empirical study presented here was publicly released and anonymized (Kuzilek et al., 2017) and certified by the Open Data Institute. The authors did not conduct any further research on human subjects. The use of OULAD is in keeping with its CC BY 4.0 license, and the Open University's published policies regarding ethical use of student data for learning analytics research.

FUTURE RESEARCH DIRECTIONS

Based on the above framework, architecture, and empirical findings, there are open questions that can guide the next step of research on GenAI and LLMs in smart education using the Metaverse. In particular, six directions seem to have important implications.

The first is about the multimodal large language models in immersive classrooms. Nowadays, LLMs are able to process and produce text, images, audio, and even structured data, and immersive environments are multimodal by nature. Comparative studies on multimodal and text-only LLMs on common learning-outcome benchmarks would help to understand the added value of multimodality relative to its high compute cost.

The second relates to real-time adaptive avatars, based on inferred learner state. With a more powerful formulation than the current architecture, avatar's pacing, expressiveness and scaffolding could be directly conditioned on continuously updated estimates of learner's cognitive and affective state. Some open questions are: what are the latency budgets where such adaptation can still be pedagogically relevant and what is the coarsest granularity at which state can reliably be estimated?

The third relates to federated/privacy-preserving learning analytics. There is a debate on the need to keep sensitive learner data within institutional boundaries, while predictive models can benefit from training data from numerous institutions. Federated learning protocols make it possible to enhance models across institutional boundaries without sharing raw data from the origin and are an active field of research with special relevance for learning analytics.

The fourth relates to study of cross-cultural and equity. Much of the empirical literature is in English, in high-income countries and with good resources. Pedagogical and ethical interactions in GenAI-supported Metaverse classrooms in lower-resourced settings and non-English language teaching contexts and diverse cultural norms of education are under-studied – methodological and equity priority.

The fifth one relates to uniform standards for the evaluation of LLM-tutors. There are no public benchmarks for the dialogue and content generation functions in the AI Engine Layer that are similar to OULAD's role for predictive analytics. Building task-aligned, pedagogically meaningful, uncontaminated benchmarks would greatly speed principled comparison of competing systems.

The sixth relates to the long-term cognitive and skill-development effects. Most of the existing empirical literature focuses on short time horizons. It will be important to conduct longitudinal studies over semesters and modes to assess whether the convergence is providing learners with enduring educational value, or just with engagement gains in the short term.

CONCLUSION

In this chapter, the convergence of generative AI, large language models, the Metaverse, and smart education has been explored and studied both theoretically and empirically, including in literature, a framework, and an architecture. A four-layer functional pedagogical framework was proposed to classify the functional roles of GenAI and LLMs in an immersive smart-education environment, and a five-component reference architecture was proposed to map the functional pedagogical framework into an engineering implementable form with Governance as a cross-cutting concern.

The empirical study assessed the predictive analytics function in stratified cross validation of the Open University Learning Analytics Dataset. The best stand-alone accuracy obtained was 93.08% on XGBoost with an AUC-ROC score of 0.9785, much higher than previous published results. A hybrid model combining tabular features and embeddings derived from DistilBERT did not outperform XGBoost, which is a natural result as LLM representations are most likely to add value when text is the medium of learner expression, and less when the text is a recap of text features already used by the baseline. The chapter concluded with a systematic analysis of bias, hallucination, privacy and academic integrity and a six principle mitigation framework.

As we look ahead, it is not so much the future development of the underlying technologies that will be crucial for the responsible use of GenAI in education and the Metaverse, but rather the development of the pedagogical, ethical, and infrastructural fields associated with these technologies. The technologies won't wait, and, as always, it's up to the human educators, researchers and institutional leaders who use them to choose to deploy them in ways that benefit students.

ACKNOWLEDGMENT

The authors acknowledge with appreciation the support provided by the Deanship of the Faculty of Information Technology, the Deanship of Scientific Research and Graduate Studies at the University of Petra, Al-Balqa Applied University, the University of Jordan, and Sultan Qaboos University in conducting this research.

REFERENCES

Ackermann, H., Henke, A., Chevalère, J., Yun, H. S., Hafner, V. V., Pinkwart, N., & Lazarides, R. (2025). Physical embodiment and anthropomorphism of AI tutors and their role in student enjoyment and performance. *NPJ Science of Learning*, *10*(1), 1. DOI: 10.1038/s41539-024-00293-z PMID: 39779711

Alfaisal, R., Hashim, H., & Azizan, U. H. (2024). Metaverse system adoption in education: A systematic literature review. *Journal of Computers in Education*, *11*(1), 259–303. DOI: 10.1007/s40692-022-00256-6

Bender, E. M., Gebru, T., McMillan-Major, A., & Shmitchell, S. (2021). On the dangers of stochastic parrots: Can language models be too big? In *Proceedings of the 2021 ACM Conference on Fairness, Accountability, and Transparency* (pp. 610–623). Association for Computing Machinery. DOI: 10.1145/3442188.3445922

Breiman, L. (2001). Random forests. *Machine Learning*, *45*(1), 5–32. DOI: 10.1023/A:1010933404324

Brown, T. B., Mann, B., Ryder, N., Subbiah, M., Kaplan, J., Dhariwal, P., Neelakantan, A., Shyam, P., Sastry, G., Askell, A., Agarwal, S., Herbert-Voss, A., Krueger, G., Henighan, T., Child, R., Ramesh, A., Ziegler, D. M., Wu, J., Winter, C., & Amodei, D. (2020). Language models are few-shot learners. *Advances in Neural Information Processing Systems*, *33*, 1877–1901. DOI: 10.48550/arXiv.2005.14165

Chen, T., & Guestrin, C. (2016). XGBoost: A scalable tree boosting system. In *Proceedings of the 22nd ACM SIGKDD International Conference on Knowledge Discovery and Data Mining* (pp. 785–794). Association for Computing Machinery. DOI: 10.1145/2939672.2939785

Devlin, J., Chang, M.-W., Lee, K., & Toutanova, K. (2019). BERT: Pre-training of deep bidirectional transformers for language understanding. In *Proceedings of the 2019 Conference of the North American Chapter of the Association for Computational Linguistics: Human Language Technologies* (pp. 4171–4186). Association for Computational Linguistics. DOI: 10.18653/v1/N19-1423

Falchuk, B., Loeb, S., & Neff, R. (2018). The social metaverse: Battle for privacy. *IEEE Technology and Society Magazine*, *37*(2), 52–61. DOI: 10.1109/MTS.2018.2826060

Fan, X., Chao, D., Zhang, Z., Wang, D., Li, X., & Tian, F. (2024). Web 3.0 metaverse turn in education. *IEEE Transactions on Learning Technologies*, *17*, 819–833. DOI: 10.1109/TLT.2024.3385505

Hlosta, M., Zdrahal, Z., & Zendulka, J. (2017). Ouroboros: Early identification of at-risk students without models based on legacy data. In *Proceedings of the 7th International Learning Analytics and Knowledge Conference* (pp. 6–15). Association for Computing Machinery. DOI: 10.1145/3027385.3027449

Holmes, W., Porayska-Pomsta, K., Holstein, K., Sutherland, E., Baker, T., Shum, S. B., Santos, O. C., Rodrigo, M. T., Cukurova, M., Bittencourt, I. I., & Koedinger, K. R. (2022). Ethics of AI in education: Towards a community-wide framework. *International Journal of Artificial Intelligence in Education*, *32*(3), 504–526. DOI: 10.1007/s40593-021-00239-1

Holon, I. Q. (2022). *10 charts for a changing education market*. https://www.holoniq.com/notes/10-charts-for-a-changing-education-market

Hwang, G.-J., & Chien, S.-Y. (2022). Definition, roles, and potential research issues of the metaverse in education: An artificial intelligence perspective. *Computers and Education: Artificial Intelligence*, *3*, 100082. DOI: 10.1016/j.caeai.2022.100082

Ji, Z., Lee, N., Frieske, R., Yu, T., Su, D., Xu, Y., Ishii, E., Bang, Y. J., Madotto, A., & Fung, P. (2023). Survey of hallucination in natural language generation. *ACM Computing Surveys*, *55*(12), 1–38. DOI: 10.1145/3571730

Kasneci, E., Sessler, K., Küchemann, S., Bannert, M., Dementieva, D., Fischer, F., Gasser, U., Groh, G., Günnemann, S., Hüllermeier, E., Krusche, S., Kutyniok, G., Michaeli, T., Nerdel, C., Pfeffer, J., Poquet, O., Sailer, M., Schmidt, A., Seidel, T., & Kasneci, G. (2023). ChatGPT for good? On opportunities and challenges of large language models for education. *Learning and Individual Differences*, *103*, 102274. DOI: 10.1016/j.lindif.2023.102274

Kuzilek, J., Hlosta, M., & Zdrahal, Z. (2017). Open University Learning Analytics dataset. *Scientific Data*, *4*(1), 170171. DOI: 10.1038/sdata.2017.171 PMID: 29182599

Lee, H.-Y., & Wu, T.-T. (2025). ChatGPT in education: A systematic review of current landscape, limitations and future directions through general system theory lens. *European Journal of Education*, *60*(4), e70262. DOI: 10.1111/ejed.70262

Lee, L.-H., Braud, T., Zhou, P., Wang, L., Xu, D., Lin, Z., Kumar, A., Bermejo, C., & Hui, P. (2021). *All one needs to know about metaverse: A complete survey on technological singularity, virtual ecosystem, and research agenda* (arXiv:2110.05352). arXiv. /arXiv.2110.05352DOI: 10.48550

Mubarak, A. A., Cao, H., & Ahmed, S. A. M. (2021). Predictive learning analytics using deep learning model in MOOCs' courses videos. *Education and Information Technologies*, *26*(1), 371–392. DOI: 10.1007/s10639-020-10273-6

Mystakidis, S. (2022). Metaverse. *Encyclopedia*, *2*(1), 486–497. DOI: 10.3390/encyclopedia2010031

Mystakidis, S., Christopoulos, A., & Pellas, N. (2022). A systematic mapping review of augmented reality applications to support STEM learning in higher education. *Education and Information Technologies*, *27*(2), 1883–1927. DOI: 10.1007/s10639-021-10682-1

Omar, K., Abu-Aishah, S., Matar, I., Al Smadi, D., Fakhouri, H., & Abuarqoub, M. (2024). Analyzing Jordanian higher education instructors' perception towards Metaverse based education. In *2024 2nd International Conference on Cyber Resilience (ICCR)* (pp. 1–6). IEEE. DOI: 10.1109/ICCR61006.2024.10533007

Omar, K., & Gómez, J. M. (2025). Metaverse-Enhanced Learning Ecosystem (MELE) framework. In *2025 1st International Conference on Computational Intelligence Approaches and Applications (ICCIAA)* (pp. 1–6). IEEE. DOI: 10.1109/ICCIAA65327.2025.11013595

Omar, K., Saleh, Y., & Issa, G. (2024). Challenges of distance learning during the Coronavirus (COVID-19) pandemic: A case study of the University of Petra. In *2024 2nd International Conference on Cyber Resilience (ICCR)* (pp. 1–6). IEEE. DOI: 10.1109/ICCR61006.2024.10533003

Park, S.-M., & Kim, Y.-G. (2022). A metaverse: Taxonomy, components, applications, and open challenges. *IEEE Access : Practical Innovations, Open Solutions*, *10*, 4209–4251. DOI: 10.1109/ACCESS.2021.3140175

Patel, K. K., & Amin, K. (2024). Predictive modeling of dropout in MOOCs using machine learning techniques. *International Journal of Intelligent Systems and Applications in Engineering*, *12*(4), 436–443. https://www.ijisae.org/index.php/IJISAE/article/view/6230

Pedregosa, F., Varoquaux, G., Gramfort, A., Michel, V., Thirion, B., Grisel, O., Blondel, M., Prettenhofer, P., Weiss, R., Dubourg, V., Vanderplas, J., Passos, A., Cournapeau, D., Brucher, M., Perrot, M., & Duchesnay, É. (2011). Scikit-learn: Machine learning in Python. *Journal of Machine Learning Research*, *12*, 2825–2830. https://www.jmlr.org/papers/v12/pedregosa11a.html

PwC. (2020). *The effectiveness of virtual reality soft skills training in the enterprise*. PwC United States. https://www.pwc.com/us/en/tech-effect/emerging-tech/virtual-reality-study.html

Radianti, J., Majchrzak, T. A., Fromm, J., & Wohlgenannt, I. (2020). A systematic review of immersive virtual reality applications for higher education: Design elements, lessons learned, and research agenda. *Computers & Education*, *147*, 103778. DOI: 10.1016/j.compedu.2019.103778

ResearchAndMarkets. (2022, February 1). *Global EdTech market outlook & forecast report 2022: Market size was valued at $254.80 billion in 2021 and is expected to reach $605.40 billion by 2027*. GlobeNewswire. https://www.globenewswire.com/news-release/2022/02/01/2376551/28124/en/Global-EdTech-Market-Outlook-Forecast-Report-2022.html

Sailer, M., Bauer, E., Hofmann, R., Kiesewetter, J., Glas, J., Gurevych, I., & Fischer, F. (2023). Adaptive feedback from artificial neural networks facilitates pre-service teachers' diagnostic reasoning in simulation-based learning. *Learning and Instruction*, *83*, 101620. DOI: 10.1016/j.learninstruc.2022.101620

Sanh, V., Debut, L., Chaumond, J., & Wolf, T. (2019). *DistilBERT, a distilled version of BERT: Smaller, faster, cheaper and lighter* (arXiv:1910.01108). arXiv. /arXiv.1910.01108DOI: 10.48550

Tlili, A., Huang, R., Shehata, B., Liu, D., Zhao, J., Metwally, A. H. S., Wang, H., Denden, M., Bozkurt, A., Lee, L.-H., Beyoglu, D., Altinay, F., Sharma, R. C., Altinay, Z., Li, Z., Liu, J., Ahmad, F., Hu, Y., Salha, S., & Burgos, D. (2022). Is metaverse in education a blessing or a curse: A combined content and bibliometric analysis. *Smart Learning Environments*, *9*(1), 24. DOI: 10.1186/s40561-022-00205-x

Touvron, H., Lavril, T., Izacard, G., Martinet, X., Lachaux, M.-A., Lacroix, T., Rozière, B., Goyal, N., Hambro, E., Azhar, F., Rodriguez, A., Joulin, A., Grave, E., & Lample, G. (2023). *LLaMA: Open and efficient foundation language models* (arXiv:2302.13971). arXiv. /arXiv.2302.13971DOI: 10.48550

Vaswani, A., Shazeer, N., Parmar, N., Uszkoreit, J., Jones, L., Gomez, A. N., Kaiser, Ł., & Polosukhin, I. (2017). Attention is all you need. *Advances in Neural Information Processing Systems*, *30*, 5998–6008. DOI: 10.48550/arXiv.1706.03762

Wang, M., Yu, H., Bell, Z., & Chu, X. (2022). Constructing an Edu-Metaverse ecosystem: A new and innovative framework. *IEEE Transactions on Learning Technologies*, *15*(6), 685–696. DOI: 10.1109/TLT.2022.3210828

Wolf, T., Debut, L., Sanh, V., Chaumond, J., Delangue, C., Moi, A., Cistac, P., Rault, T., Louf, R., Funtowicz, M., Davison, J., Shleifer, S., von Platen, P., Ma, C., Jernite, Y., Plu, J., Xu, C., Le Scao, T., Gugger, S., & Rush, A. M. (2020). Transformers: State-of-the-art natural language processing. In *Proceedings of EMNLP 2020: System Demonstrations* (pp. 38–45). Association for Computational Linguistics. DOI: 10.18653/v1/2020.emnlp-demos.6

Zhang, X., Chen, Y., Hu, L., & Wang, Y. (2022). The metaverse in education: Definition, framework, features, potential applications, challenges, and future research topics. *Frontiers in Psychology*, *13*, 1016300. DOI: 10.3389/fpsyg.2022.1016300 PMID: 36304866

Chapter 8
IoT-Enabled and Explainable Smart Experimental Platforms for Multidisciplinary STEAM Engineering Training:
IoT, XAI, and Adaptive Models for STEAM Labs

Mario Oscar Ordaz Oliver
http://orcid.org/0000-0002-9302-0988
Tecnológico Nacional de México, Pachuca, Mexico

Evelin Gutierrez-Moreno
http://orcid.org/0000-0001-7610-9318
Universidad Politécnica de Pachuca, Mexico

María Angélica Espejel Rivera
http://orcid.org/0000-0002-2565-8250
Tecnológico Nacional de México, Pachuca, Mexico

Jesús Patricio Ordaz Oliver
http://orcid.org/0000-0002-5055-2183
Universidad Autónoma del Estado de Hidalgo, Mexico

Javier Hernández Pérez
http://orcid.org/0000-0003-0371-4255

DOI: 10.4018/979-8-2600-3658-7.ch008

Universidad Politécnica de Pachuca, Mexico

ABSTRACT

This chapter, examines the pedagogical foundations of IoT-enabled intelligent experimental platforms as transformative infrastructures for multidisciplinary STEAM engineering education. The discussion progresses from the limitations of traditional laboratory models towards the emergence of smart ecosystems in which e-learning environments, IoT-based architectures, and embedded systems are reinterpreted as accessible mediators between theoretical knowledge and experimental practice. Attention is devoted to multidisciplinary data integration, cloud computing, and responsible educational technology governance. Adaptive and multimodal learning models are addressed as mechanisms for personalising experimental learning trajectories, whilst safety-aware strategies for high-risk environments are equally considered. Technological and pedagogical dimensions are examined as mutually constitutive, positioning intelligent experimental platforms as dynamic ecosystems for interdisciplinary engineering competency development aligned with Sustainable Development Goal 4.

INTRODUCTION

The accelerated technological development causes a growing need for the modification and updating of educational environments. Traditional teaching models, centred on face-to-face instruction, have evolved over time, primarily with the aim of making learning more efficient, improving the use of resources, reducing the digital divide and educational lag. Among the most significant advances in technology based learning is the emergence of e learning platforms, which have enabled greater access to communication through the reciprocal distribution of content between teachers and students, as well as interaction in virtual environments that overcome barriers of time and space.

Despite the historical benefits of face-to-face education, technological development along with the emergence of critical situations such as the COVID-19 pandemic in 2020, have evidenced the need to innovate educational environments. During the years 2020 and 2021, the use of digital platforms intensified significantly, mainly due to the restrictions imposed on face-to-face education. Organisations such as UNESCO (United Nations Educational, Scientific and Cultural Organisation) have contributed to education with educational resources available online regarding science, technology, engineering, and mathematics (STEM). The work carried out by UNESCO to strengthen online and distance education contributes to the Sustainable

Development Goals (SDGs), also known as the Global Goals, adopted by the United Nations (UN) in 2015 and whose objective is to end poverty, protect the planet, and guarantee peace and prosperity by the year 2030. The 17 SDGs are designed to be indivisible and interconnected; progress in one of the SDGs depends on the others. The direct contribution of UNESCO is focused on SDG 4: Quality Education. This goal seeks to guarantee inclusive, equitable, and quality education, in addition to promoting continuous learning opportunities (UNESCO, n.d.).

SDG 4 of the UN establishes education as a key resource that allows for breaking the cycle of poverty, reducing inequalities, and achieving gender equality; furthermore, education fosters tolerance among people and contributes to the development of more peaceful societies. One of the most viable strategies to achieve SDG 4 consists of investment in education becoming a priority for nations; additionally, the adoption of digital transformation processes is fundamental. However, for the transformation to be effective, the development of digital competences is necessary, as deficiencies in information and communication technology (ICT) skills represent a significant barrier to achieving universal and meaningful connectivity (United Nations, n.d.).

The STEAM educational approach was born in 2008, and is based on turning the teaching and learning process into an integrated, creative, interdisciplinary and transversal process that involves science (S), technology (T), engineering (E), the arts (A) and mathematics (M). It is considered that this approach is preceded by the Maker and Do It Yourself (DIY) philosophy, which is based on principles of collaboration, sharing resources, spaces and creations with other people, which encourages the creation of interest groups, where users learn by doing and sharing projects. It is considered that the STEAM educational approach is a model that allows the development of logical, scientific and mathematical thinking, and that simultaneously improves the creativity and motivation of users. The implementation of this approach allows the development of the necessary skills for today's students (García-Fuentes et al., 2023). The educational environment is ideal for people to go from the Maker philosophy, DIY, to the implementation of STEAM. The maker culture proposes the idea that anyone has the ability to devise and build objects using technological tools; from the educational point of view, this allows students to associate curricular contents with practice and therefore become protagonists of knowledge (Aleixo et al., 2021).

Unlike traditional educational approaches based on disciplinary reductionism, the STEAM approach fosters the integration of scientific, technological and artistic knowledge, which allows problems to be addressed from an integral vision. From this perspective, Guy (2013) points out that in a dynamic world, which evolves in an accelerated and complex manner, complex and constantly changing, it is not enough to resort to reductionist approaches to understand and resolve the different challenges that arise, since even small variations are capable of generating large effects. That is, it is not enough to study things separately; the implementation of a vision that contemplates a greater number of knowledge areas is needed. The STEAM approach prepares society to better face the challenges that arise (Guy, 2013).

Santillan et al. (2019) point out that the STEAM educational model can be implemented through project development, as it allows those involved to learn, discover and solve situations autonomously. Project work implies active preparation in the face of real challenges, while at the same time promoting the development of transversal competences, through the connection of classroom practices with social reality, supported by the use of available technology, since in this approach learning is carried out in an interdisciplinary manner.

The implementation of the STEAM approach in current educational environments is strengthened by the use of digital platforms. These platforms facilitate the integration of knowledge and the development of competences through interactive learning experiences. Digital platforms are tools that enable students to engage in active learning (Soroko et al., 2020).

In this regard, digital platforms form part of what is known as e learning, which refers to the use of electronic technologies to support teaching and learning processes. E learning is a broad concept that encompasses various forms of learning mediated by the use of technology, both online and offline, and includes both synchronous and asynchronous modalities. E learning, beyond the mere transmission of content, involves carrying out an interactive process with constant feedback (Thakkar & Joshi, 2015).

Despite the growing body of literature documenting the deployment of IoT technologies, digital twins, and adaptive systems in engineering education, a critical conceptual gap persists: existing proposals predominantly treat technological infrastructure as an end in itself, focusing on the sophistication of devices, connectivity protocols, and computational architectures whilst leaving undertheorised the pedagogical logic that must orchestrate their integration. As a consequence, the design of IoT-enabled experimental platforms for STEAM education remains largely fragmented, with technological components implemented in disciplinary isolation rather than as constituents of coherent learning ecosystems. This chapter directly addresses that gap by proposing a conceptual framework in which intelligent experimental platforms are reconceived as pedagogical infrastructures—structures whose value is not derived from their technological complexity, but from their capacity to mediate meaningfully between abstract disciplinary knowledge and authentic experimental practice. In doing so, this contribution seeks to provide practitioners and researchers with a theoretically grounded and practically oriented scaffold for designing smart laboratory environments that are simultaneously inclusive, adaptable, and epistemologically coherent with the interdisciplinary ambitions of contemporary STEAM engineering education.

The use of technologies such as the Internet of Things (IoT) constitutes an important foundation within the e learning environment applied to the STEAM educational approach. IoT enables the interconnection of physical devices capable of collecting, transmitting and processing data in real time, thereby expanding the possibilities for experimentation. In this way, students can interact remotely with real or simulated systems. This practice facilitates the development of practical competences in areas such as engineering. The integration of IoT into educational platforms enables the creation of intelligent and dynamic learning environments, strengthening project based learning (Abdul-Qawy et al., 2015).

In academic contexts, there is continuous discussion of the technological revolution in which we are living, initiated in the final years of the twentieth century and affecting different aspects of people's lives, the way they communicate, how society interacts, the family, the economy and how working environments evolve. According to UNESCO, the technological revolution demands a greater capacity for information processing and the development of cognitive and interpersonal skills in addition to the specific domain of professions (Lam-Byrne, 2023). Taking this perspective into account, some fundamental concepts that underpin these changes can be identified, which have been summarised in Table 1.

Table. 1 Concepts related to the digital transformation of education.

Concept	Description
STEAM	Interdisciplinary educational approach that integrates Science, Technology, Engineering, Arts and Mathematics.
Maker culture	"Maker culture" is a contemporary movement based on Do It Yourself (DIY). This movement encourages the creation, invention, and repair of physical and technological objects through active learning and promotes collaborative work.
IoT	A network of physical devices, which are integrated with sensors, software, and built-in network connectivity, enabling them to collect and share data.
Digital platform	According to UNESCO, a digital platform is an online environment that facilitates interactions, transactions, and content sharing among users.
e-learning	Learning modality characterized by the use of the internet and digital technologies for flexible and distance learning.

IOT-BASED ARCHITECTURE AND MULTIDISCIPLINARY INTEGRATION

The configuration of intelligent experimental platforms for construction in STEAM engineering transcends the traditional concepts of technological infrastructure, with the principal objective of constituting an educational ecosystem of a coherent nature, in which digital and physical resources converge to foster meaningful learning experiences. In this regard, the architecture is not defined by its technological elements, but by the logic employed in pedagogy, which organises and articulates the interaction between e-learning environments, the Internet of Things (IoT) and experimental learning activities. For their part, Tariq et al. (2024) describe in their research said convergence as a synergy between cyber-physical systems and educational environments, wherein remote laboratories, personalised learning and institutional management are articulated by means of interconnected structures that are grounded in IoT and that enhance both the flexibility and the quality of educational experiences (Auer et al., 2018).

Furthermore, the conceptual architecture of these platforms incorporates adaptive and context-sensitive mechanisms that respond to the diversity of student profiles and educational objectives. As documented by Asad et al. (2024), IoT-integrated smart labs promote student interaction, motivation, creativity, and active learning through authentic tasks, positioning the experimental platform not only as a content delivery tool but also as a dynamic environment for inquiry-based knowledge construction. This perspective aligns with the multidisciplinary orientation of STEAM pedagogy, in which technological infrastructure serves as a medium through which science, technology, engineering, the arts, and mathematics enter into a productive dialogue.

Within smart experimental platforms designed for STEAM education, sensors, actuators, and embedded systems fulfil a function that is fundamentally pedagogical, as they constitute the material basis of didactic prototypes through which disciplinary concepts, which are often abstract in nature, become observable, manipulable, and meaningful (He et al., 2016). In this same sense, the use of low-cost microcontroller-based platforms, such as Arduino and Raspberry Pi, equipped with various sensors, actuators, and algorithms, has made it possible to expand accessibility to experimental learning environments, rendering feasible the design of didactic prototypes that simultaneously address electronic, mathematical, mechanical, and computational principles (Martínez Ramírez et al., 2025).

The educational importance of these devices is particularly evident in the development of educational prototypes geared toward STEAM integration. Melgarejo et al. (2026) and Hernández Pérez et al. (2024), in their work, document the design and validation of low-cost aerodynamic and pendulum experimental systems. These systems utilize digital control algorithms integrated with signal filtering techniques and sensor-based feedback loops as practical tools for illustrating multidisciplinary engineering principles. These prototypes demonstrate how the integration of physical components such as motors, potentiometers, encoders, and inertial sensors, with computational platforms and control strategies, generates enriched and contextualised learning experiences capable of transcending disciplinary boundaries.

Industrial communication protocols, when incorporated into educational laboratory environments, further expand the scope of STEAM learning by introducing students to the standards and conventions that govern real-world cyber-physical systems. Rather than approaching these protocols as advanced technical specifications, their use in educational prototypes serves to cultivate awareness of the systemic nature of technological environments, in which data exchange, synchronisation, and interoperability among heterogeneous devices are fundamental competencies for contemporary engineering practice (Hernandez-de-Menendez et al., 2020). Consequently, the pedagogical use of sensors, actuators and embedded systems within STEAM experimental platforms prioritises accessibility, conceptual understanding and interdisciplinary integration above technical depth.

One of the most significant characteristics that intelligent experimental platforms may possess within STEAM engineering education is their capacity to facilitate the integration of data, which are commonly generated across multiple disciplinary domains of engineering. Unlike traditional laboratory environments, where data collection and analysis are confined to a single disciplinary perspective, IoT-enabled intelligent platforms allow experimental data to flow across the disciplinary boundaries of knowledge, thereby generating a series of opportunities for systemic thinking, which includes interdisciplinary problem-solving (Jantassova et al., 2022). This integration of multidisciplinary data constitutes a pedagogical strategy in itself: one that begins when students are asked to interpret signals generated by sensors from both mechanical and electrical perspectives, or to connect mathematical models with observable physical behaviours, in order to engage in the integrative reasoning that STEAM education seeks to cultivate in students (Holbrook et al, 2020), (Alkhatib et al, 2025). This perspective coincides with the characterisation of STEAM education as a sociotechnical system (Singam, 2026), in which the technical and social dimensions of knowledge are mutually constituted and cannot be fully addressed in isolation. In this context, intelligent experimental platforms, by virtue of their capacity for multidisciplinary data integration, provide numerous material conditions for a systemic and integrative mode of learning.

With the purpose of synthesising the principal structural and functional elements that constitute IoT-based intelligent experimental platforms within the framework of STEAM education, Table 2 is presented, which integrates an overview of the main components of this ecosystem, together with their educational functions and their contribution to the development of multidisciplinary competencies in students. This synthesis affords the possibility of visualising, in a structured and objective manner, how the interrelation between the technological and pedagogical dimensions described previously in this section is brought about.

Table 2. Educational components and functions in experimental IoT platforms for STEAM education.

Component of the ecosystem	Main educational function	Contribution to STEAM learning
IoT ecosystem architecture	Integrate e-learning, experimental laboratory and cyber-physical systems	It promotes active, contextualized, and interdisciplinary learning
Sensors, actuators and embedded systems	Materializing abstract concepts through didactic prototypes	They promote practical, accessible, and experiment-based learning.
Low-cost educational prototypes	Facilitating real-world experimentation in academic contexts	They democratize access and foster creativity and innovation
Integration of multidisciplinary data	Articulate data from multiple domains (mechanical, electrical, mathematical, etc.)	Develops systemic thinking and real-world problem-solving skills
IoT + Cloud Platforms	Enable virtual and remote laboratories	They expand accessibility, scalability, and flexible learning.
Edge-AI (as support)	Process data in real time and improve system response	It allows for customization and immediate feedback.
Cybersecurity and data protection	Ensuring the ethical and secure use of academic information	Promotes digital awareness and technological responsibility

The articulation of intelligent experimental platforms with cloud computing infrastructures and IoT-enabled digital environments has notably transformed the landscape of STEAM laboratory education, enabling the development of virtual and remote laboratories that extend learning beyond the physical limitations of traditional classrooms. Zhang (2025) documents in their research how the convergence of IoT devices and cloud-based platforms generates virtual laboratory environments that transcend conventional hands-on learning methods, thereby offering greater accessibility, scalability and real-time data collection capabilities, which enhance student engagement and instructional realism. This transformation is particularly significant for STEAM engineering education, where access to laboratory resources has historically been constrained by economic, spatial, and temporal factors.

Remote and virtual laboratory platforms represent one of the most important applications of IoT-cloud integration in educational contexts. Alsaleh et al. (2022) describe in their work the so-called ReImagine Lab framework, which leverages digital twin technologies and extended reality environments to bridge the gap amongst hands-on, virtual and remote laboratory modalities, thereby demonstrating how cloud-enabled platforms afford the possibility of enhancing student interaction, immersion and collaboration within geographically distributed learning communities. In a similar manner, Auer et al. (2018) document in their work the development of online laboratory systems, with modular features, which combine pedagogical rigour with technological accessibility, establishing that the effectiveness of virtual laboratory platforms depends upon both their instructional design and their technical architecture. These advances confirm that IoT-cloud platforms function primarily as educational infrastructures whose value is determined by the quality of the learning experiences they make possible.

In order to provide a structured visualisation of the conceptual interactions addressed in this section, Figure 1 presents an integrative overview of the principal elements of IoT-based intelligent experimental platforms for STEAM education. This representation aims to highlight the interaction between technological infrastructure and pedagogical processes within a multidisciplinary engineering learning ecosystem.

Figure 1. Conceptual ecosystem of IoT-based smart experimental platforms for multidisciplinary STEAM engineering education

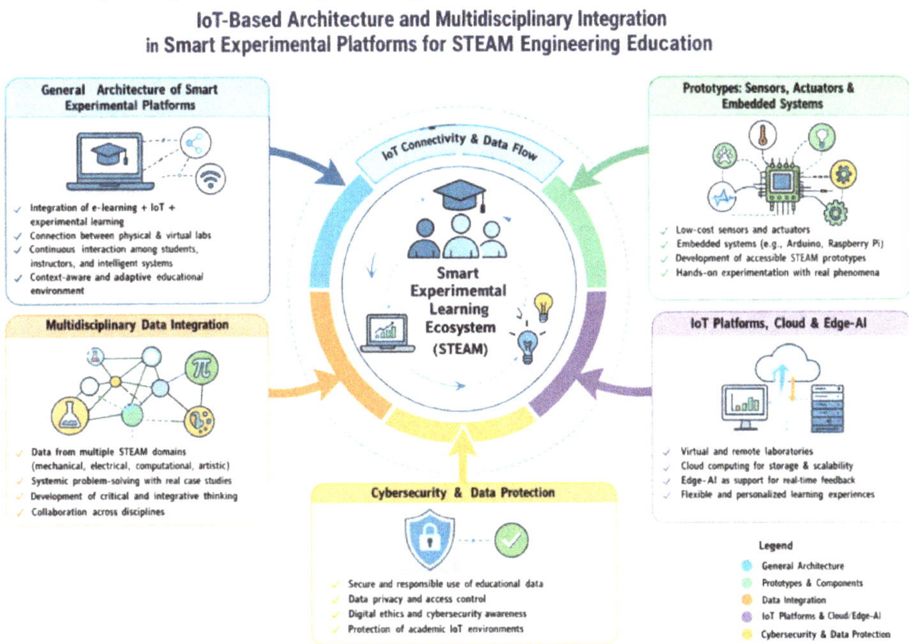

In this educational context, edge AI operates as a support layer, enabling a large number of computational processes (particularly those requiring real-time response) to run closer to the data source than in centralized cloud environments. Singh and Singh (2025) examine the application of edge AI in engineering education contexts in their research, demonstrating its potential to enhance personalized and interactive learning experiences through real-time processing of student data. However, within the context of STEAM experimental platforms, edge AI is more appropriately conceived as an infrastructure tool rather than a core educational component: its contribution lies in its ability to reduce latency, improve the responsiveness of adaptive learning systems, and support data-intensive experimental activities without requiring continuous cloud connectivity (Plakhteyev et al., 2018). The pedagogical value of these technologies lies in the enriched learning experiences they facilitate, not in the technological sophistication they incorporate.

From an academic perspective, the data generated by smart laboratories encompass not only experimental measurements, but also information that is frequently sensitive and related to students' behaviour, performance, and learning trajectories, the protection of which constitutes both an ethical imperative and a legal obligation (Delgado et al., 2023). Consequently, cybersecurity and data protection in smart laboratories must be understood not merely as technical issues, but as dimensions of a much broader commitment to responsible digital citizenship and the ethical governance of educational technology in contemporary contexts.

Rao and Elias-Medina (2024) document in their work the design of IoT laboratory courses in which cybersecurity principles are integrated into the didactic content itself, thereby demonstrating that educational environments can simultaneously serve as spaces for learning about and through secure digital practices. This dual orientation — which employs intelligent laboratory environments both to protect data and to educate students on the importance of digital security — reflects a pedagogically coherent approach in which the technological infrastructure of the laboratory becomes a context for developing digital awareness and critical competencies. When students interact with experimental platforms that incorporate authentication mechanisms, encrypted data transmission and access control protocols, they collectively acquire a practical familiarity with the security dimensions of cyber-physical systems, which will characterise their future professional environments (Demir and Suri, 2017).

The promotion of digital awareness and the responsible use of technology is, in this sense, an integral component of training in STEAM engineering in intelligent laboratory environments. Lin et al. (2023) observed in their studies that the implementation of AI systems and information technologies in educational contexts raises significant concerns regarding data privacy and security, which require sustained institutional attention as well as the active participation of students. Rather than treating cybersecurity as a peripheral technological complement, intelligent experimental platforms for STEAM education should integrate data protection principles into both their design and their operation, thereby modelling the ethical standards demanded by the responsible development and use of technology. This approach makes it possible to ensure that students not only acquire technical competencies, but also develop the reflective capacity to engage critically with the digital systems that regulate their learning and their future professional practice.

DIGITAL TWINS AND EXPLAINABLE AI FOR EXPERIMENTAL LEARNING

The development of simulation and virtual modelling technologies, derived from the concept of digital twins, represents a significant advance in education when applied to the learning and development of skills of students at different levels, since they facilitate the understanding of complex systems through interactive environments which in turn favour user safety, increase the degree to which users engage in the learning process and in some circumstances reduce the risks of certain processes (Ağca, 2023).

The definition of digital twins implies the representation of physical objects that are used to observe, analyse and simulate the behaviour of a system, their basic characteristic being the ability to exchange data with the physical object automatically (Berisha-Gawlowski et al., 2021). The concept of digital twins offers a broad perspective to involve knowledge from different areas in multidisciplinary projects, facilitating the adoption of the STEAM educational approach. As a result, different study groups have taken advantage of these benefits to promote the development of competences in students, especially at the university level.

Among the most representative academic levels in the use of digital twins are those involved in the study of engineering and related postgraduate programmes. For example, Martínez-Sanchez (2024) presented in his Mechanical Engineering final degree project the application of digital twins for the dynamic analysis of a bracket manufactured using 3D printing, employing the sensors of a mobile phone and IoT technology (Martínez Sánchez, 2024). In the Martínez-Sanchez work (2024), the application of sciences such as physics for the development of calculations can be highlighted, as well as the arts involved in the design of the part for 3D printing, which evidences the integration of multiple disciplines and, consequently, the application of the STEAM approach in the development of this type of proposal.

Calle (2022) worked on the development of a digital twin of a Modular Production System (MPS) with the aim of carrying out practical activities remotely, mainly to address needs similar to those arising from the COVID-19 pandemic. The system by Calle system integrates a physical environment with its virtual replica through the use of tools such as Factory IO for process simulation, TIA Portal for control programming, and bidirectional communication based on Node-RED, which enables real-time data exchange between the physical system and its digital model. In addition, this user employed Firebase for cloud data storage and synchronisation, ensuring remote access. The advantage of the system is that it can operate both in real time and in offline mode, from any computer, expanding its use in educational environments and achieving the researcher's objective. The developed proposal reflects the convergence of scientific, technological, engineering and mathematical disciplines, together with design components, evidencing the implementation of the STEAM educational approach in the development of the project.

Another example of the implementation of digital twins in chemical applications is presented by Martínez López (2021), who worked on the design of a system based on a digital twin of a simulated chemical plant. The system allows data monitoring and online fault diagnosis through the use of a modular communication architecture. The model, executed in a remote environment, transmits information to the cloud, facilitating access to results for real-time analysis. The system integrates Machine Learning techniques and data analysis for automatic anomaly detection. Despite the limitations identified by the author, the work validates the feasibility of integrating digital twins, intelligent algorithms and cloud platforms, evidencing the integration of scientific, technological, engineering and data analysis knowledge, in accordance with the STEAM approach, and also highlights that involving different areas of knowledge will improve proposals and achieve the intended objectives.

In the aeronautical field, the use of digital twins can also be positioned as a highly relevant tool. Mascareñas (2021) developed a digital twin of a wind turbine with integrated sensors for data acquisition. Among the sensors used in the study were an accelerometer to measure system vibrations, an anemometer and a wind vane to determine wind speed and direction, respectively; temperature, humidity and pressure sensors were also employed to record environmental variables. The sensors were integrated through an Arduino, a device that is highly useful for the development of educational projects, ranging from intermediate to advanced levels. The acquired data were sent to an IoT platform for storage and processing. Based on the obtained data, machine learning models were implemented to analyse system behaviour and predict certain variables.

Other applications of digital twins in the aeronautical field include the predictive maintenance of complex systems, such as aero-engines. Xiong et al. (2021) developed a digital twin combined with deep learning techniques for data processing and management. This approach allows not only for the representation of the system but also for the monitoring of its status, fault diagnosis, and the prediction of its remaining useful life. It is for this reason that digital twins can be considered a useful tool for the intelligent maintenance of engines.

The multidisciplinary approach, characteristic of the STEAM educational model, is also evident in industrial applications, where digital twins can be very useful for process optimisation. Min et al. (2019) point out the advantages of integrating digital twins, IoT, data mining and machine learning technologies into traditional processes to give rise to intelligent manufacturing processes. This group worked particularly on the petrochemical industry process, where they built a digital twin based on IoT and machine learning models that allows information exchange between the physical factory and its virtual representation, with the aim of optimising the production process. One of the main advantages of creating virtual models that update in real time is that they allow dynamic decision-making, enabling better results in continuous work.

Another example of the use of digital twins in the industrial environment is found in the work of Xu et al. (2019), who developed a two-phase digital-twin-assisted fault diagnosis method to be applied in the automotive industry. Their method uses deep transfer learning; this method allows for fault diagnosis in both the development phase and the maintenance phase. In the second phase, the model migrates from the virtual space to the physical space. The authors applied the developed method to an automotive production line, evidencing the feasibility of the proposed approach.

Probably the most representative area for the application of digital twins is robotics, since the knowledge acquired in this area enables the creation of virtual replicas of physical systems that facilitate simulation, monitoring and even optimisation. Vassiliev et al. (2019) employed this approach for the development of intelligent robotic systems. The methodology of the working group was based on a structure that follows a hierarchy integrating the development of virtual models of the robot with its physical implementation, passing through stages that include actuator creation, simulation and system construction. In addition to enabling robot design in a shorter time, the approach allows interdisciplinary work, one of the fundamental principles of the STEAM approach. A similar example to the contribution of Vassiliev et al. (2019) is the integration of a physical electrical system with a mechanical virtual model through the use of a digital twin, which allows the dynamics of second-order systems to be analysed interactively. In this work, Varguez Rojas et al. (2024) developed a methodology based on the interconnection of a series RLC circuit with a multibody model of a one-degree-of-freedom mass-spring-damper mechanical system, which is implemented in Simulink with Simscape Multibody, using the Arduino UNO programmable development platform for real-time data acquisition. This approach not only demonstrates the mathematical analogy between electrical and mechanical systems but also facilitates the interdisciplinary understanding of dynamic phenomena, allowing experimentation, visualisation and parameter adjustment without the need to build multiple physical prototypes. From the STEAM perspective, the proposal stands out for integrating knowledge from various disciplines, such as electronics, mechanics, programming and mathematical modelling in a unified environment, which promotes active learning, advanced simulation and the development of competences in complex systems analysis.

ADAPTIVE AND MULTIMODAL LEARNING MODELS IN SMART LABORATORIES

The development of intelligent laboratories in STEAM education has evolved towards the incorporation of adaptable learning models of a multimodal nature, which enable dynamic responses to the needs, abilities and contexts of students and their learning in contemporary settings. In this regard, the convergence between technologies such as IoT, learning analytics, artificial intelligence and advanced experimental environments affords the possibility of creating educational experiences that are personalised, contextualised and evidence-based in the acquisition of new knowledge. These models not only optimize the learning process but also promote the development of competencies of greater complexity and abstraction, which are associated with engineering in its various branches. Unlike traditional approaches, where learning follows a linear and homogeneous structure, adaptable systems permit the dynamic adjustment of content, such as activities and difficulty levels in accordance with results obtained in real time. As noted by Hu et al. (2024) in their work, in intelligent laboratories this adaptability is based upon the analysis of data generated during interaction with experimental systems, such as measurements, errors, response times, performance indices and patterns of behaviour.

This approach allows for the identification of strengths and weaknesses in a specific manner, which facilitates the personalisation of learning and, in a general context, of the educational process. For example, a student who presents difficulties in the interpretation of signals in an electrical, mechanical, or electromechanical system can receive additional reinforcement activities, which are focused on that topic, while another with greater mastery can progress towards problems of greater difficulty. This differentiation favours more efficient and significant learning, aligned with the principles of student-centred education Hazrat et al. (2023).

The pedagogical potential of IoT-based intelligent experimental platforms becomes most evident when considered from the perspective of the actors who inhabit them. In a typical undergraduate control engineering session, for instance, an instructor may configure a cloud-connected Furuta pendulum prototype so that each student workgroup receives a personalised set of initial parameters (mass distribution, damping coefficients, and target stabilisation criteria) derived from their prior performance on a mathematical modelling assessment. Rather than delivering a uniform laboratory script, the instructor monitors in real time, through a learning analytics dashboard, the divergence between each group's theoretical predictions and the sensor-generated response of the physical system, intervening selectively and formatively where systemic misconceptions emerge. Students, for their part, engage not merely as operators of equipment but as active investigators: they adjust control gains, observe the propagation of perturbations through the physical plant, interpret filtered sensor signals in light of their mathematical models, and collaboratively document the discrepancies that link abstract eigenvalue analysis to observable physical behaviour. This iterative cycle of prediction, experimentation, and reflective revision instantiates precisely the integrative epistemology that STEAM pedagogy seeks to cultivate, transforming the laboratory session from a procedural exercise into a genuine site of disciplinary convergence.

Beyond the individual session, intelligent experimental platforms afford the possibility of structuring extended, project-based learning trajectories in which students and instructors co-construct knowledge across multiple disciplinary domains over time. A multidisciplinary team comprising students from electrical, mechanical, and computer engineering programmes might collaboratively design, instrument, and validate a low-cost aerodynamic pendulum system: electrical engineering students assume responsibility for sensor integration and signal conditioning; mechanical engineering students develop and refine the dynamic model; and computer engineering students implement the embedded control algorithm and the IoT communication layer that streams experimental data to a shared cloud environment. The instructor's role shifts correspondingly, from transmitter of disciplinary content to orchestrator of interdisciplinary convergence, designing assessment rubrics that evaluate not only technical correctness but also the quality of cross-disciplinary reasoning and the coherence of the team's integrative documentation. In this configuration, the intelligent experimental platform functions as the shared material substrate through which distinct disciplinary languages enter into productive dialogue, rendering the abstract aspirations of STEAM education concrete, assessable, and institutionally reproducible.

The implementation of adaptive trajectories is enhanced by the use of multimodal learning analytics, which integrates data coming from multiple sources. In the context of intelligent laboratories, these data include not only information generated by physical sensors (temperature, pressure, level, vibration, etc.), but also student interactions with digital platforms, such as usage logs, behaviour in interfaces and even environmental variables, such as illumination, noise or environmental stress. This diversity of data allows for the construction of a more complete representation of the learning process (Kerimbayev et al., 2024).

Table 3. Core components of adaptive and multimodal learning models in intelligent STEAM laboratories for engineering education.

Component	Domain	Educational function
Adaptive learning trajectories	Pedagogy	Dynamically adjusts content, sequencing, and difficulty based on real-time individual performance, replacing homogeneous linear curricula
Multimodal learning analytics	Data science	Integrates heterogeneous data streams (sensors, platform logs, environmental variables) to construct holistic learner profiles and identify complex performance patterns
Explainable artificial intelligence (XAI)	AI / ethics	Renders adaptive system decisions legible to learners and instructors, promoting transparency, trust, and metacognitive awareness
Real-time formative feedback	Pedagogy	Provides continuous, automated diagnostic information during experimental tasks, accelerating error correction and fostering reflective, self-regulated learning
Predictive modelling	Data science	Anticipates learner difficulties prior to their occurrence, enabling proactive pedagogical intervention and reducing rates of failure and disengagement
Intelligent Tutoring Systems (ITS)	AI / pedagogy	Delivers personalised, step-by-step guidance through complex or high-risk experimental procedures by integrating domain, learner, and pedagogical models
IoT-enabled experimental environments	Engineering	Provides the empirical substrate for adaptive and analytical systems through instrumented, networked laboratory infrastructure generating continuous data streams
Digital twins	Engineering	Enables risk-free rehearsal and contextualised ITS interaction by mirroring physical system states in high-fidelity virtual representations
Safety-aware adaptive mechanisms	Safety	Detects unsafe behaviours and out-of-tolerance states, redirecting activity to mitigate risk and reinforcing a professional culture of procedural responsibility
Competency-based assessment	Pedagogy	Derives evidence-driven evaluation of higher-order engineering competencies from performance data accumulated across adaptive experimental interactions
Environmental contextualisation	Learning environment	Incorporates ambient variables (illumination, noise, thermal comfort) as covariates in learner performance modelling, producing more ecologically valid profiles
Ethical and regulatory governance	Policy / ethics	Ensures compliant, responsible use of learner data and adaptive AI systems, safeguarding autonomy, equity, and institutional accountability

The table 3 synthesises the key components of intelligent STEAM laboratories, integrating pedagogy, artificial intelligence, data science and engineering to provide adaptive, personalised and safe learning. It highlights the use of IoT and digital twins for experimentation, together with advanced analytics and real-time feedback, promoting the development of complex competences in engineering environments (Kumar et al., 2024).

Multimodal analytics, for its part, facilitates the identification of complex patterns that would not be evident through the analysis of a single data source. For example, the combination of sensor data with interaction logs can reveal how certain external factors influence experimental performance, or how certain problem-solving strategies correlate with better results (see Figure 2). This capacity for integral analysis is key to the design of more effective and contextualised educational measures towards learning (Gori et al., 2025). In this framework, explainable artificial intelligence (XAI) plays an essential role by allowing the decisions taken by adaptive systems to be comprehensible for both students and teachers. The generation of results and real-time feedback based on AI models can significantly improve learning, provided it is kept in mind that its effectiveness also depends on the users' capacity to understand the reasons behind the recommendations. XAI provides numerous tools to interpret these decisions, which promotes transparency and trust in these advanced systems (Fiok et al., 2022).

Figure 2. Conceptual framework of adaptive and multimodal learning models in IoT-enabled smart experimental laboratories for STEAM engineering education

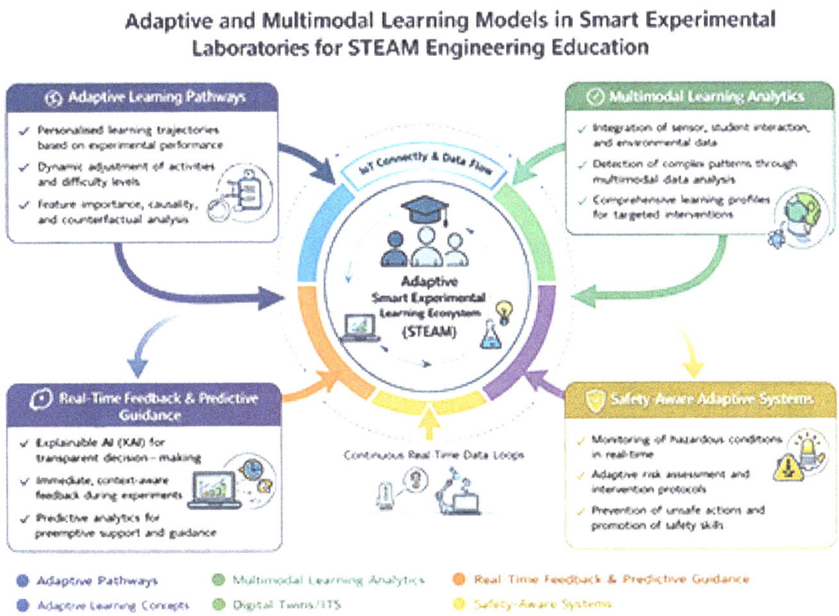

As has been mentioned, real-time feedback is one of the most valuable elements of smart laboratories. It is through the continuous analysis of data that systems can detect errors, suggest corrections, and provide guidance during the execution of laboratory practices and experimental procedures. This immediate feedback enables students to adjust their actions and better understand the effects of their decisions, fostering active and reflective learning (Afzaal et al., 2021). Furthermore, the incorporation of predictive models allows for the anticipation of difficulties and the provision of recommendations before errors or critical situations occur, enhancing the efficiency of the educational process. Intelligent Tutoring Systems (ITS) represent an advanced application of these approaches in experimental engineering environments. These advanced systems combine models of the domain, the student, and pedagogy to provide detailed and adaptive personalized instructions. In smart laboratories, ITS can guide students through experiments and laboratory practices that represent a high degree of complexity or risk, offering contextualised explanations and adapting activities based on the individual progress of the students (Asad et al., 2024).

For example, if a student attempts to operate equipment outside the safety parameters established by standards, the system can block the action, provide a warning, or redirect the activity towards a virtual simulation. Similarly, data analytics may be utilised to identify patterns of risk and adapt learning trajectories to reinforce competencies related to safety. This approach not only protects the integrity of students, but also fosters a culture of responsibility and awareness in the use of technologies.

In conclusion, the convergence between multimodal analytics, explainable artificial intelligence and adaptable systems configures a new paradigm in STEAM training, where learning becomes a dynamic, personalised process deeply connected with real experimentation. These advances not only transform the manner in which the disciplines of engineering are taught and learned, but also prepare students to face the challenges of complex technological environments in constant evolution.

CONCLUSION

The strategic integration of the Internet of Things (IoT), explainable artificial intelligence (XAI) and adaptive learning models within intelligent experimental platforms represents a paradigmatic shift in the configuration of STEAM engineering education. This chapter has synthesised the technological, pedagogical, ethical and infrastructural dimensions that characterise the emergence of smart laboratories as dynamic ecosystems capable of mediating simultaneously between theoretical knowledge and experimental practice, while at the same time fostering the development of complex and interdisciplinary competences in engineering students across different fields.

The fundamental contribution of this work lies in establishing that intelligent experimental platforms are not, in the first instance, technological innovations, but rather pedagogical infrastructures whose value derives from their capacity to instantiate inclusive, adaptable and evidence based learning ecologies. The chapter demonstrates that the architectural coherence of these ecosystems does not stem from the sophistication of their technological components, such as sensors, actuators, embedded systems or cloud infrastructure, but from the pedagogical logic that orchestrates their integration. This conceptualisation represents a significant epistemological shift with respect to traditional models of engineering education, in which disciplinary silos, linear curricula and homogeneous instructional pacing have historically constrained the development of genuinely interdisciplinary competences. The convergence of IoT with adaptive learning analytics enables the generation of continuous and multimodal data flows that make it possible to construct personalised experiential learning trajectories tailored to the heterogeneous abilities, learning styles and contextual circumstances of individual students. This adaptive orientation, grounded in real time performance analysis and predictive modelling, embodies a fundamentally student centred approach that contrasts sharply with the one size fits all pedagogies that have dominated conventional laboratory instruction.

A second important contribution concerns the pedagogical reconceptualisation of low cost didactic prototypes and sensors as accessible mediators between abstract theoretical concepts and empirically grounded experimental phenomena. The chapter has examined how platforms based on Arduino, simple electronic sensors and mechanical systems, when carefully integrated within comprehensive learning ecosystems, function not as diminished substitutes for industrial grade equipment, but as epistemologically coherent tools for fostering authentic engagement with complex engineering principles. The documented examples of Furuta pendulums, aerodynamic pendulums and wind turbine systems demonstrate that pedagogical value resides not in technological complexity per se, but in the integration of physical interaction, computational modelling and interdisciplinary conceptualisation. This democratisation of access to experimental infrastructures directly addresses persistent inequities in STEAM education, particularly within institutionally and geographically resource constrained contexts, and contributes substantially to the fulfilment of Sustainable Development Goal 4, which calls for inclusive and equitable access to education.

A third significant contribution relates to the articulation of safety aware adaptive mechanisms as integral pedagogical components rather than peripheral technical safeguards. The chapter has shown that in high risk laboratory environments (chemical, electrical and mechanical) the incorporation of context sensitive monitoring, behaviour detection and adaptive interventions not only protects student well being, but simultaneously cultivates professional competences centred on procedural responsibility, risk awareness and critical reflection on technological use. This integration of safety considerations into the core logic of adaptive learning models represents an advance in the conceptualisation of engineering education as sociotechnical formation, in which technical competence and ethical professional awareness are mutually constituted rather than compartmentalised.

A fourth contribution emerges from the systematic examination of explainable artificial intelligence (XAI) as a prerequisite for the meaningful adoption of adaptive systems in educational contexts. The chapter has articulated that, while AI driven personalisation and predictive analytics offer substantial pedagogical benefits, their educational legitimacy and effectiveness depend fundamentally on the intelligibility of system decisions for both students and instructors. This emphasis on transparency and interpretability serves to counteract logics of technological instrumentalism and instead promotes a model of educational technology governance grounded in human agency, reflective practice and institutional responsibility. The integration of XAI principles across smart laboratory ecosystems instantiates what may be termed "transparent personalisation", adaptive learning experiences whose mechanisms remain accessible to human scrutiny and critical evaluation.

The chapter has further emphasised that multimodal learning analytics, digital twin technologies and Intelligent Tutoring Systems constitute a coherent methodological ensemble for experimental engineering education only when they are designed and implemented in alignment with clearly articulated pedagogical objectives. Accumulated evidence from contemporary research demonstrates that the mere accumulation of technological sophistication does not guarantee educational effectiveness; rather, pedagogical robustness emerges through deliberate alignment between learning objectives, assessment strategies, technological affordances and instructional design. The chapter's systematic integration of pedagogical frameworks with technological specifications seeks to provide practitioners with a conceptually coherent scaffold for designing intelligent experimental platforms that optimise both learning outcomes and institutional sustainability.

Looking ahead, the institutionalisation of intelligent experimental platforms in STEAM engineering education remains contingent upon several critical developments. These include sustained investment in technological infrastructure and the development of digital competence among teaching staff; the establishment of governance frameworks that ensure the ethical, equitable and compliant use of educational data; the emergence of assessment methodologies capable of capturing the development of complex and interdisciplinary competences; and the cultivation of professional learning communities in which educators can collectively refine pedagogical practices in dialogue with advancing technological possibilities.

Notwithstanding the considerable promise of intelligent experimental platforms for STEAM engineering education, their widespread institutionalisation confronts a set of structural challenges that future research must address with empirical rigour. The economic cost of deploying and maintaining IoT-enabled laboratory infrastructure, even when based on low-cost components, remains a significant barrier in resource-constrained educational contexts, particularly in institutions operating under conditions of limited public funding and insufficient technical support capacity. Equally critical is the challenge of pedagogical readiness: the effective orchestration of adaptive, data-rich learning environments demands from instructors a level of digital and analytical competence that current teacher training programmes have not yet systematically addressed, risking the reduction of sophisticated platforms to passive technological props rather than active pedagogical instruments. The large-scale collection of behavioural and performance data generated by smart laboratories also raises unresolved questions regarding student privacy, data sovereignty, and the ethical governance of algorithmic decision-making in academic contexts, issues that require robust institutional frameworks and not merely technical compliance with existing regulations. Furthermore, the conceptual contributions advanced in this chapter rest primarily on a synthesis of existing literature and documented case studies; their transferability across diverse institutional, cultural, and disciplinary contexts remains to be validated through longitudinal empirical research conducted in real educational settings. Future lines of investigation should therefore prioritise the development of low-cost scalable deployment models, the design of competency-based instructor training programmes aligned with smart laboratory pedagogy, the establishment of ethical governance frameworks specific to educational IoT environments, and the systematic empirical evaluation of learning outcomes attributable to the integration of adaptive and multimodal technologies in STEAM engineering curricula.

In summary, this chapter has established that intelligent experimental platforms, when carefully designed and responsibly governed, constitute transformative infrastructures for STEAM engineering education. Their capacity to personalise learning, integrate multidisciplinary data, provide immediate formative feedback and foster critical engagement with technological systems positions them as valuable instruments for addressing contemporary educational challenges while advancing progress towards inclusive, equitable and quality education in accordance with the Sustainable Development Goals. The convergence of IoT, XAI and adaptive learning models configures a new pedagogical paradigm in which experiential, contextualised and evidence based learning becomes accessible at scale, thereby democratising the development of complex engineering competences increasingly demanded by dynamic, technologically mediated professional environments.

REFERENCES

Abdul-Qawy, A. S., Pramod, P. J., Magesh, E., & Srinivasulu, T. (2015). The internet of things (IoT): An overview. *International Journal of Engineering Research and Applications*, *5*(12), 71–82.

Afzaal, M., Nouri, J., Zia, A., Papapetrou, P., Fors, U., Wu, Y., Li, X., & Weegar, R. (2021). Explainable AI for data-driven feedback and intelligent action recommendations to support students self-regulation. *Frontiers in Artificial Intelligence*, *4*, 723447. DOI: 10.3389/frai.2021.723447 PMID: 34870183

Ağca, R. K. (2023). Using digital twins in education from an innovative perspective: Potential and application areas. *Education Mind*, *2*(2), 65–74. DOI: 10.58583/Pedapub.EM2306

Alkhatib, O. J. (2025). STEAM integration and engineering: Lessons from transformative approaches. In Behera, S. K., Sorayyaei Azar, A., Curle, S., & Dials, J. (Eds.), *Transformative approaches to STEAM integration in modern education* (pp. 345–374). IGI Global Scientific Publishing., DOI: 10.4018/979-8-3693-7408-5.ch015

Alsaleh, S., Tepljakov, A., Köse, A., Belikov, J., & Petlenkov, E. (2022). ReImagine lab: Bridging the gap between hands-on, virtual and remote control engineering laboratories using digital twins and extended reality. *IEEE Access : Practical Innovations, Open Solutions*, *10*, 89924–89943. DOI: 10.1109/ACCESS.2022.3199371

Alves Aleixo, A., Silva, B., & Silva Ramos, M. A. (2021). Análisis del uso de la cultura maker en contextos educativos: Una revisión sistemática de la literatura. *Educatio Siglo XXI*, *39*(2), 143–168. DOI: 10.6018/educatio.465991

Asad, M. M., Naz, A., Churi, P., & Tahanzadeh, M. M. (2024). Investigating the impact of IoT-based smart laboratories on students' academic performance in higher education. *Universal Access in the Information Society*, *23*(3), 1135–1149. DOI: 10.1007/s10209-022-00944-1 PMID: 36407564

Auer, M. E., Azad, A. K., Edwards, A., & De Jong, T. (Eds.). (2018). *Cyber-physical laboratories in engineering and science education*. Springer International Publishing. DOI: 10.1007/978-3-319-76935-6

Berisha-Gawlowski, A., Caruso, C., & Harteis, C. (2021). The concept of a digital twin and its potential for learning organizations. In *Digital transformation of learning organizations* (pp. 95–114). Springer., DOI: 10.1007/978-3-030-55878-9_6

Boy, G. A. (2013). From STEM to STEAM: *Toward a human-centred education, creativity & learning thinking.* In *Proceedings of the European Conference on Cognitive Ergonomics.* ACM. DOI: 10.1145/2501907.2501934

Calle Balarezo, S. D. (2022). *Digital twin del laboratorio MPS mediante herramientas IoT y simulación virtual para realizar prácticas de laboratorio no presenciales* [Trabajo de titulación, Universidad Politécnica Salesiana]. https://dspace.ups.edu.ec/handle/123456789/22113

Delgado, I., Sancristobal, E., Martin, S., & Robles-Gómez, A. (2023). Exploring IoT vulnerabilities in a comprehensive remote cybersecurity laboratory. *Sensors (Basel), 23*(22), 9279. DOI: 10.3390/s23229279 PMID: 38005664

Demir, K., & Suri, N. (2017). SeReCP: A secure and reliable communication platform for the smart grid. In *2017 IEEE 22nd Pacific Rim International Symposium on Dependable Computing (PRDC)* (pp. 175–184). IEEE. DOI: 10.1109/PRDC.2017.31

Fiok, K., Farahani, F. V., Karwowski, W., & Ahram, T. (2022). Explainable artificial intelligence for education and training. *The Journal of Defense Modeling and Simulation: Applications, Methodology. Technology, 19*(2), 133–144. DOI: 10.1177/15485129211028651

García-Fuentes, O., Raposo-Rivas, M., & Martínez-Figueira, M. E. (2023). El enfoque educativo STEAM: Una revisión de la literatura. *Revista Complutense de Educación, 34*(1), 191–202. DOI: 10.5209/rced.77261

Gori, K. D., Zalawadia, K., & Bhaidasna, H. (2025). Explainable AI for students performance prediction system. In *2025 IEEE Pune Section International Conference (PuneCon)* (pp. 1–6). IEEE. DOI: DOI: 10.1109/PuneCon67554.2025.11379137

Hazrat, M. A., Hassan, N. M. S., Chowdhury, A. A., Rasul, M. G., & Taylor, B. A. (2023). Developing a skilled workforce for future industry demand: The potential of digital twin-based teaching and learning practices in engineering education. *Sustainability (Basel), 15*(23), 16433. DOI: 10.3390/su152316433

He, J., Lo, D. C.-T., Xie, Y., & Lartigue, J. (2016). I*ntegrating Internet of Things (IoT) into STEM undergraduate education: Case study of a modern technology infused courseware for embedded system course.* In 2016 IEEE Frontiers in Education Conference (FIE) (pp. 1–9). IEEE. DOI: 10.1109/FIE.2016.7757458

Hernández-de-Menéndez, M., Escobar Díaz, C. A., & Morales-Menéndez, R. (2020). Engineering education for smart 4.0 technology: A review. *International Journal on Interactive Design and Manufacturing, 14*(3), 789–803. DOI: 10.1007/s12008-020-00672-x

Hernández Pérez, J., Gutiérrez Moreno, E., Ordaz Oliver, J. P., & Ordaz Oliver, M. O. (2024). LQR-based control with gravity compensation for a wind turbine pendulum system. *International Journal of Combinatorial Optimization Problems and Informatics, 15*(5), 161–180. DOI: 10.61467/2007.1558.2024.v15i5.428

Holbrook, J., Rannikmäe, M., & Soobard, R. (2020). STEAM education—A transdisciplinary teaching and learning approach. In Akpan, B., & Kennedy, T. J. (Eds.), *Science education in theory and practice* (pp. 465–477). Springer., DOI: 10.1007/978-3-030-43620-9_31

Hu, J., Huang, Z., Li, J., Xu, L., & Zou, Y. (2024). Real-time classroom behavior analysis for enhanced engineering education: An AI-assisted approach. *International Journal of Computational Intelligence Systems, 17*(1), 167. DOI: 10.1007/s44196-024-00572-y

Jantassova, D., Churchill, D., Shebalina, O., & Akhmetova, D. (2022). Capacity building for engineering training and technology via STEAM education. *Education Sciences, 12*(11), 737. DOI: 10.3390/educsci12110737

Kerimbayev, N., Adamova, K., Jotsov, V., Shadiev, R., Umirzakova, Z., & Nurymova, A. (2024). Organization of feedback in the intelligent learning systems. In *2024 IEEE 12th International Conference on Intelligent Systems (IS)* (pp. 1–7). IEEE. DOI: 10.1109/IS61756.2024.10705178

Kumar, B., & Deák, C. (2024). Evolving minds: A literature-driven and empirical exploration of STEAM skill development and learning approaches. *Journal of Innovation Management, 11*(4), 71–96. Advance online publication. DOI: 10.24840/2183-0606_011.004_0004

Lam-Byrne, A. G. (2023). El aprendizaje STEAM: Una práctica inclusiva. *Revista Científica Episteme Y Tekne, 2*(1), e466. DOI: 10.51252/rceyt.v2i1.466

Lin, C. C., Huang, A. Y. Q., & Lu, O. H. T. (2023). Artificial intelligence in intelligent tutoring systems toward sustainable education: A systematic review. *Smart Learning Environments, 10*(1), 41. DOI: 10.1186/s40561-023-00260-y

Martínez López, K. (2021). *Development of machine learning strategies for fault diagnosis in virtual plants (digital twin)* [Master's thesis, Universitat Politècnica de Catalunya]. https://hdl.handle.net/2117/358256

Martínez Ramírez, E., Diaz Ledezma, M. A., López Portillo Zuarth, D., Vicente Ortiz, A. Y., Mera Sánchez, N. R., Ordaz Oliver, M. O., & Espejel Rivera, M. A. (2025). Model of a low-cost educational prototype of the Furuta pendulum. *International Journal of Combinatorial Optimization Problems and Informatics, 16*(4), 61–78. DOI: 10.61467/2007.1558.2025.v16i4.1133

Martínez Sánchez, K. E. (2024). Digital twin para el análisis dinámico de una ménsula construida con impresión 3D utilizando los sensores del móvil [Trabajo final de grado, Universitat Politècnica de Catalunya]. https://hdl.handle.net/2117/418222

Mascareñas Brito, A. (2021). Diseño y modelado de un sistema Digital Twin [Trabajo de fin de máster, Universidad Pontificia Comillas]. http://hdl.handle.net/11531/51618

Melgarejo, Y., Perez Garcia, B., Melgarejo, M. F. M. M., Ramirez Alvarado, J. J., Gutierrez Paredes, J. A., Hernández Pérez, J., & Gutierrez Moreno, E. (2026). Closed-loop control and sensor noise reduction in a low-cost aerodynamic pendulum using digital PID and Kalman filtering on Arduino Mega. *International Journal of Combinatorial Optimization Problems and Informatics*, *17*(1), 34–47. DOI: 10.61467/2007.1558.2026.v17i1.1137

Min, Q., Lu, Y., Liu, Z., Su, C., & Wang, B. (2019). Machine learning based digital twin framework for production optimization in petrochemical industry. *International Journal of Information Management*, *49*, 502–519. DOI: 10.1016/j.ijinfomgt.2019.05.020

Plakhteyev, A., Perepelitsyn, A., & Frolov, V. (2018). Edge computing for IoT: An educational case study. In *2018 IEEE 9th International Conference on Dependable Systems, Services and Technologies (DESSERT)* (pp. 130–133). IEEE. DOI: 10.1109/DESSERT.2018.8409113

Rao, R., & Elias-Medina, A. (2024). Designing an internet of things laboratory to improve student understanding of secure IoT systems. *Internet of Things and Cyber-Physical Systems*, *4*, 154–166. DOI: 10.1016/j.iotcps.2023.10.002

Santillán Aguirre, J. P., Cadena Vaca, V. del C., & Cadena Vaca, M. (2019). Educación STEAM: Entrada a la sociedad del conocimiento. *Ciencia Digital*, 3(3.4), 212–227. DOI: 10.33262/cienciadigital.v3i3.4.847

Singam, C. A. K. (2026). Developing an integrated model of STEAM education. In Madni, A., Endsley, M., & Boy, G. A. (Eds.), *Handbook of sociotechnical systems: A human systems integration approach* (2nd ed.). CRC Press., DOI: 10.1201/9781003666431-5

Singh, K. D., & Singh, P. D. (2025). Edge-AI driven gamification in engineering education for improving student engagement. *Computer Applications in Engineering Education, 33*(1), e70076. DOI: 10.1002/cae.70076

Soroko, N. V., Mykhailenko, L. A., Rokoman, O. G., & Zaselskiy, V. I. (2020). Educational electronic platforms for STEAM-oriented learning environment at general education school. In Proceedings of the 7th Workshop on Cloud Technologies in Education (CTE 2019). *CEUR Workshop Proceedings, 2643*, 462–473. DOI: 10.55056/cte.386

Tariq, R., Casillas-Muñoz, F., Hassan, S., & Ramírez-Montoya, M. (2024). Synergy of Internet of Things and Education: Cyber-physical systems contributing towards remote laboratories, improved learning, and school management. *Journal of Social Studies Education Research, 15*(2), 305–352. DOI: 10.6084/m9.figshare.24927696

Thakkar, S. R., & Joshi, H. D. (2015). E-learning systems: A review. In 2015 IEEE Seventh International Conference on Technology for Education (T4E) (pp. 37–40). IEEE. DOI: 10.1109/T4E.2015.6

UNESCO. (2020, April 22). The UNESCO Section for Innovation and Capacity Building in Science and Engineering compiles online STEM education resources available for inclusive distance learning in response to COVID-19. https://www.unesco.org/en/articles/unesco-section-innovation-and-capacity-building-science-and-engineering-compiles-online-stem

United Nations. (n.d.). Education. https://www.un.org/sustainabledevelopment/education/

Varguez Rojas, E., Gutiérrez Moreno, E., Cornejo Cervantes, J. A., Montiel Hernández, J. F., Ordaz Oliver, M. O., & Ordaz Oliver, J. P. (2024). Interacción entre circuito RLC serie y modelo gemelo multicuerpo del sistema masa-resorte-amortiguador. In Memorias del Congreso Internacional de Mecatrónica, Control e Inteligencia Artificial (CIMCIA) (pp. 27–33). UNAM FES Cuautitlán.http://virtual.cuautitlan.unam.mx/intar/memoriascimcia/wp-content/uploads/sites/20/2024/12/4-27-33.pdf

Vassiliev, A., Samarin, V., Raskin, D., Evseev, E., Veris, V., Peschinski, I., Cabezas, D., & Kurniawan, Y. (2019). Designing the built-in microcontroller control systems of executive robotic devices using the digital twins technology. In *2019 International Conference on Information Management and Technology (ICIMTech)* (Vol. 1, pp. 256–260). IEEE. DOI: 10.1109/ICIMTech.2019.8843814

Xiong, M., Wang, H., Fu, Q., & Xu, F. (2021). Digital twin-driven aero-engine intelligent predictive maintenance. *International Journal of Advanced Manufacturing Technology, 114*(11–12), 3751–3761. DOI: 10.1007/s00170-021-06976-w

Xu, Y., Sun, Y., Liu, X., & Zheng, Y. (2019). A digital-twin-assisted fault diagnosis using deep transfer learning. *IEEE Access : Practical Innovations, Open Solutions*, *7*, 19990–19999. DOI: 10.1109/ACCESS.2018.2890566

Zhang, X. (2025). Internet of Things and cloud computing-powered virtual laboratories for enhanced STEM education. *Journal of the Institution of Engineers India Series B*, *106*(6), 1767–1776. DOI: 10.1007/s40031-024-01192-y

Chapter 9
Persistent Homology for Learning Trajectories With Cycles, Transitions, and Ruptures

Jaime Aguilar-Ortiz
http://orcid.org/0009-0003-5302-1454
Universidad Politécnica de Pachuca, Mexico

Ocotlán Díaz-Parra
Universidad Politécnica de Pachuca, Mexico

Marco A. Vera-Jiménez
http://orcid.org/0009-0009-3712-1440
Universidad Politécnica de Pachuca, Mexico

Víctor M. Zamudio-García
http://orcid.org/0000-0002-4660-8025
Universidad Politéctica Metropolitana de Hidalgo, Mexico

Carlos R. Domínguez-Mayorga
http://orcid.org/0009-0007-1018-4412
Universidad Politécnica de Pachuca, Mexico

ABSTRACT

This chapter develops and evaluates a reproducible topological workflow for modeling learning trajectories as evolving geometric objects rather than as static aggregates. Event logs are segmented into pedagogically meaningful windows, encoded as learner states, organized through similarity-based filtrations, and analyzed

DOI: 10.4018/979-8-2600-3658-7.ch009

with persistent homology, stable summaries, topology-aware latent representations, and graph-based recommendation layers. Using synthetic but theory-consistent trajectories, the results show that dimension-1 persistence identifies recurrent study-feedback-practice loops, latent-space audits expose regime shifts more clearly than conventional summaries, and rupture-sensitive indicators can be translated into interpretable recommendations for educational support. The chapter demonstrates that persistent homology reveals multiscale structural patterns in learning trajectories that conventional analytics frequently miss while preserving reproducibility, interpretability, and human-centred decision support.

1. INTRODUCTION

1.1. Learning Trajectories as Dynamic Educational Processes

Digital learning environments now record educational activity as temporally situated traces: visits to resources, assessment attempts, feedback use, help-seeking episodes, and returns to prior content. These traces make visible not only participation volume but also rhythm, sequence, and reorganization. For a trajectory-oriented study, the relevant unit is therefore the evolving pathway through which a learner stabilizes routines, shifts strategy, or loses coherence. Such a reading also prevents delay, absence, and revisitation from being treated as deficits before their temporal role is examined.

Learning trajectories are treated here as dynamic educational processes because digital environments register how actions unfold, recur, and interact across time. Contemporary learning analytics has shown that temporality and sequence are not secondary descriptors but explanatory dimensions of self-regulated learning, engagement, and performance. Empirical trace-data studies further show that observed behavioral sequences can distinguish learning strategies and self-regulatory profiles more reliably than totals or self-reports alone (Saint et al., 2022; Engelmann & Bannert, 2021; Saqr & López-Pernas, 2021; Gašević et al., 2017; Ye & Pennisi, 2022).

Under that lens, cycles, transitions, and ruptures are not simple increases or decreases in activity. They are relational configurations in which learners revisit regions of the state space, move into new regimes, or fragment away from previously coherent pathways. Because the same amount of activity can produce different shapes, the topological question is not how much a learner acts but how the states relate across time. Persistent homology is suited to that reading because it captures connected components and loops across multiple scales and remains stable under noise, an essential property for sparse and heterogeneous educational traces. Longitudinal evidence on engagement, collaboration, and self-regulated online learning supports this process-oriented view of learner pathways (Saqr & López-Pernas, 2022; Chazal & Michel, 2021; Mishra & Motta, 2023; Maldonado-Mahauad et al., 2018).

1.2. Research Gap, Objective, and Contribution

The central problem is the gap between temporally rich educational data and analytic frameworks that still privilege aggregates, short local transitions, or static learner profiles. The chapter responds to that gap by proposing a persistent-homology workflow that identifies recurrent cycles, regime transitions, and structural ruptures, and then translates those signatures into interpretable educational signals.

Recent trajectory research confirms that temporality, sequence, stability, and change are central to self-regulated learning and long-term engagement. However, many pipelines still stop at clustering, transition probabilities, or window-level summaries. These methods are informative, but they rarely evaluate whether the trajectory itself has multiscale cohesion, loop structure, or fragmentation. That limitation leaves the structural organization of learner pathways under-specified, especially when the data contain irregular pacing and repeated returns to prior resources. It also makes visible whether changes in behaviour remain locally isolated or alter the geometry of the pathway as a whole (Saint et al., 2022; Saqr & López-Pernas, 2021; Saqr et al., 2023; Bannert et al., 2014).

The objective is therefore to provide a reproducible and interpretable framework that transforms event streams into learner-state representations, constructs filtered complexes over time, computes persistence diagrams and stable summaries, and links those summaries to educational readings of cycles, transitions, and ruptures. The contribution is methodological and pedagogical: it preserves the mathematics of persistent homology while grounding the interpretation in trace-based learning analytics, empirical sequence analysis, and human-centred decision support. That grounding is essential for the reference-quality issue raised in the evaluation: technical TDA sources remain useful, but the argumentative centre of gravity should be education-facing and empirical (Chazal & Michel, 2021; Munch, 2017; Gašević et al., 2017; Ye & Pennisi, 2022).

To orient the reader before the formal development of the theoretical and methodological sections, Figure 1 synthesizes the complete analytical route followed in the chapter. The diagram makes explicit how temporal educational traces are transformed into learner states, how those states are organized through similarity and filtration operations, and how the resulting topological summaries are later translated into educational signals for cycles, transitions, ruptures, and recommendation support.

Figure 1. End-to-end research route for topological analysis of learning trajectories

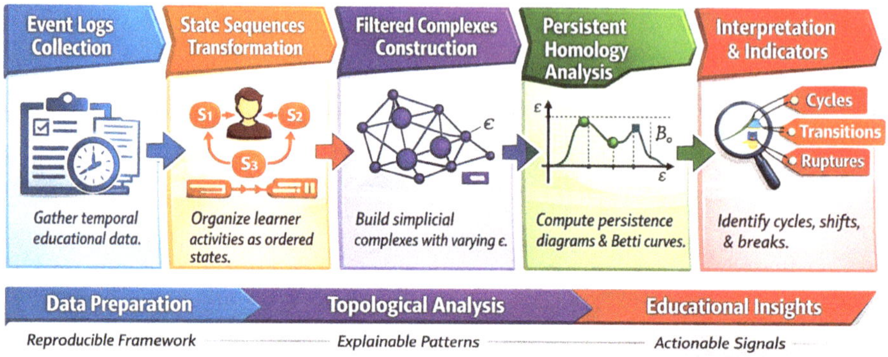

The figure summarizes the pipeline developed in the chapter, from event-log collection and weekly state construction to filtration design, persistent homology, stable summarization, and educational signal generation for cycle analysis, latent-space transition analysis, and recommendation support.

2. THEORETICAL FOUNDATIONS

2.1. Learning Analytics, Sequential Behavior, and Trajectory Modeling

Learning analytics, educational data mining, and trajectory modeling converge on the idea that learner activity is better understood as an ordered process than as a collection of disconnected counts. From that perspective, the mathematical formulation begins by preserving temporal order and by representing each learner through a trace that can later be segmented, compared, and topologically analyzed.

Learning analytics, sequential behavior, and trajectory modeling treat learning as an ordered process in which timing, recurrence, and sequential order shape the interpretation of learner activity. Rather than collapsing activity into static totals, the present approach preserves temporal position across windows and uses the learner's raw trace as an ordered event stream (Molenaar & Wise, 2022; Saint et al., 2022; Gašević et al., 2017; Kizilcec et al., 2017; Saint et al., 2020; Fan et al., 2021; Ye & Pennisi, 2022). Thus, for learner i, the event log is written as

$$E_i = \left\langle e_{i,1}, e_{i,2}, \ldots, e_{i,n} \right\rangle, e_{i,s} = \left(a_{i,s}, t_{i,s}, \boldsymbol{m}_{i,s}\right), t_{i,1} \leq t_{i,2} \leq \cdots \leq t_{i,n}.$$

Here, $a_{i,s}$ denotes the recorded educational action, $t_{i,s} = t(e_{i,s})$ its timestamp, $\boldsymbol{m}_{i,s}$ the associated contextual metadata, and n_i the number of observed events for learner i.

To preserve pedagogical rhythm, the event stream is then segmented into ordered windows, so that the r-th window is defined by

$$W_{i,r} = \{e \in E_i : \tau_{r-1} < t(e) \leq \tau_r\}$$

With boundaries chosen according to weekly modules, assessment cycles, or activity-adaptive intervals, each window becomes a temporally coherent unit of analysis. Here, the window for learner i at position r gathers all events whose timestamps fall between the opening and closing temporal boundaries of that window. The segmentation converts a continuous event stream into comparable educational units while retaining the temporal order required for later state construction and topological analysis.

$$\mathbf{x}_{i,r} = \phi(W_{i,r}) \in \mathbb{R}^p$$

In this mapping, the state vector for learner i in window r is obtained through the feature extractor φ, and p denotes the number of pedagogically selected dimensions retained for analysis. Those dimensions may summarize engagement intensity, regularity, assessment performance, help-seeking, and concept coverage. When a distributional view is preferred, the count c for category k measures the observed weight of that topic or resource inside the same window, and the normalization across K categories turns those counts into a probability profile rather than a raw frequency total.

$$p_{i,r}(k) = \frac{c_{i,rk}}{\sum_{h=1}^{K} c_{i,rh}}, \; k = 1, \ldots, K$$

From this construction, the full learning trajectory is the ordered state sequence$T_i = (\mathbf{x}_{i,1}, \mathbf{x}_{i,2}, \ldots, \mathbf{x}_{i,R})$. Unlike totals or averages, it preserves recurrence, progression, and local reorganization for interpretable analysis of cycles, transitions, and ruptures. It also aligns with empirical trace-based and temporal learning-analytics studies that treat sequences as evidence of process rather than merely as performance covariates (Engelmann & Bannert, 2021; Chen & Cui, 2020; Kizilcec et al., 2017; Saint et al., 2020; Fan et al., 2021; van Halem et al., 2020; Saqr et al., 2024; Wu et al., 2024; Bannert et al., 2014).

Once the trajectory has been encoded as an ordered sequence of states, sequential behavior can be modeled through transitions between regimes and through distances between successive or aligned windows. In the transition formulation, the numerator counts how often a window labeled u is followed by a window labeled v, whereas the denominator normalizes by all departures from u. The resulting quantity summarizes directional movement among behavioral regimes and distinguishes stable recurrence from systematic change.

$$\widehat{P}_{uv} = \frac{\sum_i \sum_{r=1}^{R-1} 1\left(s_{i,r} = u,\ s_{i,r+1} = v\right)}{\sum_i \sum_{r=1}^{R-1} 1\left(s_{i,r} = u\right)}$$

When the state vectors are continuous and covariance structure matters, a metric-consistent distance may be introduced through the Mahalanobis form. In this expression, the two arguments are learner-state vectors and Σ is the covariance matrix of the state space, so deviations along highly variable directions are discounted while deviations along statistically informative directions are emphasized. This choice is necessary when correlated educational indicators would make ordinary Euclidean distance misleading.

$$d_M(\mathbf{x}, \mathbf{y}) = \sqrt{(\mathbf{x} - \mathbf{y})^\top \Sigma^{-1} (\mathbf{x} - \mathbf{y})}$$

With that metric in place, trajectories of unequal pace can be compared by alignment-based dissimilarity, for example through a dynamic-time-warping style construction. Here, the two objects being compared are complete learner trajectories, π denotes an admissible alignment path, and the local cost is evaluated between states that are matched along that path. This alignment matters because learners may follow similar pedagogical routes at different speeds, and the comparison concerns structural evolution rather than mere clock-time synchrony.

$$D_{\mathrm{DTW}}\left(T_i, T_j\right) = \min_{\pi \in \Pi} \sum_{(r,s) \in \pi} d_M\left(\mathbf{x}_{i,r}, \mathbf{x}_{j,s}\right)$$

The set Π collects the admissible alignment paths between the two trajectories. After alignment has been defined, abrupt temporal reorganization can be localized with the stepwise change magnitude, which compares the current learner state with its immediately preceding state. That local difference provides an early marker for possible transitions or ruptures before the richer topological summaries are computed.

$$\Delta_{i,r} = d_M\left(\mathbf{x}_{i,r}, \mathbf{x}_{i,r-1}\right)$$

Under this state-space view, small repeated values of $\Delta_{i,r}$ together with recurrent transition patterns indicate stable routines, sustained directional changes suggest transitions between learning regimes, and large local jumps indicate possible ruptures;

the result is a coherent state space before persistent homology is introduced, because later topological summaries depend on explicit filtrable objects, stable distances, and robust vectorizations of multiscale structure under noise (Chazal & Michel, 2021; Barnes et al., 2021; Atienza et al., 2020; Ali et al., 2023; Mishra & Motta, 2023).

2.2. Persistent Homology and Topological Data Analysis

Persistent homology provides the formal bridge between temporally ordered learner states and multiscale structural analysis. The mathematical development that follows introduces filtrations, simplicial complexes, homology groups, Betti numbers, persistence diagrams, and stable summaries in a way that keeps the algebraic definitions close to their educational interpretation.

Persistent homology provides the mathematical core needed to transform learning trajectories into analyzable geometric objects, because it studies how structure persists across scales in a cloud of learner states rather than reducing the trajectory to isolated observations. Let the available learner states at time t be equipped with the distance induced by the chosen representation. For the point-cloud case, the Vietoris-Rips complex is a natural construction, because a simplex enters the complex only when all of its vertices are sufficiently close under the selected metric. This yields the filtration used below.

$$\mathrm{VR}_{\varepsilon}(X_t) = \{\sigma \subseteq X_t : d(x_i, x_j) \le \varepsilon \text{ for every } x_i, x_j \in \sigma\}.$$

Once this nested family has been introduced, algebraic topology acts on each complex through chain spaces and boundary operators, which specify how simplices relate across dimensions. In the boundary expression, a k-simplex is written through its ordered vertices, and each term removes one vertex with alternating sign to produce a face of one lower dimension. The operator links algebraic structure to attachment patterns, since topology depends not on isolated simplices but on how they attach to one another.

$$\partial_k[v_0, \ldots, v_k] = \sum_{i=0}^{k}(-1)^i[v_0, \ldots, \widehat{v}_i, \ldots, v_k].$$

From this point, cycles are defined as chains with zero boundary and boundaries are those cycles inherited from higher-dimensional simplices. The homology group therefore keeps only the classes that remain after boundaries have been factored out. In this quotient, the kernel of the k-th boundary operator collects closed k-chains, the image of the $(k + 1)$-st boundary operator collects those that are already explained as higher-dimensional boundaries, and the Betti number counts the independent classes that survive. This is the algebraic step that turns raw combinatorial structure into interpretable counts of components and loops.

$$H_k(K_\varepsilon) = \ker(\partial_k)/\mathrm{im}(\partial_{k+1}),\ \beta_k(\varepsilon) = \dim H_k(K_\varepsilon).$$

Within the present chapter, this formulation is especially meaningful because β_0 captures fragmentation versus cohesion among learner states, while β_1 captures loops that can be interpreted as recurrent study-feedback-practice patterns, repeated revisitation of content, or stable returns to earlier behavioral regimes; consequently, topological invariants become mathematically rigorous descriptors of cycles and emerging structural organization in educational trajectories rather than merely decorative abstractions (Wasserman, 2018; Chazal & Michel, 2021; El-Yaagoubi et al., 2023).

Persistent homology then tracks how each homology class appears and disappears as the scale parameter grows. Between two scales, the induced map between homology groups retains classes that survive from the earlier scale to the later one. The analysis therefore privileges multiscale regularities in learning trajectories and downweights brief geometric coincidences that vanish immediately as scale changes.

$$H_k^{\varepsilon,\varepsilon'} = \mathrm{im}\big(H_k(K_\varepsilon) \rightarrow H_k(K_{\varepsilon'})\big),\ \varepsilon \leq \varepsilon'.$$

Each feature receives a birth time and a death time, so persistence is read through the interval over which the feature remains visible. In the persistence diagram, each ordered pair records when a component or loop appears and when it disappears, while the index distinguishes one feature from another. The diagram compresses the filtration into a comparable record of structural emergence and disappearance.

$$\mathrm{Dgm}_k(X_t) = \{(b_j, d_j)\}_{j=1}^{m_k},\ \ell_j = d_j - b_j,$$

The lifetime of a feature is the difference between its death and birth scales, so larger lifetimes correspond to more prominent and stable structures. To compare trajectories, adjacent temporal windows, or groups of learners, stable distances between persistence diagrams are required. The bottleneck distance is especially useful when the analysis should remain sensitive to the single largest discrepancy between two structural signatures.

$$d_B(D_1, D_2) = \inf_{\gamma} \sup_{x \in D_1} \| x - \gamma(x) \|_\infty,$$

The p-Wasserstein distance complements the bottleneck perspective by accumulating all matched discrepancies rather than only the largest one. In that definition, the matching γ pairs points across the two diagrams or with the diagonal, and the exponent p controls the way those discrepancies are aggregated. This measure is valuable when many moderate topological changes together carry pedagogical meaning.

$$W_p(D_1, D_2) = \left(\inf_{\gamma} \sum_{x \in D_1} \|x - \gamma(x)\|_\infty^p\right)^{1/p},$$

Predictive and monitoring pipelines also require fixed-length summaries, so persistence diagrams are commonly vectorized through stable descriptors such as Betti curves and persistent entropy. The Betti curve counts features alive at a given filtration value, whereas persistent entropy weights each feature by normalized lifetime and summarizes whether persistence is concentrated in a few features or dispersed across the diagram.

$$\beta_k(\tau) = \sum_{(b,d) \in \mathrm{Dgm}_k} 1_{[b,d)}(\tau)$$

$$\mathrm{PE}(\mathrm{Dgm}_k) = -\sum_{j=1}^{m_k} p_j \log p_j,\ p_j = \frac{\ell_j}{\sum_{m=1}^{m_k} \ell_m}.$$

These constructions support the computational pipeline used for detecting cycles, transitions, and ruptures: they preserve multiscale shape, enable stable comparison across windows, and produce vectorizations that remain interpretable under noisy and heterogeneous educational traces (Atienza et al., 2020; Barnes et al., 2021; Ali et al., 2023; Mishra & Motta, 2023; Munch, 2017).

2.3. Educational Interpretation of Cycles, Transitions, and Ruptures

Topological quantities become educationally useful only when they can be interpreted as process signals. In that spirit, cycles are read as recurrent routines or feedback loops, transitions as movement between learning regimes, and ruptures as fragmentation or instability in the learner's trajectory.

Educationally, cycles are interpreted as recurrent returns to previously occupied regions of the learner-state space, not as mere repetition of isolated actions. Let the dimension-1 persistence diagram of learner i in window t record the loop-like features observed at that moment. The total cycle-persistence score then sums the lifetimes of those loops, so each term contributes according to how long the recurrent pathway remains visible across the filtration. This scalar provides a comparable measure of cyclic organization across learners and time windows.

$$C_{i,t} = \sum_{r=1}^{m_1^{(i,t)}} (d_r - b_r).$$

The score increases when recurrent pathways remain visible across multiple filtration scales, thereby capturing sustained educational recurrence rather than transient noise. A normalized cycle-concentration score can also be introduced by retaining loop persistence in the numerator and dividing by the overall topological mass in dimensions 0 and 1. The normalized form distinguishes trajectories dominated by a few robust cycles from trajectories whose apparent cyclicity is diluted by many weak or noisy features.

$$\widetilde{C}_{i,t} = \frac{\sum_{r=1}^{m_1^{(i,t)}} (d_r - b_r)}{1 + \left|D_0^{(i,t)}\right| + \left|D_1^{(i,t)}\right|}.$$

This normalization makes the interpretation more conservative, because it rewards persistent recurrence while penalizing topological clutter. In educational terms, high $C_{i,t}$ and high $\widetilde{C}_{i,t}$ may indicate productive recursive regulation when they co-occur with timely help-seeking, feedback use, and later mastery, but they may also reveal stalled repetition when the same loops persist together with weak performance or unresolved revisitation. For that reason, cycles are read as interpretable process signals whose pedagogical meaning depends on their temporal placement and association with outcomes, rather than as automatically positive or negative markers (Saint et al., 2022; Saqr & López-Pernas, 2021; Molenaar et al., 2023; Chazal & Michel, 2021; Munch, 2017; Ye & Pennisi, 2022; El-Yaagoubi et al., 2023).

Transitions and ruptures are separated analytically because both involve change, but only rupture implies a severe loss of structural coherence. If the Betti curve of learner i in window t and dimension k summarizes active topological structure, then a transition can be modeled by combining a persistence-diagram distance between consecutive windows with a functional difference between their Betti curves. The weight λ regulates the balance between those terms, so transition is treated as both geometric reconfiguration and change in active topological structure.

$$T_{i,t} = \sum_{k=0}^{1} W_p\left(D_k^{(i,t)}, D_k^{(i,t-1)}\right) + \lambda \sum_{k=0}^{1} \int_{\mathscr{E}} \left|\beta_k^{(i,t)}(\varepsilon) - \beta_k^{(i,t-1)}(\varepsilon)\right| d\varepsilon, \ \lambda \geq 0.$$

The transition score rises when a learner moves into a new behavioral regime, for example after an assessment, an instructional redesign, or a regulation-triggering event. Rupture, however, requires more than ordinary change: fragmentation must increase and persistent structure must be replaced by short-lived, unstable features.

The rupture index therefore combines the change in component structure, measured through dimension-0 topology, with the proportion of features whose lifetimes fall below a threshold τ, while α balances the two ingredients.

$$R_{i,t} = \alpha\left[\overline{\beta}_0^{(i,t)} - \overline{\beta}_0^{(i,t-1)}\right]_+ + (1-\alpha)\frac{\sum_{(b,d)\in D_0^{(i,t)}\cup D_1^{(i,t)}} 1(d-b<\tau)}{\left|D_0^{(i,t)}\right| + \left|D_1^{(i,t)}\right|},\ 0 \le \alpha \le 1.$$

The index flags ruptures when connected activity decomposes into many components and when topological mass shifts toward short-lived features, which is precisely the mathematical pattern expected when routines break down, disengagement becomes episodic, or a learner drifts away from previously coherent pathways. In pedagogical use, high $T_{i,t}$ suggests regime change that may still be adaptive, whereas high $R_{i,t}$ supports a more cautious reading of instability, fragmentation, or possible risk; accordingly, these signals are best used in human-in-the-loop review rather than as autonomous decisions, especially in longitudinal learning systems where behavioral change may reflect both challenge and growth (Saqr et al., 2023; López-Pernas & Saqr, 2024; Järvelä & Hadwin, 2024; Atienza et al., 2020; Ali et al., 2023; Maldonado-Mahauad et al., 2018; Sailer et al., 2024).

3. METHODOLOGY

3.1. Data Representation, Trajectory Encoding, and Similarity Design

The methodological design begins by translating event logs into learner states defined over pedagogically meaningful windows. The mathematical choices made at this stage—state representation, similarity, smoothing, and thresholding—matter because they determine the geometry on which the later topological analysis will operate.

Data representation begins by treating each learner as an ordered event stream rather than as a set of aggregated counts. The educational meaning of recurrence, pacing, and reorganization depends on temporal order and local context across pedagogically meaningful windows. To formalize that starting point, the raw trace of learner i is written as follows. In this notation, the sequence lists observed actions, timestamps, and metadata such as topic, resource, or assessment label; preserving those elements keeps state construction aligned with event meaning.

$$E_i = \left(\left(a_{i1}, t_{i1}, m_{i1}\right), \ldots, \left(a_{in_i}, t_{in_i}, m_{in_i}\right)\right).$$

After this event stream has been defined, the next step segments it into windows aligned with weekly modules, assessment phases, or activity-adaptive intervals. The window for learner i at index r contains the events that fall between its opening and closing temporal boundaries. These window-level units provide the basis for later comparison, filtration, and prediction.

$$W_{i,r} = \left\{ e \in E_i : \tau_{r-1} < t(e) \leq \tau_r \right\},\ r = 1, \ldots, R.$$

Once windows are available, each one is encoded into a learner state whose form depends on the educational question. For feature-based encoding, the state is obtained through a map φ that summarizes engagement intensity, regularity, assessment outcome, help-seeking, and concept coverage in p retained dimensions. This representation gives persistent homology comparable objects while avoiding the irregularity of raw event lists.

$$\mathrm{x}_{i,r} = \phi\left(W_{i,r}\right) \in \mathbb{R}^p.$$

After the raw feature state has been obtained, robust scaling and clipping control the effect of extreme values while keeping the temporal signal interpretable. In this transformation, each feature is centered by its median, scaled by its interquartile range, stabilized by a small constant δ, and clipped at threshold c. The procedure limits outlier influence without erasing ordinal structure.

$$z_{i,rj} = \mathrm{clip}\left(\frac{x_{i,rj} - \mathrm{med}_j}{\mathrm{IQR}_j + \delta}, -c, c \right),\ j = 1, \ldots, p.$$

When the window is represented as a probability allocation over topics or resources, the distributional state is more appropriate. The weight assigned to category k is obtained by normalizing its count or intensity within the window by the total activity across all K categories. This comparison then reflects composition rather than raw activity volume alone.

$$p_{i,r}(k) = \frac{c_{i,rk}}{\sum_{h=1}^{K} c_{i,rh}},\ k = 1, \ldots, K.$$

If the educational objective is instead to preserve the internal transition structure among actions, concepts, or resources, a graph state can be constructed through a weighted adjacency matrix. In that matrix, the entry for ordered pair (u, v) counts how often state u is followed by state v within the window. This graph formulation is appropriate when the chapter aims to preserve internal transition architecture rather than collapse behavior into independent feature totals.

$$A_{i,r}(u,v) = \sum_{\ell=1}^{|W_{i,r}|-1} 1\left(a_{i,\ell} = u,\, a_{i,\ell+1} = v\right).$$

With these alternatives in place, the learning trajectory becomes an ordered sequence of states, regardless of whether the state is vectorial, probabilistic, or graph-structured. The symbol for the state at window r denotes the representation assigned to learner i at that temporal position. The trajectory itself is therefore the object on which cycles, transitions, and ruptures are later measured.

$$T_i = \left(s_{i,1}, s_{i,2}, \ldots, s_{i,R}\right),\ s_{i,r} \in \left\{\mathrm{z}_{i,r}, p_{i,r}, A_{i,r}\right\}.$$

These representation choices preserve the temporal organization needed to identify cycles, transitions, and ruptures while remaining compatible with predictive, sequential, and multimodal learning-analytics practice in which learner behavior is modeled as an evolving process rather than as a static profile (Saint et al., 2022; Molenaar & Wise, 2022; Chen & Cui, 2020; Saqr et al., 2024; Wu et al., 2024; Molenaar et al., 2023; López-Pernas & Saqr, 2024; Bannert et al., 2014; Gašević et al., 2017; Ye & Pennisi, 2022).

Similarity design is then matched to the chosen state representation, since persistent homology depends on a meaningful notion of proximity and each data modality imposes a different geometry on the learner-state space. For feature-vector states, cosine dissimilarity compares the angle between two vectors and emphasizes directional resemblance after normalizing for magnitude. This metric is appropriate when two windows differ in activity volume but share similar behavioral composition.

$$d_{\cos}(\mathrm{u},\mathrm{v}) = 1 - \frac{\mathrm{u}^{\top}\mathrm{v}}{\|\mathrm{u}\|_2 \|\mathrm{v}\|_2}.$$

After that proportional comparison, a covariance-sensitive alternative may be incorporated through the Mahalanobis distance. In this formulation, the covariance matrix of the feature space down weights directions that vary greatly and highlights deviations that are unusual relative to the observed joint variation among variables. The metric is useful when correlated educational indicators would otherwise be counted as independent evidence of change.

$$d_M(\mathrm{u},\mathrm{v}) = \sqrt{(\mathrm{u}-\mathrm{v})^{\top}\Sigma^{-1}(\mathrm{u}-\mathrm{v})}.$$

When the state is distributional, the proximity function should respect probabilistic geometry rather than Euclidean displacement alone. A Jensen-Shannon distance can therefore be defined by comparing each distribution with their midpoint distribution. Because the Kullback-Leibler terms are taken with respect to that midpoint, the result remains symmetric and numerically stable. This is why the measure is appropriate for topic, resource, or concept-allocation states.

$$d_{\mathrm{JS}}(p,q) = \sqrt{1/2 D_{\mathrm{KL}}(p \parallel m) + 1/2 D_{\mathrm{KL}}(q \parallel m)}, \; m = 1/2(p+q).$$

Alongside that measure, a Hellinger distance can be used to compare distributions through their square-root geometry. This alternative is especially useful when the educational distributions are sparse, because the square-root transformation moderates the effect of very small probabilities while preserving meaningful compositional differences.

$$d_H(p,q) = \frac{1}{\sqrt{2}} \parallel \sqrt{p} - \sqrt{q} \parallel_2.$$

If graph states are used, structural comparison may proceed through a graph embedding obtained from spectral or diffusion information and then evaluated in an ordinary Euclidean space. The embedding maps each graph to a vector that preserves salient structural properties, and the Euclidean norm measures the resulting discrepancy. This step gives the topological pipeline a workable distance when original states are relational rather than vectorial objects.

$$d_G\left(G_{i,r}, G_{j,s}\right) = \parallel \psi\left(G_{i,r}\right) - \psi\left(G_{j,s}\right) \parallel_2.$$

Before these distances are passed to the topological stage, preprocessing makes missingness explicit and reduces spurious fluctuation. A missingness indicator marks whether feature j is unavailable for learner i in window r. The distinction matters because absence of data may represent a meaningful educational condition, such as inactivity, non-submission, or platform non-use, rather than mere measurement error.

$$m_{i,rj} = 1\left(x_{i,rj} \text{ is missing}\right).$$

After missingness has been encoded, temporal smoothing stabilizes the learner state without erasing meaningful change. In the exponentially weighted formulation, the smoothed state at the current window is a convex combination of the raw current state and the previously smoothed state, and α determines the balance between responsiveness and stability. The procedure suppresses random fluctuation while retaining genuine pedagogical transitions.

$$\overline{s}_{i,r} = \alpha s_{i,r} + (1 - \alpha)\overline{s}_{i,r-1}, \; 0 < \alpha \leq 1.$$

With denoised states in hand, minimum-activity thresholding can be used to suppress windows whose information content is too weak to sustain reliable topology. In this rule, the activity volume of the window is compared against a threshold η, and windows below that threshold are discarded from the topological stage. This safeguard prevents very sparse windows from creating artificial disconnectedness that reflects data scarcity more than learner behavior.

$$\widetilde{W}_{i,r} = \begin{cases} W_{i,r}, & \left|W_{i,r}\right| \geq \eta, \\ \varnothing, & \left|W_{i,r}\right| < \eta. \end{cases}$$

These design decisions transform heterogeneous educational traces into a metrized family of learner states whose geometry is explicit, noise-aware, and comparable across windows. That structure is the input required for stable topological summaries and for the interpretable detection of cycles, transitions, and ruptures in empirical trace-based learning analytics (Chazal & Michel, 2021; El-Yaagoubi et al., 2023; Bannert et al., 2014; Gašević et al., 2017; Saint et al., 2020; Fan et al., 2021; van Halem et al., 2020).

3.2. Filtration Construction, Topological Feature Extraction, and Evaluation Protocol

Once learner states have been defined, the next step is to construct filtrations, compute persistent homology, and convert the resulting topological information into stable descriptors for modeling and interpretation. The same subsection also keeps temporal validation, calibration, and monitoring aligned with the educational purpose of the chapter.

Filtration construction begins after each temporal window has produced a finite collection of learner states endowed with the similarity structure defined above. For point clouds, the Vietoris-Rips filtration includes a simplex at scale ε only when all of its vertices lie within the chosen distance threshold. The nested family allows the analysis to observe how isolated states merge and how loop structure appears as the scale parameter increases.

$$K_t(\varepsilon) = \mathrm{VR}_\varepsilon(X_t) = \{\sigma \subseteq X_t : d(u,v) \leq \varepsilon \text{ for all } u,v \in \sigma\}.$$

When the encoded state is graph-based rather than vector-based, the filtration can instead be induced by thresholding edge weights and then taking the clique complex of the resulting graph. Here, λ is the edge-weight threshold, the filtered graph retains only edges whose weights meet that level, and the clique complex converts fully connected subgraphs into simplices. This alternative is necessary when the primary educational information is relational rather than point-cloud based.

$$G_t^{\lambda} = \left(V, E_t^{\lambda}\right),\ E_t^{\lambda} = \left\{(u,v): w_t(u,v) \geq \lambda\right\},\ K_t^{\lambda} = \mathrm{Cl}\left(G_t^{\lambda}\right).$$

Once the filtration has been defined, the topological content in dimension k is extracted through homology. The boundary operator determines how k-dimensional simplices attach to their faces, while the corresponding Betti number counts the independent classes that survive at scale ε and time t. This algebraic step turns a filtered educational structure into interpretable counts of components and loops.

$$H_k\left(K_t^{\varepsilon}\right) = \ker\left(\partial_k\right)/\mathrm{im}\left(\partial_{k+1}\right),\ \beta_k^{(t)}(\varepsilon) = \dim H_k\left(K_t^{\varepsilon}\right).$$

The multiscale birth-and-death record of those features is encoded by the persistence diagram. For each homological dimension k and time t, the diagram stores the birth and death scales of every detected feature. This representation preserves when structure appears, how long it survives, and when it disappears, information that would be lost if the analysis kept only a single Betti number.

$$\mathrm{Dgm}_k^{(t)} = \left\{\left(b_r, d_r\right)\right\}_{r=1}^{m_k^{(t)}}$$

The diagram is then converted into stable summaries suitable for modeling and interpretation. The Betti curve counts how many features are active at filtration value u, total persistence adds the lifetimes of all recorded features, and persistent entropy measures how evenly that persistence is distributed across them. These summaries transform variable-size diagrams into fixed-length descriptors while preserving recurrence, persistence, and structural complexity.

$$\beta_k^{(t)}(u) = \sum_{r=1}^{m_k^{(t)}} 1_{[b_r, d_r)}(u),$$

$$\mathrm{TP}_k^{(t)} = \sum_{r=1}^{m_k^{(t)}} \left(d_r - b_r\right),$$

$$\mathrm{PE}_k^{(t)} = -\sum_{r=1}^{m_k^{(t)}} p_r \log p_r,\ p_r = \frac{d_r - b_r}{\sum_{m=1}^{m_k^{(t)}} \left(d_m - b_m\right)}.$$

These summaries give the pipeline fixed-length descriptors that retain multiscale information while remaining stable enough for downstream prediction, monitoring, and interpretability. They are therefore appropriate for identifying cycles, transitions, and ruptures from noisy educational traces rather than from static aggregates (Chazal & Michel, 2021; Munch, 2017; Atienza et al., 2020; Barnes et al., 2021; Ali et al., 2023; El-Yaagoubi et al., 2023).

The evaluation protocol preserves temporal causality by training on earlier windows and testing on later ones; leakage across time would inflate performance and weaken early-warning claims. In this split, τ denotes the last training window and T is the total number of observed windows. The design mirrors real deployment, where future learner behavior is unavailable at training time.

$$\mathcal{T}_{\text{train}} = \{1,\ldots,\tau\},\ \mathcal{T}_{\text{test}} = \{\tau + 1,\ldots,T\}.$$

Once topological descriptors have been extracted, they can be concatenated with conventional predictors through a vectorization map. The operator Ψ collects information from the dimension-0 and dimension-1 persistence diagrams together with their summary statistics and returns a fixed-length numerical representation. This step permits variable-size topological objects to enter downstream predictive models.

$$z_{i,t} = \Psi\left(\mathrm{Dgm}_0^{(i,t)}, \mathrm{Dgm}_1^{(i,t)}, \beta_0^{(i,t)}, \beta_1^{(i,t)}, \mathrm{TP}_0^{(i,t)}, \mathrm{TP}_1^{(i,t)}, \mathrm{PE}_0^{(i,t)}, \mathrm{PE}_1^{(i,t)}\right).$$

This representation supports both purely topological models and hybrid predictors that combine topology with engagement, performance, and behavioral covariates. In the predictive equation, the function *f* denotes the supervised model, the topological vector summarizes multiscale structure for learner *i* at time *t*, and the auxiliary covariates can add conventional predictors. This formula connects interpretable topological evidence with actionable risk estimation.

$$\hat{p}_{i,t} = f\left(z_{i,t}, x_{i,t}\right).$$

This predictive layer is judged not only by discrimination but also by calibration and subgroup reliability. The Brier score averages the squared difference between predicted probabilities and observed outcomes across N evaluated cases. The expected calibration error for subgroup g partitions cases into bins, compares empirical accuracy with average confidence inside each bin, and weights those discrepancies by subgroup counts. These quantities matter because pedagogical decisions depend on trustworthy probabilities, not only on rank ordering.

$$\mathrm{BS} = \frac{1}{N}\sum_{i=1}^{N}(\hat{p}_i - y_i)^2,$$

$$\mathrm{ECE}_g = \sum_{b=1}^{B}\frac{|B_{b,g}|}{n_g}\left|\mathrm{acc}\left(B_{b,g}\right) - \mathrm{conf}\left(B_{b,g}\right)\right|.$$

Because the chapter frames intervention as assistive under limited institutional capacity, recall under a fixed alert budget and decision-curve net benefit are also reported. In the recall expression, the operational cutoff selects the top q fraction of learners for review, so the numerator counts how many true at-risk cases are captured under that budget. In the net-benefit expression, true positives and false positives are evaluated at decision threshold c and the penalty term discounts false alarms by their relative harm. These measures show whether the model improves decision making under practical constraints.

$$\mathrm{Recall}@q = \frac{\sum_{i=1}^{N} y_i 1\left(\hat{p}_i \geq c_q\right)}{\sum_{i=1}^{N} y_i},$$

$$\mathrm{NB}(c) = \frac{TP(c)}{N} - \frac{FP(c)}{N}\frac{c}{1-c}.$$

Finally, because cycles, transitions, and ruptures are temporal objects rather than static labels, deployment monitors topological drift between adjacent windows through a diagram-distance statistic. The monitoring quantity aggregates Wasserstein distances between consecutive persistence diagrams in dimensions 0 and 1, so it functions as a longitudinal drift signal rather than as a single-window performance score.

$$M_t = \sum_{k=0}^{1} W_p\left(\mathrm{Dgm}_k^{(t)}, \mathrm{Dgm}_k^{(t-1)}\right).$$

This monitoring layer helps distinguish ordinary pedagogical evolution from abrupt structural change after assessments, curriculum redesigns, or platform updates, and it keeps the evaluation protocol aligned with interpretable, stable, and actionable educational decision support (Saint et al., 2022; Saqr et al., 2024; Riley et al., 2024; van Calster et al., 2019; Vickers & Holland, 2021; Liou et al., 2024; Maldonado-Mahauad et al., 2018; López-Pernas & Saqr, 2024).

4. COMPUTATIONAL ARCHITECTURE

4.1. Reproducible Computational Pipeline for Topological Learning Analytics

The computational architecture is organized as a closed-loop and configuration-locked pipeline in which each analytical layer preserves the temporal logic of learning while remaining auditable from data input to decision-oriented output. Raw platform traces, assessment records, feedback interactions, and support events enter the workflow as timestamped educational logs. These heterogeneous records are harmonized into a common event schema, aligned to weekly or pedagogically meaningful windows, and transformed into learner-state representations that preserve order, pacing, revisitation, engagement, performance, and support-seeking behavior. At this stage, robust scaling, smoothing, and minimum-activity thresholding reduce spurious fluctuation without eliminating the local discontinuities that later become analytically meaningful as possible transitions or ruptures.

Once temporally ordered states have been constructed, the architecture makes the geometry of the trajectory explicit. Feature-based, distributional, or graph-based states are endowed with a similarity structure consistent with the chosen representation, so that the learner pathway can be analyzed as a metrized family of objects rather than as a mere sequence of counts. Rolling windows over those states produce local point clouds or filtered graph structures from which Vietoris–Rips or clique-complex filtrations are generated. Persistent homology is then computed in low dimensions, especially H0 and H1, because component structure captures cohesion versus fragmentation and loop structure captures recurrence, revisitation, and feedback-practice cycles. The architecture does not rely on a single topological object; instead, it stores persistence diagrams, barcodes, Betti curves, total persistence, and entropy-based summaries so that structure can be inspected both visually and quantitatively.

A second computational layer connects topological summaries to representation learning and monitoring. Topology-aware latent models receive the vectorized outputs of the persistent-homology engine together with conventional behavioral features, allowing the latent space to be audited as training progresses. This makes it possible to compare the geometry of learner states before and after training and to determine whether the learned representation preserves meaningful structure or merely improves numerical fit. In parallel, adjacent temporal windows are compared through Wasserstein-style diagram distances and Betti-curve differences, which operationalize transition strength and rupture intensity as longitudinal changes in multiscale structure rather than as isolated point anomalies. The same architecture therefore supports both descriptive topology and topology-aware learning.

The final layer translates topological evidence into educationally interpretable outputs. At the analytics level, the pipeline produces cycle indicators, transition scores, rupture indices, and drift traces that can be aligned with assessments, redesign events, or episodes of disengagement. At the intervention-support level, the architecture connects learner risk states with concept-level graphs and recommendation rules, so that the system does not merely identify structural instability but also suggests which conceptual areas are most defensible as next instructional targets. All intermediate artifacts—synthetic logs, weekly states, preprocessed matrices, persistence summaries, latent audits, graph structures, figures, and tables—are serialized as reproducible outputs. In this way the architecture remains traceable, inspectable, and suitable for human-in-the-loop educational decision support rather than opaque automated classification.

An operational advantage of the architecture is that it is organized around section-ready outputs rather than only around internal computations. The workflow writes cycle-oriented figures and tables, transition-oriented latent audits, and rupture-oriented recommendation artifacts into separate result folders, so that the empirical narrative of the chapter is aligned with the execution logic of the code. This design choice is important for reproducibility because it allows the reader to trace each interpretation in Section 5 back to a concrete computational artifact instead of treating the reported evidence as a post hoc narrative summary. Equally relevant, the serialized structure separates data generation, state encoding, topology, latent auditing, and recommendation outputs. That separation limits accidental leakage between stages, makes it easier to reproduce the same figures from the same configuration file, and allows another researcher to inspect whether a reported cycle, transition, or rupture was produced by the data geometry or by a later narrative decision.

5. RESULTS AND ANALYSIS

The empirical analysis was conducted on the synthetic result package generated by the computational pipeline and organized in the section-specific folders of the accompanying output archive. Although the data are synthetic, the trajectories were explicitly designed to instantiate the three structural processes defined in the chapter cycles, transitions, and ruptures and the results therefore operate as a proof-of-concept validation of the proposed methodology. The synthetic setting is not presented as evidence of external validity; it is used to test whether the pipeline can carry the theoretical distinctions through computation without losing interpretability. The interpretation below is organized in the same order as the chapter objective: first, recurrent topology is examined as evidence of cycles; second, latent and inter-window reconfiguration is examined as evidence of transitions; third, fragmentation-sensitive signals are translated into rupture-oriented and recommendation-oriented educational outputs.

For that reason, the order of the tables and figures below follows the logic of the computational pipeline itself: recurrent topology is examined first, controlled structural reorganization second, and support-oriented rupture interpretation third.

5.1. Detection of Cycles in Learning Behavior

At the cohort level, the results support the claim that dimension-1 topology captures recurrent educational organization rather than only local variation. Table 1 shows that the cycle group obtained the highest mean H1 total persistence (0.143) and the largest mean number of H1 features (1.79), while the rupture group remained substantially lower on both measures (0.069 and 0.75, respectively). The transition group occupied an intermediate but revealing position: its mean total persistence (0.131) remained close to the cycle group, yet its average maximum lifetime (0.106) slightly exceeded the cyclic profile. This pattern suggests that transitions are not characterized by the total absence of loops but by fewer and more dominant loop-like structures, consistent with regime change rather than stable recurrence. Figure 2 confirms this reading by showing that the cycle distribution is shifted upward relative to rupture, while the transition distribution remains broad and heterogeneous.

Table 1. Cohort-level H1 summary by trajectory group.

Group	Mean H1 total persistence	SD H1 total persistence	Mean H1 max lifetime	SD H1 max lifetime	Mean H1 feature count	SD H1 feature count
Cycle	0.143	0.126	0.093	0.058	1.792	0.932
Rupture	0.069	0.089	0.061	0.083	0.750	0.676
Transition	0.131	0.120	0.106	0.089	1.333	0.761

The learner-level evidence strengthens the same conclusion. Table 2 reports the metrics for the exemplar cyclic learner CYC_019, whose trajectory contains four H1 features, a total H1 persistence of 0.567, and a maximum lifetime of 0.224. These values are much larger than the group means and indicate a trajectory in which recurrent structure does not depend on a single accidental loop, but on several loop-like features that survive across multiple scales. Figure 3 makes this visible in the persistence diagram: the H1 points are not concentrated near the diagonal, which means that the recurrent structures are not merely short-lived artifacts of noise. Figure 4 reinforces the same point in barcode form. The presence of several finite H1 bars indicates that the learner repeatedly returns to previously occupied behavioral regions, a pattern fully consistent with the educational interpretation of study-feedback-practice recursion and topic revisitation.

Table 2. Topological metrics for the exemplar cyclic learner.

Learner	Group	Final risk	H1 total persistence	H1 max lifetime	H1 feature count	Mean step change	Max step change	Transition distance	Frag-mentation increase	Late short-lived ratio	Rupture index
CYC_019	Cycle	1.000	0.567	0.224	4.000	1.114	1.388	0.121	0.000	1.000	1.000

Figure 2. Cycle persistence by trajectory group.

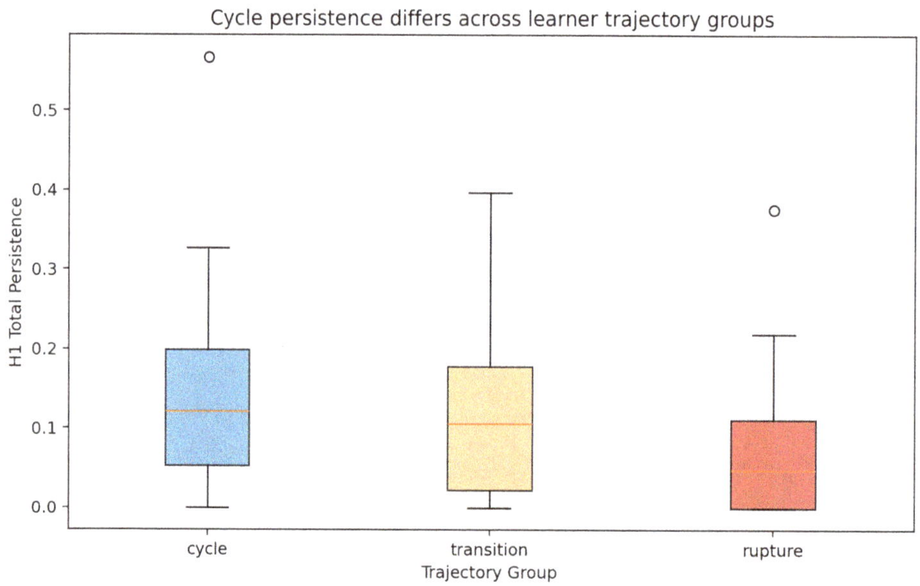

Figure 3. Persistence diagram for the exemplar cyclic learner.

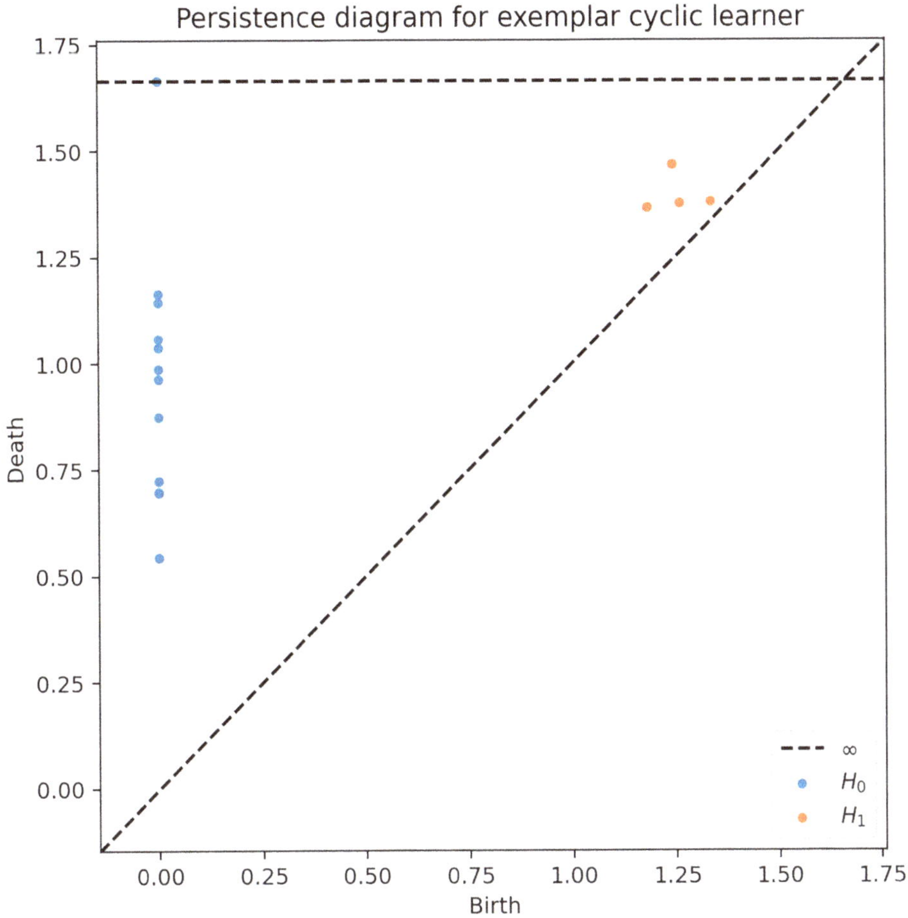

Figure 4. Topological barcode for the exemplar cyclic learner.

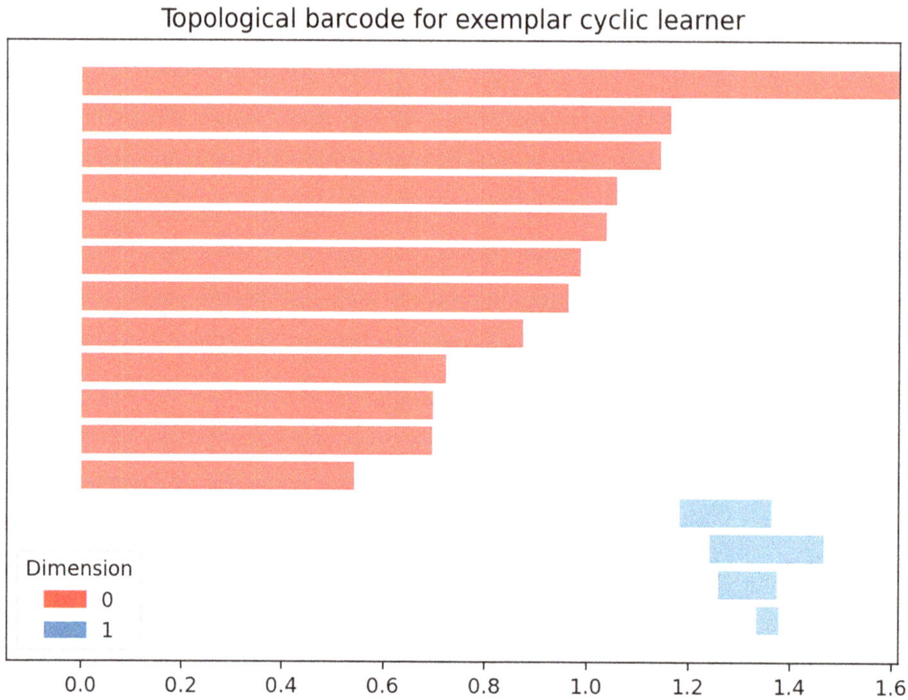

Figure 5. Average Betti-1 curves by trajectory group.

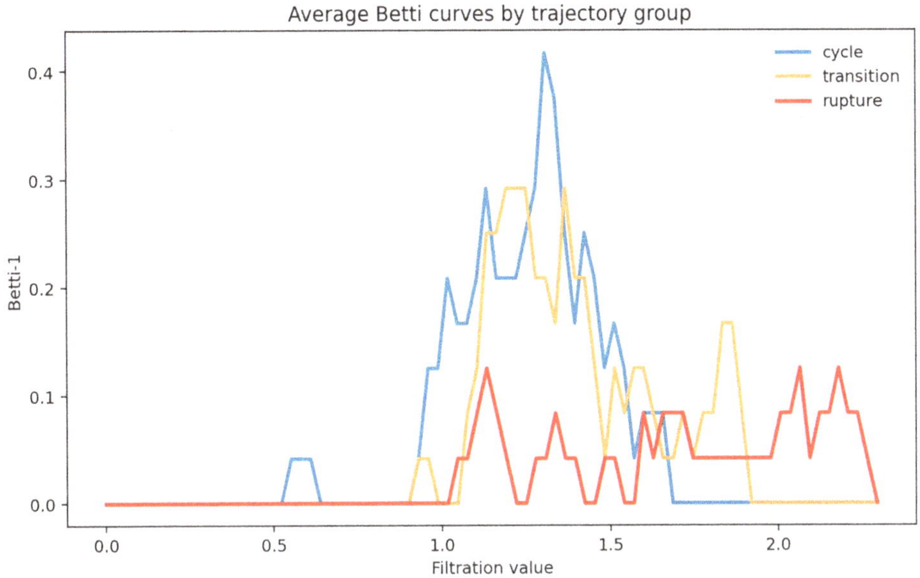

The Betti-curve comparison provides the clearest multiscale cohort-level view. In Figure 5 the cycle profile sustains the highest Betti-1 values over the broadest portion of the filtration range, especially around the mid-scale region where loop structure becomes most visible. The transition profile also exhibits loop activity, but it is more concentrated and irregular, which fits the idea that pedagogical change can temporarily create strong but less repeated structural motifs. The rupture profile, by contrast, remains comparatively low and fragmented. Its Betti-1 curve rises later, reaches smaller values, and disappears more quickly, indicating that any apparent cyclicity is weak, unstable, or overwhelmed by fragmentation.

Taken together, Table 1, Table 2, and Figures 2–5 validate the first part of the chapter objective. Persistent homology does more than confirm that activity varies over time; it reveals whether a trajectory is topologically organized around repeated returns. This matters educationally because recurrent loops can mark productive regulation when they co-occur with gradual mastery and meaningful feedback use, but they can also mark stalled repetition when recurrence persists without consolidation. The topological layer therefore contributes a structurally richer account of recurrence than the one provided by raw counts or transition frequencies alone.

5.2. Identification of Transitions Across Pedagogical States

The second empirical question concerns whether topological change can identify pedagogical transitions more clearly than conventional summaries. Figure 6 and Table 3 show that the topology-aware latent model evolves in a markedly different way from the baseline autoencoder. The baseline model begins with low H1 total persistence, but after epoch 10 its latent topology expands sharply, reaching 2.337 at epoch 16 and remaining high thereafter. The topology-aware model, by contrast, follows a more gradual and controlled trajectory, rising from 0.112 at initialization to 0.992 at epoch 18. This smoother evolution indicates that topological regularization does not eliminate structure; instead, it prevents the latent space from developing excessive and unstable loop activity that is difficult to interpret pedagogically.

Table 3. Latent-topology evolution across audited training epochs.

H1 total persistence	H1 max lifetime	H1 feature count	H1 entropy	Model	Epoch	Wasserstein vs. epoch 0	Bottleneck vs. epoch 0
0.112	0.017	28.000	4.306	Baseline	0		
0.070	0.010	18.000	3.604	Baseline	2	0.082	0.005
0.054	0.018	8.000	2.582	Baseline	4	0.116	0.009
0.110	0.042	6.000	2.148	Baseline	6	0.157	0.021
0.086	0.049	5.000	1.739	Baseline	8	0.140	0.025
0.380	0.118	11.000	2.734	Baseline	10	0.348	0.059
0.682	0.123	17.000	3.684	Baseline	12	0.562	0.062
1.996	0.321	19.000	3.616	Baseline	14	1.491	0.160
2.337	0.314	17.000	3.835	Baseline	16	1.731	0.157
1.770	0.398	14.000	3.224	Baseline	18	1.331	0.199
0.112	0.018	23.000	4.049	Topology Aware	0		
0.201	0.034	24.000	3.919	Topology Aware	2	0.124	0.016
0.218	0.023	25.000	4.123	Topology Aware	4	0.165	0.011
0.465	0.076	22.000	3.991	Topology Aware	6	0.372	0.038
0.707	0.132	17.000	3.669	Topology Aware	8	0.579	0.066
0.882	0.142	22.000	4.032	Topology Aware	10	0.703	0.071
0.787	0.165	23.000	3.694	Topology Aware	12	0.636	0.083

continued on following page

Table 3. Continued

H1 total persistence	H1 max lifetime	H1 feature count	H1 entropy	Model	Epoch	Wasserstein vs. epoch 0	Bottleneck vs. epoch 0
0.885	0.191	29.000	3.847	Topology Aware	14	0.703	0.095
1.163	0.146	28.000	4.233	Topology Aware	16	0.901	0.073
0.992	0.170	21.000	3.763	Topology Aware	18	0.781	0.085

Figure 6. Topological evolution of the latent space during training.

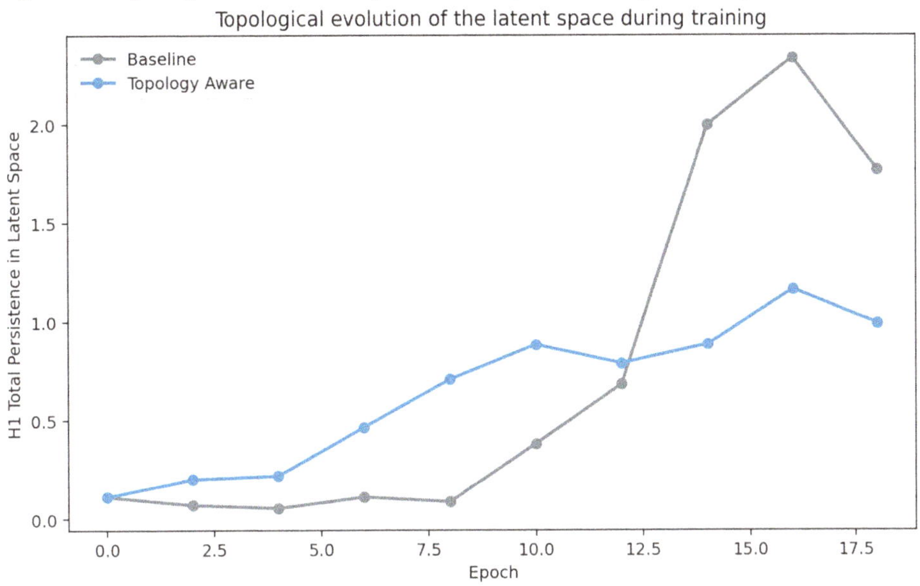

Table 4 makes the trade-off precise. The topology-aware model yields a slightly higher reconstruction error than the baseline (0.491 versus 0.461), but the structural benefit is substantial. Latent silhouette improves from 0.070 to 0.105, which means that the learned representation separates the trajectory archetypes more clearly. At the same time, Wasserstein drift relative to the initial latent topology drops from 1.331 in the baseline model to 0.781 in the topology-aware model, and bottleneck distance falls from 0.199 to 0.085. Persistent entropy also increases from 3.224 to 3.763, indicating that the topology-aware model distributes persistence more evenly instead of concentrating it in a smaller number of exaggerated latent structures. From the perspective of chapter validity, this is a central result: the topological signal becomes both more separable and more stable.

Table 4. Comparison between baseline and topology-aware latent models.

Model	Reconstruction MSE	Latent silhouette	H1 persistence before	H1 persistence after	H1 max lifetime after	H1 entropy after	Wasserstein vs. before	Bottleneck vs. before
Baseline	0.461	0.070	0.112	1.770	0.398	3.224	1.331	0.199
Topology Aware	0.491	0.105	0.112	0.992	0.170	3.763	0.781	0.085

Figure 7. Latent space before training and after topology-aware training.

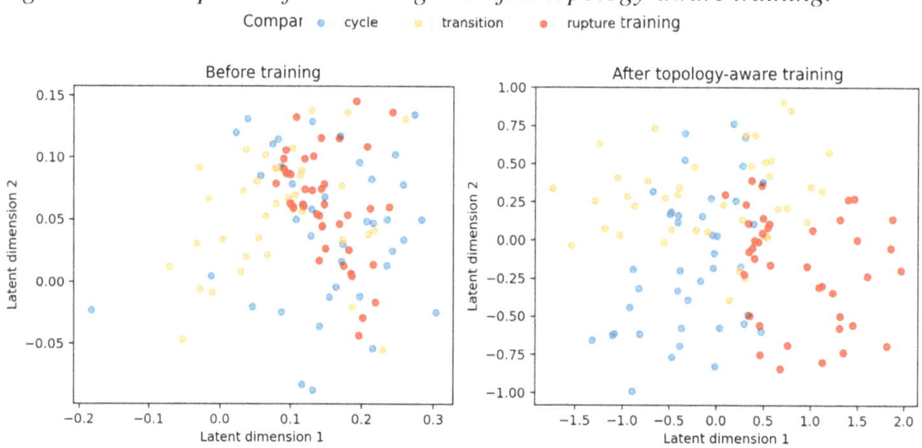

Figure 8. Before/after Betti-1 curves of the latent space.

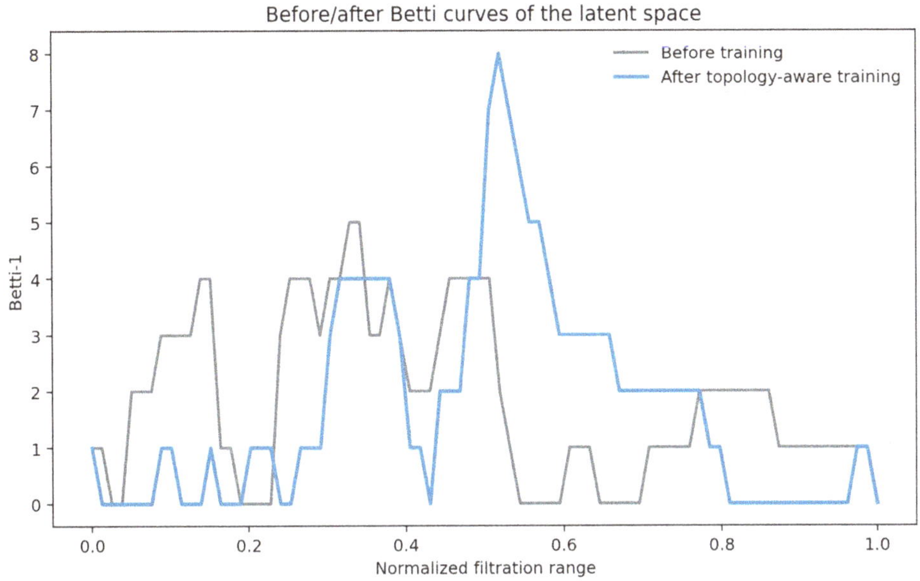

The geometric comparison in Figure 7 complements the scalar results. Before training, the latent cloud is compact and partially mixed, so the cyclic, transition, and rupture states overlap substantially. After topology-aware training, the configuration becomes more structured: the rupture states occupy a more clearly separated region, transition states remain intermediate, and cyclic states retain a relatively coherent band of positions. The visual effect is not one of perfect class separation and it should not be, because the chapter models temporal processes, not immutable categories but one of improved structural readability. The latent space begins to encode regime change as a topological rearrangement rather than as an arbitrary projection.

Figure 8 provides the most direct before/after topological comparison. The post-training Betti-1 curve becomes more concentrated in the mid-filtration range and reaches a higher, more dominant peak than the pre-training curve. This indicates that the learned latent geometry preserves a clearer loop structure over a more interpretable band of scales. In practical terms, the topology-aware model transforms transition analysis from a purely visual or statistical change-detection problem into a multiscale audit of how representations reorganize during training. That capability is especially valuable for the chapter's objective because transitions are defined here as changes in structural organization, not merely as changes in average behavior.

Together, Figure 6, Figure 7, Figure 8, Table 3, and Table 4 support the second part of the chapter objective. Topological comparison across adjacent windows and across latent training states reveals regime shifts that conventional feature summaries could flatten or misread. The evidence does not imply that topology should replace other forms of modeling; it shows that persistent-homology-informed learning can produce a more controlled and interpretable representation of pedagogical change.

5.3. Recognition of Ruptures, Risk Patterns, and Actionable Signals

The third empirical step translates topological evidence into rupture-sensitive and recommendation-oriented outputs. The most cautious reading begins with Figure 9, which contains the exploratory Mapper projection of final learner states. Under the chosen cover and clustering configuration, the mapper routine did not generate a stable node decomposition. Rather than being dismissed, this negative result is analytically informative: it shows that coarse manifold partitioning is highly sensitive to sample density and resolution and that not every topological projection is equally useful for educational decision support. In the present experiment, the decision-support layer is therefore better grounded in the concept-level simplicial structure and recommendation logic than in the mapper partition itself.

Figure 9. Mapper knowledge map of final learner states under the selected cover and clustering configuration.

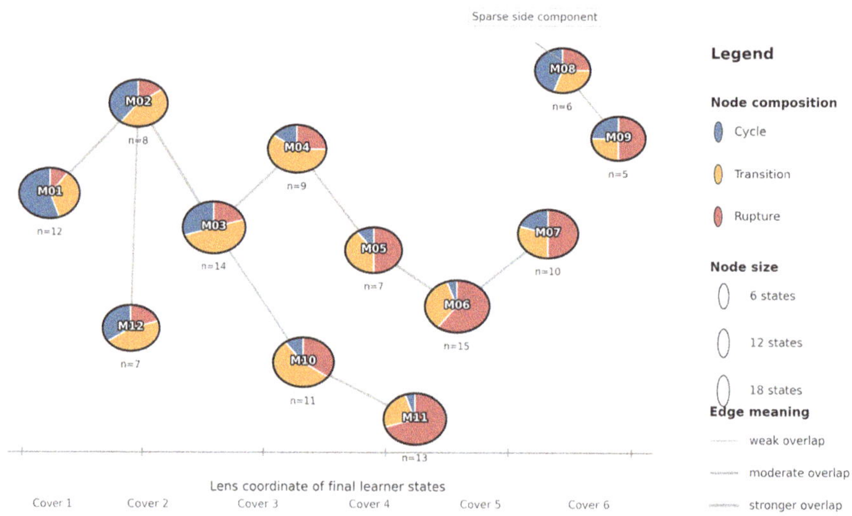

That concept-level structure is shown in Figure 10 and summarized in Table 5. The resulting topological learning graph places Event Logs at the center of the concept network with degree 7 and degree centrality 1.000, followed by State Encoding and Filtration with centrality 0.571. Similarity Design, Homology, and Persistence Diagrams occupy a second tier with centrality 0.429, while Temporal Windows and Educational Signals remain less connected but still structurally present. This pattern is pedagogically coherent: foundational concepts related to data representation and filtration act as bridges between raw traces and higher-level topological interpretation, and for that reason the recommender should not prioritize advanced topics when those bridge concepts remain weakly mastered.

Table 5. Concept-graph centrality and incidence summary.

Concept	Degree	Degree centrality	In incidence structure	Incidence rows	Incidence cols
Event Logs	7	1.000	1	8	14
State Encoding	4	0.571	1	8	14
Filtration	4	0.571	1	8	14
Similarity Design	3	0.429	1	8	14
Homology	3	0.429	1	8	14
Persistence Diagrams	3	0.429	1	8	14
Temporal Windows	2	0.286	1	8	14
Educational Signals	2	0.286	1	8	14

Figure 10. Topological learning graph derived from the concept simplices.

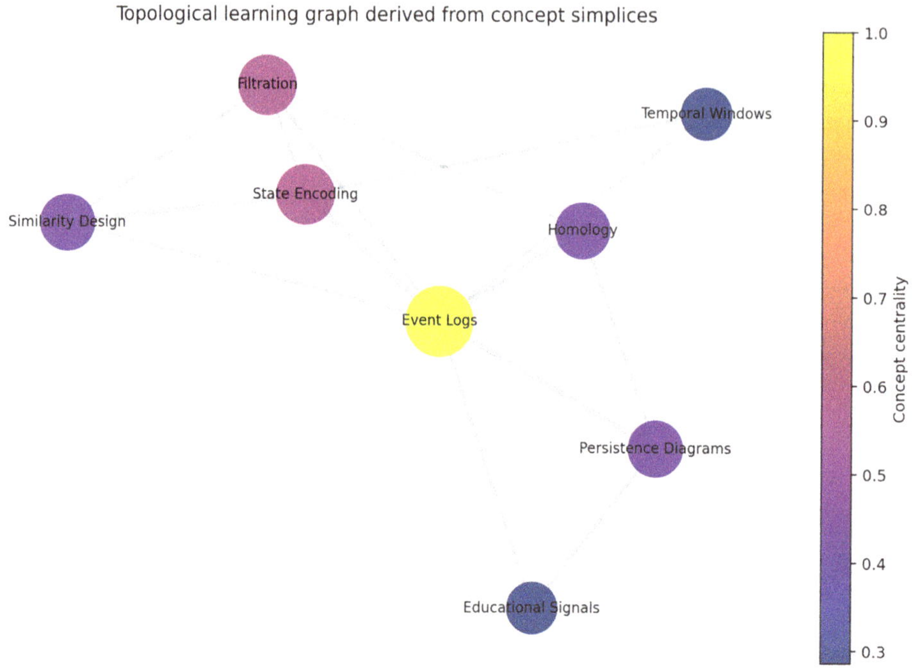

Table 6 shows that the recommendation layer behaves consistently with that structure. The highest assistive-risk states are dominated by rupture and transition learners, which is expected because those profiles exhibit the strongest fragmentation and instability. However, the appearance of one cyclic learner among the prioritized cases is equally important, because it demonstrates that risk is not reducible to the nominal trajectory archetype. The recommendations repeatedly prioritize Event Logs, State Encoding, Similarity Design, Filtration, and Temporal Windows. In other words, the system tends to recommend conceptually central and prerequisite-rich topics rather than isolated advanced targets. That behavior is consistent with a support-oriented educational interpretation: when rupture-sensitive signals are high, the most defensible action is often to stabilize the conceptual base of the pathway.

Table 6. Topology-guided recommendations for the highest-risk learner states.

Learner	Group	Assistive risk probability	Recommended concepts	Current mastery
RUP_016	Rupture	0.877	Event Logs Filtration Similarity Design	Event Logs=0.25 Filtration=0.01 Similarity Design=0.14
TRA_010	Transition	0.862	Event Logs State Encoding Temporal Windows	Event Logs=0.31 State Encoding=0.19 Temporal Windows=0.16
RUP_012	Rupture	0.855	Event Logs State Encoding Similarity Design	Event Logs=0.26 State Encoding=0.08 Similarity Design=0.04
TRA_003	Transition	0.854	Event Logs Filtration Similarity Design	Event Logs=0.27 Filtration=0.17 Similarity Design=0.21
RUP_015	Rupture	0.830	Event Logs Similarity Design Filtration	Event Logs=0.23 Similarity Design=0.08 Filtration=0.08
TRA_012	Transition	0.817	Event Logs State Encoding Temporal Windows	Event Logs=0.23 State Encoding=0.18 Temporal Windows=0.13
TRA_023	Transition	0.803	Event Logs State Encoding Similarity Design	Event Logs=0.21 State Encoding=0.21 Similarity Design=0.16
CYC_023	Cycle	0.761	Event Logs Filtration Homology	Event Logs=0.43 Filtration=0.26 Homology=0.21
RUP_018	Rupture	0.760	Event Logs Similarity Design Filtration	Event Logs=0.23 Similarity Design=0.01 Filtration=0.03
RUP_021	Rupture	0.755	Event Logs Similarity Design Filtration	Event Logs=0.23 Similarity Design=0.07 Filtration=0.09
RUP_010	Rupture	0.737	Event Logs Similarity Design State Encoding	Event Logs=0.26 Similarity Design=0.05 State Encoding=0.14
RUP_014	Rupture	0.730	Event Logs State Encoding Persistence Diagrams	Event Logs=0.23 State Encoding=0.10 Persistence Diagrams=0.00

The recommendation table also illustrates how the architecture combines different kinds of evidence. Each proposed concept is supported by current mastery gaps, prerequisite support, and topological support estimated from stronger neighborhoods or graph structure. The result is not an automatic prescription but an interpretable prioritization. For example, several rupture learners receive low-mastery recommendations concentrated on Event Logs and Filtration, whereas transition learners are more often guided toward State Encoding and Temporal Windows. This difference is meaningful: rupture cases require re-establishing coherence, while transition cases more often require consolidating the representational bridge between early and advanced material.

The evidence in Section 5.3 supports the final part of the chapter objective. Rupture-related topological information can move beyond diagnosis and become actionable, yet non-deterministic, support evidence. The contribution is not the automation of intervention, but the demonstration that the same topological framework that detects cycles and transitions can also support cautious, concept-aware, human-centred recommendations.

6. DISCUSSION AND CONCLUSIONS

6.1. Theoretical, Pedagogical, and Analytical Implications

The findings extend the theoretical reach of learning analytics by showing that temporality becomes substantially more informative when it is treated as multiscale structure rather than as a mere sequence of discrete transitions. Cycles were not inferred from repeated labels alone, but from persistent H1 features that survived across scales; transitions were not reduced to local step differences, but were made visible through diagram distances, Betti-curve change, and latent-space reorganization; ruptures were not equated with any abrupt deviation, but were interpreted as a combination of fragmentation, short-lived topology, and weak conceptual support. The theoretical value of the framework is therefore its capacity to connect educational process theory with a mathematically explicit account of persistence, recurrence, breakdown, and reorganization.

The pedagogical implications are equally important. Instructors and student-support teams gain a richer basis for interpretation when learner traces are converted into topology-aware signals. A high cycle score can indicate recursive regulation or stalled repetition depending on the surrounding evidence; a high transition score can mark movement into a new regime; and a rupture-oriented signal can justify review and support without implying deterministic failure. The key pedagogical gain is not the production of another risk number, but the possibility of asking why a learner pathway has become repetitive, displaced, or fragmented at a particular moment in the course. The recommendation layer reinforces that human-centred stance by linking rupture-sensitive states to conceptually central targets rather than to opaque risk labels. The chapter therefore supports educational analytics in which mathematical rigor and pedagogical prudence reinforce each other.

Analytically, the study demonstrates the value of integrating persistent homology with representation learning and concept-graph reasoning within a single workflow. The cycle analyses in Section 5.1, the latent audits in Section 5.2, and the recommendation logic in Section 5.3 do not behave as isolated modules; together they show that topology can serve as a unifying bridge between descriptive analysis, model auditing, and assistive decision support. Even the non-stable Mapper result is useful in this regard, because it highlights that topological outputs must be triangulated rather than accepted uncritically. That lesson strengthens, rather than weakens, the interpretability of the framework.

6.2. Conclusions, Limitations, and Responsible Use

The chapter developed a reproducible and interpretable framework that transforms event streams into learner-state representations, constructs filtrations, computes persistent-homology summaries, and translates those summaries into signals for cycles, transitions, and ruptures. The results support that objective in a coherent way. Dimension-1 persistence recovered recurrent educational structure, topology-aware latent modeling revealed regime change with greater stability, and rupture-sensitive indicators were connected to concept-aware recommendation outputs. The framework therefore operates as a proof-of-concept architecture for trustworthy topological learning analytics, provided that its outputs are interpreted as structural evidence and not as direct judgments about learner capacity, motivation, or future achievement.

At the same time, the chapter has clear limitations. The experiment is based on synthetic data, so the present results validate internal methodological coherence rather than external empirical generalization. Topological outputs also depend on the chosen state representation, distance metric, window length, filtration scale, and vectorization strategy. The non-stable Mapper result demonstrates this dependence concretely: some topological views are informative under one resolution and uninformative under another. Moreover, while persistent homology provides rigorous structural summaries, the pedagogical meaning of a loop or a rupture still requires contextual interpretation. Future empirical studies should therefore test parameter robustness, compare alternative state encodings, and examine whether instructors interpret the same topological signals in educationally consistent ways. Such tests would make the synthetic demonstration a bridge to field validation rather than a substitute for it.

Responsible use remains essential. The framework remains assistive and interpretive rather than autonomous; deployment requires temporal validation, subgroup checks, drift monitoring, and human review, especially when signals prioritize support. Educational decisions must not rest on topology alone. They require triangulation with performance, curriculum context, instructor judgment, and student voice. Under those conditions, the framework offers a defensible path toward scalable but human-centred educational analytics. In review contexts, the topological layer is an interpretive addition to established educational evidence, not a replacement for qualitative feedback, formative assessment, or curriculum-level diagnosis. This distinction improves reviewability, accountability, and reader trust.

7. FUTURE WORK

7.1. Toward Explainable, Adaptive, and Real-Time Topological Learning Systems

Future work moves in four complementary directions. First, validation on real learning-management-system traces, multimodal self-regulated-learning data, and longitudinal program-level records must test whether the same cycle, transition, and rupture patterns remain visible outside synthetic conditions. Such validation needs varied course designs, student populations, and assessment rhythms, because topology is sensitive to how learning opportunities are structured. Second, the architecture can be extended toward online or near-real-time monitoring, allowing persistence diagrams, Betti curves, and drift statistics to update as new events arrive rather than only after a complete trajectory has been observed. Third, the latent-space component requires more explicit explainable-AI mechanisms and subgroup-sensitive evaluation so structural signals remain interpretable across learner populations.

A fourth direction concerns adaptive intervention. The recommendation layer can move from concept-priority lists to experimentally evaluated support policies that combine topological evidence with pedagogical constraints, instructor dashboards, and student-facing explanations. In that setting, topological learning analytics becomes part of a broader intelligent and ethical learning ecosystem in which structural evidence, explanatory feedback, and human decision making remain aligned. Controlled pilots and qualitative studies should examine whether students experience recommendations as supportive, transparent, and fair. Evaluations should report not only predictive accuracy but also uptake, perceived usefulness, unintended burden, and whether interventions derived from topological alerts improve learning opportunities without stigmatizing learners.

The code generated to obtain all the results in this chapter can be found at the following URL:

https://github.com/JAIME6609/EDUCATION/blob/main/CODE-BOOK-15-ART-01.py

REFERENCES

Ali, D., Asaad, A., Jimenez, M.-J., Nanda, V., Paluzo-Hidalgo, E., & Soriano-Trigueros, M. (2023). A survey of vectorization methods in topological data analysis. *IEEE Transactions on Pattern Analysis and Machine Intelligence, 45*(12), 14069–14080. DOI: 10.1109/TPAMI.2023.3308391

Atienza, N., González-Díaz, R., & Soriano-Trigueros, M. (2020). On the stability of persistent entropy and new summary functions for topological data analysis. *Pattern Recognition, 107*, 107509. DOI: 10.1016/j.patcog.2020.107509

Bannert, M., Reimann, P., & Sonnenberg, C. (2014). Process mining techniques for analysing patterns and strategies in students' self-regulated learning. *Metacognition and Learning, 9*(2), 161–185. DOI: 10.1007/s11409-013-9107-6

Barnes, D., Polanco, L., & Perea, J. A. (2021). A comparative study of machine learning methods for persistence diagrams. *Frontiers in Artificial Intelligence, 4*, 681174. DOI: 10.3389/frai.2021.681174

Chazal, F., & Michel, B. (2021). An introduction to topological data analysis: Fundamental and practical aspects for data scientists. *Frontiers in Artificial Intelligence, 4*, 667963. DOI: 10.3389/frai.2021.667963

Chen, F., & Cui, Y. (2020). Utilizing student time series behaviour in learning management systems for early prediction of course performance. *Journal of Learning Analytics, 7*(2), 1–17. DOI: 10.18608/jla.2020.72.1

El-Yaagoubi, A. B., Chung, M. K., & Ombao, H. (2023). Topological data analysis for multivariate time series data. *Entropy (Basel, Switzerland), 25*(11), 1509. DOI: 10.3390/e25111509

Engelmann, K., & Bannert, M. (2021). Analyzing temporal data for understanding the learning process induced by metacognitive prompts. *Learning and Instruction, 72*, 101205. DOI: 10.1016/j.learninstruc.2019.05.002

Fan, Y., Matcha, W., Uzir, N. A., Wang, Q., & Gašević, D. (2021). Learning analytics to reveal links between learning design and self-regulated learning. *International Journal of Artificial Intelligence in Education, 31*(4), 980–1021. DOI: 10.1007/s40593-021-00249-z

Gašević, D., Jovanović, J., Pardo, A., & Dawson, S. (2017). Detecting learning strategies with analytics: Links with self-reported measures and academic performance. *Journal of Learning Analytics, 4*(2), 113–128. DOI: 10.18608/jla.2017.42.10

Järvelä, S., & Hadwin, A. (2024). Triggers for self-regulated learning: A conceptual framework for advancing multimodal research about SRL. *Learning and Individual Differences*, *115*, 102526. DOI: 10.1016/j.lindif.2024.102526

Kizilcec, R. F., Pérez-Sanagustín, M., & Maldonado, J. J. (2017). Self-regulated learning strategies predict learner behavior and goal attainment in Massive Open Online Courses. *Computers & Education*, *104*, 18–33. DOI: 10.1016/j.compedu.2016.10.001

Liou, L., Scott, E., Parchure, P., Ouyang, Y., Egorova, N., Freeman, R., Hofer, I. S., Nadkarni, G. N., Timsina, P., Kia, A., & Levin, M. A. (2024). Assessing calibration and bias of a deployed machine learning malnutrition prediction model within a large healthcare system. npj. *NPJ Digital Medicine*, *7*(1), 149. DOI: 10.1038/s41746-024-01141-5

López-Pernas, S., & Saqr, M. (2024). How the dynamics of engagement explain the momentum of achievement and the inertia of disengagement: A complex systems theory approach. *Computers in Human Behavior*, *153*, 108126. DOI: 10.1016/j.chb.2023.108126

Maldonado-Mahauad, J., Pérez-Sanagustín, M., Kizilcec, R. F., Morales, N., & Munoz-Gama, J. (2018). Mining theory-based patterns from big data: Identifying self-regulated learning strategies in Massive Open Online Courses. *Computers in Human Behavior*, *80*, 179–196. DOI: 10.1016/j.chb.2017.11.011

Mishra, A., & Motta, F. C. (2023). Stability and machine learning applications of persistent homology using the Delaunay-Rips complex. *Frontiers in Applied Mathematics and Statistics*, *9*, 1179301. DOI: 10.3389/fams.2023.1179301

Molenaar, I., de Mooij, S., Azevedo, R., Bannert, M., Järvelä, S., & Gašević, D. (2023). Measuring self-regulated learning and the role of AI: Five years of research using multimodal multichannel data. *Computers in Human Behavior*, *139*, 107540. DOI: 10.1016/j.chb.2022.107540

Molenaar, I., & Wise, A. F. (2022). Temporal aspects of learning analytics: Grounding analyses in concepts of time. In Lang, C., Wise, A. F., Merceron, A., Gašević, D., & Siemens, G. (Eds.), *Handbook of Learning Analytics* (2nd ed., pp. 66–76). Society for Learning Analytics Research., DOI: 10.18608/hla22.007

Munch, E. (2017). A User's Guide to Topological Data Analysis. *Journal of Learning Analytics*, *4*(2), 47–61. DOI: 10.18608/jla.2017.42.6

Riley, R. D., Archer, L., Snell, K. I. E., Ensor, J., Dhiman, P., Martin, G. P., Bonnett, L. J., & Collins, G. S. (2024). Evaluation of clinical prediction models (part 2): How to undertake an external validation study. *BMJ (Clinical Research Ed.)*, *384*, e074820. DOI: 10.1136/bmj-2023-074820

Sailer, M., Ninaus, M., Huber, S. E., Bauer, E., & Greiff, S. (2024). The End is the Beginning is the End: The closed-loop learning analytics framework. *Computers in Human Behavior*, *158*, 108305. DOI: 10.1016/j.chb.2024.108305

Saint, J., Fan, Y., Gašević, D., & Pardo, A. (2022). Temporally-focused analytics of self-regulated learning: A systematic review of literature. *Computers and Education: Artificial Intelligence*, *3*, 100060. DOI: 10.1016/j.caeai.2022.100060

Saint, J., Whitelock-Wainwright, A., Gašević, D., & Pardo, A. (2020). Trace-SRL: A framework for analysis of microlevel processes of self-regulated learning from trace data. *IEEE Transactions on Learning Technologies*, *13*(4), 861–877. DOI: 10.1109/TLT.2020.3027496

Saqr, M., & López-Pernas, S. (2021). The longitudinal trajectories of online engagement over a full program. *Computers & Education*, *175*, 104325. DOI: 10.1016/j.compedu.2021.104325

Saqr, M., & López-Pernas, S. (2022). How CSCL roles emerge, persist, transition, and evolve over time: A four-year longitudinal study. *Computers & Education*, *189*, 104581. DOI: 10.1016/j.compedu.2022.104581

Saqr, M., López-Pernas, S., Helske, S., Durand, M., Murphy, K., Studer, M., & Ritschard, G. (2024). Sequence analysis in education: Principles, technique, and tutorial with R. In Saqr, M., & López-Pernas, S. (Eds.), *Learning analytics methods and tutorials: A practical guide using R* (pp. 321–354). Springer., DOI: 10.1007/978-3-031-54464-4_10

Saqr, M., López-Pernas, S., & Vogelsmeier, L. V. D. E. (2023). When, how and for whom changes in engagement happen: A transition analysis of instructional variables. *Computers & Education*, *207*, 104934. DOI: 10.1016/j.compedu.2023.104934

van Calster, B., McLernon, D. J., van Smeden, M., Wynants, L., Steyerberg, E. W., Bossuyt, P., Collins, G. S., MacAskill, P., Moons, K. G. M., & Vickers, A. J. (2019). Calibration: The Achilles heel of predictive analytics. *BMC Medicine*, *17*(1), 230. Advance online publication. DOI: 10.1186/s12916-019-1466-7

van Halem, N., van Klaveren, C., Drachsler, H. J., Schmitz, M., & Cornelisz, I. (2020). Tracking patterns in self-regulated learning using students' self-reports and online trace data. *Frontline Learning Research*, *8*(3), 140–163. DOI: 10.14786/flr.v8i3.497

Vickers, A. J., & Holland, F. (2021). Decision curve analysis to evaluate the clinical benefit of prediction models. *The Spine Journal : Official Journal of the North American Spine Society, 21*(10), 1643–1648. DOI: 10.1016/j.spinee.2021.02.024

Wasserman, L. (2018). Topological data analysis. *Annual Review of Statistics and Its Application, 5*(1), 501–532. DOI: 10.1146/annurev-statistics-031017-100045

Wu, J.-Y., Liao, C.-H., Tsai, C.-C., & Kwok, O.-M. (2024). Using learning analytics with temporal modeling to uncover the interplay of before-class video viewing engagement, motivation, and performance in an active learning context. *Computers & Education, 212*, 104975. DOI: 10.1016/j.compedu.2023.104975

Ye, D., & Pennisi, S. (2022). Using trace data to enhance students' self-regulation: A learning analytics perspective. *The Internet and Higher Education, 54*, 100855. DOI: 10.1016/j.iheduc.2022.100855

Compilation of References

Abdul-Qawy, A. S., Pramod, P. J., Magesh, E., & Srinivasulu, T. (2015). The internet of things (IoT): An overview. *International Journal of Engineering Research and Applications*, *5*(12), 71–82.

ABET. (2019). *Criteria for accrediting engineering programs*. ABET Engineering Accreditation Commission.

ABET. (2025). *Criteria for accrediting engineering programs, 2025–2026*. https://www.abet.org/accreditation/accreditation-criteria/criteria-for-accrediting-engineering-programs-2025-2026/

Abnoulgid, F., Aouhassi, S., Mansouri, K., & Akef, F. (2025). Quality 4.0 in higher education: Integrating Industry 4.0 technologies in higher education quality management practices. *Frontiers in Education*, *10*, 1594377. Advance online publication. DOI: 10.3389/feduc.2025.1594377

Abras, C., Maloney-Krichmar, D., & Preece, J. (2004). User-centered design. In Bainbridge, W. S. (Ed.), *Berkshire encyclopedia of human-computer interaction* (Vol. 2, pp. 763–768). Berkshire Publishing Group.

Acemoglu, D., & Restrepo, P. (2020). Robots and jobs: Evidence from US labor markets. *Journal of Political Economy*, *128*(6), 2188–2244. DOI: 10.1086/705716

Acevedo Carrillo, M., Cabezas Torres, N. M., La Serna La Rosa, P. A., & Araujo Rossel, S. A. (2026). Desafíos y oportunidades de la inteligencia artificial en la educación superior latinoamericana: Una revisión sistemática de la literatura. *Revista InveCom*, *6*(1). Advance online publication. DOI: 10.5281/zenodo.15508755

Ackermann, H., Henke, A., Chevalère, J., Yun, H. S., Hafner, V. V., Pinkwart, N., & Lazarides, R. (2025). Physical embodiment and anthropomorphism of AI tutors and their role in student enjoyment and performance. *NPJ Science of Learning*, *10*(1), 1. DOI: 10.1038/s41539-024-00293-z PMID: 39779711

Acosta, D. I., & Haden, C. A. (2023). Supporting Latine children's informal engineering learning through tinkering and oral storytelling. *Developmental Psychology*, *59*(12), 2342–2355. DOI: 10.1037/dev0001648

Adadi, A., & Berrada, M. (2018). Peeking inside the black-box: A survey on explainable artificial intelligence (XAI). *IEEE Access : Practical Innovations, Open Solutions*, *6*, 52138–52160. DOI: 10.1109/ACCESS.2018.2870052

Adel, A. (2024). The convergence of intelligent tutoring, robotics, and IoT in smart education for the transition from Industry 4.0 to 5.0. *Smart Cities*, *7*(1), 325–369. DOI: 10.3390/smartcities7010014

Adenubi, A. O., Samuel, N., Oyenuga, A. O., & Adewale, K. A. (2024). Artificial intelligence with agile teaching strategies for personalized learning. *Nigerian Online Journal of Educational Sciences and Technology*, *6*(1), 364–379.

Afzaal, M., Nouri, J., Zia, A., Papapetrou, P., Fors, U., Wu, Y., Li, X., & Weegar, R. (2021). Explainable AI for data-driven feedback and intelligent action recommendations to support students self-regulation. *Frontiers in Artificial Intelligence*, *4*, 723447. DOI: 10.3389/frai.2021.723447 PMID: 34870183

Ağca, R. K. (2023). Using digital twins in education from an innovative perspective: Potential and application areas. *Education Mind*, *2*(2), 65–74. DOI: 10.58583/Pedapub.EM2306

Aguayo, C., Videla, R., López-Cortés, F., Rossel, S., & Ibacache, C. (2023). Ethical enactivism for smart and inclusive STEAM learning design. *Heliyon*, *9*(9), e19205. DOI: 10.1016/j.heliyon.2023.e19205 PMID: 37662760

Aheleroff, S., Huang, H., Xu, X., & Zhong, R. Y. (2022). Toward sustainability and resilience with Industry 4.0 and Industry 5.0. *Frontiers in Manufacturing Technology*, *2*, 951643. Advance online publication. DOI: 10.3389/fmtec.2022.951643

Ahmad, A., Amry, D., Chen, Z., & Hu, Y. (2026). Building entrepreneurial self-efficacy in engineering students: Towards a new methodological framework. *Entrepreneurship Education*, *9*(1), 21–56. DOI: 10.1007/s41959-025-00156-7

Airaj, M. (2024). Ethical artificial intelligence for teaching-learning in higher education. *Education and Information Technologies*, *29*(13), 17145–17167. DOI: 10.1007/s10639-024-12545-x

Ajoudani, A., Zanchettin, A. M., Ivaldi, S., Albu-Schäffer, A., Kosuge, K., & Khatib, O. (2018). Progress and prospects of the human–robot collaboration. *Autonomous Robots*, *42*(5), 957–975. DOI: 10.1007/s10514-017-9677-2

Akdemir-Beveridge, Z. G., & Zaghi, A. E. (2026). ECAT as a contextualized TTCT: Evidence of convergent validity in engineering creativity assessment. *Frontiers in Education, 11*, 1705312. Advance online publication. DOI: 10.3389/feduc.2026.1705312

Al-Ansi, A. M., Jaboob, M., Garad, A., & Al-Ansi, A. (2023). Analyzing augmented reality (AR) and virtual reality (VR) recent development in education. *Social Sciences & Humanities Open, 8*(1), 100532. DOI: 10.1016/j.ssaho.2023.100532

Alenezi, A. (2024). Evaluating the effectiveness of AI-powered adaptive learning systems in secondary schools. *International Journal on Studies in Education, 6*(4), 686–700. DOI: 10.46328/ijonse.264

Alfaisal, R., Hashim, H., & Azizan, U. H. (2024). Metaverse system adoption in education: A systematic literature review. *Journal of Computers in Education, 11*(1), 259–303. DOI: 10.1007/s40692-022-00256-6

Ali, D., Asaad, A., Jimenez, M.-J., Nanda, V., Paluzo-Hidalgo, E., & Soriano-Trigueros, M. (2023). A survey of vectorization methods in topological data analysis. *IEEE Transactions on Pattern Analysis and Machine Intelligence, 45*(12), 14069–14080. DOI: 10.1109/TPAMI.2023.3308391

Alier, M., Casañ Guerrero, M. J., Amo, D., Severance, C., & Fonseca, D. (2021). Privacy and e-learning: A pending task. *Sustainability (Basel), 13*(16), 9206. Advance online publication. DOI: 10.3390/su13169206

Alkhatib, O. J. (2025). STEAM integration and engineering: Lessons from transformative approaches. In Behera, S. K., Sorayyaei Azar, A., Curle, S., & Dials, J. G. (Eds.), *Transformative approaches to STEAM integration in modern education* (pp. 345–374). IGI Global., DOI: 10.4018/979-8-3693-7408-5.ch015

Allen, L. K., & Kendeou, P. (2024). ED-AI Lit: An Interdisciplinary Framework for AI Literacy in Education. *Policy Insights from the Behavioral and Brain Sciences, 11*(1), 3–10. DOI: 10.1177/23727322231220339

Alomá Bello, M., Crespo Díaz, L. M., González Hernández, K., & Estévez Pérez, N. (2022). Fundamentos cognitivos y pedagógicos del aprendizaje activo. *Mendive. Review of Education, 20*(4), 1353–1368. https://mendive.upr.edu.cu/index.php/MendiveUPR/article/view/3128

Alsaleh, S., Tepljakov, A., Köse, A., Belikov, J., & Petlenkov, E. (2022). ReImagine lab: Bridging the gap between hands-on, virtual and remote control engineering laboratories using digital twins and extended reality. *IEEE Access : Practical Innovations, Open Solutions, 10*, 89924–89943. DOI: 10.1109/ACCESS.2022.3199371

Alves Aleixo, A., Silva, B., & Silva Ramos, M. A. (2021). Análisis del uso de la cultura maker en contextos educativos: Una revisión sistemática de la literatura. *Educatio Siglo XXI*, *39*(2), 143–168. DOI: 10.6018/educatio.465991

Alves-Oliveira, P., Sequeira, P., Melo, F. S., Castellano, G., & Paiva, A. (2019). Empathic robot for group learning: A field study. *ACM Transactions on Human-Robot Interaction*, *8*(1), 3. Advance online publication. DOI: 10.1145/3300188 PMID: 33829148

Amabile, T. M. (1996). *Creativity in context: Update to The social psychology of creativity*. Westview Press.

Amo-Filvà, D., Alier, M., García-Peñalvo, F. J., Fonseca, D., & Casañ, M. J. (2020). Privacidad, seguridad y legalidad en soluciones educativas basadas en blockchain: Una revisión sistemática de la literatura. *RIED. Revista Iberoamericana de Educación a Distancia*, *23*(2), 213–236. DOI: 10.5944/ried.23.2.26388

Analuisa-Sánchez, J. J., López Chica, J. A., & Macías Loor, C. A. (2025). Las ecuaciones diferenciales como pilar metodológico en la interpretación y representación de sistemas dinámicos dentro de la educación superior: Aplicaciones en el ámbito de la ingeniería y las matemáticas avanzadas. *Revista Social Fronteriza*, *5*(4), e833. Advance online publication. DOI: 10.59814/resofro.2025.5(4)833

Araújo, A. A., Kalinowski, M., & Baldassarre, M. T. (2025). Embracing experiential learning: Hackathons as an educational strategy for shaping soft skills in software engineering. In *2025 IEEE Conference on Software Engineering Education and Training (CSEE&T)* (pp. 319–324). IEEE. DOI: 10.1109/CSEET66350.2025.00040

Arce Rangel, L. M. (2024). Habilidades blandas en la gestión cultural: nuevos retos [Soft skills in cultural management: New challenges]. *Córima. Revista de Investigación en Gestión Cultural*, *9*(17), 1–27. Advance online publication. DOI: 10.32870/cor.a9n17.7472

Asad, M. M., Naz, A., Churi, P., & Tahanzadeh, M. M. (2024). Investigating the impact of IoT-based smart laboratories on students' academic performance in higher education. *Universal Access in the Information Society*, *23*(3), 1135–1149. DOI: 10.1007/s10209-022-00944-1 PMID: 36407564

Atienza, N., González-Díaz, R., & Soriano-Trigueros, M. (2020). On the stability of persistent entropy and new summary functions for topological data analysis. *Pattern Recognition*, *107*, 107509. DOI: 10.1016/j.patcog.2020.107509

Attaran, M. (2017). The rise of 3-D printing: The advantages of additive manufacturing over traditional manufacturing. *Business Horizons*, *60*(5), 677–688. DOI: 10.1016/j.bushor.2017.05.011

Atzori, L., Iera, A., & Morabito, G. (2010). The Internet of Things: A survey. *Computer Networks*, *54*(15), 2787–2805. DOI: 10.1016/j.comnet.2010.05.010

Auer, M. E., Azad, A. K., Edwards, A., & De Jong, T. (Eds.). (2018). *Cyber-physical laboratories in engineering and science education*. Springer International Publishing. DOI: 10.1007/978-3-319-76935-6

Avendano-Uribe, B. E., Lombana-Bermudez, A., Flórez, L. V., Chaparro, E., Hernandez-Morales, A. C., Archbold, J., Buitrago-Casas, J. C., & Porras, A. M. (2022). Engaging Scientific Diasporas in STEAM Education: The Case of Science Clubs Colombia. *Frontiers in Research Metrics and Analytics*, *7*, 898167. Advance online publication. DOI: 10.3389/frma.2022.898167

Aznarte, J. L. (2020). Consideraciones éticas en torno al uso de tecnologías basadas en datos masivos en la UNED. *RIED. Revista Iberoamericana de Educación a Distancia*, *23*(2), 237–252. DOI: 10.5944/ried.23.2.26590

Baalsrud Hauge, J. M., Stanescu, I. A., Arnab, S., Moreno-Ger, P., Lim, T., Serrano-Laguna, Á., Lameras, P., Hendrix, M., Kiili, K., Ninaus, M., de Freitas, S., Mazzetti, A., Dahlbom, A., & Degano, C. (2015). Learning analytics architecture to scaffold learning experience through technology-based methods. *International Journal of Serious Games*, *2*(1). Advance online publication. DOI: 10.17083/ijsg.v2i1.38

Bailey, D. E. (2022). Emerging Technologies at Work: Policy Ideas to Address Negative Consequences for Work, Workers, and Society. *Industrial & Labor Relations Review*, *75*(3), 527–551. DOI: 10.1177/00197939221076747

Bandura, A. (1977). Self-efficacy: Toward a unifying theory of behavioral change. *Psychological Review*, *84*(2), 191–215. DOI: 10.1037/0033-295X.84.2.191 PMID: 847061

Bannert, M., Reimann, P., & Sonnenberg, C. (2014). Process mining techniques for analysing patterns and strategies in students' self-regulated learning. *Metacognition and Learning*, *9*(2), 161–185. DOI: 10.1007/s11409-013-9107-6

Barnes, D., Polanco, L., & Perea, J. A. (2021). A comparative study of machine learning methods for persistence diagrams. *Frontiers in Artificial Intelligence*, *4*, 681174. DOI: 10.3389/frai.2021.681174

Barnes, M., Lafferty, K., & Li, B. (2024). Assessing twenty-first century competencies: Can students lead and facilitate the co-construction process? *Educational Review*, *76*(4), 691–709. DOI: 10.1080/00131911.2022.2142524

Barr, V., & Stephenson, C. (2011). Bringing computational thinking to K–12. *ACM Inroads.*

Bascopé, M., Reiss, K., Morales, M., Robles, C., Reyes, P., Duque, M. I., & Andrade, J. C. (2020). Latin American STEM policy: A review of recent initiatives on STEM education in four Latin American countries. In Johnson, C. C., Mohr-Schroeder, N. J., Moore, T. J., & English, L. D. (Eds.), *Handbook of research on STEM education* (pp. 443–458). Routledge., https://doi.org/https://doi.org/10.4324/9780429021381-41 DOI: 10.4324/9780429021381-41

Basilotta-Gómez-Pablos, V., Matarranz, M., Casado-Aranda, L.-A., & Otto, A. (2022). Teachers' digital competencies in higher education: A systematic literature review. *International Journal of Educational Technology in Higher Education*, *19*(1), 8. DOI: 10.1186/s41239-021-00312-8

Baxter, G., & Sommerville, I. (2011). Socio-technical systems: From design methods to systems engineering. *Interacting with Computers*, *23*(1), 4–17. DOI: 10.1016/j.intcom.2010.07.003

Bayer, J. K. (1996). Social competence and social skills training for children and adolescents: A literature review. *Australian Journal of Guidance & Counselling*, *6*(S1), 1–14.

Belbase, S., Mainali, B. R., Kasemsukpipat, W., Tairab, H., Gochoo, M., & Jarrah, A. (2022). At the dawn of science, technology, engineering, arts, and mathematics (STEAM) education: Prospects, priorities, processes, and problems. *International Journal of Mathematical Education in Science and Technology*, *53*(11), 2919–2955. DOI: 10.1080/0020739X.2021.1922943

Belpaeme, T., Kennedy, J., Ramachandran, A., Scassellati, B., & Tanaka, F. (2018). Social robots for education: A review. *Science Robotics*, *3*(21), eaat5954. Advance online publication. DOI: 10.1126/scirobotics.aat5954 PMID: 33141719

Bender, E. M., Gebru, T., McMillan-Major, A., & Shmitchell, S. (2021). On the dangers of stochastic parrots: Can language models be too big? In *Proceedings of the 2021 ACM Conference on Fairness, Accountability, and Transparency* (pp. 610–623). Association for Computing Machinery. DOI: 10.1145/3442188.3445922

Bergasa Sariego, C. A. (2024). *Mejorando la equidad en algoritmos de aprendizaje automático usando un enfoque de transporte óptimo* [Master's thesis, Universidad de Chile]. DOI: 10.58011/5cew-3z19

Berisha-Gawlowski, A., Caruso, C., & Harteis, C. (2021). The concept of a digital twin and its potential for learning organizations. In *Digital transformation of learning organizations* (pp. 95–114). Springer., DOI: 10.1007/978-3-030-55878-9_6

Bermúdez, A. (2023). Modelos matemáticos en la industria. Universidad de La Laguna. https://imarrero.webs.ull.es/sctm03.v2/modulo3/ABermudez.pdf

Bhattacharjya, M. (2025). Future-proofing education: Developing transdiscipllinary STEAM models to prepare learners for a workforce in the forthcoming era of automation. *Transdisciplinary Journal of Engineering & Science, 16*(6), 67–97. DOI: 10.22545/2025/00271

Bicchi, A., Peshkin, M., & Colgate, J. E. (2008). Safety for physical human–robot interaction. In Siciliano, B., & Khatib, O. (Eds.), *Springer handbook of robotics* (pp. 1335–1348). Springer., DOI: 10.1007/978-3-540-30301-5_58

Biggs, J., Tang, C., & Kennedy, G. (2022). *Teaching for quality learning at university* (5th ed.). McGraw-Hill Education.

Birdthistle, N., Riverola, C., Boorer, L., & Ekberg, S. (2022). Empowering STEAM academics to adopt enterprise pedagogies. In Henry, C., Gabriel, B. F. C. C., Sailer, K., Bernadó-Mansilla, E., & Lahikainen, K. (Eds.), *Strategies for the creation and maintenance of entrepreneurial universities* (pp. 142–167). IGI Global., DOI: 10.4018/978-1-7998-7456-0.ch007

Blikstein, P., & Worsley, M. (2016). Multimodal learning analytics and education data mining: Using computational technologies to measure complex learning tasks. *Journal of Learning Analytics, 3*(2), 220–238. DOI: 10.18608/jla.2016.32.11

Bokhari, H., & Awuni, E. T. (2024). Digital inequalities in North Africa: Examining employment and socioeconomic well-being in Morocco and Tunisia. *Convergence (London), 30*(3), 1149–1169. DOI: 10.1177/13548565231209673

Borg Preca, C., Baldacchino, L., Briguglio, M., & Mangion, M. (2023). Are STEM Students Creative Thinkers? *Journal of Intelligence, 11*(6), 106. DOI: 10.3390/jintelligence11060106

Boud, D., Keogh, R., & Walker, D. (Eds.). (1985). *Reflection: Turning experience into learning*. Kogan Page.

Boy, G. A. (2013). From STEM to STEAM: *Toward a human-centred education, creativity & learning thinking.* In *Proceedings of the European Conference on Cognitive Ergonomics*. ACM. DOI: 10.1145/2501907.2501934

Bracho-Fuenmayor, P. L. (2024). Ética y moral en la educación superior: Una revisión bibliométrica. *Revista de Ciencias Sociales, 30*(3), 553–568. DOI: 10.31876/rcs.v30i3.42695

Brahimi, T., & Sarirete, A. (2024). Transforming learning in STEAM: How AI tools and language models catalyze educational advancement. In Baroudi, S., & Lytras, M. D. (Eds.), *Transformative leadership and sustainable innovation in education: Interdisciplinary perspectives* (pp. 39–58). Emerald Publishing Limited., DOI: 10.1108/978-1-83753-536-120241004

Breiman, L. (2001). Random forests. *Machine Learning, 45*(1), 5–32. DOI: 10.1023/A:1010933404324

Brennan, K., & Resnick, M. (2012). New frameworks for studying and assessing the development of computational thinking. In *Proceedings of the 2012 Annual Meeting of the American Educational Research Association*. AERA., Available https://scratched.gse.harvard.edu/ct/files/AERA2012.pdf

Breque, M., De Nul, L., & Petridis, A. (2021). Industry 5.0: Towards a sustainable, human-centric and resilient European industry. European Commission. https://data.europa.eu/doi/10.2777/308407

Brookhart, S. M. (2010). *How to assess higher-order thinking skills in your classroom*. ASCD.

Brown, D., Hanson, R., & Christian, W. (2024). Tracker Video Analysis and Modeling Tool (Version 6.3) [Computer software]. Open Source Physics. https://opensourcephysics.github.io/tracker-website

Brown, T. (2008). Design thinking. *Harvard Business Review, 86*(6), 84–92. https://hbr.org/2008/06/design-thinking PMID: 18605031

Brown, T. B., Mann, B., Ryder, N., Subbiah, M., Kaplan, J., Dhariwal, P., Neelakantan, A., Shyam, P., Sastry, G., Askell, A., Agarwal, S., Herbert-Voss, A., Krueger, G., Henighan, T., Child, R., Ramesh, A., Ziegler, D. M., Wu, J., Winter, C., & Amodei, D. (2020). Language models are few-shot learners. *Advances in Neural Information Processing Systems, 33*, 1877–1901. DOI: 10.48550/arXiv.2005.14165

Brynjolfsson, E., & McAfee, A. (2017). *Machine, platform, crowd: Harnessing our digital future*. W. W. Norton & Company.

Bugallo-Rodríguez, Á., & Vega-Marcote, P. (2020). Circular economy, sustainability and teacher training in a higher education institution. *International Journal of Sustainability in Higher Education, 21*(7), 1351–1366. DOI: 10.1108/IJSHE-02-2020-0049

Bustelo Gracia, J. L. (2025). Hacia una gobernanza algorítmica transparente: Auditoría de sesgo. Estudio de caso. *Cuadernos de Gobierno y Administración Pública, 12*(1), e97604. Advance online publication. DOI: 10.5209/cgap.97604

Bybee, R. W. (2013). *The case for STEM education: Challenges and opportunities.* NSTA Press.

C3 UNAM. (2022). Sistemas complejos. Centro de Ciencias de la Complejidad, Universidad Nacional Autónoma de México. https://www.c3.unam.mx/noticias/noticia222.html

Calder, B. J., He, S., & Sternthal, B. (2023). Using theoretical frameworks in behavioral research. *Journal of Business Research, 161*, 113758. DOI: 10.1016/j.jbusres.2023.113758

Calero López, I., González-Peiteado, M., & Rodríguez-López, B. (2024). Are creativity, L2 motivation and soft skills related? A study in VET students. *Education Sciences, 14*(3), 214. Advance online publication. DOI: 10.3390/educsci14030214

Calle Balarezo, S. D. (2022). *Digital twin del laboratorio MPS mediante herramientas IoT y simulación virtual para realizar prácticas de laboratorio no presenciales* [Trabajo de titulación, Universidad Politécnica Salesiana]. https://dspace.ups.edu.ec/handle/123456789/22113

Campero-Jurado, I., Quintanar Gomez, J., Vargas-Buitrón, O. D., Trejo-Macotela, F. R., Robles-Camarillo, D., & Simancas-Acevedo, E. (2019). Embedded system based on IoT and V2X for smart cities. *International Journal of Combinatorial Optimization Problems and Informatics, 10*(3), 50–58. https://ijcopi.org/ojs/article/view/128

Cannistrà, M. (2023). Reducing dropout rates: the challenge of learning analytics in higher education institutions.

Carrillo-Velarde, M. V. (2020). La ética y los valores en la educación superior. *Dominio de las Ciencias, 6*(3), 1108–1117. DOI: 10.23857/dc.v6i3.1340

Caspari-Sadeghi, S. (2023). Artificial intelligence in technology-enhanced assessment: A survey of machine learning. *Journal of Educational Technology Systems, 51*(3), 372–386. DOI: 10.1177/00472395221138791

CAST. (2024). *CAST Universal Design for Learning Guidelines version 3.0.* https://udlguidelines.cast.org/

Castillo Galicia, A. M., & Barajas Zúñiga, Z. (2024). Integrando inteligencia artificial en la capacitación técnica para la empresa ART. *DIDAC*, (84), 75–83. DOI: 10.48102/didac.2024..84_JUL-DIC.214

Castillo-Castillo, M. (2025). Adaptación y aplicación de la metodología STEAM en entornos educativos con recursos limitados. *Episteme Koinonía*, *8*(16), 437–459. DOI: 10.35381/e.k.v8i16.4641

Cervantes-Juarez, E., & Sanchez-Guzman, D. (2022). Developing computational thinking in engineering students. In *IEEE Frontiers in Education Conference (FIE)*.

Chappell, K., Hetherington, L., Juillard, S., Aguirre, C., & Duca, E. (2025). A framework for effective STEAM education: Pedagogy for responding to wicked problems. *International Journal of Educational Research Open*, *9*, 100474. DOI: 10.1016/j.ijedro.2025.100474

Chazal, F., & Michel, B. (2021). An introduction to topological data analysis: Fundamental and practical aspects for data scientists. *Frontiers in Artificial Intelligence*, *4*, 667963. DOI: 10.3389/frai.2021.667963

Chen, F., & Cui, Y. (2020). Utilizing student time series behaviour in learning management systems for early prediction of course performance. *Journal of Learning Analytics*, *7*(2), 1–17. DOI: 10.18608/jla.2020.72.1

Chen, J.-C., Huang, Y., Lin, K.-Y., Chang, Y.-S., Lin, H.-C., Lin, C.-Y., & Hsiao, H.-S. (2020). Developing a hands-on activity using virtual reality to help students learn by doing. *Journal of Computer Assisted Learning*, *36*(1), 46–60. DOI: 10.1111/jcal.12389

Chen, T., & Guestrin, C. (2016). XGBoost: A scalable tree boosting system. In *Proceedings of the 22nd ACM SIGKDD International Conference on Knowledge Discovery and Data Mining* (pp. 785–794). Association for Computing Machinery. DOI: 10.1145/2939672.2939785

Clapp, E. P. (2018). *La creatividad como proceso participativo y distribuido: Implicación en las aulas.* Narcea.

Coeckelbergh, M. (2024). What is digital humanism? A conceptual analysis and an argument for a more critical and political digital (post)humanism. *Journal of Responsible Technology*, *17*, 100073. DOI: 10.1016/j.jrt.2023.100073

Coello Pisco, S., Rodríguez Gómez, B., González Cañizalez, Y., & Hidalgo Crespo, J. (2021). Habilidades profesionales STEM e industria 4.0 para estudiantes de Física Aplicada en proyectos disciplinarios I+D+i. Revista de Investigación, Formación y Desarrollo. *Generando Productividad Institucional*, *9*(3), 1–18.

Correa, J., Ulloa-Leon, F., Vergara-Perucich, F., Aguirre-Nuñez, C., & Truffello, R. (2023). Infrastructural inequality: Exploring the emergence of digital classes in the Metropolitan Area of Santiago, Chile. *Bulletin of Geography. Socio-Economic Series*, (62), 107–122. DOI: 10.12775/bgss-2023-0037

Cortizo Pérez, J. C., Carrero García, F. M., Monsalve Piqueras, B., Velasco Collado, A., Díaz del Dedo, L. I., & Pérez Martín, J. (2011). Gamificación y docencia: Lo que la universidad tiene que aprender de los videojuegos. In *VIII Jornadas Internacionales de Innovación Universitaria: Retos y oportunidades del desarrollo de los nuevos títulos en educación superior*. Universidad Europea de Madrid. http://hdl.handle.net/11268/1750

Costantino, T. (2018). STEAM by another name: Transdisciplinary practice in art and design education. *Arts Education Policy Review*, *119*(2), 100–106. DOI: 10.1080/10632913.2017.1292973

Cropley, A. J. (2006). In praise of convergent thinking. *Creativity Research Journal*, *18*(3), 391–404. DOI: 10.1207/s15326934crj1803_13

Cruzes, S. (2025). Data centers in the age of AI: A tutorial survey on infrastructure, sustainability, and emerging challenges. *Authorea Preprints*.

Cummings, D., Cheeks, L., & Robinson, R. (2018). Culturally-Centric Outreach and Engagement for Underserved Groups in STEM. *Proceedings of the 49th ACM Technical Symposium on Computer Science Education, SIGCSE '18*, 447–452. DOI: 10.1145/3159450.3159565

Dahal, N. (2022). Transformative STEAM education as a praxis-driven orientation. *Journal of STEAM Education*, *5*(2), 167–180. DOI: 10.55290/steam.1098153

Damayanti, N. A., Yus, A., & Mahya, V. A. (2024). Assessment rubric based on Guilford's creativity theory. In *Proceedings of the 2nd International Conference on Chemistry & Chemical Education (ICCCE)*. https://journal.ar-raniry.ac.id/index.php/ICCCE/article/view/5372

Darling-Hammond, L., Schachner, A., & Edgerton, A. K. (with Badrinarayan, A., Cardichon, J., Cookson, P. W., Jr., Griffith, M., Klevan, S., Maier, A., Martinez, M., Melnick, H., Truong, N., & Wojcikiewicz, S.). (2020). *Restarting and reinventing school: Learning in the time of COVID and beyond*. Learning Policy Institute. https://learningpolicyinstitute.org/product/restarting-reinventing-school-covid

Dastane, O., Turner, J., & Nankervis, A. (2024). The trajectory of artificial intelligence for competency-based personalised learning: Past, present and future. *The International Journal of Information and Learning Technology*, *41*(5), 473–489. DOI: 10.1108/IJILT-07-2024-0162

Daugherty, P. R., & Wilson, H. J. (2018). *Human + machine: Reimagining work in the age of AI*. Harvard Business Review Press.

Davis, B., & Sumara, D. (2006). *Complexity and education: Inquiries into learning, teaching, and research*. Lawrence Erlbaum Associates.

Davis, F. D. (1989). Perceived usefulness, perceived ease of use, and user acceptance of information technology. *Management Information Systems Quarterly*, *13*(3), 319–340. DOI: 10.2307/249008

De Angelis, R., & Ianulardo, G. (2025). Walking the talk on education for sustainable development: The value of circular economy education in the age of complexity. *Circular Economy and Sustainability*, *5*(4), 3305–3316. DOI: 10.1007/s43615-025-00577-5

Deák, C., & Kumar, B. (2024). A systematic review of STEAM education's role in nurturing digital competencies for sustainable innovations. *Education Sciences*, *14*(3), 226. DOI: 10.3390/educsci14030226

Decorte, B., & Vlieghe, J. (2024). Towards a pedagogical conception of imagination in STEAM education. *Ethics and Education*, *19*(2), 218–232. DOI: 10.1080/17449642.2024.2361560

Delgado, I., Sancristobal, E., Martin, S., & Robles-Gómez, A. (2023). Exploring IoT vulnerabilities in a comprehensive remote cybersecurity laboratory. *Sensors (Basel)*, *23*(22), 9279. DOI: 10.3390/s23229279 PMID: 38005664

Delgado-Quintero, D. J., Sepúlveda-López, J. J., Pineda Romero, M. M., & Santos-Mendez, D. J. (2025). Mapping the ethical landscape in AI: A bibliometric analysis with educational insights. *INTELETICA*, *2*(3), 1–16. DOI: 10.4114/INTELETICA.vol2iss3pp1-16

Demir, K., & Suri, N. (2017). SeReCP: A secure and reliable communication platform for the smart grid. In *2017 IEEE 22nd Pacific Rim International Symposium on Dependable Computing (PRDC)* (pp. 175–184). IEEE. DOI: 10.1109/PRDC.2017.31

Devlin, J., Chang, M.-W., Lee, K., & Toutanova, K. (2019). BERT: Pre-training of deep bidirectional transformers for language understanding. In *Proceedings of the 2019 Conference of the North American Chapter of the Association for Computational Linguistics: Human Language Technologies* (pp. 4171–4186). Association for Computational Linguistics. DOI: 10.18653/v1/N19-1423

Dintén, R., López Martínez, P., & Zorrilla, M. (2021). Arquitectura de referencia para el diseño y desarrollo de aplicaciones para la Industria 4.0. *Revista Iberoamericana de Automática e Informática Industrial, 18*(3), 300–311. DOI: 10.4995/riai.2021.14532

Domínguez Osuna, P. M., Olivares Carmona, K. M., Rodríguez Elías, O. M., & Gutiérrez Franco, E. (2019). Retos de ingeniería: Enfoque educativo STEM+A en la revolución industrial 4.0. *Innovación Educativa (México, D.F.), 19*(80), 15–32.

Đorđević, B., Zbiljić, S. M., & Radosavljević, M. (2025). Impact of the digital skills on employability: Cross-sectional analysis. *Economies (Basel), 13*(7), 196. Advance online publication. DOI: 10.3390/economies13070196

Doss, T. P., Poursharif, G., Price, H., & Buck, L. (2024). Education for Industry 5.0 and ESD: Co-creation of engineering design challenges with industry. In *2024 IEEE Global Engineering Education Conference (EDUCON)* (pp. 1–6). IEEE. DOI: 10.1109/EDUCON60312.2024.10578850

Dost, G. (2024). Students' perspectives on the "STEM belonging" concept at A-level, undergraduate, and postgraduate levels: An examination of gender and ethnicity in student descriptions. *International Journal of STEM Education, 11*(1), 12. DOI: 10.1186/s40594-024-00472-9

Drnas de Clément, Z. (2022). Inteligencia artificial en el derecho internacional, Naciones Unidas y Unión Europea. *Revista Estudios Jurídicos. Segunda Época, 22*(22). Advance online publication. DOI: 10.17561/rej.n22.7524

Durlak, J. A., Weissberg, R. P., Dymnicki, A. B., Taylor, R. D., & Schellinger, K. B. (2011). The impact of enhancing students' social and emotional learning: A meta-analysis of school-based universal interventions. *Child Development, 82*(1), 405–432. DOI: 10.1111/j.1467-8624.2010.01564.x PMID: 21291449

Dym, C. L., Agogino, A. M., Eris, O., Frey, D. D., & Leifer, L. J. (2005). Engineering design thinking, teaching, and learning. *Journal of Engineering Education, 94*(1), 103–120. DOI: 10.1002/j.2168-9830.2005.tb00832.x

Elaby, M., Mohamed, H., Wafa, M., & Sweilam, S. (2023). Impact of full-scale models on students' creativity in basic design course. *Creativity Studies*, *16*(2), 411–432. DOI: 10.3846/cs.2023.15718

El-Yaagoubi, A. B., Chung, M. K., & Ombao, H. (2023). Topological data analysis for multivariate time series data. *Entropy (Basel, Switzerland)*, *25*(11), 1509. DOI: 10.3390/e25111509

Engelmann, K., & Bannert, M. (2021). Analyzing temporal data for understanding the learning process induced by metacognitive prompts. *Learning and Instruction*, *72*, 101205. DOI: 10.1016/j.learninstruc.2019.05.002

Engelman, S., Magerko, B., McKlin, T., Miller, M., Edwards, D., & Freeman, J. (2017). Creativity in authentic STEAM education with EarSketch. In *Proceedings of the 2017 ACM SIGCSE Technical Symposium on Computer Science Education* (pp. 183–188). Association for Computing Machinery. DOI: 10.1145/3017680.3017763

Ervik, A. (2023). Generative AI and the collective imaginary: The technology-guided social imagination in AI-imagenesis.

European Commission, Directorate-General for Research and Innovation. (2021). Industry 5.0, a transformative vision for Europe: Governing systemic transformations towards a sustainable industry. Publications Office of the European Union. https://data.europa.eu/doi/10.2777/17322

European Commission. (2022). *Communication from the Commission to the European Parliament, the Council, the European Economic and Social Committee and the Committee of the Regions on a European strategy for universities* (COM(2022) 16 final). https://eur-lex.europa.eu/legal-content/EN/TXT/?uri=CELEX:52022DC0016

Euskadi, S. T. E. A. M. (2023). *Funghi Thinking: Programa de economía circular y STEAM*. Departamento de Educación del Gobierno Vasco.

Facler, M. (2023). The personal learner profile, as the key component for shaping a personalized learning journey, in a learning management system in the digital era. In *INTED2023 Proceedings* (pp. 1336-1344). IATED. DOI: 10.21125/inted.2023.0387

Falchuk, B., Loeb, S., & Neff, R. (2018). The social metaverse: Battle for privacy. *IEEE Technology and Society Magazine*, *37*(2), 52–61. DOI: 10.1109/MTS.2018.2826060

Fan, X., Chao, D., Zhang, Z., Wang, D., Li, X., & Tian, F. (2024). Web 3.0 metaverse turn in education. *IEEE Transactions on Learning Technologies*, *17*, 819–833. DOI: 10.1109/TLT.2024.3385505

Fan, Y., Matcha, W., Uzir, N. A., Wang, Q., & Gašević, D. (2021). Learning analytics to reveal links between learning design and self-regulated learning. *International Journal of Artificial Intelligence in Education, 31*(4), 980–1021. DOI: 10.1007/s40593-021-00249-z

Felder, R. M., & Brent, R. (2016). *Teaching and learning STEM: A practical guide*. Jossey-Bass.

Fernández-Cárdenas, J. M., & Santillán-Rosas, I. M. (2025). Learning critical thinking through dialogic STEAM educational activities: A case of high school students in northeastern Mexico during pandemic times. *SAGE Open, 15*(4), 21582440251388756. Advance online publication. DOI: 10.1177/21582440251388756

Ferrada Ferrada, C., & Márquez Triviño, C. (2025). Explorando el impacto de las tecnologías emergentes en la educación STE(A)M: Un análisis bibliométrico de las publicaciones en la base de datos Scopus. *Ducere: Revista de Investigación Educativa, 4*(1), e202503. DOI: 10.61303/2735668X.v4i1.73

Ferrara, E. (2024). Fairness and bias in artificial intelligence: A brief survey of sources, impacts, and mitigation strategies. *Sci, 6*(1), 3. Advance online publication. DOI: 10.3390/sci6010003

Fiallo Rodríguez, J. (2001). *La interdisciplinariedad en la escuela: Un reto para la calidad de la educación*. Pueblo y Educación.

Fiok, K., Farahani, F. V., Karwowski, W., & Ahram, T. (2022). Explainable artificial intelligence for education and training. *The Journal of Defense Modeling and Simulation: Applications, Methodology. Technology, 19*(2), 133–144. DOI: 10.1177/15485129211028651

Flores Marín, J. A., & González Castillo, S. (2024). Competencias STEM para la Industria 4.0: Una revisión sistemática. *Congreso Internacional de Investigación Academia Journals, 638*, 1–10.

Flores Ramírez, A., Bradley, R., Andrade Flores, L., Guerrero Carrillo, A., González-Escamilla, A., Ponce, P., Ramírez-Cedillo, E., & Anthony, B. W. (2026). Immersive cognitive factory twin: Optimizing industry 5.0 with an integrated VR, ML, and LLM framework. In *Production and Manufacturing Research* (Vol. 14, Issue 1). DOI: 10.1080/21693277.2026.2664909

Florida, R. (2002). *The rise of the creative class: And how it's transforming work, leisure, community and everyday life*. Basic Books.

Floridi, L., & Cowls, J. (2019). A unified framework of five principles for AI in society. *Harvard Data Science Review*, *1*(1). Advance online publication. DOI: 10.1162/99608f92.8cd550d1

Floridi, L., Cowls, J., Beltrametti, M., Chatila, R., Chazerand, P., Dignum, V., Luetge, C., Madelin, R., Pagallo, U., Rossi, F., Schafer, B., Valcke, P., & Vayena, E. (2018). AI4People—An ethical framework for a good AI society: Opportunities, risks, principles, and recommendations. *Minds and Machines*, *28*(4), 689–707. DOI: 10.1007/s11023-018-9482-5 PMID: 30930541

Fogaça, D. R., Grijalvo, M., & Sacomano Neto, M. (2025). What are Industry 4.0 and Industry 5.0 all about? An integrative institutional model for the new industrial paradigms. *Administrative Sciences*, *15*(4), 118. Advance online publication. DOI: 10.3390/admsci15040118

Forcael, E., Garcés, G., & Orozco, F. (2022). Relationship Between Professional Competencies Required by Engineering Students According to ABET and CDIO and Teaching–Learning Techniques. *IEEE Transactions on Education*, *65*(1), 46–55. DOI: 10.1109/TE.2021.3086766

Ford, S., & Despeisse, M. (2016). Additive manufacturing and sustainability: An exploratory study of the advantages and challenges. *Journal of Cleaner Production*, *137*, 1573–1587. DOI: 10.1016/j.jclepro.2016.04.150

Fraga do Nascimento, A. (2024). How can we rethink the digital space in online programs with the support of an Empathic AI to promote inclusion, designing enriched learning experiences that foster deeper connections between students and teachers?.

Freeman, S., Eddy, S. L., McDonough, M., Smith, M. K., Okoroafor, N., Jordt, H., & Wenderoth, M. P. (2014). Active learning increases student performance in science, engineering, and mathematics. *Proceedings of the National Academy of Sciences of the United States of America*, *111*(23), 8410–8415. DOI: 10.1073/pnas.1319030111 PMID: 24821756

Fullan, M. (2020). *Liderar en una cultura de cambio* (J. G. Ross, Trans.). Ediciones Morata. https://edmorata.es/producto/liderar-en-una-cultura-de-cambio/

Fundación Chile. (2021). *Aprendizaje basado en proyectos: Un enfoque pedagógico para potenciar aprendizajes*. Educarchile. https://www.educarchile.cl/sites/default/files/2021-09/ABP-un-enfoque-pedagogico-para-potenciar-aprendizajes.pdf

Gallegos-Rejas, V. M., Thomas, E. E., Kelly, J. T., & Smith, A. C. (2023). A multi-stakeholder approach is needed to reduce the digital divide and encourage equitable access to telehealth. *Journal of Telemedicine and Telecare, 29*(1), 73–78. DOI: 10.1177/1357633X221107995

Gandini, F. (2018). Metacognición y aprendizaje. In A. M. Palacios, M. A. Pedragosa, & M. Querejeta (Coords.), *Encuentro en la encrucijada: Psicología, cultura y educación*. EDULP. https://www.memoria.fahce.unlp.edu.ar/libros/pm.4860/pm.4860.pdf

Garavito-Hernández, Y., Villamizar-Mancilla, A. F., & Castañeda-Villamizar, L. P. (2024). Importancia de las habilidades blandas en el contexto laboral: Una revisión de la literatura académica. *Innova Research Journal, 9*(3), 1–24. DOI: 10.33890/innova.v9.n3.2024.2531

García-Aranda, C., Molina-García, A., & Balsera, M. del C. M., Martínez-Cuevas, S., Hurtado, E. R., Rodríguez, J. P., Rodríguez-Chueca, J., Fungairiño, Y. T., Hernández, M. R., Miquel, M. G., Moreno, F. I. D., Gómez, E. J. G., García-Soto, M. del M. de la F., Giannakis, S., González, I. del C., Núñez, M. M., Contreras, F. B., & García, P. C. I. (2020). Creativity and innovation skills in university STEM education: The CHET Project approach. In *Sixth International Conference on Higher Education Advances* (pp. 679–687). Universitat Politècnica de València. DOI: 10.4995/HEAd20.2020.11127

García-Blancas, J., Domínguez-Ramírez, O. A., Rodríguez-Torres, E. E., Ramirez-Zamora, J. D., & Rodriguez-Hernandez, E. (2025). A technological proposal for a robot brain computer interface for neurorehabilitation purposes. *The European Physical Journal. Special Topics, 234*(1), 195–223. DOI: 10.1140/epjs/s11734-024-01463-1

García-Fuentes, O., Raposo-Rivas, M., & Martínez-Figueira, M. E. (2023). El enfoque educativo STEAM: Una revisión de la literatura. *Revista Complutense de Educación, 34*(1), 191–202. DOI: 10.5209/rced.77261

Garg, N., Kaur, A., Ahmad, F., & Dutta, R. (2025). Augmenting Education: The Transformative Power of AR, AI, and Emerging Technologies. *Human Behavior and Emerging Technologies, 2025*(1), 5681184. DOI: 10.1155/hbe2/5681184

Gašević, D., Jovanović, J., Pardo, A., & Dawson, S. (2017). Detecting learning strategies with analytics: Links with self-reported measures and academic performance. *Journal of Learning Analytics, 4*(2), 113–128. DOI: 10.18608/jla.2017.42.10

Gavari-Starkie, E., Espinosa-Gutiérrez, P.-T., & Lucini-Baquero, C. (2022). Sustainability through STEM and STEAM Education Creating Links with the Land for the Improvement of the Rural World. *Land (Basel), 11*(10), 1869. DOI: 10.3390/land11101869

Gavari-Starkie, E., Espinosa-Gutiérrez, P.-T., Lucini-Baquero, C., & Pastrana-Huguet, J. (2024). Importance of STEM and STEAM Education for Improvement of the Land in the RURAL Environment: Examples in Latin America. *Land (Basel), 13*(3), 274. DOI: 10.3390/land13030274

Gibson, I., Rosen, D., & Stucker, B. (2021). *Additive manufacturing technologies* (3rd ed.). Springer., DOI: 10.1007/978-3-030-56127-7

Gil Iranzo, R., Gutiérrez-Ujaque, D., & Teixidó Cairol, M. (2024). De la ansiedad al empoderamiento: Impacto del uso de la inteligencia artificial en la percepción de los estudiantes en educación superior. *REDU. Revista de Docencia Universitaria, 22*(2), 85–104. DOI: 10.4995/redu.2024.22009

Gilhooly, K. J., Fioratou, E., Anthony, S. H., & Wynn, V. (2007). Divergent thinking: Strategies and executive involvement in generating novel uses for familiar objects. *British Journal of Psychology, 98*(4), 611–625. DOI: 10.1111/j.2044-8295.2007.tb00467.x PMID: 17535464

Gindin, I. L., Cingolani, G., & Rodríguez-Amat, J. R. (2021). Autoridades interpretativas: Una perspectiva teórica sobre datificación y producción de sentido. *Palabra Clave (La Plata), 24*(3), e2436. Advance online publication. DOI: 10.5294/pacla.2021.24.3.6

Goedhart, N. S., Verdonk, P., & Dedding, C. (2022). "Never good enough." A situated understanding of the impact of digitalization on citizens living in a low socioeconomic position. *Policy and Internet, 14*(4), 824–844. DOI: 10.1002/poi3.315

Gonzalez-Islas, J.-C., Dominguez-Ramirez, O. A., Lopez-Ortega, O., & Pena Ramirez, J. (2024). Crouch gait recognition in the anatomical space using synthetic gait data. *Applied Sciences (Basel, Switzerland), 14*(22), 10574. Advance online publication. DOI: 10.3390/app142210574

Goodfellow, I., Bengio, Y., & Courville, A. (2016). *Deep learning*. MIT Press.

Gore, S. N., Chidhakwa, J., Mlilo, M., Magede, M., & Mpofu, V. (2023). Towards an Upper Middle-Class Economy: An Analysis of Zimbabwe's STEAM Education and Education 5.0 Frameworks. *Journal of Emerging Trends in Educational Research and Policy Studies, 14*(3), 122–130.

Gori, K. D., Zalawadia, K., & Bhaidasna, H. (2025). Explainable AI for students performance prediction system. In *2025 IEEE Pune Section International Conference (PuneCon)* (pp. 1–6). IEEE. DOI: DOI: 10.1109/PuneCon67554.2025.11379137

Graetz, G., & Michaels, G. (2018). Robots at work. *The Review of Economics and Statistics, 100*(5), 753–768. DOI: 10.1162/rest_a_00754

Gras, A., & Alí, L. (2023). *Educación STEM y su aplicación*. Editorial Académica.

Groen, A. J., & Walsh, S. T. (2013). Introduction to the Field of Emerging Technology Management. *Creativity and Innovation Management, 22*(1), 1–5. DOI: 10.1111/caim.12019

Grover, S., & Pea, R. (2013). Computational thinking in K–12: A review of the state of the field. *Educational Researcher, 42*(1), 38–43. DOI: 10.3102/0013189X12463051

Grybauskas, A., Stefanini, A., & Ghobakhloo, M. (2022). Social sustainability in the age of digitalization: A systematic literature review on the social implications of Industry 4.0. *Technology in Society, 70*, 101997. Advance online publication. DOI: 10.1016/j.techsoc.2022.101997

Guan, X., Feng, X., & Islam, A. Y. M. (2023). The dilemma and countermeasures of educational data ethics in the age of intelligence. *Humanities & Social Sciences Communications, 10*(1), 138. DOI: 10.1057/s41599-023-01633-x

Gubbi, J., Buyya, R., Marusic, S., & Palaniswami, M. (2013). Internet of Things: A vision, architectural elements, and future directions. *Future Generation Computer Systems, 29*(7), 1645–1660. DOI: 10.1016/j.future.2013.01.010

Gueye, B., & Exposito, E. (2020). Universidad 4.0: El paradigma de la industria 4.0 aplicado a la educación. In *Proceedings of CONTE 2020* (pp. 1–6). ACM. https://doi.org/DOI: 10.1145/3434780.3436620

Gutiérrez Martínez, F., & Mateos Sanz, M. M. (2006). El desarrollo de los conocimientos y habilidades metacognitivas. In F. Gutiérrez Martínez, J. A. García Madruga, & N. Carriedo López (Coords.), *Psicología evolutiva II: Desarrollo cognitivo y lingüístico* (Vol. 2, pp. 93–128). Universidad Nacional de Educación a Distancia.

Gu, X., Tong, D., Shi, P., Zou, Y., Yuan, H., Chen, C., & Zhao, G. (2023). Incorporating STEAM activities into creativity training in higher education. *Thinking Skills and Creativity, 50*, 101395. DOI: 10.1016/j.tsc.2023.101395

Guyotte, K., Sochacka, N., Costantino, T., Kellam, N., & Walther, J. (2015). Collaborative Creativity in STEAM: Narratives of Art Education Students' Experiences in Transdisciplinary Spaces. *International Journal of Education & the Arts*, *16*(15), 1–38. DOI: 10.59236/ijea16n15

Guzmán-Brand, V. A., & Gélvez-García, L. E. (2024). La ética y la responsabilidad en la implementación de la inteligencia artificial: Revisión sistemática. *Revista Ingeniería. Matemáticas y Ciencias de la Información*, *11*(22), 107–118. DOI: 10.21017/rimci.1081

Haddadin, S., De Luca, A., & Albu-Schäffer, A. (2017). Robot collisions: A survey on detection, isolation, and identification. *IEEE Transactions on Robotics*, *33*(6), 1292–1312. DOI: 10.1109/TRO.2017.2723903

Hake, R. R. (1998). Interactive-engagement versus traditional methods: A six-thousand-student survey of mechanics test data. *American Journal of Physics*, *66*(1), 64–74. DOI: 10.1119/1.18809

Haoran, Z. (2025). Bridging Digital Divide: How the Digital Economy Affects Health Care in Developed and Developing Nations. *World Medical & Health Policy*, *17*(4), 767–774. DOI: 10.1002/wmh3.70040

Harden, R. M., Grant, J., Buckley, G., & Hart, I. R. (1999). BEME Guide No. 1: Best evidence medical education. *Medical Teacher*, *21*(6), 553–562. DOI: 10.1080/01421599978960 PMID: 21281174

Hasani, N., Hosseini, A., Ashjazadeh, Y., Diederichs, V., Ghotb, S., Riggio, M., Hansen, E., & Nasir, V. (2025). Outlook on human-centred design in industry 5.0: Towards mass customisation, personalisation, co-creation, and co-production. *International Journal of Sustainable Engineering*, *18*(1), 2486343. DOI: 10.1080/19397038.2025.2486343

Hasan, M. A., Noor, N. F. M., Rahman, S. S. B. A., & Rahman, M. M. (2020). The transition from intelligent to affective tutoring system: A review and open issues. *IEEE Access : Practical Innovations, Open Solutions*, *8*, 204612–204638. DOI: 10.1109/ACCESS.2020.3036990

Hazrat, M. A., Hassan, N. M. S., Chowdhury, A. A., Rasul, M. G., & Taylor, B. A. (2023). Developing a skilled workforce for future industry demand: The potential of digital twin-based teaching and learning practices in engineering education. *Sustainability (Basel)*, *15*(23), 16433. DOI: 10.3390/su152316433

He, J., Lo, D. C.-T., Xie, Y., & Lartigue, J. (2016). *Integrating Internet of Things (IoT) into STEM undergraduate education: Case study of a modern technology infused courseware for embedded system course*. In 2016 IEEE Frontiers in Education Conference (FIE) (pp. 1–9). IEEE. DOI: 10.1109/FIE.2016.7757458

Helm-Stevens, R., Hanshaw, G. O., & Kim, J. (2019). The Hanshaw Helm-Stevens rapid prototype instructional design model: Examining the dimensions of structure and dialogue within the framework of higher education. *American Journal of Economics and Business Administration*, *11*(1), 35–46. DOI: 10.3844/ajebasp.2019.35.46

Henriksen, D. (2017). Creating STEAM with design thinking: Beyond STEM and arts integration. *The STEAM Journal*, *3*(1), 11. Advance online publication. DOI: 10.5642/steam.20170301.11

Hernández Arteaga, R., Téllez Vargas, L. N., Ramírez Zamora, J. D., & Domínguez Ramírez, O. A. (2025). Diseño e implementación de una estación de monitoreo ambiental basada en ESP32 para laboratorios académicos. Ibero Ciencias. *Revista Científica y Académica*, *4*(4), 418–446. DOI: 10.63371/ic.v4.n4.a389

Hernández Pérez, J., Gutiérrez Moreno, E., Ordaz Oliver, J. P., & Ordaz Oliver, M. O. (2024). LQR-based control with gravity compensation for a wind turbine pendulum system. *International Journal of Combinatorial Optimization Problems and Informatics*, *15*(5), 161–180. DOI: 10.61467/2007.1558.2024.v15i5.428

Hernández-de-Menéndez, M., Escobar Díaz, C. A., & Morales-Menéndez, R. (2020). Engineering education for smart 4.0 technology: A review. *International Journal on Interactive Design and Manufacturing*, *14*(3), 789–803. DOI: 10.1007/s12008-020-00672-x

Herranz Sánchez, E., & Colomo-Palacios, R. (2012). La gamificación como agente de cambio en la ingeniería del software. *Revista de Procesos y Métricas*, *9*(2), 30–56.

Hestenes, D., Wells, M., & Swackhamer, G. (1992). Force Concept Inventory. *The Physics Teacher*, *30*(3), 141–158. DOI: 10.1119/1.2343497

Hirzel, T. (2023). AI-empowered Learning Models in Economy 5.0: Fostering Meaning Creation Beyond Literacy.

Hlosta, M., Zdrahal, Z., & Zendulka, J. (2017). Ouroboros: Early identification of at-risk students without models based on legacy data. In *Proceedings of the 7th International Learning Analytics and Knowledge Conference* (pp. 6–15). Association for Computing Machinery. DOI: 10.1145/3027385.3027449

Holbrook, J., Rannikmäe, M., & Soobard, R. (2020). STEAM education—A transdisciplinary teaching and learning approach. In Akpan, B., & Kennedy, T. J. (Eds.), *Science education in theory and practice* (pp. 465–477). Springer., DOI: 10.1007/978-3-030-43620-9_31

Holcombe, E. M., Kezar, A. J., Elrod, S., & Ramaley, J. A. (Eds.). (2023). *Shared leadership in higher education: A framework and models for responding to a changing world.* Routledge., DOI: 10.4324/9781003446965

Hollnagel, E. (2014). *Safety-I and Safety-II: The past and future of safety management.* CRC Press., DOI: 10.1201/9781315607511

Holmes, W., Porayska-Pomsta, K., Holstein, K., Sutherland, E., Baker, T., Buckingham Shum, S., Santos, O. C., Rodrigo, M. T., Cukurova, M., Bittencourt, I. I., & Koedinger, K. R. (2022). Ethics of AI in education: Towards a community-wide framework. *International Journal of Artificial Intelligence in Education, 32*(3), 504–526. DOI: 10.1007/s40593-021-00239-1

Holon, I. Q. (2022). *10 charts for a changing education market.* https://www.holoniq.com/notes/10-charts-for-a-changing-education-market

Huang, B., Jong, M. S.-Y., Tsai, C.-C., & Shang, J. (2025). Unlocking students' creative potential in designing technological-enriched design solutions. *Journal of Research on Technology in Education, 57*(5), 1044–1060. DOI: 10.1080/15391523.2024.2342915

Huang, Z., Fu, X., & Zhao, J. (2025). Research on AIGC-Integrated Design Education for Sustainable Teaching: An Empirical Analysis Based on the TAM and TPACK Models. *Sustainability (Basel), 17*(12), 5497. DOI: 10.3390/su17125497

Hu, J., Huang, Z., Li, J., Xu, L., & Zou, Y. (2024). Real-time classroom behavior analysis for enhanced engineering education: An AI-assisted approach. *International Journal of Computational Intelligence Systems, 17*(1), 167. DOI: 10.1007/s44196-024-00572-y

Humayed, A., Lin, J., Li, F., & Luo, B. (2017). Cyber-physical systems security—A survey. *IEEE Internet of Things Journal, 4*(6), 1802–1831. DOI: 10.1109/JIOT.2017.2703172

Hwang, G.-J., & Chien, S.-Y. (2022). Definition, roles, and potential research issues of the metaverse in education: An artificial intelligence perspective. *Computers and Education: Artificial Intelligence, 3*, 100082. DOI: 10.1016/j.caeai.2022.100082

Ifenthaler, D., & Yau, J. Y.-K. (2020). Utilising learning analytics to support study success in higher education: A systematic review. *Educational Technology Research and Development, 68*(4), 1961–1990. DOI: 10.1007/s11423-020-09788-z

International Organization for Standardization. (2016). ISO/TS 15066:2016 robots and robotic devices—Collaborative robots. https://www.iso.org/standard/62996.html

International Organization for Standardization. (2019). ISO 9241-210:2019 ergonomics of human-system interaction—Part 210: Human-centred design for interactive systems. https://www.iso.org/standard/77520.html

International Organization for Standardization. (2025). ISO 10218-1:2025 robotics—Safety requirements—Part 1: Industrial robots. https://www.iso.org/standard/73933.html

International Organization for Standardization. (2025). ISO 10218-2:2025 robotics—Safety requirements—Part 2: Industrial robot applications and robot cells. https://www.iso.org/standard/73934.html

Isomöttönen, V., Daniels, M., Cajander, Å., Pears, A., & McDermott, R. (2019). Searching for global employability: Can students capitalize on enabling learning environments? *ACM Transactions on Computing Education*, *19*(2), 11. Advance online publication. DOI: 10.1145/3277568

Ivanov, D., & Dolgui, A. (2020). Viability of intertwined supply networks: Extending the supply chain resilience angles towards survivability. A position paper motivated by COVID-19 outbreak. *International Journal of Production Research*, *58*(10), 2904–2915. DOI: 10.1080/00207543.2020.1750727

Izquierdo Izquierdo, M., Gómez Calero, C., & García Lázaro, D. (2022). Design thinking, una metodología para fomentar el aprendizaje significativo. *Revista Ingeniería Industrial*, *21*, 1–20. DOI: 10.22320/S07179103/2022.01

Jamro, M. Y., & Jamro, F. A. (2023). AI matters: Chatbot integration in holistic STEM Education.

Jantassova, D., Churchill, D., Shebalina, O., & Akhmetova, D. (2022). Capacity building for engineering training and technology via STEAM education. *Education Sciences*, *12*(11), 737. DOI: 10.3390/educsci12110737

Järvelä, S., & Hadwin, A. (2024). Triggers for self-regulated learning: A conceptual framework for advancing multimodal research about SRL. *Learning and Individual Differences*, *115*, 102526. DOI: 10.1016/j.lindif.2024.102526

Jatnkoon, T., Jantakun, K., Jantakun, T., & Pasmala, R. (2025). STEAM Microlearning Model based on Massive Open Online Courses with Augmented Reality Technology to enhance Creativity and Innovation. *Higher Education Studies*, *15*(2), 321. DOI: 10.5539/hes.v15n2p321

Ji, D., & She, H. (2026). Digital divide revisited during and beyond COVID-19. *Media Culture & Society*, *48*(1), 191–207. DOI: 10.1177/01634437251363779

Jing, Y., Zhao, L., Zhu, K., Wang, H., Wang, C., & Xia, Q. (2023). Research landscape of adaptive learning in education: A bibliometric study on research publications from 2000 to 2022. *Sustainability (Basel)*, *15*(4), 3115. Advance online publication. DOI: 10.3390/su15043115

Ji, Z., Lee, N., Frieske, R., Yu, T., Su, D., Xu, Y., Ishii, E., Bang, Y. J., Madotto, A., & Fung, P. (2023). Survey of hallucination in natural language generation. *ACM Computing Surveys*, *55*(12), 1–38. DOI: 10.1145/3571730

Jobin, A., Ienca, M., & Vayena, E. (2019). The global landscape of AI ethics guidelines. *Nature Machine Intelligence*, *1*(9), 389–399. DOI: 10.1038/s42256-019-0088-2

Johnson, D. W., Johnson, R. T., & Johnson Holubec, E. (1999). *El aprendizaje cooperativo en el aula*. Paidós.

Johnson-Green, E., Lee, C., & Flannery, M. (2020). A Musical Perspective on STEM: Evaluating the EcoSonic Playground Project from a Co-Equal STEAM Integration Standpoint. *International Journal of Education & the Arts*, *21*(14). https://doi.org/doi.org/10.26209/ijea21n14

Jones, A., & Castellano, G. (2018). Adaptive robotic tutors that support self-regulated learning: A longer-term investigation with primary school children. *International Journal of Social Robotics*, *10*(3), 357–370. DOI: 10.1007/s12369-017-0458-z

Jora, M. B., & Basnet, H. B. (2025). ICT Integration in the 21st Century's Classroom Teaching and Learning. *Rupantaran: A Multidisciplinary Journal, 9*, 9–20. (Education). DOI: 10.3126/rupantaran.v9i01.89333

Juandi, D.. (2024). Computational thinking in mathematics instruction integrated with STEAM education. *Journal of Physics: Conference Series*.

Juárez Chavero, M. I., Rodríguez Hernández, E., Domínguez-Ramírez, O. A., Villafuerte Segura, R., & Jarillo Silva, A. (2026). Prueba piloto de una plataforma exergaming bimanual para tareas de neurorehabilitación. Pädi Boletín Científico de Ciencias Básicas e Ingenierías del ICBI, 14(Especial), 46–58. https://doi.org/DOI: 10.29057/icbi.v14iEspecial.15496

Julian, D., & Smith, R. (2019). Developing an intelligent tutoring system for robotic-assisted surgery instruction. *The International Journal of Medical Robotics + Computer Assisted Surgery : MRCAS*, *15*(6), e2037. DOI: 10.1002/rcs.2037 PMID: 31509636

Julio, Y. R., Viloria-Núñez, C., Galindo-Jaramillo, J.-F., Mangones, A. P., & Correa, C. C. R. (2024). Innovation Strategies for Training Management with STEAM, IoT, and AI through Design Thinking. *2024 IEEE Eighth Ecuador Technical Chapters Meeting (ETCM)*, 1–6. DOI: 10.1109/ETCM63562.2024.10746011

Juškevičienė, A., Dagienė, V., & Dolgopolovas, V. (2021). Integrated activities in STEM environment: Methodology and implementation practice. *Computer Applications in Engineering Education*, *29*(1), 209–228. DOI: 10.1002/cae.22324

Kaihara, T., Nishino, N., Ueda, K., Tseng, M., Váncza, J., Schönsleben, P., Teti, R., & Takenaka, T. (2018). Value creation in production: Reconsideration from interdisciplinary approaches. *CIRP Annals*, *67*(2), 791–813. DOI: 10.1016/j.cirp.2018.05.002

Kasneci, E., Sessler, K., Küchemann, S., Bannert, M., Dementieva, D., Fischer, F., Gasser, U., Groh, G., Günnemann, S., Hüllermeier, E., Krusche, S., Kutyniok, G., Michaeli, T., Nerdel, C., Pfeffer, J., Poquet, O., Sailer, M., Schmidt, A., Seidel, T., & Kasneci, G. (2023). ChatGPT for good? On opportunities and challenges of large language models for education. *Learning and Individual Differences*, *103*, 102274. DOI: 10.1016/j.lindif.2023.102274

Kerimbayev, N., Adamova, K., Jotsov, V., Shadiev, R., Umirzakova, Z., & Nurymova, A. (2024). Organization of feedback in the intelligent learning systems. In *2024 IEEE 12th International Conference on Intelligent Systems (IS)* (pp. 1–7). IEEE. DOI: 10.1109/IS61756.2024.10705178

Kizilcec, R. F., Pérez-Sanagustín, M., & Maldonado, J. J. (2017). Self-regulated learning strategies predict learner behavior and goal attainment in Massive Open Online Courses. *Computers & Education*, *104*, 18–33. DOI: 10.1016/j.compedu.2016.10.001

Klein, J. T. (2021). *Beyond interdisciplinarity: Boundary work, communication, and collaboration*. Oxford University Press., DOI: 10.1093/oso/9780197571149.001.0001

Korostelina, K. V., & Barrett, J. (2023). Bridging the digital divide for Native American tribes: Roadblocks to broadband and community resilience. *Policy and Internet*, *15*(3), 306–326. DOI: 10.1002/poi3.339

Kotis, K., Angoura, E., & Lyngri, E.-I. (2025). Emerging Technologies in Smart Libraries for Visually Impaired People: Challenges and Design Considerations. *Journal on Computing and Cultural Heritage*, *18*(3), 1–37. DOI: 10.1145/3727965

Kotsis, K. T. (2024). ChatGPT in teaching physics hands-on experiments in primary school. *European Journal of Education Studies*, *11*(10). Advance online publication. DOI: 10.46827/ejes.v11i10.5549

Kristanto, Y. D.. (2023). Integrating STEAM education and computational thinking. *Journal of Physics: Conference Series.*

Kritzinger, W., Karner, M., Traar, G., Henjes, J., & Sihn, W. (2018). Digital twin in manufacturing: A categorical literature review and classification. *IFAC-PapersOnLine*, *51*(11), 1016–1022. DOI: 10.1016/j.ifacol.2018.08.474

Kuh, G. D., Kinzie, J. L., Buckley, J. A., Bridges, B. K., & Hayek, J. C. (2006). *What matters to student success: A review of the literature.* National Postsecondary Education Cooperative.

Kumar, B., & Deák, C. (2024). Evolving minds: A literature-driven and empirical exploration of STEAM skill development and learning approaches. *Journal of Innovation Management*, *11*(4), 71–96. Advance online publication. DOI: 10.24840/2183-0606_011.004_0004

Kusiak, A. (2018). Smart manufacturing. *International Journal of Production Research*, *56*(1–2), 508–517. DOI: 10.1080/00207543.2017.1351644

Kuzilek, J., Hlosta, M., & Zdrahal, Z. (2017). Open University Learning Analytics dataset. *Scientific Data*, *4*(1), 170171. DOI: 10.1038/sdata.2017.171 PMID: 29182599

Lai, X., Ye, J., & Wong, G. K. W. (2023). Effectiveness of collaboration in developing computational thinking skills: A systematic review of social cognitive factors. *Journal of Computer Assisted Learning*, *39*(5), 1418–1435. DOI: 10.1111/jcal.12845

Lam-Byrne, A. G. (2023). El aprendizaje STEAM: Una práctica inclusiva. *Revista Científica Episteme Y Tekne, 2*(1), e466. DOI: 10.51252/rceyt.v2i1.466

Lampou, R. (2024). The role of STEAM education in curriculum 5.0. PENSAR MÁS ALLÁ EN EDUCACIÓN THINKING OUTSIDE THE BOX IN EDUCATION, 57.

Lancheros-Cuesta, D. J., Carrillo-Ramos, Á., & Pavlich-Mariscal, J. A. (2014). Content adaptation for students with learning difficulties: Design and case study. *International Journal of Web Information Systems*, *10*(2), 106–130. DOI: 10.1108/IJWIS-12-2013-0040

Lara-Prieto, V., Prieto-Hinojosa, A. I., Galindo-Cota, E., Galvan, J. A., & Swain-Oropeza, R. (2023). Challenge-Based Learning and the Industry Liaison as Educational Partners. In *2023 IEEE IFEES World Engineering Education Forum and Global Engineering Deans Council: Convergence for a Better World: A Call to Action, WEEF-GEDC 2023—Proceedings.* DOI: 10.1109/WEEF-GEDC59520.2023.10344279

Lara-Prieto, V., Ruiz-Cantisani, M. I., Arrambide-Leal, E. J., de la Cruz-Hinojosa, J., Mojica, M., Rivas-Pimentel, J. R., & Membrillo-Hernández, J. (2023). Challenge-Based Learning Strategies Using Technological Innovations in Industrial, Mechanical and Mechatronics Engineering Programs. *International Journal of Instruction, 16*(1), 1. DOI: 10.29333/iji.2023.16115a

Larman, C., & Basili, V. R. (2003). Iterative and incremental development: A brief history. *Computer, 36*(6), 47–56. DOI: 10.1109/MC.2003.1204375

Lasi, H., Fettke, P., Kemper, H.-G., Feld, T., & Hoffmann, M. (2014). Industry 4.0. *Business & Information Systems Engineering, 6*(4), 239–242. DOI: 10.1007/s12599-014-0334-4

Lasota, P. A., Fong, T., & Shah, J. A. (2017). A survey of methods for safe human–robot interaction. *Foundations and Trends in Robotics, 5*(4), 261–349. DOI: 10.1561/2300000052

Lavasani, M. G., Afzali, L., & Afzali, F. (2011). Cooperative learning and social skills. *Cypriot Journal of Educational Sciences, 6*(4), 186–193.

Le Blanc, P., Ulfert, A.-S., Peeters, M., Rispens, S., & Scherer, S. (2024). How emerging technologies shape the future of work. *European Journal of Work and Organizational Psychology, 33*(2), 115–119. DOI: 10.1080/1359432X.2024.2324937

Leavy, A., Dick, L., Meletiou-Mavrotheris, M., Paparistodemou, E., & Stylianou, E. (2023). The prevalence and use of emerging technologies in STEAM education: A systematic review of the literature. *Journal of Computer Assisted Learning, 39*(4), 1061–1082. DOI: 10.1111/jcal.12806

Lee, E. A. (2008). Cyber physical systems: Design challenges. In 2008 11th IEEE International Symposium on Object and Component-Oriented Real-Time Distributed Computing (ISORC) (pp. 363–369). IEEE. https://doi.org/DOI: 10.1109/ISORC.2008.25

Lee, L.-H., Braud, T., Zhou, P., Wang, L., Xu, D., Lin, Z., Kumar, A., Bermejo, C., & Hui, P. (2021). *All one needs to know about metaverse: A complete survey on technological singularity, virtual ecosystem, and research agenda* (arXiv:2110.05352). arXiv. /arXiv.2110.05352DOI: 10.48550

Lee, H.-Y., & Wu, T.-T. (2025). ChatGPT in education: A systematic review of current landscape, limitations and future directions through general system theory lens. *European Journal of Education, 60*(4), e70262. DOI: 10.1111/ejed.70262

Lee, J., Bagheri, B., & Kao, H.-A. (2015). A cyber-physical systems architecture for Industry 4.0-based manufacturing systems. *Manufacturing Letters*, *3*, 18–23. DOI: 10.1016/j.mfglet.2014.12.001

Lei, M. (2025). Research on the Application of Artificial Intelligence Pattern Recognition Technology in University Training Laboratory. *International Journal of Advance in Applied Science Research*, *4*(8), 67–72.

Leyzberg, D., Ramachandran, A., & Scassellati, B. (2018). The effect of personalization in longer-term robot tutoring. *ACM Transactions on Human-Robot Interaction*, *7*(3), 19. Advance online publication. DOI: 10.1145/3283453

Li, L. (2024). Reskilling and Upskilling the Future-ready Workforce for Industry 4.0 and Beyond. *Information Systems Frontiers*, *26*(5), 1697–1712. DOI: 10.1007/s10796-022-10308-y

Lin, C. C., Huang, A. Y. Q., & Lu, O. H. T. (2023). Artificial intelligence in intelligent tutoring systems toward sustainable education: A systematic review. *Smart Learning Environments*, *10*(1), 41. DOI: 10.1186/s40561-023-00260-y

Liou, L., Scott, E., Parchure, P., Ouyang, Y., Egorova, N., Freeman, R., Hofer, I. S., Nadkarni, G. N., Timsina, P., Kia, A., & Levin, M. A. (2024). Assessing calibration and bias of a deployed machine learning malnutrition prediction model within a large healthcare system. npj. *NPJ Digital Medicine*, *7*(1), 149. DOI: 10.1038/s41746-024-01141-5

Liu, L. (2020). STEAM platform: Transforming youth leadership for a smart circular economy. In B. Panth and R. Maclean (Eds.), *Anticipating and preparing for emerging skills and jobs* (pp. 297–304). Springer. DOI: 10.1007/978-981-15-7018-6_36

Liu, M., & Yu, D. (2023). Towards intelligent E-learning systems. *Education and Information Technologies*, *28*(7), 7845–7876. DOI: 10.1007/s10639-022-11479-6 PMID: 36532790

Lizzio, A. (2025). From Artificial to Humane Intelligence (HI)–A Sociotechnical Framework for Co-Evolving AI. Available at *SSRN* 5373124. DOI: 10.2139/ssrn.5373124

Llano Arana, L., Gutiérrez Escobar, M., Stable Rodríguez, A., Núñez Martínez, M. C., Masó Rivero, R. M., & Rojas Rivero, B. (2016). La interdisciplinariedad: Una necesidad contemporánea para favorecer el proceso de enseñanza aprendizaje. *Medisur*, *14*(3), 320–327. https://medisur.sld.cu/index.php/medisur/article/view/3233

López, B. S., & Recio, H. (1998). *Creatividad y pensamiento crítico* (1.ª ed.). Trillas.

López-Pernas, S., & Saqr, M. (2024). How the dynamics of engagement explain the momentum of achievement and the inertia of disengagement: A complex systems theory approach. *Computers in Human Behavior, 153*, 108126. DOI: 10.1016/j.chb.2023.108126

Lu, Y., Zheng, H., Chand, S., Xia, W., Liu, Z., Xu, X., Wang, L., Qin, Z., & Bao, J. (2022). Outlook on human-centric manufacturing towards Industry 5.0. *Journal of Manufacturing Systems*, *62*, 612–627. DOI: 10.1016/j.jmsy.2022.02.001

Mackinlay, J. D. (1987). Automating the design of graphical presentations of relational information. *Communications of the ACM*, *30*(6), 902–910.

Maity, S., & Deroy, A. (2024). Generative AI and its impact on personalized intelligent tutoring systems [Preprint]. arXiv. https://arxiv.org/abs/2410.10650

Maldonado-Mahauad, J., Pérez-Sanagustín, M., Kizilcec, R. F., Morales, N., & Munoz-Gama, J. (2018). Mining theory-based patterns from big data: Identifying self-regulated learning strategies in Massive Open Online Courses. *Computers in Human Behavior*, *80*, 179–196. DOI: 10.1016/j.chb.2017.11.011

Marín Juarros, V. I., & Tur Ferrer, G. (2023). La privacidad de los datos en tecnología educativa: Resultados de una revisión de alcance. *Edutec. Revista Electrónica de Tecnología Educativa*, *83*(83), 7–23. DOI: 10.21556/edutec.2023.83.2701

Martínez López, K. (2021). *Development of machine learning strategies for fault diagnosis in virtual plants (digital twin)* [Master's thesis, Universitat Politècnica de Catalunya]. https://hdl.handle.net/2117/358256

Martínez Ramírez, E., Diaz Ledezma, M. A., López Portillo Zuarth, D., Vicente Ortiz, A. Y., Mera Sánchez, N. R., Ordaz Oliver, M. O., & Espejel Rivera, M. A. (2025). Model of a low-cost educational prototype of the Furuta pendulum. *International Journal of Combinatorial Optimization Problems and Informatics*, *16*(4), 61–78. DOI: 10.61467/2007.1558.2025.v16i4.1133

Martínez Sánchez, K. E. (2024). Digital twin para el análisis dinámico de una ménsula construida con impresión 3D utilizando los sensores del móvil [Trabajo final de grado, Universitat Politècnica de Catalunya]. https://hdl.handle.net/2117/418222

Mascareñas Brito, A. (2021). Diseño y modelado de un sistema Digital Twin [Trabajo de fin de máster, Universidad Pontificia Comillas]. http://hdl.handle.net/11531/51618

Mejias, S., Thompson, N., Sedas, R. M., Rosin, M., Soep, E., Peppler, K., Roche, J., Wong, J., Hurley, M., Bell, P., & Bevan, B. (2021). The trouble with STEAM and why we use it anyway. *Science Education*, *105*(2), 209–231. DOI: 10.1002/sce.21605 PMID: 33250574

Melgarejo, Y., Perez Garcia, B., Melgarejo, M. F. M. M., Ramirez Alvarado, J. J., Gutierrez Paredes, J. A., Hernández Pérez, J., & Gutierrez Moreno, E. (2026). Closed-loop control and sensor noise reduction in a low-cost aerodynamic pendulum using digital PID and Kalman filtering on Arduino Mega. *International Journal of Combinatorial Optimization Problems and Informatics*, *17*(1), 34–47. DOI: 10.61467/2007.1558.2026.v17i1.1137

Mhlongo, S., Mbatha, K., Ramatsetse, B., & Dlamini, R. (2023). Challenges, opportunities, and prospects of adopting and using smart digital technologies in learning environments: An iterative review. *Heliyon*, *9*(6), e16348. DOI: 10.1016/j.heliyon.2023.e16348 PMID: 37274691

Miah, M. T., Erdei-Gally, S., Dancs, A., & Fekete-Farkas, M. (2024). A systematic review of Industry 4.0 technology on workforce employability and skills: Driving success factors and challenges in South Asia. *Economies (Basel)*, *12*(2), 35. Advance online publication. DOI: 10.3390/economies12020035

Miao, F., Holmes, W., Huang, R., & Zhang, H. (2021). *AI and education: Guidance for policy-makers*. UNESCO., DOI: 10.54675/PCSP7350

Min, Q., Lu, Y., Liu, Z., Su, C., & Wang, B. (2019). Machine learning based digital twin framework for production optimization in petrochemical industry. *International Journal of Information Management*, *49*, 502–519. DOI: 10.1016/j.ijinfomgt.2019.05.020

Mishra, A., & Motta, F. C. (2023). Stability and machine learning applications of persistent homology using the Delaunay-Rips complex. *Frontiers in Applied Mathematics and Statistics*, *9*, 1179301. DOI: 10.3389/fams.2023.1179301

Mishra, P., Terry, C. A., & Henriksen, D.Deep-Play Research Group. (2013). Square Peg, Round Hole, Good Engineering. *TechTrends*, *57*(2), 22–25. DOI: 10.1007/s11528-013-0641-5

Molenaar, I., de Mooij, S., Azevedo, R., Bannert, M., Järvelä, S., & Gašević, D. (2023). Measuring self-regulated learning and the role of AI: Five years of research using multimodal multichannel data. *Computers in Human Behavior*, *139*, 107540. DOI: 10.1016/j.chb.2022.107540

Molenaar, I., & Wise, A. F. (2022). Temporal aspects of learning analytics: Grounding analyses in concepts of time. In Lang, C., Wise, A. F., Merceron, A., Gašević, D., & Siemens, G. (Eds.), *Handbook of Learning Analytics* (2nd ed., pp. 66–76). Society for Learning Analytics Research., DOI: 10.18608/hla22.007

Mondaini, G., & Rosciani, M. (2021). Adaptive environments: New spaces for learning. In Scaradozzi, D., Guasti, L., Di Stasio, M., Miotti, B., Monteriù, A., & Blikstein, P. (Eds.), *Makers at school, educational robotics and innovative learning environments* (pp. 367–373). Springer., DOI: 10.1007/978-3-030-77040-2_49

Monroy-Peláez, Á. R., Juarez-Acosta, I., Miralrio, A., & Montes de Oca, S. (2025). Implementation of 3D printing as a didactic tool for problem solving of engineering systems and devices. In *Frontiers in Education* (Vol. 10). DOI: 10.3389/feduc.2025.1541586

Montés, N., Barquero, S., Martínez-Carbonell, A., Aloy, P., Ferrer, T., Romero, P. D., Millan, M., & Salazar, A. D. S. (2024). Redefining STEAM to STEAM∀ H (STEAM for all humanity) in higher education. *Education Sciences*, *14*(8), 888. DOI: 10.3390/educsci14080888

Moraes, E. B., Kipper, L. M., Hackenhaar Kellermann, A. C., Austria, L., Leivas, P., Moraes, J. A. R., & Witczak, M. (2023). Integration of Industry 4.0 technologies with Education 4.0: Advantages for improvements in learning. *Interactive Technology and Smart Education*, *20*(2), 271–287. DOI: 10.1108/ITSE-11-2021-0201

Morales González, E., & Del Moral Zamudio, Y. A. (2022). Los objetos de diseño desde una mirada cognitiva. *Cuadernos del Centro de Estudios en Diseño y Comunicación. Ensayos*, *172*(172). Advance online publication. DOI: 10.18682/cdc.vi172.7122

Morin, E. (1992). *El método IV: Las ideas: Su hábitat, su vida, sus costumbres, su organización* (Sánchez, A., Trans.). Cátedra.

Msambwa, M. M., Zhang, W., & Kangwa, D. (2025). The impact of AI on the personal and collaborative learning environments in higher education. *European Journal of Education*, *60*(1), e12909. DOI: 10.1111/ejed.12909

Mubarak, A. A., Cao, H., & Ahmed, S. A. M. (2021). Predictive learning analytics using deep learning model in MOOCs' courses videos. *Education and Information Technologies*, *26*(1), 371–392. DOI: 10.1007/s10639-020-10273-6

Mukuni, J. (2023). Behold the Fourth Industrial Revolution and How to Keep Pace with Workplace Competencies in an Ever-Changing World of Work! In El-Farr, H. (Ed.), *The Changing Landscape of Workplace and Workforce*. IntechOpen., DOI: 10.5772/intechopen.1002648

Mulvey, K. L.. (2022). The role of inclusion, discrimination, and belonging for adolescent STEM engagement. *Journal of Research in Science Teaching*, *59*(8), 1447–1464. DOI: 10.1002/tea.21762

Munch, E. (2017). A User's Guide to Topological Data Analysis. *Journal of Learning Analytics, 4*(2), 47–61. DOI: 10.18608/jla.2017.42.6

Muslim, R. (2024). STEAM-Based Learning for Mechanical Engineering. *Journal of Mathematics and Mathematics Education, 13*(2), 221. DOI: 10.20961/jmme.v13i2.91848

Myburgh, S., & Tammaro, A. M. (2013). Constructing a theoretical framework. In *Exploring Education for Digital Librarians* (pp. 133–172). Chandos Publishing., DOI: 10.1016/B978-1-84334-659-3.50007-4

Mystakidis, S. (2022). Metaverse. *Encyclopedia, 2*(1), 486–497. DOI: 10.3390/encyclopedia2010031

Mystakidis, S., Christopoulos, A., & Pellas, N. (2022). A systematic mapping review of augmented reality applications to support STEM learning in higher education. *Education and Information Technologies, 27*(2), 1883–1927. DOI: 10.1007/s10639-021-10682-1

Nahavandi, S. (2019). Industry 5.0—A human-centric solution. *Sustainability (Basel), 11*(16), 4371. Advance online publication. DOI: 10.3390/su11164371

National Research Council. (2012). *A framework for K–12 science education: Practices, crosscutting concepts, and core ideas*. National Academies Press., DOI: 10.17226/13165

Negri, E., Fumagalli, L., & Macchi, M. (2017). A review of the roles of digital twin in CPS-based production systems. *Procedia Manufacturing, 11*, 939–948. DOI: 10.1016/j.promfg.2017.07.198

Ngo, T. D., Kashani, A., Imbalzano, G., Nguyen, K. T., & Hui, D. (2018). Additive manufacturing: 3D printing. A review of materials, methods, applications and challenges. *Composites. Part B, Engineering, 143*, 172–196. DOI: 10.1016/j.compositesb.2018.02.012

Nieto-Miguel, I., Sanz-Camarero, R., Ortiz-Revilla, J., & Greca, I. M. (2023). La Potencialidad de la Educación STEAM Integrada y el Papel del Arte para la Internacionalización de la Formación Docente. *Journal of International Students, 13*(S1). Advance online publication. DOI: 10.32674/jis.v13iS1.6600

Nnadi, L. C., Ding, D., Godwin-Ojukwu, E. D., Watanobe, Y., & Naruse, K. (2025). Strategic Human Resource Development for Emerging Technologies: A Scoping Review in ICT, Robotics, Data Science, and CPS. *IEEE Access : Practical Innovations, Open Solutions, 13*, 133994–134013. DOI: 10.1109/ACCESS.2025.3592301

Norman, D. A. (2013). The design of everyday things (Rev. and expanded ed.). Basic Books.

Nozato López, M. J. (2024). La inteligencia artificial en educación: Consideraciones éticas y fomento al pensamiento crítico. *RECIE. Revista Electrónica Científica de Investigación Educativa, 8*, e2357. DOI: 10.33010/recie.v8i0.2357

Núñez-Naranjo, A. F. (2025). *Educación 4.0 y competencias STEAM: Nuevas estrategias para la enseñanza del futuro*. Editorial Universidad Tecnológica Indoamérica.

Obaid, A., & Alak, G. (1989). Application of spreadsheet programs in the learning of numerical methods. *Computers & Education, 13*(1), 25–31. DOI: 10.1016/0360-1315(89)90035-3

Oberländer, M., Beinicke, A., & Bipp, T. (2020). Digital competencies: A review of the literature and applications in the workplace. *Computers & Education, 146*, 103752. DOI: 10.1016/j.compedu.2019.103752

OECD. (2018). The future of education and skills [OECD Publishing.]. *Education*, •••, 2030.

OECD. (2020). *Curriculum (re)design: A series of thematic reports from the OECD Education 2030 project—Overview brochure*. OECD. https://www.oecd.org/education/2030-project/contact/Curriculum_Redesign_Thematic_Reports.pdf

Oh, S., PhD, DiNitto, D. M., PhD, & Powers, D. A., PhD. (. (2020). Spillover Effects of Job Skills Training on Substance Misuse Among Low-Income Youths With Employment Barriers: A Longitudinal Cohort Study. *American Journal of Public Health, 110*(6), 900–906. *ProQuest One Academic*, (2404088206). Advance online publication. DOI: 10.2105/AJPH.2020.305631

Oliveros Ruiz, M. A. (2021). Panorama of teaching in higher education institutions under science, technology, engineering and mathematics (STEM) programs. *Revista Científica (Maracaibo), 40*(1), 2–12. DOI: 10.14483/23448350.16764

Oliveros, M. A. (2019). STEAM como herramienta para fomentar los estudios de ingeniería. *Revista Científica (Maracaibo), 35*(2), 158–166.

Omar, K., & Gómez, J. M. (2025). Metaverse-Enhanced Learning Ecosystem (MELE) framework. In *2025 1st International Conference on Computational Intelligence Approaches and Applications (ICCIAA)* (pp. 1–6). IEEE. DOI: 10.1109/ICCIAA65327.2025.11013595

Omar, K., Abu-Aishah, S., Matar, I., Al Smadi, D., Fakhouri, H., & Abuarqoub, M. (2024). Analyzing Jordanian higher education instructors' perception towards Metaverse based education. In *2024 2nd International Conference on Cyber Resilience (ICCR)* (pp. 1–6). IEEE. DOI: 10.1109/ICCR61006.2024.10533007

Omar, K., Saleh, Y., & Issa, G. (2024). Challenges of distance learning during the Coronavirus (COVID-19) pandemic: A case study of the University of Petra. In *2024 2nd International Conference on Cyber Resilience (ICCR)* (pp. 1–6). IEEE. DOI: 10.1109/ICCR61006.2024.10533003

Organisation for Economic Co-operation and Development. (2023). *OECD digital education outlook 2023: Towards an effective digital education ecosystem.* OECD Publishing., DOI: 10.1787/c74f03de-

Ortiz-Martínez, G., Vázquez-Villegas, P., Ruiz-Cantisani, M. I., Delgado-Fabián, M., Conejo-Márquez, D. A., & Membrillo-Hernández, J. (2023). Analysis of the retention of women in higher education STEM programs. *Humanities & Social Sciences Communications, 10*(1), 101. DOI: 10.1057/s41599-023-01588-z

Page, S. E. (2007). *The difference: How the power of diversity creates better groups, firms, schools, and societies.* Princeton University Press.

Panadero, E., & Alonso-Tapia, J. (2014). ¿Cómo autorregulan nuestros alumnos?: Modelo de Zimmerman sobre autorregulación del aprendizaje. *Anales de Psicología, 30*(2), 450–462. DOI: 10.6018/analesps.30.2.167221

Panadés Zafra, R., Amorós Parramond, N., Albiol-Perarnaub, M., & Yuguero Torres, O. (2024). Análisis de retos y dilemas que deberá afrontar la bioética del siglo XXI, en la era de la salud digital. *Atencion Primaria, 56*(7), 102901. Advance online publication. DOI: 10.1016/j.aprim.2024.102901 PMID: 38452658

Pandey, P. (2025). Role of Digital Technology for Advancing STEAM Learning. In Behera, S. K., Sorayyaei Azar, A., Curle, S., & Dials, J. G. (Eds.), (pp. 159–182). Advances in Educational Technologies and Instructional Design. IGI Global., DOI: 10.4018/979-8-3693-7408-5.ch007

Papadopoulou, E. A. (2024). Advancements in STEAM education for 21st century learners. *International Journal of Education, 16*(4), 39–70. DOI: 10.5296/ije.v16i4.22270

Park, S.-M., & Kim, Y.-G. (2022). A metaverse: Taxonomy, components, applications, and open challenges. *IEEE Access : Practical Innovations, Open Solutions, 10*, 4209–4251. DOI: 10.1109/ACCESS.2021.3140175

Paśko, Ł., Mądziel, M., Stadnicka, D., Dec, G., Carreras-Coch, A., Solé-Beteta, X., Pappa, L., Stylios, C., Mazzei, D., & Atzeni, D. (2022). Plan and Develop Advanced Knowledge and Skills for Future Industrial Employees in the Field of Artificial Intelligence, Internet of Things and Edge Computing. *Sustainability (Basel)*, *14*(6), 3312. DOI: 10.3390/su14063312

Patel, K. K., & Amin, K. (2024). Predictive modeling of dropout in MOOCs using machine learning techniques. *International Journal of Intelligent Systems and Applications in Engineering*, *12*(4), 436–443. https://www.ijisae.org/index.php/IJISAE/article/view/6230

Pedregosa, F., Varoquaux, G., Gramfort, A., Michel, V., Thirion, B., Grisel, O., Blondel, M., Prettenhofer, P., Weiss, R., Dubourg, V., Vanderplas, J., Passos, A., Cournapeau, D., Brucher, M., Perrot, M., & Duchesnay, É. (2011). Scikit-learn: Machine learning in Python. *Journal of Machine Learning Research*, *12*, 2825–2830. https://www.jmlr.org/papers/v12/pedregosa11a.html

Pedrosa de Souza, D., & Sivini Ferreira, H. (2025). Potentials of the Science, Technology, Engineering, Arts and Mathematics (STEAM) education for gender inclusion in science: A systematic literature review. *Revista Electrónica de Enseñanza de las Ciencias*, *24*(1), 186.

Pegoraro, R., & Curzel, E. (2023). Convocatoria de Roma por la ética de la IA: El nacimiento de un movimiento. *Medicina y Etica : Revista Internacional de Bioética, Deontología y Etica Médica*, *34*(2), 315–349. DOI: 10.36105/mye.2023v34n2.01

Peng, J.. (2025). Cultivating computational thinking in STEM courses. *Education and Information Technologies*. Advance online publication. DOI: 10.1007/s10639-025-13716-0

Perales, F. J., & Aróstegui, J. L. (2024). The STEAM approach: Implementation and educational, social and economic consequences. *Arts Education Policy Review*, *125*(2), 59–67. DOI: 10.1080/10632913.2021.1974997

Pérez-Domínguez, L. A., López García, J. C., & Aguilar Molina, R. (2023). Industria 4.0 vs. 5.0: Contexto, fundamentos y una revisión de la literatura. *Mundo FESC*, *13*(S1), 1–20.

Perignat, E., & Katz-Buonincontro, J. (2018). From STEM to STEAM: Using Brain-Compatible Strategies to Integrate the Arts: by David A. Sousa and Tom Pilecki. (2013). Thousand Oaks, CA: Sage. 280 pp. *Arts Education Policy Review*, *119*(2), 107–110. DOI: 10.1080/10632913.2017.1300970

Perignat, E., & Katz-Buonincontro, J. (2018). STEAM in practice and research: An integrative literature review. *Thinking Skills and Creativity*, *31*, 31–43. DOI: 10.1016/j.tsc.2018.10.002

PhET Interactive Simulations. (n.d.). *The Moving Man*. University of Colorado Boulder. https://phet.colorado.edu

Pinilla Gamboa, M. A. (2014). Dar sentido a las posibilidades: Síntesis y prototipo en diseño. *Iconofacto, 10*(15), 22–34. https://dialnet.unirioja.es/servlet/articulo?codigo=5204359

Pinilla, M. A., Parra, C., & Rojas, E. (2011). El prototipo en el diseño: Actitud creativa de cambio. *Dearq, 8*, 18–31. https://www.redalyc.org/articulo.oa?id=341630317004

Plakhteyev, A., Perepelitsyn, A., & Frolov, V. (2018). Edge computing for IoT: An educational case study. In *2018 IEEE 9th International Conference on Dependable Systems, Services and Technologies (DESSERT)* (pp. 130–133). IEEE. DOI: 10.1109/DESSERT.2018.8409113

Pollard, V., Hains-Wesson, R., & Young, K. (2018). Creative teaching in STEM. *Teaching in Higher Education*, *23*(2), 178–193. DOI: 10.1080/13562517.2017.1379487

Ponce de Leon-Sanchez, E. R., Dominguez-Ramirez, O. A., Herrera-Navarro, A. M., Rodriguez-Resendiz, J., Paredes-Orta, C., & Mendiola-Santibañez, J. D. (2023). A deep learning approach for predicting multiple sclerosis. *Micromachines*, *14*(4), 749. Advance online publication. DOI: 10.3390/mi14040749 PMID: 37420982

Ponce, P., Anthony, B., Bradley, R., Maldonado-Romo, J., Méndez, J. I., Montesinos, L., & Molina, A. (2024). Developing a virtual reality and AI-based framework for advanced digital manufacturing and nearshoring opportunities in Mexico. *Scientific Reports*, *14*(1), 11214. DOI: 10.1038/s41598-024-61514-4

Presno Linera, M. Á., & Meuwese, A. (2024). La regulación de la inteligencia artificial en Europa. *Teoría y Realidad Constitucional*, *54*(54), 131–161. DOI: 10.5944/trc.54.2024.43310

Pressick-Kilborn, K., Silk, M., & Martin, J. (2021). STEM and STEAM education in Australian K–12 schooling. In *Oxford research encyclopedia of education*. Oxford University Press., DOI: 10.1093/acrefore/9780190264093.013.1684

Prince, M., & Felder, R. (2006). Inductive teaching and learning methods: Definitions, comparisons, and research bases. *Journal of Engineering Education*, *95*(2), 123–138. DOI: 10.1002/j.2168-9830.2006.tb00884.x

PwC. (2020). *The effectiveness of virtual reality soft skills training in the enterprise*. PwC United States. https://www.pwc.com/us/en/tech-effect/emerging-tech/virtual-reality-study.html

Quintana-Zaez, J. C., Vázquez-Villegas, P., & Valdes-Ramirez, D. (2025). Identifying Key Predictors of Students' Competency Achievement Using Machine Learning Models: A Bioengineering Case Study. *IEEE Access : Practical Innovations, Open Solutions*, *13*, 168855–168877. DOI: 10.1109/ACCESS.2025.3613250

Radianti, J., Majchrzak, T. A., Fromm, J., & Wohlgenannt, I. (2020). A systematic review of immersive virtual reality applications for higher education: Design elements, lessons learned, and research agenda. *Computers & Education*, *147*, 103778. DOI: 10.1016/j.compedu.2019.103778

Rajabi, K. I. (2025). Beyond the LMS: How a Multi-Platform, AI-Enhanced Ecosystem Boosts Motivation, Interaction, Deep Learning, and Design Competence among Arabic-Speaking Graduate Students.

Ramachandran, A., Sebo, S. S., & Scassellati, B. (2019). Personalized robot tutoring using the Assistive Tutor POMDP (AT-POMDP). *Proceedings of the AAAI Conference on Artificial Intelligence*, *33*(01), 8050–8057. DOI: 10.1609/aaai.v33i01.33018050

Ramachandran, M. (2025). AI Ethics by Design with AI Reference Architecture: Embedding Ethics by Design in AI Architecture. In *Engineering Ethics of AI by Design: Principles, Practices, and Frameworks for Responsible Artificial Intelligence* (pp. 409–464). Springer Nature Singapore.

Ramírez Chávez, M. A., & Manjarrez Fuentes, N. N. (2022). Habilidades blandas y habilidades duras, clave para la formación profesional integral. *Revista de Ciencias Sociales y Económicas*, *6*(2), 27–37. DOI: 10.18779/csye.v6i2.590

Ramírez-Cedillo, E., Armendáriz-Rodríguez, M., García-Ávila, J., Quintero-Sánchez, D., Ortiz-Espinoza, A. A., & Vargas-Martínez, A. (2025). Student 5.0: Immersive learning in next-gen Automation of Manufacturing Systems courses for the Industry 5.0 era. *Frontiers in Education*, *10*, 1416761. Advance online publication. DOI: 10.3389/feduc.2025.1416761

Ramírez-Montoya, M.-S., Zavala, G., Patiño, A., & Ibarra-Vázquez, G. (2025). STEAM Education of the Future in the Framework of Complexity: Case of Good Practice in OER LATAM Community. *Academic Journal of Interdisciplinary Studies*, *14*(4), 7. DOI: 10.36941/ajis-2025-0054

Rao, R., & Elias-Medina, A. (2024). Designing an internet of things laboratory to improve student understanding of secure IoT systems. *Internet of Things and Cyber-Physical Systems*, *4*, 154–166. DOI: 10.1016/j.iotcps.2023.10.002

Real Academia Española. (n.d.). Autosuficiencia. In *Diccionario de la lengua española*. Retrieved February 10, 2026, from https://dle.rae.es/autosuficiencia

ResearchAndMarkets. (2022, February 1). *Global EdTech market outlook & forecast report 2022: Market size was valued at $254.80 billion in 2021 and is expected to reach $605.40 billion by 2027*. GlobeNewswire. https://www.globenewswire.com/news-release/2022/02/01/2376551/28124/en/Global-EdTech-Market-Outlook-Forecast-Report-2022.html

Reyes-Angona, S., Pattier Bocos, D., & López Moreno, I. (2025). *Guía didáctica hackathon educativo*. Universidad Complutense de Madrid. https://docta.ucm.es/entities/publication/b20d9225-f299-4150-bef7-ec77cfb3d4ea

Riley, R. D., Archer, L., Snell, K. I. E., Ensor, J., Dhiman, P., Martin, G. P., Bonnett, L. J., & Collins, G. S. (2024). Evaluation of clinical prediction models (part 2): How to undertake an external validation study. *BMJ (Clinical Research Ed.)*, *384*, e074820. DOI: 10.1136/bmj-2023-074820

Ritter, B. A., Small, E. E., Mortimer, J. W., & Doll, J. L. (2018). Designing management curriculum for workplace readiness: Developing students' soft skills. *Journal of Management Education*, *42*(1), 80–103. DOI: 10.1177/1052562917703679

Rizakhojayeva, G., Ramankulov, S., Akeshova, M., Nurizinova, M., Tuyakov, Y., & Abdrakhmanov, R. (2025). STEM-based approaches to soft skills development: A synthesis of meta-analytic findings and empirical evidence. *Frontiers in Education*, *10*, 1663155. Advance online publication. DOI: 10.3389/feduc.2025.1663155

Robinson, J. P., Winthrop, R., & McGivney, E. (2016). *Millions learning: Scaling up quality education in developing countries*. Brookings Institution.

Robles Gutiérrez, M. P., Mendoza Diaz, N. V., Del Razo Robles, L. E., & Maria Jimenez Romero, A. (2024). WIP:Perceptions of Use and Requirements for Digital Competencies of Engineers According to Employers in Central Mexico. *2024 IEEE Frontiers in Education Conference (FIE)*, 1–8. DOI: 10.1109/FIE61694.2024.10893060

Robles Gutiérrez, M. P., Mendoza Diaz, N. V., Del Razo Robles, L. E., Dominguez-Ramirez, O. A., & Guerrero Azpeitia, L. A. G. (2025). *Identification of Digital Competencies to Strengthen the Graduation Profile of Students Close to Graduation From a Polytechnic University in Central Mexico*. 1–8. DOI: 10.1109/FIE63693.2025.11328313

Rodríguez-Rey, R., & Cantero-García, M. (2020). Albert Bandura: Impacto en la educación de la teoría cognitiva social del aprendizaje. *Padres y Maestros*, *384*(384), 72–76. DOI: 10.14422/pym.i384.y2020.011

Rodriguez, V., Rojas, N. M., Rabadi-Raol, A., Souto-Manning, M. V., & Brotman, L. M. (2022). Silent expectations: An exploration of women pre-Kindergarten teachers' mental health and wellness during Covid-19 and beyond. *Early Childhood Research Quarterly*, *60*, 80–95. DOI: 10.1016/j.ecresq.2021.12.006 PMID: 34955598

Rojas-Noguera, E., Revelo-Sánchez, O., & Jiménez-Toledo, J. A. (2026). Exploring computational thinking through collaborative work in secondary education: A systematic literature review. *TecnoLógicas*, *29*(65), e3537. DOI: 10.22430/22565337.3537

Romano, A. L., Henrique Dos Santos, C., Koch, C., Lourenço Ubeda, C., Rorato Fogaça, D., César Almada Santos, F., & Freitas, V. (2025). Startups in the Era of Industry 4.0 and 5.0: Technologies, Decisions, Framing, and Competences. *IEEE Access : Practical Innovations, Open Solutions*, *13*, 187042–187057. DOI: 10.1109/ACCESS.2025.3627113

Russell, S., & Norvig, P. (2021). *Artificial intelligence: A modern approach* (4th ed.). Pearson.

Rüütmann, T., & Läänemets, U. (2025). Generating Curricula: A Human-Centred Perspective in the Era of Artificial Intelligence. In International Baltic Symposium on Science and Technology Education. Scientia Socialis Ltd. 29 K. Donelaicio Street, LT-78115 Siauliai, Republic of Lithuania. DOI: 10.33225/BalticSTE/2025.180

Ryalat, M., Franco, E., Elmoaqet, H., Almtireen, N., & Al-Refai, G. (2024). The Integration of Advanced Mechatronic Systems into Industry 4.0 for Smart Manufacturing. *Sustainability (Basel)*, *16*(19), 8504. DOI: 10.3390/su16198504

Sailer, M., Bauer, E., Hofmann, R., Kiesewetter, J., Glas, J., Gurevych, I., & Fischer, F. (2023). Adaptive feedback from artificial neural networks facilitates pre-service teachers' diagnostic reasoning in simulation-based learning. *Learning and Instruction*, *83*, 101620. DOI: 10.1016/j.learninstruc.2022.101620

Sailer, M., Ninaus, M., Huber, S. E., Bauer, E., & Greiff, S. (2024). The End is the Beginning is the End: The closed-loop learning analytics framework. *Computers in Human Behavior*, *158*, 108305. DOI: 10.1016/j.chb.2024.108305

Saint, J., Fan, Y., Gašević, D., & Pardo, A. (2022). Temporally-focused analytics of self-regulated learning: A systematic review of literature. *Computers and Education: Artificial Intelligence*, *3*, 100060. DOI: 10.1016/j.caeai.2022.100060

Saint, J., Whitelock-Wainwright, A., Gašević, D., & Pardo, A. (2020). Trace-SRL: A framework for analysis of microlevel processes of self-regulated learning from trace data. *IEEE Transactions on Learning Technologies, 13*(4), 861–877. DOI: 10.1109/TLT.2020.3027496

Saira Banu, K. A., & Kalai Lakshmi, T. R. (2025). Bridging the gap: Aligning soft skills with industry demands for enhanced employability: Challenges and insights from training professionals in engineering colleges of Ernakulam, Kerala. *TPM. Testing, Psychometrics, Methodology in Applied Psychology, 32*(S6), 1186–1195. https://tpmap.org/submission/index.php/tpm/article/view/1955

Salas-Pilco, S. Z. (2024). K-12 STEAM Education in Latin America: A Systematic Review. *2024 IEEE World Engineering Education Conference (EDUNINE)*, 1–6. DOI: 10.1109/EDUNINE60625.2024.10500534

Salvendy, G. (Ed.). (2012). *Handbook of human factors and ergonomics* (4th ed.). Wiley., DOI: 10.1002/9781118131350

Sánchez Carlessi, H. H., Reyes Romero, C. A., & Mejía Sáenz, K. B. (2018). *Manual de términos en investigación científica, tecnológica y humanística*. Universidad Ricardo Palma. https://www.urp.edu.pe/pdf/id/13350/n/libro-manual-de-terminos-en-investigacion.pdf

Sánchez Islas, M., & Rodríguez Betanzos, A. (2026). Exploración del uso de la inteligencia artificial en estudiantes universitarios. *Cuaderno de Pedagogía Universitaria, 23*, e713. Advance online publication. DOI: 10.29197/cpu.v23i.739

Sánchez Mendiola, M., & Martínez González, A. (Eds.). (2020). *Evaluación del y para el aprendizaje: Instrumentos y estrategias*. Universidad Nacional Autónoma de México, Coordinación de Desarrollo Educativo e Innovación Curricular. https://cuaed.unam.mx/descargas/investigacion/Evaluacion_del_y_para_el_aprendizaje.pdf

Santillán Aguirre, J. P., Cadena Vaca, V. del C., & Cadena Vaca, M. (2019). Educación STEAM: Entrada a la sociedad del conocimiento. *Ciencia Digital*, 3(3.4), 212–227. DOI: 10.33262/cienciadigital.v3i3.4.847

Saqr, M., & López-Pernas, S. (2021). The longitudinal trajectories of online engagement over a full program. *Computers & Education, 175*, 104325. DOI: 10.1016/j.compedu.2021.104325

Saqr, M., & López-Pernas, S. (2022). How CSCL roles emerge, persist, transition, and evolve over time: A four-year longitudinal study. *Computers & Education, 189*, 104581. DOI: 10.1016/j.compedu.2022.104581

Saqr, M., López-Pernas, S., Helske, S., Durand, M., Murphy, K., Studer, M., & Ritschard, G. (2024). Sequence analysis in education: Principles, technique, and tutorial with R. In Saqr, M., & López-Pernas, S. (Eds.), *Learning analytics methods and tutorials: A practical guide using R* (pp. 321–354). Springer., DOI: 10.1007/978-3-031-54464-4_10

Saqr, M., López-Pernas, S., & Vogelsmeier, L. V. D. E. (2023). When, how and for whom changes in engagement happen: A transition analysis of instructional variables. *Computers & Education, 207*, 104934. DOI: 10.1016/j.compedu.2023.104934

Schirpke, U., Ghermandi, A., Sinclair, M., Van Berkel, D., Fox, N., Vargas, L., & Willemen, L. (2023). Emerging technologies for assessing ecosystem services: A synthesis of opportunities and challenges. *Ecosystem Services, 63*, 101558. DOI: 10.1016/j.ecoser.2023.101558

Scholapurapu, P. K. (2025). Artificial intelligence-powered learning analytics and student feedback mechanisms for dynamic curriculum enhancement and continuous quality improvement in outcome-based education. *SSRN, 10*, 9789349552531–06. DOI: 10.2139/ssrn.5382140

Schouten, G. (2017). On meeting students where they are: Teacher judgment and the use of data in higher education. *Theory and Research in Education, 15*(3), 321–338. DOI: 10.1177/1477878517734452

Schwab, K. (2017). *The fourth industrial revolution*. Currency.

Selwyn, N. (2019). Should robots replace teachers? AI and the future of education. *Polity*.

Serrano Corkin, D. M., Ekmekci, A., & Fisher, A. (2020). Integrating Culture, Art, Geometry, and Coding to Enhance Computer Science Motivation Among Underrepresented Minoritized High School Students. *The Urban Review, 52*(5), 950–969. DOI: 10.1007/s11256-020-00586-8

Servicio de Innovación Educativa de la Universidad Politécnica de Madrid. (2020). *Gamificación en el aula*. Universidad Politécnica de Madrid. https://innovacioneducativa.upm.es/sites/default/files/guias/Guia-Gamificaci%C3%B3n.pdf

Shabalala, N. P. (2025). Global citizenship education as a strategy for social, justice and identity: Achieving balance for meaningful social impact. *Globalisation, Societies and Education, 0*(0), 1–13. DOI: 10.1080/14767724.2025.2537371

Shavelson, R. J. (2010). On the measurement of competency. *Empirical Research in Vocational Education and Training, 2*(1), 41–63. DOI: 10.1007/BF03546488

Shernoff, D. J. (2024). *Integrative STEM and STEAM education for Real-Life learning*. Springer. DOI: 10.1007/978-3-031-69824-8

Shute, V. J., Sun, C., & Asbell-Clarke, J. (2017). Demystifying computational thinking. *Educational Research Review*, *22*, 142–158. DOI: 10.1016/j.edurev.2017.09.003

Siemens, G. (2013). Learning analytics: The emergence of a discipline. *The American Behavioral Scientist*, *57*(10), 1380–1400. DOI: 10.1177/0002764213498851

Silva-Hormazábal, M., & Alsina, Á. (2023). Educación STEAM para la sostenibilidad en un contexto rural: Una experiencia integradora. *Revista Iberoamericana de Educación*, *25*(39), 188–210. DOI: 10.35362/rie2539188

Singam, C. A. K. (2026). Developing an integrated model of STEAM education. In Madni, A., Endsley, M., & Boy, G. A. (Eds.), *Handbook of sociotechnical systems: A human systems integration approach* (2nd ed.). CRC Press., DOI: 10.1201/9781003666431-5

Singh, A., Madaan, G., Hr, S., & Kumar, A. (2023). Smart manufacturing systems: A futuristics roadmap towards application of industry 4.0 technologies. *International Journal of Computer Integrated Manufacturing*, *36*(3), 411–428. DOI: 10.1080/0951192X.2022.2090607

Singh, K. D., & Singh, P. D. (2025). Edge-AI driven gamification in engineering education for improving student engagement. *Computer Applications in Engineering Education*, *33*(1), e70076. DOI: 10.1002/cae.70076

Solehuddin, M., Sopandi, E., Saputra, D. G., Dhaniswara, E., Yulianto, S., Zhang, W., & Xu, S. (2023). Development of adaptive e-learning content to increase learning effectiveness. *Journal International Inspire Education Technology*, *2*(2), 101–112. DOI: 10.55849/jiiet.v2i2.457

Soomro, S. A., Casakin, H., Nanjappan, V., & Georgiev, G. V. (2023). Makerspaces Fostering Creativity: A Systematic Literature Review. *Journal of Science Education and Technology*, *32*(4), 530–548. DOI: 10.1007/s10956-023-10041-4

Soori, M., Dastres, R., Arezoo, B., & Jough, F. K. G. (2024). Intelligent robotic systems in Industry 4.0: A review. *Journal of Advanced Manufacturing Science and Technology*, *4*(3), 2024007. Advance online publication. DOI: 10.51393/j.jamst.2024007

Soroko, N. (2024). Features of organizing steam educational projects using immersive technologies. *Physical and Mathematical Education*, *39*(2), 51–59. DOI: 10.31110/fmo2024.v39i2-07

Soroko, N. V., Mykhailenko, L. A., Rokoman, O. G., & Zaselskiy, V. I. (2020). Educational electronic platforms for STEAM-oriented learning environment at general education school. In Proceedings of the 7th Workshop on Cloud Technologies in Education (CTE 2019). *CEUR Workshop Proceedings*, *2643*, 462–473. DOI: 10.55056/cte.386

Sotomayor, C., Vaccaro, C., & Téllez, A. (2021). *Aprendizaje basado en proyectos: Un enfoque pedagógico para potenciar aprendizajes*. Fundación Chile. https://fch.cl/wp-content/uploads/2021/10/ABP-un-enfoque-pedagogico-para-potenciar-aprendizajes.pdf

Spyropoulou, N., & Kameas, A. (2025). AI and the future of teaching in STEAM: Competences, challenges, and opportunities. INTED2025 Proceedings, 4421-4427.

Spyropoulou, N., & Kameas, A. (2024). Leveraging communities of practice for STEAM education: A study on engagement and professional development. *European Journal of Education*, *59*(4), e12806. DOI: 10.1111/ejed.12806

Suherman, S.. (2025). The role of STEM teaching in enhancing creativity and computational thinking. *Computers*.

Sun, J., Zhang, Z., Hong, L., OuYang, L., & Lu, C. (2025). Collaborative optimization for interdisciplinary intelligent education systems: Algorithm design and application. In *Proceedings of SPIE* (Vol. 13808, Article 138081A). SPIE. DOI: 10.1117/12.3082466

Suresh Babu, C. V., Nithika Scree, R., & Varshini, R. (2025). The role of artificial intelligence in personalized STEAM education: Enhancing student-centered learning. In Son, N. D. (Ed.), *Integrating personalized learning methods into STEAM education* (pp. 169–188). IGI Global., DOI: 10.4018/979-8-3693-7718-5.ch008

SWARGIARY, K. (2026). EDUCATION 6.0: Envisioning the Symbiotic Future of Learning and Innovation. ATLANTIS PUBLICATION HOUSE (RUSSIA).

Szilágyi, S., Körei, A., & Vaičiulyté, I. (2024). An innovative STEAM-based method for teaching cycloidal curves in engineering higher education. *Education Sciences*, *14*(10), 1087. DOI: 10.3390/educsci14101087

Tao, F., Zhang, H., Liu, A., & Nee, A. Y. C. (2019). Digital twin in industry: State-of-the-art. *IEEE Transactions on Industrial Informatics*, *15*(4), 2405–2415. DOI: 10.1109/TII.2018.2873186

Tariq, R.. (2025). Computational thinking in STEM education: A systematic review of pedagogical approaches. *Frontiers of Computer Science*.

Tariq, R., Casillas-Muñoz, F., Hassan, S., & Ramírez-Montoya, M. (2024). Synergy of Internet of Things and Education: Cyber-physical systems contributing towards remote laboratories, improved learning, and school management. *Journal of Social Studies Education Research*, *15*(2), 305–352. DOI: 10.6084/m9.figshare.24927696

Thakkar, S. R., & Joshi, H. D. (2015). E-learning systems: A review. In 2015 IEEE Seventh International Conference on Technology for Education (T4E) (pp. 37–40). IEEE. DOI: 10.1109/T4E.2015.6

Tlili, A., Huang, R., Shehata, B., Liu, D., Zhao, J., Metwally, A. H. S., Wang, H., Denden, M., Bozkurt, A., Lee, L.-H., Beyoglu, D., Altinay, F., Sharma, R. C., Altinay, Z., Li, Z., Liu, J., Ahmad, F., Hu, Y., Salha, S., & Burgos, D. (2022). Is metaverse in education a blessing or a curse: A combined content and bibliometric analysis. *Smart Learning Environments*, *9*(1), 24. DOI: 10.1186/s40561-022-00205-x

Topali, P., Ortega-Arranz, A., Rodríguez-Triana, M. J., Er, E., Khalil, M., & Akçapınar, G. (2025). Designing human-centered learning analytics and artificial intelligence in education solutions: A systematic literature review. *Behaviour & Information Technology*, *44*(5), 1071–1098. DOI: 10.1080/0144929X.2024.2345295

Torbaghan, M. E., Sasidharan, M., Jefferson, I., & Watkins, J. (2023). Preparing Students for a Digitized Future. *IEEE Transactions on Education*, *66*(1), 20–29. DOI: 10.1109/TE.2022.3174263

Torres-Rivera, A. D., Díaz-Torres, S. T., & Díaz-Torres, L. A. (2025). ENGINEERING EDUCATION FOR SOCIETY 5.0: A STEAM-BASED, ETHICAL AND SUSTAINABLE LEARNING MODEL INSPIRED BY THE "AULA SUSTENTABLE". In EDULEARN25 Proceedings (pp. 9127-9136). IATED.

Torres-Rivera, A. D., Rendón Peña, A. A., Díaz-Torres, S. T., & Díaz-Torres, L. A. (2025). Ethical integration of AI and STEAM pedagogies in higher education: A sustainable learning model for society 5.0. *Sustainability (Basel)*, *17*(19), 8525. DOI: 10.3390/su17198525

Trump, B. D., Hristozov, D., & Linkov, I. (2018). An introduction to Environment Systems and Decisions' Special Issue on Emerging Technologies. *Environment Systems & Decisions*, *38*(2), 161–162. DOI: 10.1007/s10669-018-9689-2

Tsarkos, A. (2024). Navigating Change in Education 5.0: A Model for Successful Digital Transformation. In Chemsi, G., Elimadi, I., Sadiq, M., & Radid, M. (Eds.), (pp. 265–290). Advances in Educational Marketing, Administration, and Leadership. IGI Global., DOI: 10.4018/979-8-3693-3045-6.ch015

Uddin, Z. (2017). Teaching physics using Microsoft Excel. *Physics Education*, •••, 52.

Udina, N. N., & Atabekova, A. A. (2012). Interdisciplinary approach to teaching language for specific purposes. *RUDN Journal of Law*, *16*(1), 226–229.

Ulbrich, E., Da Cruz, M., Anđić, B., Tejera, M., Dana-Picard, N. T., & Lavicza, Z. (2024). Cross-cultural examination of 3D modelling and 3D printing in STEAM education: Comparing results from teachers in Montenegro and Austria. *London Review of Education*, *22*(1). Advance online publication. DOI: 10.14324/LRE.22.1.12

UNESCO Institute for Lifelong Learning. (2022). *Making lifelong learning a reality: A handbook*. UNESCO Institute for Lifelong Learning.

UNESCO. (2017). *Educación para los objetivos de desarrollo sostenible: Objetivos de aprendizaje*. UNESCO., DOI: 10.54675/CZBA9153

UNESCO. (2020, April 22). The UNESCO Section for Innovation and Capacity Building in Science and Engineering compiles online STEM education resources available for inclusive distance learning in response to COVID-19. https://www.unesco.org/en/articles/unesco-section-innovation-and-capacity-building-science-and-engineering-compiles-online-stem

UNESCO. (2021). *Reimagining our futures together: A new social contract for education*. UNESCO., DOI: 10.54675/ASRB4722

Uniminuto Virtual. (2024, August 15). La educación STEAM logra capacitar profesionales integrales. Corporación Universitaria Minuto de Dios. https://virtual.uniminuto.edu/blog/la-educacion-steam-logra-capacitar-profesionales-integrales/

United Nations News. (2024, September 19). *La regulación mundial de la IA es necesaria*. https://news.un.org/es/story/2024/09/1532941

United Nations. (n.d.). Education._https://www.un.org/sustainabledevelopment/education/

Université de Montréal. (2018). *Déclaration de Montréal pour un développement responsable de l'intelligence artificielle*. https://declarationmontreal-iaresponsable.com/

van Calster, B., McLernon, D. J., van Smeden, M., Wynants, L., Steyerberg, E. W., Bossuyt, P., Collins, G. S., MacAskill, P., Moons, K. G. M., & Vickers, A. J. (2019). Calibration: The Achilles heel of predictive analytics. *BMC Medicine*, *17*(1), 230. Advance online publication. DOI: 10.1186/s12916-019-1466-7

van Halem, N., van Klaveren, C., Drachsler, H. J., Schmitz, M., & Cornelisz, I. (2020). Tracking patterns in self-regulated learning using students' self-reports and online trace data. *Frontline Learning Research*, *8*(3), 140–163. DOI: 10.14786/flr.v8i3.497

Van Laar, E., Van Deursen, A. J., Van Dijk, J. A., & De Haan, J. (2017). The relation between 21st-century skills and digital skills: A systematic literature review. *Computers in Human Behavior, 72*, 577–588. DOI: 10.1016/j.chb.2017.03.010

Varguez Rojas, E., Gutiérrez Moreno, E., Cornejo Cervantes, J. A., Montiel Hernández, J. F., Ordaz Oliver, M. O., & Ordaz Oliver, J. P. (2024). Interacción entre circuito RLC serie y modelo gemelo multicuerpo del sistema masa-resorte-amortiguador. In Memorias del Congreso Internacional de Mecatrónica, Control e Inteligencia Artificial (CIMCIA) (pp. 27–33). UNAM FES Cuautitlán.http://virtual.cuautitlan.unam.mx/intar/memoriascimcia/wp-content/uploads/sites/20/2024/12/4-27-33.pdf

Vassilakopoulou, P., & Hustad, E. (2023). Bridging Digital Divides: A Literature Review and Research Agenda for Information Systems Research. *Information Systems Frontiers, 25*(3), 955–969. DOI: 10.1007/s10796-020-10096-3

Vassiliev, A., Samarin, V., Raskin, D., Evseev, E., Veris, V., Peschinski, I., Cabezas, D., & Kurniawan, Y. (2019). Designing the built-in microcontroller control systems of executive robotic devices using the digital twins technology. In *2019 International Conference on Information Management and Technology (ICIMTech)* (Vol. 1, pp. 256–260). IEEE. DOI: 10.1109/ICIMTech.2019.8843814

Vaswani, A., Shazeer, N., Parmar, N., Uszkoreit, J., Jones, L., Gomez, A. N., Kaiser, Ł., & Polosukhin, I. (2017). Attention is all you need. *Advances in Neural Information Processing Systems, 30*, 5998–6008. DOI: 10.48550/arXiv.1706.03762

Vercelli, A. (2025). Las inteligencias artificiales y sus regulaciones internacionales: Análisis de las resoluciones de la Asamblea General de la ONU en 2024. *SADIO Electronic Journal of Informatics and Operations Research, 24*(2), 110–119. DOI: 10.24215/15146774e081

Veytia Bucheli, M. G., & Contreras Fuentes, Y. B. (2025). Tendencias investigativas acerca del método STEAM en México: Mapeo sistemático de la literatura. *Transdigital, 6*(11), e422–e422. DOI: 10.56162/transdigital422

Viberg, O., Hatakka, M., Bälter, O., & Mavroudi, A. (2018). The current landscape of learning analytics in higher education. *Computers in Human Behavior, 89*, 98–110. DOI: 10.1016/j.chb.2018.07.027

Vickers, A. J., & Holland, F. (2021). Decision curve analysis to evaluate the clinical benefit of prediction models. *The Spine Journal : Official Journal of the North American Spine Society, 21*(10), 1643–1648. DOI: 10.1016/j.spinee.2021.02.024

Villani, V., Pini, F., Leali, F., & Secchi, C. (2018). Survey on human–robot collaboration in industrial settings: Safety, intuitive interfaces and applications. *Mechatronics, 55*, 248–266. DOI: 10.1016/j.mechatronics.2018.02.009

Vygotski, L. S. (1979). *El desarrollo de los procesos psicológicos superiores*. Crítica. (Original work published 1978)

Vygotsky, L. S. (1995). *Pensamiento y lenguaje* (Kozulin, A., Ed.). Paidós.

Wamba, S. F., Gunasekaran, A., Akter, S., Ren, S. J., Dubey, R., & Childe, S. J. (2017). Big data analytics and firm performance: Effects of dynamic capabilities. *Journal of Business Research, 70*, 356–365. DOI: 10.1016/j.jbusres.2016.08.009

Wang, D., & Chen, G. (2024). Making AI accessible for STEM teachers: Using explainable AI for unpacking classroom discourse analysis. *IEEE Transactions on Education, 67*(6), 907–918. DOI: 10.1109/TE.2024.3421606

Wang, D., & Huang, X. (2025). Transforming education through artificial intelligence and immersive technologies: Enhancing learning experiences. *Interactive Learning Environments, 33*(7), 4546–4565. DOI: 10.1080/10494820.2025.2465451

Wang, M., Yu, H., Bell, Z., & Chu, X. (2022). Constructing an Edu-Metaverse ecosystem: A new and innovative framework. *IEEE Transactions on Learning Technologies, 15*(6), 685–696. DOI: 10.1109/TLT.2022.3210828

Wan, J., Tang, S., Shu, Z., Li, D., Wang, S., Imran, M., & Vasilakos, A. V. (2016). Software-defined industrial Internet of Things in the context of Industry 4.0. *IEEE Sensors Journal, 16*(20), 7373–7380. DOI: 10.1109/JSEN.2016.2565621

Wasserman, L. (2018). Topological data analysis. *Annual Review of Statistics and Its Application, 5*(1), 501–532. DOI: 10.1146/annurev-statistics-031017-100045

Weintrop, D., Beheshti, E., Horn, M., Orton, K., Jona, K., Trouille, L., & Wilensky, U. (2016). Defining computational thinking for mathematics and science classrooms. *Journal of Science Education and Technology, 25*(1), 127–147. DOI: 10.1007/s10956-015-9581-5

Weller, J. (2020). Las transformaciones tecnológicas y el empleo en América Latina: Oportunidades y desafíos. *Revista de la CEPAL, 2020*(130), 7–27. DOI: 10.18356/ce83a6d1-es

Weng, X., Ng, O.-L., Cui, Z., & Leung, S. (2023). Creativity Development With Problem-Based Digital Making and Block-Based Programming for Science, Technology, Engineering, Arts, and Mathematics Learning in Middle School Contexts. *Journal of Educational Computing Research*, *61*(2), 304–328. DOI: 10.1177/07356331221115661

Werbach, K., & Hunter, D. (2014). *Gamificación: Revoluciona tu negocio con las técnicas de los juegos* (Educación, P., Trans.). Vuelapluma. (Original work published 2012)

Wing, J. M. (2006). Computational thinking. *Communications of the ACM*, *49*(3), 33–35. DOI: 10.1145/1118178.1118215

Wolf, T., Debut, L., Sanh, V., Chaumond, J., Delangue, C., Moi, A., Cistac, P., Rault, T., Louf, R., Funtowicz, M., Davison, J., Shleifer, S., von Platen, P., Ma, C., Jernite, Y., Plu, J., Xu, C., Le Scao, T., Gugger, S., & Rush, A. M. (2020). Transformers: State-of-the-art natural language processing. In *Proceedings of EMNLP 2020: System Demonstrations* (pp. 38–45). Association for Computational Linguistics. DOI: 10.18653/v1/2020.emnlp-demos.6

Wong, B. T. M. (2017). Learning analytics in higher education: An analysis of case studies. *Asian Association of Open Universities Journal*, *12*(1), 21–40. DOI: 10.1108/AAOUJ-01-2017-0009

Woodford, P. (2022). What are STEAM proponents thinking? on creativity, excellence, and measurement. *Diálogos Sonoros*, *1*(1), 1–15.

World Economic Forum. (2020). *The future of jobs report 2020*. https://www.weforum.org/publications/the-future-of-jobs-report-2020/

World Economic Forum. (2020). The future of jobs report 2020. https://www.weforum.org/reports/the-future-of-jobs-report-2020/

World Economic Forum. (2023). The future of jobs report 2023. https://www.weforum.org/publications/the-future-of-jobs-report-2023/

World Health Organization. (2021). *Ethics and governance of artificial intelligence for health*. World Health Organization. https://www.who.int/publications/i/item/9789240029200

Wuest, T., Weimer, D., Irgens, C., & Thoben, K.-D. (2016). Machine learning in manufacturing: Advantages, challenges, and applications. *Production & Manufacturing Research*, *4*(1), 23–45. DOI: 10.1080/21693277.2016.1192517

Wu, J.-Y., Liao, C.-H., Tsai, C.-C., & Kwok, O.-M. (2024). Using learning analytics with temporal modeling to uncover the interplay of before-class video viewing engagement, motivation, and performance in an active learning context. *Computers & Education, 212*, 104975. DOI: 10.1016/j.compedu.2023.104975

Xiong, M., Wang, H., Fu, Q., & Xu, F. (2021). Digital twin-driven aero-engine intelligent predictive maintenance. *International Journal of Advanced Manufacturing Technology, 114*(11–12), 3751–3761. DOI: 10.1007/s00170-021-06976-w

Xu, L. D., Xu, E. L., & Li, L. (2018). Industry 4.0: State of the art and future trends. *International Journal of Production Research, 56*(8), 2941–2962. DOI: 10.1080/00207543.2018.1444806

Xu, X., Lu, Y., Vogel-Heuser, B., & Wang, L. (2021). Industry 4.0 and Industry 5.0—Inception, conception and perception. *Journal of Manufacturing Systems, 61*, 530–535. DOI: 10.1016/j.jmsy.2021.10.006

Xu, Y., Sun, Y., Liu, X., & Zheng, Y. (2019). A digital-twin-assisted fault diagnosis using deep transfer learning. *IEEE Access : Practical Innovations, Open Solutions, 7*, 19990–19999. DOI: 10.1109/ACCESS.2018.2890566

Yakman, G. (2008). STEAM education: An overview of creating a model of integrative education. *Purdue University Conference Proceedings.*

Yang, M., Wang, T., & Lim, C. P. (2017). E-portfolios as digital assessment tools in higher education. In Spector, M. J., Lockee, B. B., & Childress, M. D. (Eds.), *Learning, design, and technology: An international compendium of theory, research, practice, and policy*. Springer., DOI: 10.1007/978-3-319-17727-4_83-1

Yannier, N., Hudson, S. E., Chang, H. Y., & Koedinger, K. R. (2024). AI adaptivity in a mixed-reality system improves learning. *International Journal of Artificial Intelligence in Education, 34*(4), 1541–1558. DOI: 10.1007/s40593-023-00388-5

Yaqub, M. Z., & Alsabban, A. (2023). Industry-4.0-Enabled Digital Transformation: Prospects, Instruments, Challenges, and Implications for Business Strategies. *Sustainability (Basel), 15*(11), 8553. DOI: 10.3390/su15118553

Ye, D., & Pennisi, S. (2022). Using trace data to enhance students' self-regulation: A learning analytics perspective. *The Internet and Higher Education, 54*, 100855. DOI: 10.1016/j.iheduc.2022.100855

Yeni, S. (2024). Computational thinking integrated in school subjects. *Computers and Education Open.*

Yusufjanovna, T. Z. (2026). Creating a socially beneficial product within STEAM clubs and its educational effectiveness. *International Journal of Pedagogics, 6*(1), 123–128. DOI: 10.37547/ijp/Volume06Issue01-27

Zavala Ortiz, S. A. (2020). Modelado matemático. Tecnológico Nacional de México. https://rinacional.tecnm.mx/bitstream/TecNM/5627/1/LIBRO_ModeladoMat_SAUL%20ZAVALA%20%281%29.pdf

Zhang, C., Chen, Y., Chen, H., & Chong, D. (2021). Industry 4.0 and its implementation: A review. *Information Systems Frontiers, 26*(5), 1773–1783. DOI: 10.1007/s10796-021-10153-5

Zhang, X. (2025). Internet of Things and cloud computing-powered virtual laboratories for enhanced STEM education. *Journal of the Institution of Engineers India Series B, 106*(6), 1767–1776. DOI: 10.1007/s40031-024-01192-y

Zhang, X. M., Li, B., & Huang, L. (2026). 'Brain + X': Interdisciplinary health professions education for the AI era. *Medical Teacher, 48*(3), 434–443. DOI: 10.1080/0142159X.2025.2560570

Zhang, X., Chen, Y., Hu, L., & Wang, Y. (2022). The metaverse in education: Definition, framework, features, potential applications, challenges, and future research topics. *Frontiers in Psychology, 13*, 1016300. DOI: 10.3389/fpsyg.2022.1016300 PMID: 36304866

Zhou, D., Liu, Y., Huang, J., Xiang, Y., Gu, R., & Liu, B. (2022). An intelligent tutoring system enhancing transdisciplinary problem-finding in design-led integrated STEM education. In *Proceedings of the International Conference on Intelligent Computing and Artificial Intelligence in Education (IC-ICAIE 2022)* (pp. 943–949). Atlantis Press. DOI: 10.2991/978-94-6463-040-4_142

Zhu, Z., Dhokia, V., Nassehi, A., & Newman, S. T. (2017). A review of hybrid manufacturing processes—State of the art and future perspectives. *International Journal of Computer Integrated Manufacturing, 30*(4–5), 349–371. DOI: 10.1080/0951192X.2012.749530

Zou, D., Xie, H., & Kohnke, L. (2025). Navigating the future: Establishing a framework for educators' pedagogic artificial intelligence competence. *European Journal of Education, 60*(2), e70117. DOI: 10.1111/ejed.70117

Zuboff, S. (2019). *The age of surveillance capitalism: The fight for a human future at the new frontier of power*. PublicAffairs.

About the Contributors

Jorge A. Ruiz-Vanoye is a Professor and Researcher at Universidad Politécnica de Pachuca (UPP), a National Researcher under the Secretaria de Ciencia, Humanidades, Tecnología e Innovación program, and an Adjunct Researcher at the National Laboratory of Autonomous Vehicles and Exoskeletons (LANAVEX). Additionally, he holds the title of Lecturer-level Researcher for the Agency for the Quality of the University System of Catalonia (Generalitat de Catalunya). His research interests include Smart Cities, Smart Water, Smart Education, Smart Government, Smart Healthcare, Smart Farming, Smart Energy, Smart Sports, Smart Food, Smart Tourism, Algorithmic Finance, Algorithmic Portfolio Management, Applications and Theory of Algorithms, Bio-inspired Algorithms, Combinatorial Optimization Problems, Compilers, Computational Intelligence, Computational Complexity Theory, Computational Financial Intelligence, Complexity of Algorithms, Complexity of Instances, Computational Statistics, Computer Networks, Computer Science Security, Cybercrimes, Data Mining, Education, Evolutionary Computation, Heuristic Optimization Techniques in Bioinformatics, Hybrid Evolutionary Algorithms, Hybrid Optimization Algorithms, Machine Learning, Meta-heuristics, Operations Research, Operations Management, Parallel & Distributed Computing, Production Planning and Logistics Optimization, Project Scheduling Problems, Software Engineering, and Transgenic Algorithms.

Francisco Rafael Trejo-Macotela received the PhD degree in Electronics from the National Institute of Astrophysics, Optics and Electronics (INAOE), Puebla, Mexico. He is a Certified LabVIEW Associate Developer (CLAD) accredited by National Instruments and holds professional competence certifications in the EC0477 and EC0217 standards issued by the National Council for Standardisation and Certification of Competencies (CONOCER). He is currently Professor and Researcher in the Master's programmes in Mechatronics and Information and Communication Technologies, and the PhD programme in Advanced Science and

Technology, at the Polytechnic University of Pachuca (UPP), Mexico. During his academic career at UPP, he has held several leadership positions, including Director of Mechatronics Engineering (2007–2009), Director of Research, Innovation and Postgraduate Studies (2015–2023), and Coordinator of the Master's Programme in Information and Communication Technologies (2023–2024). He also served as Professor and Researcher in the Departments of Mechatronics (2006–2007) and Telematics (2009–2015). He has contributed to numerous research and innovation projects and has participated in more than eight evaluation processes for master's and doctoral programmes within the National Postgraduate System (SNP) of the Secretariat of Science, Humanities, Technology and Innovation (SECIHTI). He is an Adjunct Researcher at the SECIHTI National Laboratory for Autonomous Vehicles and Exoskeletons (LANAVEX). He currently serves as an evaluator for the Interinstitutional Committees for the Evaluation of Higher Education (CIEES), the Engineering Education Accreditation Council (CACEI–COPAES), and the Higher Education Evaluation and Accreditation System (SEAES) through the Peer Registry for Diagnostic and Formative Evaluation (REPEV) of the Mexican Ministry of Public Education (SEP). In 2019, he served as an External Peer Evaluator for the accreditation of Ecuadorian universities and polytechnic institutions under the Higher Education Quality Assurance Council (CACES). He has also acted as a peer evaluator for postgraduate programmes within the National Postgraduate System (SNP) and as a project evaluator for the Innovation Incentives Programme (PEI) of SECIHTI. He is currently a Level 1 member of the National System of Researchers (SNI) of SECIHTI. His research interests include Integrated Circuit Design, Analogue and Digital Electronics, Automation, Embedded Systems, Cyber-physical Systems, Internet of Things, Telecommunications, Smart Cities, Smart Water, Precision Agriculture, Educational Technology, Artificial Intelligence, Machine Learning, Autonomous Navigation, and Optimisation.

Martha Patricia Robles Gutiérrez has collaborated on projects funded by PEI-CONACYT in the field of business innovation, developing digital applications and educational materials for higher education. She participated in the creation of MOOCs under the Mexico-France CODAES program and in the 2015 SINED-ANUIES assessment of distance higher education. She is a member of the RIDMAE network (Mexico, Andorra, and Spain) and holds CONOCER certifications in business incubation. She has served as a business mentor for Harvard University, the Binational University Innovation Node (2019), and the Wadhwani Foundation (2023). She is currently a member of the SNI. Their research focuses on the effective use of ICT for study and work, with presentations at universities in Mexico and abroad, including FIE events in Texas, Cincinnati, and Nashville. Notable achievements include the STEAM-focused scientific and technological mentoring project—presented at LACCEI 2026 in Santiago Chile and the 2025.

***

Jaime Aguilar-Ortiz holds a Ph.D. in Mathematical Sciences (CINVESTAV–IPN, Mexico) and serves as a professor and researcher in the fields of Mathematics, Artificial Intelligence, and Project Management, with academic involvement also extending to the Universidad Politécnica Metropolitana de Hidalgo. He additionally leads innovation-driven initiatives as Director General of CICAINTE and TEDNOVA GROUP, bridging rigorous academic work with applied technological development and institutional impact. His prior scholarly and editorial contributions include the preparation and/or editing of a substantial body of books and educational resources spanning mathematics education, financial mathematics, programming, and technology-based learning, complemented by the creation of audiovisual materials, educational platforms, and serious-game applications aimed at strengthening learning outcomes. His academic production further includes dozens of peer-reviewed articles and book chapters addressing themes at the intersection of smart cities, education, and AI, together with sustained experience in research mentoring, curriculum development, and interdisciplinary collaboration. These achievements, combined with recognized academic credentials and a consistent record of knowledge dissemination and capacity building, position him as a strong editor for a high-impact scholarly volume with methodological rigor, cross-sector relevance, and measurable educational and societal value.

Pedro José Argumedo Teuffer is an aeronautical engineer who graduated in 1999 from the Higher School of Mechanical and Electrical Engineering (ESIME), Ticomán Unit, at the National Polytechnic Institute (IPN). He holds a Master of Science degree in Mechanical Engineering from ESIME, Zacatenco Unit (IPN), and a Doctorate in Educational Sciences from INECUH University in Tizayuca, Hidalgo. He has 10 years of experience in the aerospace and energy sectors, having worked for companies such as Mexicana de Aviación and General Electric (in the Transportation/Aircraft Engines and Energy divisions); he has also participated in PEMEX-related projects involving turbomachinery for the transport of LPG, natural gas, and crude oil. With 18 years of experience in aerospace education, he was part of the founding team for the national aeronautical engineering program within the system of polytechnic and technological universities (CGUTYP). Locally, he is the founder and dean of the aeronautical engineering program at the Metropolitan Polytechnic University of Hidalgo (located in Tolcayuca, Hidalgo), where he has participated in various curriculum design and redesign initiatives since the program's inception. He has co-directed student projects at institutions such as NASA's Ames Research Center in San Jose, California, and has collaborated on projects with various institutions and research centers, including CIDESI and CYCATA in Querétaro, Mexico. He has led projects to strengthen his academic program by developing two open-circuit subsonic wind tunnel systems for the institution's aerodynamics laboratory: one with a 40 x 40 cm test section (70 km/h wind speed) and another with an 80 x 80 cm test section (200 km/h wind speed).

Erika Cervantes Juárez received her B.Sc. in Applied Physics (2014), M.Sc. in Applied Physics (Cum Laude, 2016), and Ph.D. in Applied Physics (Cum Laude, 2020) from the Benemérita Universidad Autónoma de Puebla (BUAP), Mexico. She is currently a Professor at the Unidad Profesional Interdisciplinaria de Ingeniería "Alejo Peralta" (UPIIAP), Instituto Politécnico Nacional (IPN), where she teaches Physics and Mathematics to engineering students. Her research focuses on materials science, including luminescent materials, glass materials, energy-efficient systems for solar cells, and environmental remediation, as well as physics education and innovative teaching methodologies. She has authored eight JCR-indexed publications, presented her work at more than 15 national and international conferences, and actively supervises undergraduate research projects. Dr. Cervantes Juárez received the PACSURF Students Award in 2018 and has been a Level I Researcher in Mexico's National System of Researchers (SNII) since 2022. She also serves as a reviewer for scientific journals and has contributed to the organization of international conferences, including Frontiers in Education (FIE).

Ocotlán Diaz-Parra is a Professor and Researcher at Universidad Politécnica de Pachuca (UPP), a National Researcher under the Secretaria de Ciencia, Humanidades, Tecnología e Innovación program, and an Adjunct Researcher at the National Laboratory of Autonomous Vehicles and Exoskeletons (LANAVEX). His research interests include Smart Cities, Smart Water, Smart Education, Smart Government, Smart Healthcare, Smart Farming, Smart Energy, Smart Sports, Smart Food, Smart Tourism, Algorithmic Finance, Algorithmic Portfolio Management, Applications and Theory of Algorithms, Bio-inspired Algorithms, Combinatorial Optimization Problems, Compilers, Computational Intelligence, Computational Complexity Theory, Computational Financial Intelligence, Complexity of Algorithms, Complexity of Instances, Computational Statistics, Computer Networks, Computer Science Security, Cybercrimes, Data Mining, Education, Evolutionary Computation, Heuristic Optimization Techniques in Bioinformatics, Hybrid Evolutionary Algorithms, Hybrid Optimization Algorithms, Machine Learning, Meta-heuristics, Operations Research, Operations Management, Parallel

& Distributed Computing, Production Planning and Logistics Optimization, Project Scheduling Problems, Software Engineering, and Transgenic Algorithms.

Carlos Domínguez-Mayorga holds a Ph.D. in Sciences specializing in Artificial Intelligence, with a foundational background in Physics and Mathematics. His research focuses on Deep Learning, NLP, neural networks, and the development of predictive models. He has an extensive track record in scientific publications and graduate program management, applying cutting-edge data science techniques to engineering and sustainability projects.

Omar A. Dominguez Ramirez received the Ph.D. degree in Electrical Engineering with a specialization in Mechatronics from the Mechatronics Section of the Center for Research and Advanced Studies of the National Polytechnic Institute (CINVESTAV-IPN), Zacatenco Unit, Mexico, in 2005. He obtained the M.Sc. degree in Electrical Engineering (Automatic Control) from the Graduate and Research Division of the Technological Institute of La Laguna in 1999, and the B.Sc. degree in Electrical Engineering with a specialization in Industrial Applications from the Technological Institute of Pachuca in 1994. He is a member of Mexico's National System of Researchers (SNI) and has been a Full-Time Research Professor at the Research Center for Information Technologies and Systems of the Autonomous University of the State of Hidalgo since 1995. His research interests include human–robot interaction systems, cognitive robotics, haptic interfaces, biomechanics, and control of biomedical mechatronic systems.

María Ingeniera Eléctrica egresada del Instituto Tecnológico de Pachuca (ITP), con Maestría en Ingeniería Eléctrica y Doctorado en Optomecatrónica. Su trayectoria académica y profesional se centra en el desarrollo y aplicación de tecnologías en automatización industrial, sistemas de control y robótica. Asimismo, ha incursionado en el aprendizaje automático aplicado a la ingeniería eléctrica, integrando enfoques inteligentes para la optimización de procesos y sistemas.

Hussam Fakhouri is an Assistant Professor of Data Science at Al-Balqa Applied University (BAU) in Jordan, a position he has held since 2025. He earned his Ph.D. in Computer Science from the University of Jordan in 2020, where his doctoral research focused on data science. Dr. Fakhouri's research interests span multiple domains within artificial intelligence and data science, including metaheuristic algorithms, optimization, data analysis, data exploration, data engineering, machine learning, and deep learning. He has authored approximately 100 research papers in reputable international journals and conference proceedings. In addition, Dr. Fakhouri contributes to the scholarly community as an academic editor and reviewer. Dr. Fakhouri has also undertaken significant academic leadership roles. He has also participated in Erasmus Programs such as doctoral schools hosted by universities in Denmark, Germany, and Russia.

Evelin Gutiérrez Moreno studied Chemical Engineering at the Technological Institute of Pachuca (ITP), later received a master's degree and doctorate in Chemistry at the Autonomous University of the State of Hidalgo (UAEH). Evelin is currently a professor at the Polytechnic University of Pachuca (UPP). Her research interests are related to analytical chemistry, modeling, prediction and inhibition of corrosion, design of experiments and construction of low-cost devices for chemical-experimental analysis.

Faten Hamad is an Associate Professor in the Department of Information Studies at Sultan Qaboos University (Oman), where she has served since September 2021. She earned her Ph.D. in Information Science from Aberystwyth University (UK) in 2013, following an M.Sc. in Computer Science from the University of Jordan (2006) and a B.Sc. in Computer Science from Yarmouk University (2004). Her research interests span advanced metaheuristic optimization and AI-driven data analytics, applied to engineering design, cybersecurity, and intelligent systems, and extend to digital transformation, accessibility, and resilience in academic libraries and education.

Mustafa Kayyali is an ardent advocate for excellence in higher education, driven by a relentless pursuit of quality, recognition, and innovation. Their journey in academia started with a Master's in Quality Management and Evaluation in Higher Education from Universitat Oberta de Catalunya, followed by a Ph.D. in Quality Management from Azteca University. These academic pursuits have laid a strong foundation for their expertise in Accreditation, Quality Assurance, and Higher Education Rankings. As an entrepreneur, researcher, translator, and publisher, they are deeply involved in various facets of the academic world. Their diverse interests encompass Management, Translation, Interpretation, and Academic consulting, contributing to a well-rounded understanding of the industry. Throughout their career, they have made significant contributions to academic literature, with more than 40 published papers and 30 book chapters to my name. Additionally, they take pride in having translated 6 books, bridging language gaps, and promoting knowledge exchange on a global scale. They are committed to fostering positive change in higher education and contributing to its continuous improvement.

Jesús Patricio Oliver obtained the title of engineer in Electronics and Telecommunications from the Autonomous University of the State of Hidalgo and the M.Sc. in Automatic Control at the same university. In 2012, he received the PhD in Sciences in Automatic Control at CINVESTAV, Mexico City. His research interests are intelligent systems, adaptive control, nonlinear control, robust control, system identification and observation. He is currently a Professor at the Autonomous University of the State of Hidalgo, Pachuca, Mexico.

Khalil Omar is an assistant professor at the University of Petra in Jordan. He received his Ph.D. degree in computer science from the University of Oldenburg, Germany, in 2018. His academic focus is on distance learning and e-learning in combination with software engineering, mobile applications, usability design, adaptive interfaces, and ERP systems.

Mario Ordaz Oliver holds a doctorate in Science in Automation and Control from the Autonomous University of the State of Hidalgo, where optimal discrete-time control techniques were developed and validated on multirotor unmanned aerial vehicles for agricultural applications. With over ten years of teaching experience across multiple engineering programmes, delivered courses include control theory, advanced control, modelling and simulation, digital control systems, and industrial automation. Research interests focus on classical and modern control strategies applied to robotic systems, haptic interfaces and unmanned aerial vehicles. The author currently serves as part-time professor at the Pachuca Institute of Technology and has contributed to rehabilitation systems for individuals with motor disabilities and to energy optimisation in industrial robotics processes.

Alma Delia Paz Gómez is a doctoral student in Education at Pablo Latapí Sarre University. She holds a Master's degree in Education, specializing in higher education, from La Salle University in Pachuca, Mexico, as well as a Bachelor's degree in Education. She currently works as an adjunct professor at the Metropolitan Polytechnic University of Hidalgo (UPMH), where she teaches human development courses to students in the Aeronautical Engineering program. Her main lines of research focus on the analysis of education in the twentieth-century press, as well as on topics related to professional ethics. She is also interested in the history of aviation and aeronautics, the inclusion of women in the aeronautical industry, and aeronautical psychology.

Juan-Carlos Rojas is an Assistant Professor with a research focus at the School of Architecture, Art and Design (EAAD) at Tecnológico de Monterrey, Campus Monterrey, and a Researcher at the Institute for the Future of Education (IFE). He is a member of the Mexican National System of Researchers (SNI) at the Candidate level (SECIHTI, Mexico). He holds a Ph.D. in Design, Management, and Development of Industrial Projects from the Universitat Politècnica de València (UPV), Spain, awarded with cum laude distinction, as well as a Master's degree in Industrial Design and Innovation Processes from Tecnológico de Monterrey.

His research lies at the intersection of emotional design, neurotechnologies, and educational innovation. He focuses on understanding how visual, cognitive, and affective factors influence perception, decision-making, and learning processes in design contexts, using tools such as eye-tracking, neurophysiological analysis, and generative artificial intelligence.

Daniel Sánchez Guzmán is professor at the Instituto Politécnico Nacional at the Unidad Profesional Interdisciplinaria de Ingeniería, campus Guanajuato in México, teaching postgraduate courses in Physics Education and Advance Technology, his activities also include teaching Physics and Computer Science in engineering courses. He leads research projects, research theses, and technology applications. His research focuses on technology-mediated learning processes in Physics, Science and Engineering.

Eric Simancas-Acevedo (Phd. in Electro-communications), graduated from the Postgraduate Studies and Research Section (SEPI-ESIME Culhuacan) of the National Polytechnic Institute (IPN) in 2015; he had a postgraduate study stays in Tokyo, Japan 2001-2003; He is currently a Senior Research Professor and Posgraduate teacher at the Polytechnic University of Pachuca in Engineering and Graduate degrees. His research interests are: Signal and image processing, artificial intelligence, neuroengineering, adaptive filters, neural networks, fuzzy logic, stochastic models, embedded systems, machine learning, security and control systems based on biometric features and embedded systems.

Patricia Vázquez-Villegas is a Food Industry Engineer and PhD in Engineering Sciences from Tecnológico de Monterrey, Professor at the School of Engineering and Sciences, and Researcher at the Institute for the Future of Education at Tecnologico de Monterrey, in the Effective and Engaging Learning Models Research Unit; Member of the National System of Researchers (SNI), level 1 of SECIHTI, Mexico; Member of the Mexican Academy of Sciences as a Young Academician; Research stays at the University of British Columbia (2012) and the University of Texas at Austin (2024-25).

Mario Alejandro Vega Navarrete earned a Ph.D. in Educational Sciences from INECUH University in 2022. He obtained a Master of Science degree in Automation and Control from the Autonomous University of the State of Hidalgo in 2013, and a Bachelor's degree in Electronics and Telecommunications Engineering from the same university in 2010. He is currently a full-time professor at the Metropolitan Polytechnic University of Hidalgo. His research interests include the development of robotic prototypes and aerial vehicles with applications in artificial intelligence, as well as the impact of technology development and its applications in education, particularly in enhancing learning processes, fostering innovation, and integrating emerging technologies into educational environments.

Index

A

C

D

E

G

H

I

L

M

P

R

S

T

www.ingramcontent.com/pod-product-compliance
Lightning Source LLC
LaVergne TN
LVHW080907300926
849162LV00003B/587